THE SHADOW OF THE WINTER PALACE

By the same author

JOSEPH CONRAD: Aspects of the Art of the Novel

VIENNA: The Image of a Culture in Decline

BRITAIN AND RUSSIA

RUSSIA AND THE RUSSIANS

RUSSIA BY DAYLIGHT

THE FORSAKEN IDEA: A Study of Viscount Milner

GESTAPO: Instrument of Tyranny

RUSSIA WITHOUT STALIN

KHRUSHCHEV'S RUSSIA

THE NEW COLD WAR: Moscow *v*. Pekin

THE FALL OF THE HOUSE OF HABSBURG

KHRUSHCHEV: A Biography

MARIA THERESA

THE HABSBURGS

TOLSTOY: The Making of a Novelist

Novels

NINA LESSING

WHAT GLORY?

THE CREEDY CASE

The Shadow of the Winter Palace

RUSSIA'S DRIFT TO REVOLUTION
1825–1917

Edward Crankshaw

WITHDRAWN

DA CAPO PRESS

Copyright © 1976 by Edward Crankshaw

Library of Congress Cataloging in Publication Data to come

ISBN 0-306-80940-0

The author and publishers wish to thank the following who have kindly given permission for the use of copyright material:
Barrie & Jenkins and Praeger Publishers Inc. for an extract from *Selected Essays on Music* by Vladimir Vasilevich Stasov, translated by Florence Jonas; Cambridge University Press for an extract from 'Nicholas I and the Partition of Turkey' by G. H. Bolsover, taken from *The Slavonic and East European Review*, No. 69, 1948; Chatto & Windus Limited and Alfred A. Knopf Inc. for an extract from *My Past and Thoughts: the Memoirs of Alexander Herzen* translated by Constance Garnett; Constable & Company Limited for extracts from *Sir Arthur Nicolson, Bart, First Lord Carnock* by Harold Nicolson; Oxford University Press for *The Testament* by Lermontov from the Introduction to *The Oxford Book of Russian Verse* chosen by Maurice Baring; University of California Press for extracts from *The First Russian Revolution, 1825* by Anatole G. Mazour, copyright © 1937 by The Regents of the University of California.
    The publishers have made every effort to trace the copyright-holders but if they have inadvertently overlooked any, they will be pleased to make the necessary arrangement at the first opportunity.

First Da Capo Press Edition 2000

Reprinted by arrangement with Viking Penguin, a division of Penguin Books USA, Inc.

Published by Da Capo Press
A Member of the Perseus Books Group
http://www.dacapopress.com

1 2 3 4 5 6 7 8 9 10——04 03 02 01 00

To the Emperor of All the Russias belongs the supreme and unlimited power. Not only fear, but also conscience commanded by God Himself, is the basis of obedience to this power.

Article 1 of the Fundamental Laws of Imperial Russia

Russia's past is admirable; her present more than magnificent; as to her future, it is beyond the grasp of the most daring imagination. That is the point of view . . . from which Russian history must be conceived and written.

Count A. K. Benckendorff, Chief of Police, to P. I. Chaadayev, 1836

The whole of our administration is one vast system of malfeasance raised to the dignity of state government.

A. M. Unkovsky, Provincial Marshal of the Nobility of Tver, 1859

Contents

A Note on Dates and Spelling

Until 1918 the Russians used the Julian calendar, which runs behind our own Gregorian calendar – twelve days in the nineteenth century and thirteen days in the twentieth. This makes for awkwardness and confusion. It explains why, for example, Lenin's revolution, which took place on 25 October 1917, is now celebrated on 7 November. There is no painless way out of this situation. I myself have used the Old Style dating for internal Russian events and the New Style for external events, including wars.

A different sort of confusion may arise from the fact that the foreign brides of future Emperors, or Tsars, were required to submit to baptism into the Orthodox Church, changing their names as well as their religion. Princess Charlotte of Prussia, for example, when married to the future Nicholas I became the Grand Duchess Alexandra Feodorovna.

As for spelling, with every respect for the labours of the systematisers, it seems to be impossible to devise an entirely consistent system of transliteration from the Cyrillic to the Roman alphabet without introducing tiresome awkwardnesses and pedantries. It seems to me that so long as the meaning is clear and the spirit of our own language not affronted there is no need to worry about this. I have not felt myself bound by any hard and fast rules but have followed current usage most of the time, varying it for my own satisfaction or because of hallowed tradition – e.g. the continued spelling of Tchaikovsky instead of Chaikovsky. Christian names have been anglicised where this could be done without awkwardness.

E.C.

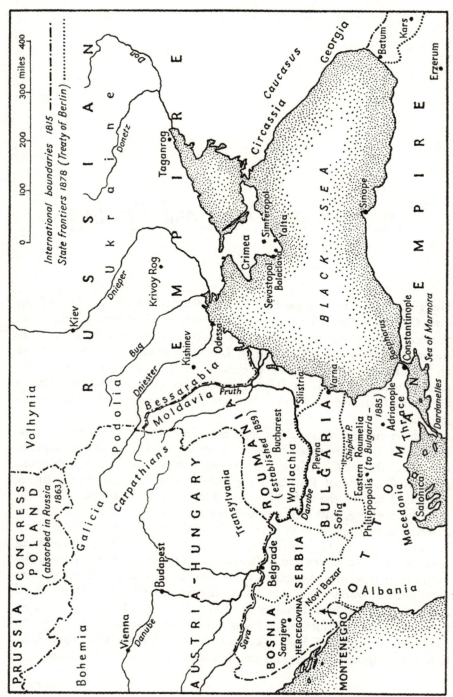

The Balkans and the Black Sea

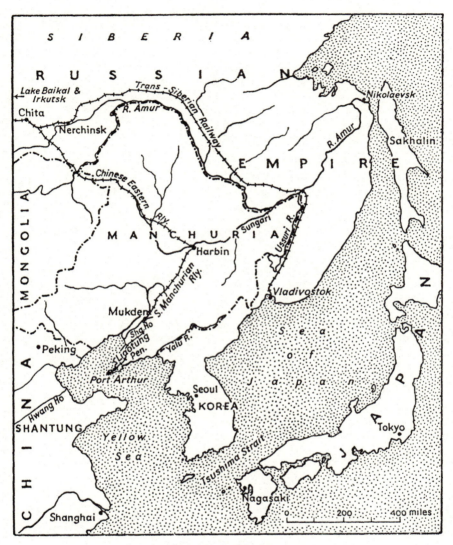

Russia and Japan

THE SHADOW OF THE WINTER PALACE

CHAPTER ONE

A Moment of History

I

THE extraordinary scene on the Senate Square in St Petersburg on 14 December 1825 had an almost dreamlike quality of inconsequence and unreason; so that what should have been, on the day of the new Tsar's accession, the climax of the first serious attempt to destroy the Tsarist autocracy, plotted in laborious but imperfect secrecy by so many ardent souls, appeared less like a revolution in the making than a premature and tentative rehearsal of the first act of a play still uncompleted, one of those epic dramas designed to be enacted under open skies with great crowd-scenes against an architectural setting. Some of the principals had not turned up at all, having decided overnight that they did not like their parts, though omitting to inform the others; some had not even begun to learn their lines and fluffed about the arena, while the patient ranks of supers stood stolidly waiting for their cue which never came.[1]

But it was not a rehearsal, it was the real thing, and it ended in bloodshed and killing. The chief actors were officers of the Imperial Army, some belonging to the most noble families in the land, who, together with a handful of liberal-minded civilians, had been for years conspiring with passion but little cohesion to liberate their country from the dead hand of autocracy. The supers who stood and waited consisted of the Moscow Regiment of Foot with elements of the Grenadiers and the Marine Guard, some three thousand in all, incited to mutiny by their own officers. The revolutionary leaders, together with their fellow-conspirators a thousand miles to the south, who at that very moment were supposed to be seizing Kiev and other towns, were divided in their aims. Some wanted to force a constitution on the Tsar, others to depose him and proclaim a republic, others to kill him. They were united only in their determination to put an end to autocratic rule. But it was characteristic that when appealing to the garrison troops upon whom they depended for the force which was to usher in a new age of freedom, human dignity and reason, they had found

it necessary to lie. The troops were incited with promises of easier conditions and more pay to revolt not against the autocracy as such but against
the person of the new Tsar. Nicholas I, in favour of his elder brother,
Constantine.

It was a long time before reality broke in. The troops had been told that
Nicholas was a usurper; that under the will of the dead Emperor,
Alexander I, his brother Constantine in Warsaw should succeed; that this
will, in the keeping of the Senate, would be read out publicly on the Senate
Square. But first thing that morning the Senate had already met to swear
their oath to Nicholas and then dispersed. There was, indeed, a will but
it named Nicholas as heir, explaining that Constantine had abdicated his
right to the throne some years before. The revolutionary headquarters
which should have been set up on the square never came into being
because the admired leader of the revolt, the provisional 'dictator', Prince
Sergei Trubetskoy, had had a change of heart and slipped away, first
secretly to swear his own allegiance to the man he was sworn to depose,
then to hide in the Austrian Embassy. His second-in-command, Colonel
Bulatov, also vanished from the scene: he too swore allegiance to Nicholas,
then gave himself up, confessing eloquently and gratuitously the iniquity
of his sins, later committing suicide by smashing his head against his
prison wall. Alexander Yakubovich, a brilliant figure from the Caucasus,
an officer spectacularly brave in action, flamboyant and terrible in his
proclaimed revolutionary intention, went one better. Having paraded
briefly in the forefront of the mutinying troops, shouting 'Hurrah for
Constantine!' with his hat on his raised sword, as soon as the order was
given to the Moscow Regiment to load, he pleaded a sudden intolerable
headache (he had indeed been wounded in the head fighting against
mountain tribesmen) and fell back through the ranks. In no time at all
he made his way round to the far side of the square and presented himself
most humbly to his Tsar to declare his devoted loyalty and sacrificial zeal.
Having received the Tsar's thanks this double-renegade promptly returned
to the ranks of the mutineers, this time to urge them to hold fast
because, he said, Nicholas was afraid. Then he went home, gave orders
that he was not to be disturbed, locked himself in his room, loaded
his revolver, and sat waiting for what would happen next. What happened was that many hours later in the depths of the night the police
came for him and led him away, his revolver unfired. Men under stress
behave strangely, some Russians, it seems hardly too much to say, more
strangely than most. The new Tsar, as we shall see, had been behaving
strangely too, but on this first day of his reign he rose to the occasion.

The Senate Square lies off the Neva embankment between the fairly
undistinguished Senate building and Sakharov's Admiralty with its

exquisite needle spire. Beyond the Admiralty, and hidden by it, stands the Winter Palace. The north side of the square lies open to the river Neva, heavily frozen over on that December day. The south side was then bounded by the untidy bulk of St Isaac's Cathedral, only half built. The whole was dominated, as now, by Catherine's great bronze memorial to Peter, seated on the rearing horse with trampling hooves, Falconnet's masterpiece, raised up on its colossal plinth of Finnish granite. The square had been chosen as the focus of the revolution because troops stationed there cut off the Senate from the Winter Palace. The three thousand mutineers were drawn up with their backs to the Admiralty and facing the Senate. While they waited for their orders a vast and potentially dangerous crowd of onlookers grew constantly behind them and on either flank. There was a good deal of cheerful fraternisation with the crowd, who plied the troops, hungry and very cold, with vodka and hunks of bread and sausage. There were ragged cheers for Constantine. There was random shooting into the air, while the rebel leaders did their best to keep the lines steady, rather desperately waiting for something to happen. For a long time nothing much happened. Across the square, and facing them, and also blocking all the entrances to the square, were nine thousand loyal troops with cavalry and artillery. As the day wore on Nicholas, the new Tsar, himself appeared, braving the desultory shooting from the rebel side. He was twenty-nine, an immense figure of a man, finely built, coldly handsome, resplendent on horseback, helmeted, surrounded by his staff. He was determined, if humanly possible, to avoid shedding blood on this first day of his reign. He held his fire when the mutineers themselves started firing, sporadically, loosely, but dangerously, largely to keep their spirits up while the few brave leaders left to them argued about what to do next and who was to command in the absence of the chosen commanders – and while others toured the barracks, rebuffed by some units, but extracting promises of support from others when they could move under cover of darkness. These revolutionary leaders never thought of appealing to the vast civilian crowd or trying to organise them. They simply let their troops stand, hungry and shivering in the icy wind that swept across the Neva from the Arctic. Nicholas still held his fire even when it became clear that somewhere in that waiting, indeterminate throng there was at least a handful who meant business and were prepared to go to extremes.

The first show of wholly destructive violence came when the Governor-General of St Petersburg, one of the new Tsar's closest and most trusted advisers, General Miloradovich, rode across the square to address the mutineers and urge them to return to barracks. Miloradovich was not by any means a hated figure. He was a much decorated hero of the 1812 campaign against Napoleon; genial and given to laughter, he had been chosen by the Emperor Alexander as a watchdog against sedition precisely because he had a reputation for fairness and decency; even that dedicated revolutionary, Alexander Herzen, had warm childhood memories of him.[2] Now this distinguished veteran found himself in the service of his master face to face with a member of one of the oldest families in the land, Prince Eugene Obolensky, who had been persuaded to take command of the rebellion in the absence of its original leader, and being warned sharply that if he valued his life he had better not interfere. Quickly realising that he could do no good, Miloradovich prepared to return the way he had come but as he turned his horse he was shot in the back and killed. The man who did the shooting was a civilian, Peter Kakhovsky, a gifted intellectual of extreme purity of motive in whom the conviction of the necessity of regicide burned with a gem-like flame. Determined to kill, expecting to die, this brilliant and terrible apparition, his slender form bundled up in a sheepskin coat, his delicate features surmounted by a shabby top hat, shot to kill with that indiscriminate ruthlessness which was later to characterise a whole generation of revolutionary terrorists. If he could not yet murder the Tsar, he would do the next best thing.

The extraordinary aspect of this cold-blooded public execution is that it passed almost unnoticed. It neither inflamed nor shamed Kakhovsky's fellow rebels. It evoked no immediate response from the Tsar or his generals or the loyal troops across the square. Everybody went on standing and waiting, until, as in a dream, the whole operation was repeated in almost precise detail: another senior officer cantered over to the rebels, reined in his horse, was warned, turned away and was shot and fatally wounded by this same dire figure in the beaver hat. And even then the Tsar held his hand. Now it was the turn of the Metropolitan Serafim, magnificent in full canonicals, to make his way across the square to instil into the rebels the fear of God. He too was firmly told to go away and was allowed to depart in peace. There was one last attempt even now at peaceful persuasion. The Tsar's younger brother, the Grand Duke Michael, very bravely offered himself in a last appeal to reason, but he was immediately shouted down, shot at (not this time by Kakhovsky but by another civilian intellectual, a poet, Küchelbecker), and was lucky to escape with his life.

The short winter day was approaching its close. Nicholas was afraid, and with reason, that when darkness fell the rebels would be joined by other regiments. But still he refused to allow his troops to open fire. Instead he decided to clear the square with a cavalry charge, even though it might mean casualties from rebel fire. What followed was pure farce. The horses were not properly shod and slipped and floundered and fell on the icy cobbles, while the rebels jeered. There was another pause when the cavalry had reformed and retired from the stage. Even then Nicholas would not shoot. He sent another unfortunate general, the commander of the Guards Artillery, General Sukhozanet, to address the rebels, to tell them that all would be forgiven if only they would return to barracks. He too was shot at, but not hit, and at last the dream was becoming reality. The insurgent troops still stood and waited, but the civilian crowd showed signs of feeling its strength and getting out of hand. There was much more wild firing. The Tsar himself was under fire, but he still kept his head. It was only under the most urgent pressure from his generals that he at last consented to call up the artillery. Three guns were brought forward and loaded with case-shot. 'You want me to shed the blood of my subjects on the first day of my reign?' Nicholas had asked a little earlier. Now he exclaimed: 'This is a fine beginning to my reign!'³

It nearly came to a fight. Some of the rebels wanted to rush the guns which now faced them point-blank. Others thought it too risky. Still more, wholly wrapped in the dream, were sure that their comrades would never fire on them. They were wrong. The dream came to an end as, after warning shots, the three guns fired straight into the mass over open sights. At once all was chaos. Bloody reality broken in with a shock that was all the greater for being withheld so long. There was no resistance, the great crowd broke and fled. Dead and wounded lay scattered on the square. More shots tore into the fleeing mass as it tried to break out of the square down narrow streets. Others ran for the ice on the Neva, where they tried to regroup. But the gunners went on, now using cannon-balls to smash the ice and the bodies of the defeated. Nobody ever knew how many were killed as the darkness closed in on the stone heart of the great city. But all that night the police went silently about collecting the corpses and pushing them down with poles through holes in the ice – and with them many of the wounded. All that night the loyal troops bivouacked round their camp fires on the square which flickered and flared to illumine the rearing figure of the terrible bronze horseman. All that night other police and officers of the Guards went about their silent business of hunting out and arresting the leaders of the conspiracy, including those who had kept away from the drama on the Senate Square. And all that night the prisoners were brought one by one to the Winter Palace to Nicholas himself, who never went to bed at all but sat up to interrogate the ringleaders, to see for himself who they were, to ask what they thought they had been doing.

This was the start of a personal inquisition which was to continue for many weeks. Instead of distancing himself from the whole disastrous affair, instead of leaving the interrogations, the trials, the sentencing, to the relevant military and civil authorities, intervening only to confirm the sentences or to show clemency, the new Tsar chose to preside in detail over the humiliation of the defeated, questioning them individually and at length, lecturing them, pleading with them, threatening them, as he saw fit, prescribing for each his cell in the fortress of St Peter and St Paul across the river from the Winter Palace, the way he was to be treated, how he was to be fed. By the time it was all over and some had been hanged, others sent to eternal exile, he had established himself, at twenty-nine, as the chief policeman of his realm. He was never to look back.

2

The suppressed insurrection, the failed revolution of the Decembrists, so called after the dead winter month in which their hopes were shattered, was something new in Russian history. It was the first truly political movement ever to be directed against the established system. Tsars had been struck down before – how many times! – but always in the course of palace revolutions, designed to replace the reigning sovereign with another. Peasant revolts there had been in plenty, at least four of them frightening in power and menace – but always blind convulsions of rage by down-trodden slaves who had been driven too hard. In these there was never any popular movement against the Tsar. On the contrary, in the minds of the people the legitimate Tsar was the fixed point, the sun, the source of all beneficence and light. Their wrath was directed against the Tsar's officials and the landowners, whose corruption and greed came between them and the light of the sun. Thus Stenka Razin in the late seventeenth century urged his followers to march on Moscow and 'to stand for the Lord Sovereign and remove the traitors',[4] while Pugachev, a hundred years later, under Catherine the Great, actually presented himself as the true Tsar, Peter III, Catherine's murdered husband.

The Decembrist uprising, small, ill-led and quickly broken, was different in kind from the innumerable upheavals of the past: the autocracy itself was the target, to be destroyed and replaced by a constitutional monarchy, if not a republic – even though the troops, peasant conscripts, had no idea of this and believed they were striking a blow for the true Tsar Constantine against the false Tsar Nicholas. Thus the drama on the Senate Square marked, in the most literal way, the start of a new era in Imperial Russia, the first era of active political protest. Only a very few individuals were consciously involved in this great act of change. But these individuals started a process which was to continue, to develop, to ramify, gathering into itself the loftiest ideals, the unreal theorising of men turned into intellectual eunuchs by their exclusion from any share of political responsibility, the violence of frustration, envy and sometimes downright demonism, and, finally, the mindless desperation of sullen, hungry masses, until almost a century later the autocracy was swept away. The scene on the Senate Square on 14 December 1825 marked the beginning of this tremendous process which was to end in a global convulsion. To borrow from Frederick the Great, writing to Voltaire in a very different context (the premature death of the Emperor Charles VI): 'This small event . . . is the little stone which Nebuchadnezzar saw in his dream, loosening itself, and rolling down on the Image made of the Four Metals, which it shivers into ruins.'

CHAPTER TWO

The Doomed Conspiracy

I

BEFORE moving forward it is necessary to go back a little in order to discover what lay behind the December tragedy and why it happened when it did. The immediate cause was the failure of the Emperor Alexander I, the Blessed, to live up to his early promise as a reforming Tsar. That promise had been limitless. In the first year of the new century he was so eager, so beaming, so largely handsome and outgoing, that it required a major effort of the imagination to accept the fact of the complicity of this amiable young giant in the murder of his father, the miserable Paul, strangled in his bedroom in the fortress-like Michael Palace, built by him as a safe refuge.

Alexander was then twenty-four. Everyone knew of his determination to let in the light, reverse his father's repressive decrees and transform the rigid autocracy into a constitutional monarchy. From his Swiss tutor, Frédéric-César Laharpe, engaged for him towards the end of her nominally liberal phase by his overwhelming grandmother, Catherine II, the Great, he had absorbed ideas derived from Rousseau about the ideal society and his own duty, as future Emperor, to work towards their realisation. He was not unconscious of the difficulties involved. Indeed, as a youth he thought of renouncing the throne in favour of his brother Constantine and retiring to the banks of the Rhine together with his young bride, the very pretty Princess Marie Louise of Baden, to whom he had been precociously married at sixteen. Even up to the moment of his accession, and beyond, he insisted that he would abdicate once he had established an enlightened government and endowed his country with a constitution.

But he was a man most profoundly divided against himself, soon notoriously so. Catherine exclaimed in a moment of exasperation that he was a bundle of contradictions; and she was right. Napoleon was in due course to feel the same, so were all his brother sovereigns and their ministers at the Congress of Vienna. Not to put too fine a point on it, the great hero of 1812, the conqueror of Napoleon, the arbiter of Europe, won the reputation of an arch-dissembler: as with all natural actors, however, it was impossible to tell how much he consciously deceived others, how much he deceived himself.

Even in those very early days, while dreaming of renouncing the world and sinking into remote and rural obscurity, he was the darling of the St Petersburg drawing-rooms and an ardent womaniser. When faced with the exorbitant and conflicting demands of his devouring grandmother and his darkly lunatic father he did not, as might have been expected, retreat into himself but contrived to keep on terms with both, agreeing with their diametrically opposed ideas and moving with perfect fluency between the brilliant and libertine extravagances of Catherine's court and the barrack-room asperities of his father's establishment at Gatchina. The split went even deeper than that: the young Alexander was truly devoted to Laharpe with his dreams of a Russian Utopia, but at the same time he developed a close friendship with his father's right-hand man, Count A. A. Arakcheyev.

This dire and sinister creature, the only man who knew how to manage Paul, was an army officer, then in his late twenties, who had been dismissed from a staff appointment for excessive brutality and an uncontrollable temper: a noteworthy achievement in the Russia of that time. He was said to have bitten off the ear of a recruit on the parade ground in one of his frequent rages. But he had a virtue: he was loyal to his master, absolutely and unspeculatively as a savage police-dog is loyal to its handler. Loyal to Paul at the turn of the century, he was to prove himself equally loyal to Alexander when, in the later part of the reign, he rose to great eminence – to be the virtual ruler of Russia indeed, while Alexander travelled, or indulged in mystical communion with the infinite – and gave his name to an epoch of extreme oppression.

The ambiguity in Alexander's nature was reflected with especial clarity in the matter of his father's murder in March 1801. When the resentment of the nobility against Paul's tyranny culminated in a conspiracy to get rid of him in the time-honoured Russian manner, a palace revolution conducted by officers of the monarch's own Guard, the plot was confided to Alexander by one of its prime movers, the Governor-General of St Petersburg. He reluctantly lent the conspirators the cloak of his authority, but was careful to insist that no physical harm must come to his father. It should have been clear to him that if Paul resisted arrest, as he certainly would, he would die. But nobody knows to this day whether Alexander in fact understood this and was simply covering himself with a formal, empty stipulation, or whether he genuinely managed to deceive himself.

It was not a good beginning to the reign of a man who was determined to bring Russia into the nineteenth century. Instead of firmly breaking with the past, he brought that past with its centuries-long tradition of dynastic murder bloodily into the present. The outside world was shocked by yet another proof of Russian barbarity, but the Russians themselves found little to wonder at and rejoiced at the end of Paul's harsh reign. With his cruelty, violence and megalomania he had reduced the country to a vast barrack-square, or prison-yard, in the end excluding all foreigners, forbidding thought, burning books, substituting military discipline for government, treating his ministers and his nobles like serfs. It was this last offence, of course, which was the greatest. As far as the mass of the people were concerned, the peasants, one Tsar was very like another; but the nobles, flattered, pampered and exalted by Catherine, were beside themselves with bitterness and resentment. Catherine herself, for all her liberal protestations and her flirtations with Voltaire and Diderot, had reduced the peasantry to a condition of servitude more absolute and ignominious than at any time in Russian history. Few of the great Russian magnates objected to this: they profited by it, and only exceptional individuals had the sense, or the goodwill, to perceive that their own welfare and prosperity must depend in the long run on the welfare and prosperity of the country as a whole. But it was a different matter when it came to the curtailment of their own privileges and standing, and so Paul had to go.

To Paul's murderers, and those who thought like them, Alexander was the young Emperor who would restore the glories and privileges of Catherine's Russia. But there were others, and these included men who ardently desired reform not for selfish reasons but for the common good. Four of these, youthful friends of the new Emperor, were brought together to form a sort of advisory inner cabinet, known as the Private Committee. Very quickly they put an end to Alexander's dreams of a constitution. Russia, they insisted, could be run only on the autocratic principle: 'The least weakening of the autocracy would lead to the separation of many provinces, the weakening of the state, and countless disasters to the nation.'[1] What was needed was a benevolent autocrat, and this Alexander would be. He was the pledge for the present and the hope of the future. With his fine physique, he looked the part, very tall, open of countenance and fair. He was just the man to kindle the imagination of, for example, the romantic historian Karamzin, who convinced himself, together with other enthusiastic ideologues, that the real task was not to abolish the system, or even to amend it radically, but to restore it to what they believed to be its proper condition, defining the duties, obligations, privileges, the style, indeed, of a true and enlightened autocrat. Karamzin was to exercise himself deeply over such definitions. Following Montesquieu, he taught that the essence of the autocrat was that while he compelled order he was himself a part of it, adhering to the laws or codes of conduct which he himself imposed or inherited from his forebears, these ancient precedents being changed only for the most weighty reasons. The despot, on the other hand, considered himself above the law. It was a quasi-mystical concept, and, what is more, sharply at variance with the inborn Russian attitude towards the law.

The Russian people, as a whole, over-compensating for their profound anarchical tendencies, gloried in the mystique of autocracy. The Russian nobility bowed willingly to it on the strict understanding that the monarch would reward them for their subservience. Only a very few seemed to realise that the assumption of absolute authority by a solitary individual breeds irresponsibility in him, and often worse in all the rest.

Apart from the immediate repeal of Paul's repressive decrees, the movement for reform was limited in those first years of the century to the field of education and certain institutional arrangements which in no way restricted the Emperor's powers or invited men of talent or substance to play a part in policy-making. The members of the Private Committee took the poorest view of their aristocratic and landowning contemporaries. In the words of Paul Stroganov, a member of the family which had done most to open up Siberia and become fabulously wealthy in the process: 'Our nobility consists of a quantity of individuals who are gentlemen (*gentilshommes*) only by virtue of service, who are totally uneducated, who think exclusively in terms of the Emperor's power . . . They form a class distinguished for extreme ignorance, debauchery and stupidity . . .'[2]

Stroganov was a good and intelligent man with a genuine passion for reform; but reform, as he saw it, must come from the autocrat. Alexander had nothing to fear from his nobles, he said in effect. But he had everything to fear from the peasants, ill-used and oppressed, who regarded their masters with bitter and ineradicable hatred. In the eyes of the peasants, he went on, the Crown and the Crown alone was their bulwark against the depredations of landowners and officials. Weaken in the slightest degree the power of the Autocrat and the peasants will see only a strengthening of the enemy, an invitation to bloody rebellion. Therefore the autocracy must be retained in full rigour. This was to be an obsessional theme until 1861, and in a slightly amended form thereafter.

An unsympathetic observer might have put this another way: The system is rotten. The Autocrat is ultimately responsible for that system. It is in his interest, however, that he should appear to stand aloof from and loftily above the officials and the landowners, the men who are doing the dirty work for him, even though this means delivering the peasant masses entirely into their hands.

It was indeed on this confidence trick that Alexander based his rule. His first mildly reforming activity was interrupted by the outbreak of war with Napoleon in 1805. But there was a brief period, after the disasters of Austerlitz and Friedland and the subsequent Treaty of Tilsit in 1807, when he showed every sign of acting more radically. In the following year the unexpected figure of Michael Speransky was suddenly seen to dominate the whole field of domestic policies. And Speransky belonged to a new breed, not well-born like the members of the Private Committee (one of whom was his sponsor), but the son of a village priest who had made a startlingly brilliant career in the civil service, come under the notice of the Tsar at thirty-four, and in no time at all so won Alexander's favour and trust that for the next four years he was the Tsar's right-hand man, his mentor indeed in all matters affecting the civilian administration.

Speransky brought a brilliance, a lucidity, a practical sense, a capacity to strike at the roots of a problem, which put him in a class by himself. In addition, he possessed a quality rare among Russians of all epochs – not only rare but also instinctively abhorred by them: a sense of measure, an appreciation of the difference between the desirable and the possible, a belief in the virtue of compromise.[3]

With all this he was neither a prepossessing nor an attractive personality. His splendid qualities were exclusively of the intellect. He was contemptuous of the aristocracy and at the same time he kept at arm's length his most intelligent colleagues simply because like so many powerful and quick-thinking men of action, he could not be bothered to argue a case he knew to be right. He did enough work for ten men and off duty he preferred to surround himself with applauding sycophants, turning others away with a chilly handshake, a meaningless smile, an empty platitude. These personal failings are usually held to have accounted for his fall, taken together with his passion for French institutions displayed at a time when Alexander himself was arousing growing dissatisfaction by his policy of co-operation with Napoleon. The Emperor did in fact dismiss him in March 1812 when he needed a united country in face of the threat of renewed conflict with France.

But it is impossible to believe that Speransky could have got his way, Napoleon or no Napoleon, even had his personality been more sympathetic. His whole cast of mind, his approach to problems of government, was so alien to the Russian habit that the wonder is not that he fell so soon but that he was allowed to get as far as he did with the elaborate drafting of legislative, administrative and educational reforms. His supreme contribution was a proposed Statute of State Laws which proposed a brand-new governmental apparatus distinguished above all by an institution to be known as the Duma. The legislative body was to consist of four tiers of these elective assemblies. Working with these there was to be a fully-fledged executive body run by responsible ministers and a judiciary guided by the Senate. Above this whole complex was an assembly of elder statesmen known as the Council of State to advise the Emperor in person. The Tsar alone could appoint ministers, but every proposed law must be debated in the State Duma, which could reject it by majority vote. Any law passed by the Duma had to be confirmed by the Tsar, who could also, however, dissolve the Duma if the Council of State saw fit.[4]

It was a very long way from parliamentary government, but it was even farther from nakedly autocratic rule or, indeed, from the proposals of the Private Committee to which Speransky owed his chance. Had this statute been adopted it would have given a fair opportunity for the best men in the country to develop political consciousness and learn political skills. More than this, it would have offered the brighter spirits of a new generation, who were soon to show themselves radically-minded, an outlet for their enthusiasm and idealism other than the conspiratorial operations into which they were to be forced.

It was not adopted. The Council of State was set up in, as it were, a void, and the ministerial system, for what it was worth, was revised and improved. But the idea of an elective assembly, to say nothing of an assembly with powers of veto, remained a dream. It was a dream, moreover, which was shared by very few Russians and actively spurned by some, feared by more – including, almost certainly, the Tsar himself. For even while Alexander was giving Speransky his head as a civilian planner, he appointed and entrusted the military organisation of his realm to the man best calculated to work against all that Speransky stood for: his father's favourite, Count Arakcheyev. Speransky's unfortunate personality and the coming war with France between them provided the occasion for jettisoning the man and his work, but in the light of Alexander's character as it was soon to be manifested and of the profound Russian distrust of both reason and common sense in politics, if not in other things, which will be so striking a feature of the story unfolded in these pages, it is hard to believe that the Speransky plan would have been allowed to come to anything. In fact, almost exactly a century was to pass before a Duma came into existence, and then much too late, under the impact of the abortive revolution of 1905.

2

Speransky was dismissed in March 1812. In June of that year Napoleon crossed the Niemen into Russia and the whole country was united as perhaps never before to resist the invader. In March 1814, with the *grande armée* destroyed, Alexander entered Paris in the wake of his troops. Against the advice of his generals, he had insisted on the pursuit of the enemy beyond the borders of Russia, cost what it might: Napoleon had to be broken once and for all, and Russia in the person of her Emperor must demonstrate her determination from now on to operate as a great European power. She was no longer to be the embodiment of an obscure but menacing portent looming indistinctly through the mists of the vast Eurasian plain, no longer an apparently inexhaustible reservoir of peasant manpower to be converted by foreign subsidies into armies to fight foreign wars, no longer a supernumerary. She was now, with France prostrate, to take her place as an integral part of the European system, actively concerned with the refashioning of that system and able to make her voice heard, if she chose, on all matters affecting the peace and security of the whole, from the Western Mediterranean to the Black Sea, from the Aegean to the Baltic and beyond.

This was splendid for Alexander, now at a pinnacle of glory unapproached by any Russian monarch, dominating the Vienna Congress, seized with the noble mission to organise the European monarchies into a Holy Alliance for the regulation of international relations in accordance with Christian principles, in 'the name of the Most Holy and Indivisible Trinity' to operate under 'the eternal law of God the Saviour'. Even when, a few years later, this exalted concept was modified, or perverted, into a trade union of monarchs pledged to act in concert against sedition and subversion, the ruling idea was still that Russian nobility of purpose backed by Russian might would provide just that moral stiffening needed to raise the tone of the cynical, short-sighted, small-minded councils of the West and introduce an element of vision into the conduct of international affairs.

It was indeed splendid for Alexander, but it was not at all splendid for Russia. The Emperor's visionary enthusiasm, which had once been concentrated on domestic reform, was now directed entirely to the welfare of far-away countries. And the Russia which was going to save Europe from itself and preside over a golden age of equity and concord remained, unfortunately, the Russia whose wretched condition still demanded immediate and deep reforms. All Alexander now asked of his own people was that they should keep quiet and well-behaved while he addressed himself to his European mission. Few people in the west at first realised that while the Tsar was preaching enlightenment abroad, arranging the details of a constitutional monarchy for France, granting a constitution to the new kingdom of Poland within his own empire, he had entrusted the overlordship of his own vast land to the arch-reactionary and brute, Arakcheyev.

3

This is not the place to dwell upon the endlessly fascinating questions of the character and motives of one of the most impenetrable rulers in the history of Europe. The important thing in the context of this narrative is that the reactionary attitudes of his last decade prepared the ground for the Decembrist revolt in 1825. By taking his armies into the heart of Europe, Alexander accelerated the very process he most dreaded.

Consciousness of the backwardness of Russia, the corruption of her bureaucracy, her multitudinous ills, above all the evil of serfdom which created a gulf, as between men and animals, between the shockingly small ruling class – landowners and officials – and the great mass of the people, nine-tenths of the population of this country whose monarch was now telling Europe how to set its house in order – had first found expression, less than fifty years before Napoleon's march on Moscow, in the writings of Radishchev and Novikov under Catherine the Great. These men had been punished for speaking out. The conservative serf-owner Radishchev, who fell under the influence of Rousseau and gave a vivid and painful account of contemporary conditions in his *Journey from St Petersburg to Moscow*, was sent to Siberia. The Freemason Novikov who, with his primary schools, his famine relief, his scholarships for study abroad, was the Russian pioneer of enlightened charity, finished up in the Schlüsselburg prison. These men were the first of a long procession of gifted Russians sent into limbo for daring to say a little of what they felt and saw. It is a procession, already winding through two hundred years, the tail of which has still not come into view. In 1825 it was to be heavily reinforced. Since Alexander's first mild reforms a new generation had grown up.

Its members came of age in time to take part in the 1812 campaign. In their early youth, they had been encouraged by the Tsar himself to think in terms of the urgent need for radical reforms; they were conscious, as their seniors were not, of the dead weight of the serf system as it stifled the development of industry and agriculture (some of them had seen at first-hand on their parents' estates the ruinous effects of the continental blockade and deduced the inability for Russia to keep solvent when virtually her only income came from primary exports, above all of grain). They were already discussing ways and means of improvement among themselves, first in Masonic lodges, then in countless small clubs and societies, when they were suddenly and so resoundingly called to arms. Then two things happened. In the first place the ardours of the campaign against Napoleon brought them more closely than ever before to their own people, peasants in uniform, and filled them with a quite new sense of nationhood. In the second place their first sight of another world brought home to them the magnitude of the gulf between Russia and the West, spiritual as well as material, which until then they had only sensed. It was not a matter of comparative brilliance and show: there was brilliance and show in St Petersburg. What impressed them was not a comparison between Versailles, Potsdam, Schönbrunn and Tsarskoe Selo: nothing could surpass the splendours of St Petersburg. What impressed them was the relative prosperity of a relatively free peasantry, the importance and range of the great middle class, the freedom and flexibility (even in Metternich's Vienna) of the aristocracy, and, above all, the ferment of ideas: here were societies, far freer than their own, demanding yet more freedom and on the way to getting it. These wondering visitors from the East were intelligent and cultivated; they encountered some of the finest intellects of the West, conversing with them; they held their own. But they knew that these intellects were representative, whereas they, the visitors, represented nothing but themselves.

Remembering their peasant soldiers, remembering their sycophantic elders at home, they were filled with a burning sense of shame. But they still had a hope. To these ardent spirits the great hope was Alexander. He was the supreme Russian hero, invested with a prestige greater than that achieved by any Tsar before or since. He was the ruler over a land of slaves, who had proved in battle that they were more than slaves. Things could never be the same again.

But they were immediately the same again. An early sign of this was when the citizens of St Petersburg and other towns were beaten back by the police when they turned out to welcome their returning heroes – who were brought back to their native soil under cover of darkness and dispersed to their scattered garrisons before anyone knew they had come home.[5] Alexander might present himself as the benign and enlightened patron of Restoration Europe; he could endow his new kingdom of Poland with its own constitution; he could underwrite the new constitutional monarchy under Louis XVIII in France; but his own people whose brave and sacrificial loyalty had carried him to victory and power and glory were to be whipped back into their kennels – by an Arakcheyev. The fact that Alexander had in effect been forced by powerful conservative elements to banish Speransky, relegate to the pigeon-hole his elaborate plans for reform and abandon all ideas about the abolition of serfdom by the aristocracy, the fathers and uncles of the young men in revolt, in no way absolved him of guilt in their eyes. On the contrary: with a tyrannical monarch who decreed reactionary policies out of profound personal conviction one would at least know where one was. But what was the use of a monarch of goodwill held prisoner, bound hand and foot, by the blindest and most selfish elements in the land? The young men were fighting their fathers and they looked to the Tsar, the father of them all, to help them. He failed them. The autocracy thus itself had failed them and had to go.

4

And so the conspiracy gradually took shape, hampered in its development not only because the conspirators themselves covered such a wide range of opinion, but also because, most of them being army officers, they were subject to sudden postings and re-postings. It was purely accidental that the most determined and radical of the leaders found themselves based not in St Petersburg, which was the key to any successful revolt, but far away to the south.

The first serious and purposeful organisation was founded in St Petersburg in 1816 as the Union of Salvation or Society of True and Faithful Sons of the Fatherland. It was initially composed of a handful of close friends, all Guards officers: Alexander and Nikita Muraviev, Ivan Yakushkin, Matvei and Sergei Muraviev-Apostol, and Prince Sergei Trubetskoy. To these were soon added a few others, most importantly a brilliant young officer, Pavel Ivanovich Pestel, who, at twenty-four, immediately began to take control and force the pace. The son of a notoriously corrupt and brutal Governor-General of Western Siberia, he had been educated in Germany before winning outstanding honours at the St Petersburg Military Academy, had then fought and been seriously wounded at Borodino and afterwards was appointed A.D.C. to General Wittgenstein. The young Pushkin, who met him in 1821, when at twenty-seven he had just been promoted to colonel in command of the Viatsky regiment, called him 'a wise man in the complete sense of the word . . . One of the most original minds I know'.[6] He was indeed an extraordinary man, a natural leader, bursting with controlled vitality, with a passion for politics in the broadest sense, born into a country where only one leader could be recognised and politics was a forbidden land. So his politics turned, almost inevitably, to conspiracy, his natural intolerant authority to Jacobinism. The story of the development of the Decembrist conspiracy from 1817 to 1825 was very largely the story of Pestel's relentless campaign to get rid of all who opposed his own radical solutions and put heart and steel into those who, while accepting in principle the necessity for breaking the autocracy, up to and including regicide if necessary, were yet reluctant fellow-travellers.

Dissension was persistent. Pestel was regarded by many of the rebels as a dangerous man, a threat to the maintenance of any sort of order, a would-be dictator even – above all by men like N. I. Turgenev and Nikita Muraviev, who were chiefly concerned with analysing the economic reasons for Russia's backwardness and suggesting solutions for economic and institutional reforms within the framework of a constitutional monarchy. Such men had no love for Alexander and his advisers, but they feared obsessively the breakdown of civil order, accompanied by uncontrollable peasant risings, which could result from a frontal attack on existing authority. Pestel and his followers, however, were greatly assisted by the crass excesses of Arakcheyev and the virulent obscurantism of Alexander's 'educationists' – the reactionary Michael Magnitsky and Dmitri Runich, who, between them, virtually destroyed the universities of Kazan and St Petersburg.

A still deeper cause for concern was the almost revolutionary situation in Alexander's notorious military settlements designed to replace the normal barrack-life of the peacetime army. There was no regular conscription in Russia at that time. The great military machine, which so disconcerted the West by drawing upon an apparently limitless reservoir of recruits, was organised in a wholly arbitrary manner, very much in accordance with the principles of the impressment which for so long sustained the British fleet, but on a huge scale and with every landowner his own press-gang. The Government simply demanded from landowners and village communes an *ad hoc* quota of bodies, fluctuating according to the demands of the moment, to be delivered up for army service. The official term of this service was twenty-five years. As a rule this meant for life. It was nothing but chance, or ill-will, which determined the victim, who, once nominated, would be seized and taken away from his village and his family and wholly lost to them. There was no such thing as leave. There were no disability pensions. Anyone tough enough to survive his term of service would be worn out, forgotten, rejected, with no place in his village. Alexander was determined to put an end to this system. It was arbitrary, inhuman, wasteful and expensive. How much better all round if soldiers in peacetime could live together with their families in special settlements on the land, helping with the farmwork in the intervals of training.

This magniloquent and 'hare-brained' scheme led to nothing but woe. It was opposed even by Arakcheyev who said that if the Tsar wished to ameliorate the lot of his troops it would be better to reduce their term of service by five or six years. But Alexander was stubborn and, of course, it was left to Arakcheyev to implement the system, to which he brought the sort of discipline he understood. Whole regiments were settled on Crown lands and set to work to build their own huts and cultivate the soil. Wives and children were subject to the same barrack-room discipline as the men. Their lives were regulated by bugle-calls. There were regular kit inspections of household goods (every pot and pan had to be stowed in the prescribed manner). Wash-days were detailed, the meals for each day minutely regulated. Children were put into uniform. The field workers were marched to their tasks, deployed by numbers and marched home again. Men had to marry at eighteen, girls at sixteen: if they showed reluctance their spouses were chosen by lot. The least infringement of the rules was savagely punished, and floggings were frequent.[7]

Alexander thought he was imitating the system obtaining in Hungary, whereby the Austrians had sought to guard against the encroachment of the Turks by settling soldier farmers in a wide belt along the Danube. He was proud of his settlements, and Arakcheyev contrived to present him on his tours of inspection with settlements run, apparently, on idyllic lines, populated by prosperous, industrious, clean and contented villagers. On the frequent occasions when discontent seethed into bloody rebellion he was deeply hurt by the ingratitude of the men for whom he had done so much, ascribed the trouble to 'the spirit of evil' which was spreading all over Europe, and authorised the use of the harshest measures to teach the offenders a lesson. The system, combining the economics of serfdom and conscription, continued: at the time of Alexander's death over three hundred thousand soldiers with their families were frozen into it. And it was this institution, added to longer-established evils, which was to bring the milder members of the Union of Welfare to the conclusion that the autocracy must be destroyed if the country itself was not to go up in a revolutionary explosion.

Then, in 1821, occurred the incident which convinced many that the Tsar himself must be mad.

The Semyonovsky Guards were one of the proudest, most venerated and devotedly loyal regiments in the Russian army. They and the Preobrazhensky Guards derived immediately from the two regiments of 'toy soldiers' created by the future Peter the Great when, as a boy, he was sequestered, out of harm's way, in the country outside Moscow (the Izmailovsky Guards were created by the Empress Anna as a personal bodyguard, commanded by a Scot and largely officered by Baltic Germans;

the Pavlovsky Guards by the Emperor Paul who insisted that all must have snub-noses like his own). In 1821 several companies of the Semyonovsky Guards, driven to desperation by a commanding officer noted for his cruelty and with a German name, refused to obey a certain order, which was in fact illegal. It was a purely local and spontaneous affair, and it petered out with no violence shown. The ringleaders put up no resistance to arrest, and the affair should have ended with a court of inquiry, a reprimand and a re-posting for Colonel Schwarz, and short, sharp disciplinary action against the offenders. Instead, it got out of hand.[8] Alexander was, as so often, away from home. He was, in fact, at Troppau in Silesia, conferring with the Austrians, the Prussians and the French about the future of the Holy Alliance. Alarmed by revolutionary movements abroad, he had come to the conclusion that this alliance must be hardened into a union of monarchs pledged to support the monarchial principle by intervening with force anywhere in Europe where sedition showed its head. The immediate danger, as he conceived it, came from the Italian secret society, the Carbonari, which had just deposed the King of Naples. When he received the news of the Semyonovsky 'mutiny' Alexander was immediately seized with the conviction that the Carbonari had penetrated into the fastness of Holy Russia: how else could the spirit of evil, *le génie du mal*, have contaminated the loyalest of the loyal? His first thought was that he must return immediately to St Petersburg to confront the peril in person. But he changed his mind and, instead, sent instruction after instruction as to the punishment of the ringleaders – already safely sentenced and locked away in the Schlüsselburg. Imprisonment was not enough. They must receive six thousand lashes. On top of that it was clear that new watch-dogs were required, and a special and secret military police arm was set up to penetrate the regiments of the Guards and listen for seditious talk.

This was enough to steel the hearts of many patriotic officers of the Guards, who knew just what had happened, and why. So far indeed was this famous regiment from infection by any spirit of revolution that only four years later it was to stand firmly behind the new Tsar on the Senate Square, refusing to join the mutineers.

5

From now onwards talk of regicide was frequent. But still the conspirators were deeply divided, their differences polarised by new and rival constitutions drawn up by Nikita Muraviev in the north and Pestel in the south. The Muraviev constitution was, like the Green Book of the

Union of Welfare, still essentially reformist: it saw the future of the Empire in an ordered federation, the central government machine presided over by a constitutional monarch vested with certain quasi-presidential powers. Pestel's constitution was genuinely revolutionary in the context of the time. Embodied in the celebrated document which he entitled *Russkaya Pravda, Russian Justice*, a deliberate echo of the comparatively enlightened medieval code of Kiev Russia before the Tartar invasion, it provided for the deposition of the Tsar, the abolition of the monarchy, and its substitution by a republican form of government and a free-enterprise, free-trade economy.[9] Neither constitution went very far towards making life easier for the masses. Muraviev made much use of the concept of democracy, but what he envisaged was a very limited democracy: far more individuals than hitherto would be drawn into the business of government, but on the basis of rigid and steeply graded property qualifications. Pestel objected very strongly to this, holding that an aristocracy of wealth was even more deplorable than an aristocracy of birth: it apparently did not occur to him that his own projected solution of unrestricted free enterprise was bound to produce its own aristocracy of wealth. In fact free enterprise could never have flourished in the sort of society he envisaged. Simply to maintain order while the republic was being established there would have to be a dictatorship – provisional, it goes without saying. It is hard to see how such a dictatorship could have found the way to surrender its powers over a state so highly and rigorously centralised as the model conceived by Pestel, whose concern for individual liberties did not extend to the susceptibilities and aspirations of national and cultural minorities. For this ardent and brilliant Jacobin had no use for small nations and peoples. He was indeed the first exponent of total russification. The Russian conquests in the Caucasus and Transcaucasia were still incomplete, those in Turkestan were yet to come. But these troublesome borderland states, up to and including Mongolia, which he considered too weak to maintain their own independence, must be conquered and annexed to Russia and their multitudinous peoples, thrown into the melting pot with Ukrainians, Finns, Tartars, Lithuanians, Letts, Esthonians and countless smaller eastern tribes and turned into Russian citizens, renouncing their own pasts and their cultural inheritance. Jews were to be either assimilated or else deported *en masse* to Asia Minor to establish their own independent state. Gypsies could either become Orthodox Christians and settle down like good peasants or else get out. In a word, there was to be only one category of citizen: Russian. And all Russian citizens were to be equal under the law. Only one nation was to be exempted, and that was Poland, a special case, with a history of independence going back centuries before the eighteenth-century partitions. But even the Poles must agree to adopt a republican constitution which would be a replica of the Russian one; what is more, in a formal eternal alliance with Russia, they were to place their army at the disposal of the Russian Government. The Russian Government itself was to emphasise its identification with the great popular mass by moving from St Petersburg, not to Moscow, but to Nizhni Novgorod on the middle Volga, which was to be renamed Vladimir after the ancient town which was the cradle of the Muscovite state. Order was to be kept by a secret police force more powerful and better organised than previous bodies of this kind.

While Pestel was composing his constitution with its uncanny pre-echo of Stalinism, affairs were moving to a climax. The southern society was gaining allies, joining forces with a Polish secret society and also with a socialistically inclined society of small gentry who looked beyond the borders of Russia and called themselves the United Slavs. By the beginning of 1825 it was generally agreed that there must be decisive action in the following year. Even Prince Trubetskoy, N. I. Turgenev and Nikita Muraviev had come round to this view, though still far from agreeing with Pestel and his new and most devoted follower, Sergei Muraviev-Apostol, on the means and the aims. The northern will to radical action had lately been strengthened by the addition of certain civilian recruits, notably the romantic and highly idealistic poet, Ryleyev, who lent recklessness and rhetoric to the movement and saw eye to eye with Pestel and Muraviev-Apostol on the need for action for action's sake, even at the cost of temporary failure. For Pestel himself was beginning to see that it might take more than one blow to make a revolution and that martyrs might be needed too. Ryleyev, moving in a state of perpetual exaltation, was a leading exponent of the concept of a *garde perdue*, ready to sacrifice themselves and lose their lives for the awakening of the country. But he was level-headed enough to perceive the need to preserve himself and the society intact if action failed. Thus it was that when he was approached by other enthusiasts, most notably the fanatical Kakhovsky, who were determined to assassinate the Tsar and begged for the privilege of sacrificing their own lives in this cause, he encouraged them but refused to allow them to join the society. Kakhovsky, or Yakubovich, or whoever, should have the inestimable privilege of killing Alexander, but the society would be able to disown them.

This was, roughly, the position in November 1825, when the activities of the society were betrayed to the Tsar, who had less than a month to live. Even before Alexander was dead, a full-scale enquiry was proceeding, which led to Pestel's arrest on the very day before the northern revolt of 14 December. The northern revolt itself was precipitated by a local betrayal. And just as it was the discovery by Nicholas of a widespread conspiracy dedicated to the overthrow of the autocracy which made him at last move quickly to accept the crown, so the conspirators themselves were driven to go off at half-cock, with no time to co-ordinate their activities with their colleagues in the south, by the necessity of exploiting the heaven-sent interregnum.

The interregnum itself was due to the extraordinary hesitation of Nicholas before accepting the crown. The natural heir, since Alexander was childless, was his brother the Grand Duke Constantine. But Constantine quite lacked the imperial style. Coarse, off-hand, inflexibly self-centred, pug-nosed like his murdered father, he had blotted his copybook by insisting on marrying a plebeian mistress and found full satisfaction for his limited ambitions in the Governorship of Poland. Installed in Warsaw, a potentate in an alien land, he could enjoy the privileges of virtually absolute power without the burden of responsibility towards his own people which it was incumbent upon a Russian autocrat to shoulder. Years before, Alexander had signed a binding document excluding Constantine from the succession and confirming as his heir his much younger brother, Nicholas. For reasons best known to himself this document was sealed and hidden away, its very existence kept secret from all but a few members of the imperial family. Nicholas knew about it, though, when the time came and Alexander died suddenly at Taganrog when he was still only forty-seven, but he pretended not to know and insisted immediately on swearing his oath of allegiance to Constantine as his sovereign. There followed a ludicrous comedy which lasted for nearly three weeks. Couriers dashed back and forth between Moscow and Warsaw: Nicholas prostrated himself before his brother; Constantine replied that this was absurd, since he, Nicholas, was Tsar; Nicholas begged Constantine again and again to come to Moscow; Constantine refused to budge; he was comfortable where he was, the sooner Nicholas got himself crowned the better.[10]

Nobody knows just what went on in the mind of Nicholas. He insisted, like so many hereditary rulers – like most elected ones too – that the very idea of ruling filled him with dismay: he wanted to be left alone to get on with his military career and his domestic life. But some of those closest to him held that for years past he had been determined to rule. And, indeed, in the light of his character as it later revealed itself, it is impossible to believe that this born tyrant, dedicated to the point of fanaticism to his holy calling, seized with the sense of his own God-given superiority to the rest of mankind, would ever have been prepared to serve in the shadow of his cheerfully coarse-grained brother, who put his home comforts, palatial as indeed these were, above his duty to his country and his dynasty.

The true answer to the mystery is probably the obvious one, frequently suggested, that Nicholas was extremely unpopular with his fellow officers, and knew it; knew also something of the active discontent in the corps of officers and of the disrepute into which his revered brother, Alexander, had fallen, and considered it desirable to give no hostages to fortune by appearing to put himself forward to be labelled in hostile circles as an usurper. In a word, he was determined to be drafted, and to be seen to have been drafted.

It was a mistake nevertheless and very nearly a disastrous one. Had Nicholas allowed himself to be proclaimed immediately after his brother's death the most active conspirators would have been hard put to it to push through any sort of action directed at a young and brilliantly handsome Tsar sustained by all the emotionalism of popular acclaim and with no black marks against him beyond his notoriously martinet behaviour as a serving army officer. It was the long period of wavering, together with the knowledge that the conspiracy was in the process of being uncovered in detail, which gave the Decembrists the courage to act at all. And the final spur came from the news which went round on 13 December that Nicholas had at last decided to be sworn in next day. Even then, the more determined southern society, shocked by the arrest of Pestel on the thirteenth, did not move into action until 19 December when they heard for the first time of the northern insurrection – too late. As things turned out, the belated southern revolt was far more serious, dangerous and widespread than the brief action in St Petersburg. Led by Muraviev-Apostol in Pestel's absence, this revolt took on the character of a major military operation, which failed after ten days of agonised suspense, partly because of faulty liaison with the Poles, more particularly because of the almost mystical idealism of Muraviev-Apostol. Unlike his northern colleagues he was not prepared to hoodwink his troops into believing that they were fighting for a legitimate Tsar who would bring them more pay and improved conditions: he saw himself as the leader of a crusade, and wasted much time in a quasi-ritualistic attempt to turn his peasant soldiers into an army of crusaders for liberty and justice. He should have taken Kiev, and had he succeeded in this the country might well have been embroiled in a major civil war, involving also Poland, with results impossible to foresee. But he was doomed to failure and he failed magnificently, afterwards shaming so many of his northern colleagues by insisting on taking the whole blame for the uprising and dying bravely for it.[11]

CHAPTER THREE

The Autocratic Inheritance

I

The Russian autocracy as we see it now is a thing apart. It is impossible to assign to it any rational origin in the vices, the misfortunes, the necessities, or the aspirations of mankind.

This is the novelist, Joseph Conrad, writing in 1905 about the Russian débâcle in the war with Japan. He continues:

This despotism has neither a European nor an Oriental parentage: more, it seems to have no root either in the institutions or the follies of this earth. What strikes one with a sort of awe is just this something inhuman in its character. It is like a visitation, like a curse from heaven falling in the darkness of ages upon the immense plains of forest and steppe lying dumbly on the confines of two continents: a true desert harbouring no Spirit either of the East or the West.[1]

This despairing cry of a Pole whose country had suffered so much from Russia, whose mother's early death had been hastened by exile in Vologda, deep in the northern forest, because of the part his father had played in preparing for the insurrection of 1863, reflects with terrible clarity the feelings which at times, when contemplating this or that episode of overwhelming inhumanity, have seized and cast down most visitors to Russia from the sixteenth century to the present day. To make any sense at all of the Russian tragedy it is a mood to be resisted.

Perhaps the first account of the impact of the Russian autocracy on a Western European occurs in the notes of the Emperor Charles V's envoy to Moscow, first published in 1549. Commenting on the arbitrary and absolute power of the Tsar over all his subjects, including the highest dignitaries of the Orthodox Church, Baron von Herberstein remarked: 'It is a matter of doubt whether the brutality of the people has made the prince a tyrant, or whether the people themselves have become thus brutal and cruel through the tyranny of their prince.'[2] This question was to echo in the minds of Western observers for centuries to come. It is one of the first questions many visitors to Soviet Russia find themselves asking to this day.

The Russian autocracy in its most positive manifestations has always been so spectacular in its absolutism that it has compelled the myth of omnipotence with almost hypnotic force. No doubt its most gifted and energetic exponents, Ivan the Terrible, Peter the Great, as well as less dynamic rulers, managed at times to convince themselves and their subjects too that they were indeed all-powerful. But they behaved very frequently as though in their more lucid moments they knew they were nothing of the kind. The more total their pretensions, the more crippling was the fear that rode their lives – so that the dark, hallucinated brooding of the music provided by Mussorgsky for the dying Godunov may stand for the secret, sometimes not so secret, thoughts and fears and crises of conscience of the autocracy incarnate. These autocrats ruled by favour, and in their hearts they knew it. The real answer to Herberstein's question is that the state of Russia was, and is, the outcome of the interplay between the subject people who, not once but again and again, invited the general idea of autocratic rule while quarrelling with particular manifestations of that rule, and the autocracy which sought to impose in detail its absolute will over the subject people. Each brutalised the other.

For the autocracy was not, as Conrad felt, a visitation, a blight, imposed upon the Russian peoples by occult forces: it was a response to a popular demand – which is far from saying that the people liked what they had asked for when they got it. It was not, of course, an active demand. At the moment, above all other moments, when the Russian people, or the nobility, or both, could have taken their destinies into their own hands, at the ruinous 'Time of Troubles' after the death of Boris Godunov in 1605, the men who could have put Muscovy on a new course seem to have found the strain of attempted self-government too great. Tradition proved stronger than the will to reform, and the profound, assuaging, self-mortifying, self-indulgent yearning for a 'natural' Tsar prevailed. The chronicler Abraham Palitsyn wrote of the Time of Troubles, through which he himself lived, that the great destruction of the State of Muscovy had been brought about by nothing else than a deep national apathy: there was no speaking up, no determined effort on the part of the people to become masters of their fate. 'For this national apathy, for the thoughtless silence of the whole land, the country was punished.'[3]

In 1613 Michael Romanov was installed, with no checks and counter balances, as the first head of a new dynasty to rule over not only a people but also a stiff-necked aristocracy who, after all they had suffered at the hands of previous Tsars, still preferred to wear the yoke of tyranny rather than carry the awkward burden of responsibility. After 1613 the country was to be punished again and again through the centuries, and for the same cause: 'the thoughtless silence of the whole land'.

With the passage of time, the momentum and weight of the autocratic system itself so corrupted Russian society that the demand became a need. The workings of the autocracy ensured that a people subjected to it over the ages could not exist without it. Thus in the early nineteenth century a rebellious spirit, Pushkin himself, saw nothing strange in the equation of the great Tsars with the spirit of revolution. Change was a fact of life, it had to be: but who other than the Tsar could authorise it? The remarkable thing is that the nineteenth-century Tsars had very little Russian blood. Like so many of their most able officials, they were almost wholly German. The Emperor Paul was at most half Russian (Catherine being his mother, nobody could tell for certain who his father was). He married a German princess, as did his sons, Alexander I and Nicholas I, and his grandson, Alexander II. And yet all of them absorbed the Russian tradition and carried it on.

Obedience to an authority which embodies, or personifies, no matter how imperfectly, fixed principles of conduct is one thing; obedience to a ruler, or a hierarchy of rulers, lacking any guiding principles whatsoever, their conduct governed by expediency, is obviously quite another. Few Russians have shown awareness of this distinction, though many have sought unconsciously to conceal the absence of principle in their autocracy, whether monarchial or dictatorial, by placing exaggerated stress on the concept of orthodoxy, but orthodoxy, astonishingly, ingeniously indeed, existing in, as it were, a void and itself constructed of nothing at all but an imposed and man-made churchly ritual, lacking ethical content; or, at a later period, an imposed man-made catechism, the almost insolent simplification by a man of action of the teaching of a great German philosopher-economist who knew next to nothing about people.

Thomas Carlyle, who should have known better, also failed to perceive this distinction. For him obedience was all, the *sine qua non* of order. In one of the most bizarre exchanges it is possible to imagine he wrote in April 1855 – that is to say, at the height of the Crimean War – to thank Alexander Herzen for the English translation of the exiled revolutionary's pamphlet: 'On the Development of Revolutionary Ideas in Russia.'

In your vast country – which I have always respected as a huge dark 'Birth of Providence', the meanings of which are not yet known – there is evident, down to this time, one talent in which it has the pre-eminence, giving it potency far beyond any other nation: the talent (indispensable to all Nations and all creatures, and inexorably required of them all, under penalties), *the talent of obeying* – which is much out of vogue in other quarters just now! And I never doubt, or can doubt, but the want of *it* will be amerced to the last farthing, sooner or later; and bring about huge bankruptcies, wherever persevered in. Such is my sad creed in these revolutionary times.[4]

This authoritarian worshipper of rebellious heroes saw in the great masses, whom he despised, obedient instruments of the hero's will. But he should have been able to see that Nicholas I was not by any stretch of the imagination a hero and thus to have questioned the spirit of obedience which enabled him to rule, or at least to seem to rule, more absolutely than, for example, Frederick the Great, or Cromwell, both of whom commanded a large measure of positive obedience in the interests of a cause, whether admirable or not. The obedience of the Russian people was something other. It was negative, or passive, obedience. It was an abdication of responsibility. In only the most limited sense could the Russian autocrats command: except in moments of extreme national peril they could only repress. And they themselves were thus in one way to be seen as the puppets of an inarticulate people who paid them in suffering as the price for freedom to contract out of nation-building activity. The central government of Russia with its tightly organised provincial apparatus extending over unimaginable distances was, in so far as it affected the governed, less the administrative nexus of a unified nation than the colonial service of an occupying power, having no organic connection with the subject people – an analogy pointed up in post-Petrine Russia by the choice of St Petersburg as the seat of government. One person and one person alone, in the eyes of the subject people, stood above the detested government and was at the same time its victim; and he, whose supreme office did indeed reflect the people's need, was the very man who believed that he was the government: the Tsar.

2

This was the tradition inherited unquestioningly by Nicholas I when he succeeded his elder brother on that sad December morning in 1825. He was the very embodiment of the autocratic principle in looks, manner, character and thinking. He was twenty-nine and had not been educated to rule but within a matter of days he was laying down the law to his Council of State as to the manner born: 'I cannot permit', he declared, 'that any individual should dare defy my wishes, once he knows what they are.'[5] This was an almost exact repetition of his first order of the day, promulgated seven years earlier, after his youthful appointment to be Inspector-General of Military Engineers. 'The slightest infringement of the regulations,' he had then declared, 'will be punished with all the force of the law: no pardon will be granted.'[6] He went on like that all his life.

He was formidable to a degree. When in his full middle age, in the early summer of 1844, the young Queen Victoria of England received him at Windsor, she was deeply impressed with his looks and the grace and dignity of his manner. She was also made uneasy by him. She was twenty-five. The Tsar of All the Russias was forty-eight and had ruled for nearly twenty years. He stood for absolutism of the most repressive and sometimes savage kind.

The young Queen had not looked forward to this visit; but Nicholas, six feet three inches tall, finely proportioned and carrying himself superbly, was without question the most handsome monarch alive, and Victoria, as so often, found herself warming to a fine figure of a man. His profile, she thought (and wrote to her uncle Leopold in Brussels) was 'beautiful'. She must have been most affected by the fine, continuous line of forehead and nose, which indeed had a classic quality, while overlooking the thrusting, too heavy jaw and the small, tight mouth. The eyes worried her most: '. . . the expression of the eyes is formidable, and unlike anything I ever saw before.'[7] Alexander Herzen, who hated Nicholas and despised him, was also struck by those same eyes. He commented on the lower jaw as well; but for him the main thing about the face, the face of the first Gendarme of Europe, was again the eyes: 'entirely without warmth, without a trace of mercy, wintry eyes.'[8]

Victoria, not a subject of this terrible man but a fellow monarch, soon found that his eyes could soften: 'the sternness of the eyes goes very much off when you know him, and changes according to his being put out . . . or not, and also from his being heated, as he suffers from congestions to the head.' He fascinated her, and after a few days she found it impossible not to like him; but he still disturbed her: he was so much 'the greatest of all earthly Potentates' that she found difficulty in taking him in; and she could never quite get away from those eyes: '. . . he seldom smiles, and when he does the expression is not a happy one.'

Another observer, the celebrated French traveller, the Marquis de Custine, had earlier reported of Nicholas, with whom he had had long conversations, that 'he cannot smile with his eyes and his mouth at the same time'; his characteristic expression, he wrote, was one of 'worried severity'.[9] This also struck Victoria, who tried in vain to understand why an autocrat whose word was law, who had every physical and material advantage, who appeared to see things naturally in black and white and was active to a degree, could yet give such an impression of troubled melancholy. 'He is stern and severe – with fixed principles of duty which *nothing* on earth will make him change: very *clever* I do *not* think him, and his mind is an uncivilised one; his education has been neglected; politics and military concerns are the only things he takes great interest in; the arts and all softer occupations he is insensible to, but he is sincere, I am certain, *sincere* even in his most despotic acts, from a sense that it *is* the *only* way to govern.' She recorded with sympathy his kindness and courtesy to individuals around him, his delight in children. She was surprised by his lively eye for feminine beauty. Above all, however, she was impressed by a quality not as a rule associated with men of power: 'His anxiety to be *believed* is very *great*.'

This was a key observation. Ten years earlier de Custine had been almost overwhelmed by the passionate desire of this so exalted monarch to justify himself and plead the purity of his motives – not before God, but before anyone who would listen. Earlier than that, a number of the December conspirators were faced with the same manifestation when taken from prison and confronted by the potentate they had attempted to destroy. Kakhovsky, the murderer of Miloradovich, was so affected that he wrote afterwards from his prison cell: 'Sovereign, I cannot and do not wish to flatter; but since last night I have felt myself drawn to you as a man and with my whole heart wish to love in you, my Monarch and the Father of my country.'[10]

Victoria had reason to feel uneasy. She was right about the Tsar's sincerity; but what she did not understand was that this sincerity amounted to a burning conviction, by normal human standards bordering on the insane, of the absolute rectitude, the divine virtue of his own views, and of the wrong-headedness, frivolity, or sheer bad faith of all who called them in question.

And yet, with this conviction there went a profound, concealed uncertainty. Nicholas protested too much. There was not the slightest need for him to emphasise his supremacy, either as a young Grand Duke in command of a branch of the army, or as Tsar of all Russia. It was taken for granted by all the world. Only Nicholas himself had to go on proving it, pursuing with those baleful and petrifying eyes throughout all the thirty years of his reign every deviation from good conduct as prescribed by him. Nobody seemed to realise, least of all himself, that there was something demeaning in these constant assertions of personal power on the part of the most powerful monarch in the world, no less than in the passionate desire to be believed on the part of a man who should have been above caring whether others believed him or not. They went hand in hand with inexhaustible self-pity. The whole strange complex of arrogance, pleading and self-pity was to be exhibited to perfection on the eve of the Crimean War in the extraordinary correspondence between Nicholas, then approaching sixty, and the youthful Emperor Franz Joseph of Austria, who owed a profound debt of gratitude to the Tsar, but who nevertheless found himself unable to believe his protestations of perfect altruism in moving against Turkey in the Balkans:

'Can you believe,' urged Nicholas, 'that a man of honour is double-tongued, or that he would go back upon what he has once declared to be his intention? . . . Is there not something hatefully superfluous in permitting oneself to doubt his word, once given, or in asking him to reaffirm it?' Self-righteousness, affronted, leads on to the darkly minatory: 'Are you truly to make the Turks' cause your own? Emperor Apostolical, does your conscience permit it? If it be so, well and good; then Russia alone shall raise the Holy Cross and follow its commandments. If you were to range yourself with the Crescent against me, then I say to you, that would be a parricidal war.'[11]

3

A distinguishing feature of the history of nineteenth-century Russia when compared with other European monarchies was the absence of any constructive interplay between the monarch and his subjects. The development of other monarchies at least reflected the running conflict between the will of the monarch and the expressed ideas and demands of the highly articulate interest groups over which he presided. Thus there was a long story of compromise and adjustment, expressing itself in constant movement and manoeuvre, and tending always, now rapidly, now slowly, towards one clearly recognisable end: the visible broadening of the base of a once feudal society to take account of the needs and aspirations of a steadily broadening spectrum of the subject peoples. This dynamic conflict was weak in Imperial Russia; under Nicholas I it simply did not exist. The Tsar did not manoeuvre: he laid down the law, and there could be no effective public questioning of that law – though whether the law was obeyed was another matter. There was thus no gradual and organic evolution, no public preparation for inevitable change.

The most striking aspect of the reign of Nicholas I was, precisely, the absence of movement. It started with tragedy and ended, with the Crimean War, in disaster. A great many things happened in between, from the crushing of the Poles to the building of the first railways, but there was no sense of momentum, of development, of learning from past mistakes. From the historian's point of view this makes for difficulty in the elementary organisation of narrative. What happened next? Why? How did such and such an action, or conflict, produce this or that consequence? And so on. In fact, except in purely chronological terms, nothing happened over a span of nearly thirty years. Nicholas did not grow. He allowed nothing else to grow. And the consequences of his actions, with the major exception of the Crimean War, were not felt until after he was dead. This means that in describing his reign it is impossible to isolate a main narrative line, a forward movement in which the advances and setbacks may clearly be seen as stages in the conscious striving of a dominant individual, or a ruling caste, towards a distant goal, however dimly apprehended. The reign of Nicholas I was not a development; it was a prolonged situation.

Towards the end of his life one of the most devoted servants of the State, the ex-serf A. V. Nikitenko, an enlightened civil servant worn out with frustration, could declare: 'The main failing of the reign of Nicholas Pavlovich was that it was all a mistake.'[12] This is another way of saying that Russia in 1855 was in all important particulars identical with the Russia of 1825, materially stronger because of certain industrial developments (but not relatively stronger compared with the rest of Europe), morally and intellectually weaker because of the bleak discouragement not only of ideas but also of individual character and sense of responsibility.

It is impossible to establish just when Nicholas stopped growing. The precise date (it must have been in his late teens) does not matter. The Inspector-General of Engineers who, at twenty-two, announced to his new command that all deviations from the rules would be punished without mercy was the same man as the young Emperor who appeared before the rebels on the Senate Square, now twenty-nine, fully armed in all his formidable magnificence. He was also the same man who nearly twenty years later impressed the young Victoria with his uneasy might and grandeur – and his lack of cleverness. He was so complete and untouchable in his outward appearance of certainty that it is hard to visualise him at a time when he was not very self-consciously the potentate of potentates. But he was not brought up to be Tsar and his childhood years must have been extremely difficult. If it is hard to think of Alexander as the son of poor, mad Paul, it is even harder to think of Nicholas in that company. But so it was. Nicholas was only five years old when his sad and terrible father was strangled in the Michael Palace and his brother, Alexander, became the marvellous new Tsar. Alexander was then twenty-four, Constantine twenty-two. So there was an unbridgeable generation gap between the two elder brothers on the one side and Nicholas and his younger brother, Michael, on the other.

That is to say, all through his childhood Nicholas grew up in the shadow of his brilliant brother. As he toiled, stubbornly resisting, at wide-ranging but badly taught studies, he had to watch that brother soar into the empyrean. He was ten years old when Alexander, after Austerlitz, met

Napoleon at Tilsit; sixteen in 1812, desperate to join the army. He got into uniform before the end of the campaign, but was kept away from danger.

4

When the call came, Nicholas was completely set in his ways as far as the outside world was concerned. But the outside world knew nothing, guessed nothing, of the tensions produced by the imposition of a bleakly rigid exterior on a sentimental, highly emotional nature which was also subject to seizures of almost apoplectic fury when crossed. For in childhood this great disciplinarian had kicked against all discipline, and as he grew up to recognise the need for self-discipline he evolved a mystique of duty, essentially romantic. Order and harmony became the most important elements in the eyes of a man who seethed to choking point with angry passions. The young Victoria saw into him more acutely than most, but she was wrong in one particular: Nicholas was by no means insensible to the softer emotions. Like so many neurotics noted for tyrannical behaviour, he was easily moved to tears. He was only eighteen when, in Berlin, he fell head over heels in love with the Prussian princess who had already been marked down in both St Petersburg and Potsdam as the most suitable bride for the young Grand Duke. Princess Charlotte, young, beautiful, sentimental, gay, was enraptured to find that her stupendously handsome fiancé apparently shared her tastes in music and the theatre, to say nothing of the charms of nature as displayed in the Potsdam woods and heathland where they wandered hand in hand. As the years passed, however, it became apparent that neither Beethoven nor Schiller had struck deep roots in his soul. Although the mature sovereign prided himself on his patronage of the arts and, indeed, enjoyed domestic evenings with a little music, what he looked for was a reflection, however banal, of order and symmetry, that same order and symmetry which, heightened by a sense of personal power, transformed the spectacle of drilling regiments into the deepest aesthetic experience known to him.

The quasi-aesthetic aspect of army command has been underrated by historians who are usually temperamentally alien to militarism. Nicholas followed Frederick of Prussia and Napoleon, preceded the young Franz Joseph of Austria and William II of Germany, in reversing the proper order of things by regarding their armies not as necessary and regrettably expensive shields for the civilian state but as the supreme expressions of the state for the support of which the civilian economy was designed. In building up these colossal machines they created hosts which only a genius could command and effectively deploy. On parade, the army of Nicholas was superb. Tens of thousands of peasants and their officers were colourfully arrayed and drilled to perfection. On every possible occasion Nicholas himself, surrounded by his aides and senior commanders, would ride out in the uniform of one of his own regiments of Guards to preside over massed evolutions. He knew every button, every twist of gold braid, on every uniform (many he had himself designed). He interfered at every level, even to the point of finding time to assign new recruits to the various household regiments. It is easy to laugh at this mania. Indeed it was absurd. But the absurdity should not be allowed to conceal the high romantic impulse behind the obsession with minutiae. Nicholas had his dream. His dream was of a Utopia in which all men knew their place and were organised for their own good in a blessed hierarchy commanded by the Tsar who himself took his orders from God on high. The army with its rigid chain of command and perfect obedience was not only the visible expression of this harmony; it was also the model to which civilian society must aspire.

5

The shock to a limited man of this cast of mind when he discovered on the first day of his reign that elements of his army were not only disaffected but actively treacherous, was almost past bearing. When the prisoners were brought to him he was appalled by the extent of the conspiracy now uncovered. Whom, now, could he trust? To faithful old Miloradovich, the first casualty of the revolt, he owed the bad advice to wait before accepting the crown. In the forefront of the conspirators were representatives of some of the most ancient families in the land – a Trubetskoy, an Orlov, an Obolensky, no fewer than nine members of the Muraviev clan. All these families, rejecting their own traitors, were to distinguish themselves again and again in years to come. But how was Nicholas to know that this would happen? The closing of the ranks of the nobility as they disowned their fallen sons was no doubt reassuring, but it could not be immediately convincing. Whom could he believe? The rot had gone very deep. Although until the last months the conspirators had formed a close and secretive circle, their general attitude had been shared by many outside that circle. Pushkin himself, when directly questioned, admitted to Nicholas bravely that had he been in St Petersburg instead of in exile he would have joined the conspirators (in fact he had not been invited only because there were doubts about his discretion).[13] The future dictatorial Prime Minister of Austria, Prince Felix zu Schwarzenberg, then serving in the Austrian Embassy, had been so close to the Decembrists that Nicholas insisted on his recall: the Austrian Ambassador himself was a cousin of Prince Trubetskoy, who fled to him for sanctuary on the morning of 14 December.[14] Something of the bitterness the young Tsar felt against the officers of his Guard was shown less by the severity of the immediate punishments than by the refusal to pardon the survivors as the decades went by.

The initial punishments, indeed, do not appear to Western eyes outrageous in the context of the times. Five of the ringleaders were hanged, 200 more sent off into exile in Siberia, while many of the soldiers, victims really of their own officers, were flogged. But, when all is said, assassins and would-be regicides have invited death or imprisonment for life in most countries at most times. What was disturbing about these punishments was less the fact than the manner – and the attitude behind the manner – above all the passionate and personal involvement of the Emperor in a process which had best been left to appointed and impersonal guardians of the security of the realm. He involved himself here as he was to involve himself in everything for thirty years to come, and so publicly that he denied himself the freedom of action, the liberty to profit by the mistakes and experience of subordinates, to nourish second thoughts and to manoeuvre accordingly, in which lies the strength of the commander who knows how to delegate. If Nicholas ever had second thoughts about anything he was powerless to profit by them without publicly reversing positions already taken up when a wiser man would have committed himself to nothing.

The process started on that bitter winter night when Nicholas had the first prisoners brought to him at the Winter Palace, into which he had only moved with his family from the Annichkov Palace that morning. These extraordinary confrontations continued for days, for weeks, and in the course of them the new Tsar displayed the theatrical streak which was to mark so many of his utterances and actions, now threatening, now coaxing, now speaking more in sorrow than in anger.

The unfortunate Prince Trubetskoy broke down completely and sought to cover the feet of the Tsar with kisses: he was sent into exile for life. Kakhovsky, the murderer of Miloradovich, caught the interest of the Tsar by his bearing and his arguments. 'Kakhovsky spoke to me with great daring and frankness,' Nicholas wrote. 'His words were bitter and positive. He was a young man full of love for his country but pledged to the most criminal actions.'[15] It made no difference to the final issue. Kakhovsky was hanged. So was Pestel, brilliant, and admired by Pushkin, 'a blackguard in the full meaning of the word, such as is rarely found: his face had a bestial expression, his demands made with arrogant impudence and not a show of remorse.'[16] So was Alexander Bestuzhev, who gallantly took all blame on himself, and wrote most movingly from prison to Nicholas personally, explaining the nature of the ideals which had guided the conspirators. The poet Ryleyev was hanged, but Nicholas afterwards went out of his way to see that his wife and child were well provided for.

Pending trial and conviction, Nicholas gave exact orders for the individual treatment of each prisoner. They were incarcerated in the damp and gloomy cells of the Peter and Paul Fortress just across the Neva river from the Winter Palace. The long, low silhouette of Peter the Great's creation, the hub and centre as well as the bastion of his new city, is dominated by the light and slender spire of Rastrelli's cathedral, in which all but one of the Romanov Tsars from Peter to Alexander III lie buried in tombs of remarkable simplicity. Entering the fortress today and walking to the cathedral under summer trees one has not the least sense of being inside a prison, and, indeed, the notorious Alexander ravelin, the original dungeon block, was done away with under Nicholas III. It was here that Peter the Great had his own son imprisoned and tortured to death. It was here that Radishchev was kept before being sent off to Siberia by Catherine, and it was here that Nicholas consigned the Decembrist conspirators, to await death or exile – and, later, the novelist Dostoevsky and other members of the Petrashevsky Circle; later still, the anarchist Bakunin. It was a terrible place, a separate world, wholly surrounded by water within the fortress, itself surrounded by water. The cells of the much bigger prison in the Trubetskoy bastion, which became notorious in the late nineteenth century as the living graves of countless radicals and revolutionaries of every complexion, are gloomy enough, seeming to be hewn, like caves, out of solid stone, with the iron rings for the chains heavily stapled to the walls. But the Trubetskoy bastion was a model prison compared with the dreadful old Alexander ravelin, stygian, dripping wet. It was in these cells that the Decembrists managed to compose their appeals, their self-justifications, their confessions, for the Tsar. And while they were so doing Nicholas must have looked out from the splendours of Elizabeth's vast Winter Palace across the narrow, misty waters to that long, low wall which hid his prisoners from his own sight and the brilliant life of the great city.

The people [wrote Kakhovsky] have conceived a sacred truth – that they do not exist for governments, but that governments must be organised for them. This is the cause of the struggle, in all countries. Peoples, after testing the sweetness of enlightenment and freedom, strive towards them; and governments, surrounded by millions of bayonets, make efforts to push these peoples back into the darkness of ignorance.[17]

Bestuzhev wrote:

Finally, Napoleon invaded Russia and then only, for the first time, did the Russian people become aware of their power: only then was awakened in their hearts a feeling of independence, at first political and then national. That was the beginning of free thinking in Russia. The Government itself spoke such words as 'Liberty, Emancipation!' It had itself sown the idea of abuses springing from the unlimited power of Napoleon, and the appeal of the Russian monarch resounded on the banks of the Rhine and the Seine. The war was still on when the soldiers, upon their return home, for the first time spread discontent among the masses. 'We shed our blood,' they would say, 'and now we are forced once more to sweat under feudal obligations. We freed the Fatherland from the tyrant, and now we ourselves are tyrannised over by the ruling class ... Did we free Europe in order to be put in chains ourselves? Did we grant France a constitution in order that we dare not talk about it, and did we buy at the price of our blood pre-eminence among nations in order that we might be humiliated at home?'[18]

Even when they were dead, or had been dispersed on that long hard journey to Siberia, followed often by their wives who were allowed to accompany them as a special act of grace – elegant, urbanised, sometimes highly frivolous women of noble birth, braving the remote unknown of their own free will – even when they were dead or exiled, these men were never for long out of the Emperor's mind. He had their appeals, their depositions, copied out and bound in a costly leather volume which he kept always at hand in the Winter Palace. In the years to come he seems to have brooded time and again over these so varied manifestations of the awakening consciousness of social obligation. There can be no doubt that he himself was stirred by them, and troubled. Indeed, it is not too much to say that beneath that preposterously grand and marmoreally cold exterior, the obsessional, the theatrical sense of duty was warmed by a genuine sense of social obligation. Of course, there was fear, and Nicholas fed his fear by reminding himself constantly of the treacherous hostility that might be concealed behind the smooth countenances and glittering uniforms of the men who were supposed to guard and sustain his person. More than this, there was anger, almost incoherent in its suppressed intensity: men of his own Guard, who owed to the Crown all their privileges, their very existences, had conspired to kill the wearer of the Crown. Of course, behind the blandness of perfect manners, there was a passion of bad temper and a streak of raw sadism. Obsessed with the dignity of his position, Nicholas lacked dignity of soul: only a man deficient in self-respect could have mounted the charade of 1849, when he deliberately allowed Dostoevsky and his companions to be put before the firing squad blindfolded, dressed in their shrouds, knowing that at the eleventh hour his messenger would gallop up to bring them their reprieve. One of them went mad.

But this remarkable complex of fear, bitterness, incomprehension and uncontrollable passions (it was only his features that he knew how to control) was, it seems almost wholly certain, exacerbated beyond measure by a sense of personal betrayal expressed in profound self-pity: these abominable and detestable creatures, his own contemporaries (Trubetskoy, thirty-two, was the oldest) had taken it upon themselves to give premature and half-baked expression to ideas which were, at least in part, already taking shape in his own mind, and had thus, as it were, pre-empted and ruinously perverted, rendering null, a movement towards social reform, the initiation of which was the prerogative of the Tsar and of nobody else at all.

Nicholas, although he ardently desired the betterment of his realm, lacked the intelligence required to tell him what must be done . . . And when, inhibited by fear of the unknown, ignorance and intellectual incapacity, he failed to think of anything effective to do and was too proud, too frightened of men with good brains, to seek advice and listen to it, he could blame this failure on men now dead, or living far away in exile; men who, by their wicked treachery, had tied his hands.

The loneliness of a hereditary autocrat who is not especially gifted is not easily imagined. Nicholas I of Russia, had he not been born into the ruling house, might have risen to command a brigade, certainly no higher. Just as he had absorbed himself, as Grand Duke, wholly in the parade-ground aspect of his military command, so, when he became Emperor, he was happiest when making tours of inspection, ranging swiftly, far and tirelessly, with a deadly eye for cook-houses, pipe-clay and the proper layout of kit. He would inspect schools as well, bringing classes to a standstill by interrupting the form-masters and putting irrelevant questions to the pupils: once he was so incensed when a pupil, not idling but listening intently, so far forgot himself as to lean an elbow on his desk in his august presence, that he demanded the instant dismissal of the unfortunate master in charge.[19] This sort of hysteria was never far below the surface. He found distraction in restless travelling, fulfilment in barrack-room inspections, relaxation with his wife and children – later in life also with his mistress, Barbara Nelidova, by whom he had a number of children, all scrupulously cared for – under the wing of his Minister of Communications, the notorious bully, Count Kleinmikhel. But to none of these could he look for the least assistance when it came to making the political decisions required of him every day. He was temperamentally far too unsure of himself ever to seek a confidant to whom he could admit inadequacy. He could, and did, however, pour out his feelings to his family, and it is through his correspondence that we may glimpse the devouring self-pity of a man who did not know how to seek relief from a burden which was too heavy for him.

Thus, after the formal sentences had been pronounced upon the December conspirators, he wrote to his mother, the Dowager Empress Marie Feodorovna, the widow of mad Tsar Paul:

> My dear and good Mama, the verdict has been pronounced. It is hard to express what I am feeling: it is as though I were shaken by a fever.... Added to this I feel extreme anguish, at the same time gratitude to God who has allowed me to bring this horrible case to an end. My head swims. I am bombarded with letters, some of them desperate, others written in a state bordering on madness. Only the idea of a terrible duty enables me to endure such a martyrdom.[20]

But endure it he did. The hangings took place. Next day there was a ceremonial service of atonement and thanksgiving held in the open on the Senate Square. That night the Petersburg balls started up again, and while the whole of high society converged, blazing with orders and jewels, on the Kotchubey Palace, the first convoy of prisoners, which included close relatives of some of the guests, was setting out from the fortress of St Peter and St Paul across the river on the long march to Siberian limbo.

The reign had now settled into its stride. There were to be no more plots among the officers of the Guard and the nobility. What Nicholas, with all his brooding, never began to understand was that the Decembrist revolt was not a conspiracy of army officers as such; it was a conspiracy of the founding members of a new intelligentsia, who were, or had been, army officers for the simple reason that the army offered the only universally respected career for a young man of good birth. If Nicholas had understood this he would have felt more secure; and, at the same time, he could have taken steps, the army in full sympathy at his back, to undermine in advance the positions soon to be taken up by the intellectual successors of the loyal opposition, the new and rootless bourgeoisie, who were not loyal at all.

History has been justly hard on Nicholas, who has been made a scapegoat for the sins of his predecessors, to say nothing of his successors, and, in some degree for the sins of the Russian people. He was not an attractive man. He had a streak of violence, of sadism even, and more than a touch of paranoia. He attitudinised to excess. He behaved cruelly towards the Poles, but no more cruelly than his successor, Alexander II, the Tsar Liberator. He set himself up in cold and bleak opposition to all those who questioned the workings of the autocracy, but he himself sought more actively and purposefully and consistently – though not at all sensibly

– to make those workings more humane. He was indeed the first Russian monarch to display a social conscience in action as distinct from words.

There was also in him a streak of rather disconcerting silliness. For a man of his position, bearing and majestic appearance he was, as already observed, curiously lacking in dignity. He talked far too much, holding forth unnecessarily and unwisely whenever the mood took him. In this there is a distinct likeness to William II of Germany, translated into terms of an earlier epoch and a different mental climate. Thus, when revolution broke out all over Europe (but not in Russia) in 1848, Nicholas issued his notorious manifesto, refusing to amend a word when his chief advisers demurred, which filled the chancellories of Europe with wild surmise:

> Insolence, no longer recognising any limits, is in its madness threatening even our Russia entrusted to us by God.
> But let this not be!
> Following the sacred example of our Orthodox forefathers, after invoking the help of God Almighty, we are ready to meet our enemies, wherever they may appear, and, without sparing ourselves, we shall, in indissoluble union with our Holy Russia, defend the honour of the Russian name and the inviolability of our borders.
> We are convinced that every Russian, every loyal subject of ours, will respond gladly to the call of his monarch; that our ancient battle cry: 'For Faith, Tsar and Fatherland' will now once more show us the way to victory, and that then with feelings of reverent gratitude, as now with feelings of sacred trust in Him, we shall all exclaim:
> 'God is with us! Understand this, O nations, and submit, for God is with us!'[21]

Nevertheless, he tried very hard with his so inadequate intellectual equipment. For the sake of domestic order, as he conceived it, and legitimacy abroad, he was ready to make almost any sacrifice. His misfortune was that he was the first Russian monarch who was called upon to cope with a coherent movement of social criticism. The iniquities of his reign were fixed for ever in the brilliant images and polemics of Alexander Herzen, and it was the Herzen legacy which was to nurture generation on generation of liberals and revolutionaries, so that Nicholas came to be seen as the very pattern of the arch-tyrant, malignant, cruel and obscurantist.

Bound up with this, there was an element of profound national feeling. Alexander I, so free with the lofty expression of still loftier ideals, had been more heartless, more hurtful by far than his duller younger brother. But Alexander was a conquering warrior, a shining symbol, therefore, of national unity in face of the invader, an inseparable aspect of a new patriotic legend from which not even a Tolstoy was immune. Alexander had talked about abolishing the knout; it was Nicholas who acted. Alexander set up the system of military settlements; Nicholas did away with them. Alexander handed over the government of his realm to the brute Arakcheyev; Nicholas got rid of him. Alexander threw the brilliant reformer, Speransky, to the wolves; Nicholas brought him back to make a grand codification and revision of the laws. Alexander ruled without principle, without direction; Nicholas was the slave of principle and strove to impose a positive system of government reflecting the principle of benevolent despotism. His benevolence was not an empty profession. And he was brave. He proved his bravery on many occasions. He proved it under fire in the war against Turkey; he proved it during the great cholera epidemic of 1832 when he went out to face a rioting mob ravening for the blood of doctors and nurses who, they said, were poisoning the sick in the hospitals; he proved it in the great fire which burned down the Winter Palace in 1837.

But he spoilt everything. His personal intervention in his first war with Turkey was so disastrous that he himself had to recognise, with bitterness in his heart, his inadequacies as a commander. In the cholera epidemic in Moscow he dismissed the doctor in charge of a hospital which reported more deaths than the others; and no deaths were reported anywhere for long after that. After the great fire, in which thirty or forty of the fire-fighters died, he commanded the rebuilding of the vast palace within a year, and it was because of this insensate speed that workmen were suffocated to death in rooms overheated to dry the plaster quickly.

But the rigid adherence to dogmatic principle, principle degenerated into a series of *idées fixes*, was half the trouble, and perhaps the chief of all the reasons for the traditional Russian hatred of Nicholas.

At the very end of his life, when the shocking failures in the Crimea had brought home to him his own failure to clean up the rottenness and corruption of the whole bedizened, epauletted, bureaucratic and military establishments, faced with a particular betrayal of trust, he could stare out into nothingness, think back to the terrible start of his reign, and murmur: 'Ryleyev and Bestuzhev would never have served me like this.'[22]

CHAPTER FOUR

The State of the Empire

THE St Petersburg inherited by Nicholas in 1825 was very different from the city left behind him by its founder on his death in 1725. Cruel, brutish, insufferable in his titanic way, but also a visionary of genius, Peter the Great thought he was westernising Russia and bringing enlightenment to his people when what in fact he was doing was raiding the West for its technical skills, which he then sought to graft on to the ancient Muscovite stock.

The sudden, convulsive violence which he brought to this task was to shock and affront the Russian spirit without changing it. With his contempt for inherited privilege, his transformation of the nobility into a regiment of carefully graded placemen and the Church into an arm of government, he brought to the surface, institutionalised indeed, the latent schizophrenia which had characterised the Russian attitude towards the Western world since the Tartar conquest in the thirteenth century, which had effectively cut Russia off from Renaissance Europe for two hundred and fifty years. The existence of St Petersburg itself was to reflect and symbolise thereafter this painful division in the national psyche.

Here was a centre of brilliance, a great city raised on piles in a northern swamp, its impersonal and colossal elegance pressing down on the bodies of innumerable slaves, the casualties of a constantly replenished workforce of forty thousand souls dragged from their homes to toil beneath the knout until they died laying the foundations for the architectural splendours of successive monarchs, the Russians Anne and Elizabeth, above all the German Catherine, all turning their backs on traditional Russian styles and looking for inspiration to Western models. And yet even though from the reign of Anne onwards St Petersburg was the seat of government and the chief residence of the monarch, even though untold sums were expended throughout the eighteenth century not only on turning the city itself into one of the show-pieces of the world, but also on the stupendously extravagant fantasies of the outlying palace complexes at Peterhof with its terraces and fountains overlooking the Baltic, Tsarskoe Selo with its marvellous palace by Cameron, its lesser palaces and countless imperial villas and pavilions, it still counted only as the second capital of Russia. Moscow was the first. Emperors and Empresses were buried in Peter's fortress church, but they were crowned in the Moscow Kremlin. Almost every other building in St Petersburg was a palace or a barracks; in Moscow almost every other building was a church. The people still clung to the ancient Muscovite spirit, while the nobility looked to the West and forgot how to speak their own Russian tongue.

It was towards Moscow and beyond that the Tsar had to look from his study in the Winter Palace. To the north across the Neva, frozen for half the year, lay the inescapable presence of Peter's fortress and beyond that only Finland stretching far into the Arctic. To the west was the Gulf of Finland and beyond it Lake Onega and the non-Slav Baltic provinces. To the east, Lake Ladoga, thereafter thousands of miles of nothingness, barely populated forest-land stretching beyond the Urals and Tobolsk to the mountains of eastern Siberia and the Pacific, shading into barren tundra, with Archangel the only considerable port – all those northern waters like the Neva itself frozen for half the year. It was to the south, a little to the south-west with White Russia and Russian Poland, and almost infinitely to the south-east that the vast realm effectively unfolded.

But even then it was a closed view. There was something symbolic about the way in which the autocrats' view to the south from the windows of the immense Winter Palace (painted in those days not green as now, but dark red) was closed by the large, crescent-shaped bulk of the General Staff building, still unfinished when Nicholas came to the throne, across the Palace Square. When complete it was to house the Ministry of Finance and the Ministry of Foreign Affairs, as well as the General Staff. This immense complex which came in more senses than one between the monarch and his people was pierced by a triumphal archway, affording a passage from the Palace Square to the Nevsky Prospect; and it was up and down this great street, quite straight for two miles of its three-mile length, that all the business of the Empire had to pass until the railway to Moscow was opened by Nicholas in 1851. The Tsar, his ministers, his army commanders and his civilian governors, all couriers, all officers and officials secular and religious, civilian and military, coming into St Petersburg to report, or going out to Moscow and far beyond to convey decrees, to begin tours of inspection, to take up new appointments, passed up and down this street at the beginning or the end of journeys which would certainly take days and very often weeks.

There were no stage-coaches in Russia at any time, either before the advent of railways or afterwards, to cover those vast areas where the railways did not penetrate. But all along the very sparse and poor main roads there was an organised system of posting stations which combined primitive and often verminous accommodation with staging points for changing horses. The grandees passed in their heavy travelling carriages or, for faster, shorter journeys in smart outfits; but lesser men set out on their arduous journeys in a peculiar sort of unsprung cart in summer, the telega which had no seats behind the driver: travellers sat on the luggage or lay in straw. It was in a telega that the young Count Leo Tolstoy and his servant travelled from Kazan to the Caucasus in 1849, the journey he later described in the opening pages of *The Cossacks*. The tarantas, a rather crude sort of victoria, with a hood, was used for family travel by gentry who could not afford a coach. The most frequent of all the vehicles were the little two-seater carriages on wheels in summer, on runners in winter, very fast, in which even the Tsar himself might make quite long journeys, exposed to the elements, accompanied by a single aide.

The Russia which began to open out at the Alexander Nevsky Monastery was divided into great administrative areas known as Governments, each under a Governor as the Tsar's representative. The Governments were to increase in number as the century wore on, and on the eve of the Revolution there were fifty-nine of them in European Russia alone. Besides the Governments there were Territories, which were in effect purely colonial areas – Asian provinces under direct military rule. Under Nicholas I Russia proper was flanked by the General Government of Western Siberia, which comprehended several ordinary Governments and was ruled over by a very great potentate indeed, and in the south by the Viceroyalty of the Caucasus, which extended from Tiflis to Baku. Certain major cities had their own administrations under a City Governor. The provincial Governments were divided into Districts, Towns and Rural Cantons, and here the chief functionaries were the chief policemen, all responsible to the Governor, who had prefectorial powers. For the simple reason that all power stemmed from the Tsar, which meant that all his officials were the Tsar's representatives, there was never any clear definition of local powers. For all practical purposes provincial police chiefs could do as they liked unless and until, for whatever reason, they were called to order by the Governor – or by the overriding authority, derived directly from the Tsar's Private Chancery, of the representative of the Third Section of the Chancery, the Gendarmerie, or secret police, assigned to each Government.

It is obvious that in a land of such vast distances with communications so poor, governed in theory by a highly centralised bureaucracy swarming round the seat of absolute authority, any hope of good government must depend very much on the individual qualities of the provincial chieftains.

When these are neither vested with a defined measure of responsible autonomy nor bound by any precise code covering all contingencies, the opportunities both for passing awkward decisions back to the centre and for arbitrary action must between them create that ambience of uncertainty which is far more favourable to the development of tyranny than the harshest code of laws: for with a precise code of laws, no matter how repressive, the subject knows where he is and can take evasive action. Under the Russian system nobody at all knew where he was: nobody therefore dared move. Absolute repression was thus imposed with a minimum of statutory prohibition.

Nicholas I achieved nothing approaching the thoroughness and uniformity of terror which, a century later, was to be imposed by Stalin. Nor did he wish to do so. He imagined that he was ruling benevolently, though strictly, through a clearly defined chain of command, with the secret police, the Third Section of his private Imperial Chancery, acting as watch-dog and protector in his name. But under that system almost anything could happen and most things did. The farther from St Petersburg the more absolute was the power of the formal provincial governors. These might be wholly vicious, oppressing and plundering with systematic, evil-minded rigour, like the notorious General Pestel, the father of the hanged Decembrist, in Western Siberia. Or they might be jolly rogues, cheerfully corrupt, like General Bronevsky in Irkutsk, effective monarch of Eastern Siberia, who used to amuse himself and his cronies by firing cannon-balls into the town from a neighbouring vantage point 'when he was merry'.[1] Others, quite a numerous class, would start off with the best of intentions, determined to rule wisely and well, only to throw up their hands in despair in face of the impenetrable jungle of bribery and blackmail in which provincial officialdom lived and had its being. It has often enough been said that the only thing that made the Tsarist system tolerable and workable was the easy-going slackness of the typical official: if the rules had been applied with teutonic thoroughness the machinery would simply have seized up – or there would have been bloody revolution a hundred years earlier. And this may well be true, just as it has been true of the centrally planned Soviet Union, which can only live and breathe by ignoring the plan and resorting to the ancient tradition of greasing the wheels with favours and bribes and short-circuiting the official channels. Herzen himself observed that Russians on the whole are incapable of sustained and single-minded repression: they tend to get bored. This also is true, with plenty of exceptions (more today than in the nineteenth century). But this fitfulness cuts both ways. Russians of goodwill, again with exceptions, are also incapable of sustaining for very long the struggle against evil; they are too easily discouraged. A few then resign, far more simply give up trying, take on protective colouring, and continue in their posts.

The worst evils, of course, arose directly from the institution of serfdom. Contained within the framework of the bureaucratic hierarchy, and nominally subject to it, were the landowners. And the landowners for all practical purposes were the Tsar's representatives on their own estates. They were untrammelled by even the vestige of a code, except that they might not kill – although they sometimes did.

2

When it came to the internal development of Russia, the great tragedy of Nicholas arose from his failure to harness all available talent and to fashion a new administration and social framework which could respond both to the humanitarian impulses of the age and to the needs of industry, trade and agriculture in the dawning era of steam.

Jealousy of his own position of autocrat, natural enough, was aggravated by a profound distrust of the nobility as a whole and an acute consciousness of the venality and corruption of the bureaucracy. Yet the system he constructed was calculated almost to perfection to increase the alienation of men of talent, goodwill and critical intelligence, and to deliver the business of justice and administration into the suffocating toils of an underpaid bureaucracy.

This was due in the first place to the rigid centralisation of the government apparatus. There were no institutions of local government in which the landowner could play an effective part. All power and responsibility moved outwards and downwards from the centre. Nicholas was content that the landowners should be responsible for their own serfs and nothing more. Instead of involving them, large or small, in the affairs of their own districts and thus building up a class of active-minded citizens familiar with the elementary rules of responsible public service – a reservoir, too, of potential recruits with experience of practical administration to the central government apparatus – the Tsar for all practical purposes excluded them from the community, which was administered (for want of a better word) by careerists, all of them looking upwards (never outwards to the people) through a close-ranked hierarchy to the Governor, who himself looked to St Petersburg.

The Russian landowner could share in the running of his country only if he stopped being a country gentleman, left his estates in the hands of stewards, and entered the imperial service as a professional bureaucrat. This was not a career likely to appeal to the better landowners, who would hesitate, unless compelled by ambition or by some domestic crisis such as imminent bankruptcy, to commit themselves to a service notorious for corruption, incompetence, back-biting and intrigue. So they stayed on their estates, or idled in St Petersburg or Moscow, disenfranchised in the largest sense, a dead loss to their country.

Even to those who, for whatever reason, had chosen government service, Nicholas was reluctant to delegate responsibility. He found himself unable to contemplate a form of government which called for true and formalised ministerial responsibility. The idea that his ministers should operate as a collegium, or cabinet, discussing policy among themselves, perhaps organising cabals, combining to thwart or divert his directives, he found intolerable. He must be his own prime minister. Each minister must report to him personally and in private – as a rule once a week; and each minister would concern himself exclusively with his own field, the necessary exception being the Minister of Finance, to whom the other ministries had to look for their budgetary allocations. In theory this meant that he, the Tsar, would be the only person in the realm to possess a complete picture of all the affairs of the realm. But in practice, as should have been perfectly obvious – as indeed it was to Nicholas himself – it did not work out like that at all. What happened was that he found himself, with his ministers, so overwhelmed by small details that major decisions had to be shelved and forgotten, or left to junior officials to be dealt with urgently. Each separate ministry was thus a bureaucrat's paradise, and the system of bribery and corruption inevitable in any underpaid bureaucracy was allowed to grow and flourish in these claustrophobic enclaves of officialdom to an unheard of degree.

No man could have exerted himself more determinedly than Nicholas to put the administration on a healthier footing, but although his stern and rigorous presence in St Petersburg had a salutary effect in checking corruption at the centre, outside the capital he was powerless to intervene, and it is hardly too much to say that throughout the length and breadth of Russia there were very few judges or officials who could not be bought, if not with crude bribes, then by the promise of favours to come from rich and influential landowners, or of easy promotion or threats of professional ruin for covering up or failing to cover up the misdeeds of superiors who had themselves been bought. It was difficult for the honest man, and the Tsar knew it.

This rather than an excess of martial ardour was the main reason for the remarkable preponderance of military men among the Emperor's advisers. Apart from the diplomatic service, the army was traditionally the only respectable career open to the well-born Russian. It contained not only the most intelligent servants of the Crown but also, as we have seen, its most determined critics. Towards the end of the reign, for example, the young Leo Tolstoy, unaware of his genius, and faced with the business of choosing a career, could contemplate only three courses: he could use his very grand connections to secure him an appointment as A.D.C. to the Tsar; he could study for the diplomatic service, which called for a fairly high level of accomplishment; or he could take a law degree and obtain a sinecure post in the government service. Even when Nicholas was dead, the military tradition was so strong that we find it penetrating into the most unexpected places. Thus, when we come to consider the marvellous flowering of Russian music in the second half of the century we shall find that Mussorgsky was an officer of the Guards; Borodin an army doctor and chemist of distinction; Rimsky-Korsakov a seagoing naval lieutenant; César Cui who, besides composing fluently and copiously did so much to promote the music of his contemporaries, made up in military distinction what he lacked in musical genius: an engineer officer, he became a leading authority on fortifications and rose to be a lieutenant-general.

For Nicholas, of course, the army was his natural world and the only one he understood. Once in a while he would seize upon a civilian who impressed him with a combination of administrative ability and devotion to the mystique of the autocracy. But his instinct was to distrust civilians on principle: they did not understand the meaning of obedience; they had not been drilled. Alas they could never be drilled; but Nicholas at least managed to get the whole country into uniform, devoting happy hours to choosing or personally designing the distinguishing features of the uniform of this or that branch of service, profession, university or school.

Not content with surrounding himself with soldiers, men he thought he understood and could trust, Nicholas went one step further in his restless and foredoomed determination to subordinate the whole population of Russia to his stern but benevolent discipline. He developed an exaggerated passion for those special *ad hoc* committees traditionally a feature of Romanov rule to deal with any matter that caught his attention, cutting clean across the usual ministerial channels and reporting directly to him. He used his corps of personal A.D.C.s in much the same way – suddenly, without warning, detailing this or that young officer of good family to embark on some mission of inspection or investigation.

Above all he elevated the sovereign's private office, His Imperial Majesty's Own Chancery, into a formidable centre of power. Hitherto this office had provided the Tsar's personal secretariat and the administration of the magnificent private foundations and charities of the Dowager Tsaritsa, the widow of the murdered Paul. But Nicholas saw in it his own incorruptible instrument. The First Section was still his personal secretariat; the Second Section was created to codify the laws; Marie Feodorovna's charities were looked after by the Fourth Section; later, a newly created Fifth Section was charged with ameliorating the lot of the state peasants. But the pride and glory of the Private Chancery was the Third Section, soon to be notorious as the higher command of the Gendarmerie, the secret political police.

Nicholas meant so well. By elevating the Private Chancery he sought to combat the corruption, inertia and inward-lookingness of the formal government machine. In fact he only made things worse. He could have opened up the government machine by allowing his ministers more joint responsibility, thus not only cross-fertilising the ideas of the separate departments but also exposing their procedures to the critical gaze of colleagues whose own individual performance would then be seen to depend very largely on the performance of others. Instead, he drove them still further in upon themselves by superimposing upon them yet another series of private empires.

Thus, the Emperor's trusted Third Section, for many years the private empire of Count Benckendorff, soon became for all practical purposes a ministry in its own right, cutting deeply into the activities of the Ministry of the Interior, the Ministry of Education, and others.

The Third Section was seen by him not as an arm of arbitrary repression, but as a dedicated organisation, staffed by an élite untarnished by the corruption and venality of the bureaucratic machine, certainly equipped to act as watch-dogs against sedition, but more particularly to set a good example, to save honest subjects from the contamination of dangerous ideas, and, indeed, to save from themselves men of talent who might all too easily fall victim to their own unbalanced natures. The ideal state, to which Nicholas aspired, might have found its inspiration in Dr Arnold's Rugby, with the monarch as headmaster, the ministers and bureaucrats as tolerated but not wholly trusted housemasters, form-masters and ushers, and the Third Section as a monstrous corps of shining prefects dedicated to the honour of the school. It did not work out like that because the Russians were human and also very Russian. So was Nicholas himself.

Nicholas believed that the Third Section was commanded in detail by Benckendorff, his dear and trusted friend, amiable to a degree, snobbish to a degree, his imperturbable idleness, philandering habits (he could not keep away from actresses), and mild venality disguised by an expression of benevolent uprightness softened by his very fine eyes. This ballroom secret policeman was supposed to hold in his white-gloved hands all the threads of internal government, to be accessible to all petitioners whom the Tsar could not see himself, to have his finger on the pulse of the nation. And indeed he managed to convince his master that this was the case. Nobody knew better than Benckendorff how to reassure his master of the essential health of the realm; nobody knew better how to find a convincing explanation for this or that scandal or bloody revolt; nobody knew better how to show himself to petitioners, appear to listen with the utmost benevolence to their complaints, wipe away tears – and then go off duty without having taken in a word. His absent-mindedness was legendary; it was said that on occasion he forgot his own name. But this was protective colouring of a very high order. Nobody knew better how to leave the running of his all-important department in the hands of his subordinates. Nicholas's lack of cleverness, which so struck Queen Victoria, was reflected very exactly in his failure to appreciate that this sort of thing must happen: namely, that if he, the Tsar, refused to delegate responsibility, insisting on 'ruling' through chosen favourites who knew how to please him, the delegating would be done by those favourites, who would concede effective power to men the Tsar had scarcely heard of.

Thus the Third Section was run for a great many years not by Benckendorff at all, but first by a not very interesting secret-police officer, M. I. von Vock, then by a highly sophisticated official, General Dubbelt, whose creation the famous Gendarmerie really was and who, as a reflection of his own nature, gave the Third Section its strange, ambivalent aura. Dubbelt was one of those twilight figures for whom the very concept of a secret service seems to have been invented. A career soldier, he had fought and been wounded at Borodino, married the liberal-minded niece of Admiral Mordvinov, came under suspicion of involvement in the Decembrist conspiracy, survived, and was promoted to colonel. Then, a man of violent temper, he had quarrelled with his divisional general and retired from the service. Herzen, the dedicated foe of the Third Section and all it stood for, characterised him as 'more intelligent than all the sections of His Majesty's Private Imperial Chancery put together'.[2] He had a reputation for wit and preened himself as a littérateur. The conflict in his soul came to a head when he accepted an appointment in the new Corps of Gendarmes, the executive arm of the Third Section. His wife was horrified and did her best to dissuade him. In one of his innumerable letters of self-justification he wrote:

Do not be a gendarme, you say; but do you understand . . . ? If by entering the Corps of Gendarmes, I were to become an informer, an eavesdropper, then, assuredly, my good name would be sullied. But if, on the other hand, not mixing in cases that relate to the internal police, I became a bulwark for the poor, a shield for the unfortunate . . . Would I not then deserve to be admired?[3]

A few years later this man had become the all-powerful Chief of Staff who turned Benckendorff's Third Section into the secret police as traditionally understood. He did not himself eavesdrop and inform, but he organised and perfected the vast network of spies and informers which was to be a model for future generations. He first developed to a fine art the technique of using venal agents, whom he treated with contempt while talking man to man with their victims – as though accuser and accused were equally the prisoners of a system deplorable itself, but an unfortunate fact of life. In achieving this he developed what Herzen also called 'the sense of romance of the police', a kind of mystique in which victim and executioner were sometimes joined by a profound inner understanding, and which was again to set the tone for generations to come.

The more one contemplates the Tsar's advisers, the more one is struck not, as one might expect, by their narrow-minded insistence on the routine pedantries of government but, on the contrary, by an incessant and restless harking back to first principles. These men had an immense and backward country to run and to bring forward so that it could take its place in a Europe being violently transformed by the industrial revolution. They spent a great deal of their time not taking empirical decisions in the light of common sense, but in comparing memoranda which raised the largest questions, frequently with agonising soul-searching.

Thus, for example, the Minister of Education, S. S. Uvarov, has become a byword for his celebrated slogan long held to characterise the obscurantism of Nicholas's reign: 'Orthodoxy, Autocracy, and the National Way of Life'.⁴ But in inventing that phrase Uvarov was not a reactionary official laying down the law from on high: he was an eager careerist, not without ideals, making his way up the ladder of promotion, lacking the security attached to noble birth on the one hand or profound personal convictions on the other, but well intentioned, and trying very hard to improve the outlook of the ministry to which he belonged. He was fighting against the anti-intellectualism of Alexander's frightened old Minister of Education, Admiral Shishkov, which had led to the virtual suppression of university life, and trying to rationalise the more liberal principles of his new superior, Prince Lieven, who had no intellectual pretensions at all but a good deal of common sense. He was submitting a report to the Tsar on the state of Moscow University, and found it necessary to define his ideas on the aims of education – the transformation of students into 'useful and zealous instruments of the government'. The main task of his ministry as he saw it must be to encourage and nourish 'a warm faith in the truly Russian conservative principles of Orthodoxy, Autocracy, and the National Way of Life – which form the ultimate anchor of our salvation and the truest pledge of the strength and greatness of our Fatherland.'⁵ The Emperor was so deeply impressed by this formulation that Uvarov himself was soon made Minister.

It was as though the Russians were approaching problems of government for the first time, as though nobody had ever considered such problems before. And, indeed, in a sense this was true. These men knew enough about the outer world to be aware that they had inherited a problem which was unique in Europe: a vast and hopelessly backward land based on slavery. And they were deeply divided as to what to do about it.

3

Nowhere did this division, this preoccupation with first principles, come out more strongly than in the debate over the industrialisation of Russia which had started under Alexander and continued under Nicholas. Both the character and the timing of this debate reflected the anomalous position into which Russia had allowed herself to drift by taking the line of least resistance in all domestic affairs since the days of Peter the Great. The line of least resistance had been, of course, to cosset, or appease, the nobility by granting them unearned privileges, land and serfs, and the situation of the serf had correspondingly worsened at a time when a steady effort should have been made to improve it.

The debate was, broadly, the familiar-sounding argument between the protectionists and the free-traders. But whereas in England the protectionists were conservative and the free-traders radical, in Russia it was the other way round. Protection in England in the early nineteenth century meant protection for agriculture and tariffs against imported food; free trade meant cheap imported food in return for a vast open market for English manufactures. In Russia it was precisely the opposite. There protection meant the raising of a tariff wall against manufactured products (as in an earlier period of English history) to encourage the development of native industries; free trade meant the free import of manufactured products in return for a vast open market for Russian grain. Thus, on the whole, it was the great conservative landowners (not all) who stood for free trade, while the factory and mill owners stood for protection.

The arguments of the protectionists were obvious: Russian industry must be encouraged by every means if the country were to emerge into the nineteenth century. But the free-traders were also able to advance a powerful justification: Russia had developed on wholly individual lines;

her great strength was in her peasantry; her great wealth grain; her great virtue a stable autocratic order. Certainly industry must be developed, but slowly and in Russia's own time. A rapid expansion of the factory population, the consequent rapid extension of the communications system, would all too easily undermine the natural order and at the same time imperil the country's greatest asset, the production of grain.

This is a gross over-simplification. The views of the chief proponents of both sides covered a wide spectrum and were marked by sharply differing emphases. Among the most lucid, trenchant and enlightened of the protectionists was the liberal Admiral N. S. Mordvinov, who had come under suspicion at the time of the Decembrist purge, but survived to be not only a State Councillor under Nicholas, but also the uncle-in-law of the police chief, Dubbelt. He had visited America as a sailor and was the first Russian to perceive the future challenge of American industrial might. He was, indeed, a supreme example of a practical Westerniser, urging that Russia could not do better than model her development in detail on England, starting with protective tariffs (as England had done) to encourage the accumulation of private capital, putting her energies into building canals and roads, applied science, the capturing of colonial raw materials and the banking system. Only by following the English path could Russia hope one day to free her own domestic market from foreign, above all English, exploitation and enjoy the fruits of her own latent wealth.

Perhaps the best example of the contradictions and confusions of early nineteenth-century Russian thought about industrialisation is to be found in the teaching of the first serious Russian economist, university professor and tutor to the imperial family, Heinrich Storch, the most vocal and convinced of the free-traders.[6] Taking Adam Smith's *The Wealth of Nations* as his bible and applying its theory to Russian affairs, Storch concluded that Russia would be flouting her destiny if she allowed her resources to be diverted from agriculture to industry. And because he passionately believed that a highly productive soil would pay for all the imports of manufactured goods that the country could absorb, he came out boldly for the complete abolition of serfdom since it was an impediment to agricultural development.

Storch's views were shared by the Decembrist, N. I. Turgenev, but by few others. For most of those who favoured free trade based on agriculture were impelled less by a vision of immense possibilities than by fear of the forces bound to be let loose in an industrialised society and, on a higher level, by a quasi-mystical clinging to the old Russian tradition, expressed sometimes, not least by the Tsar himself, in a profound repugnance for the excesses of the industrial revolution in the West. The

Russian peasant under serfdom, the argument ran, was as a rule better off morally and physically than the English factory worker, driven off the land and reduced to the depths of dehumanised misery by the brutality of predatory capitalists and the tyranny of the machine.

Certainly the great liberal, Count P. D. Kiselev, placed by Nicholas in charge of the Fifth Section of his Private Chancery, thought along these lines, and many others with him. There was a sharp awareness of the iniquities of the English capitalist system among many Russians long before Friedrich Engels began to publish his own shocked findings. It was an awareness which was to possess a little later the Slavophile intellectuals and at the same time to disturb their opponents, including such ardent Westernisers and downright opponents of the autocracy as Alexander Herzen – none of whom seemed able to comprehend the disconcerting fact that Russia was well on the way to getting the worst of both worlds. That is to say, there was already a great deal of industry in Russia, and had been since the days of Peter the Great; that industry was developing all the time and was bound to develop (a fact accepted by the most convinced free-traders); and that the conditions of the worker under Russian industry were in fact every bit as bad as in England. Neither were they seemingly able to register another fact: namely that the rural ideal to which they clung was a dream which had never existed in reality and never could exist.

One result of this uninhibited theorising was, as might have been foreseen, the deadlocking of the projected policies of men of genuine vision and the capturing of the middle ground by frequently inferior individuals who at least knew how to deal with day-to-day affairs. The man who in the end determined Russian industrial policy under Nicholas was the Minister of Finance, Count E. F. Kankrin. The middle ground he captured was, quite simply, the preservation of the *status quo*: not rapid industrialisation, from which he recoiled in horror; not the enlightened development of agriculture, which would call for radical change of another kind; but simple stasis. Nobody, certainly no class, was to be trusted: the peasant masses were inflammable; the merchant classes were greedy and all too liable to get above themselves; the great landowners had quite enough power as things were; the existing great industrialists had too much. In any case Russia could not industrialise rapidly without relying too much on foreign experts and foreign loans. There was no prospect of accumulating either the requisite skills or capital without risking the break-up of the traditional society. Russia was a going concern. She had survived the Napoleonic wars. Her name was respected throughout the world. All she had to do was sit tight and slowly grow.

This conservative ideal suited Nicholas to perfection. So long as Kankrin was there (and the Ministry of Finance, like Treasury Departments everywhere, had negative powers over other ministries which made it supreme) the day-to-day running of the country was in safe hands. More than that, this splendid man had the inevitable defects of his qualities. Left to himself he would not move at all. Whereas he, Nicholas, the Tsar, clearly perceived the necessity for movement from time to time. It would be his task to overrule Kankrin on occasion in the interests of activism. One of these occasions was provided in the years after the Tsar's accession when Kankrin was stubbornly holding out against the building of railways, seen gloomily by him as a devil's invention to disrupt a settled society. Russia was in no hurry. Russia was virtually self-sufficient; with good management she could be completely so. The secret of her strength lay in stagnation. There were virtually no roads: never mind, the river and canal system offered all the transport required and quite enough fluidity of movement. Nicholas thought otherwise. It took three months by the river route to get iron from the Urals to the Baltic. There had to be railways. And it was the Tsar himself who brushed aside Kankrin's stubborn opposition and decreed that the sixteen-mile experimental line from St Petersburg to the imperial summer headquarters of Tsarskoe Selo, opened in 1837, be followed by the building of the 400-mile line between St Petersburg and Moscow. There is a tenacious legend to the effect that when the experts differed about the route the line should take Nicholas put an end to the matter by using his sword as a ruler to join the two cities on the map. He drew a straight line between them which the railway obediently followed, even though the line sometimes led through swamps and passed nowhere near the townships it should have served.

4

This tremendous undertaking offers a first-class example of the Russian way of doing things.[7] The moving spirit was a brilliant Russian engineer, Paul Melnikov, who had never seen a railway and had the sense to persuade Nicholas to invite to Russia a distinguished American army railway engineer as chief technical adviser. This was Major George Washington Whistler, father of the painter, James McNeill Whistler, who spent his childhood and early schooldays in St Petersburg – where he might have stayed much longer if his father had not died in the cholera epidemic of 1848. The railway was begun in 1842 and finished in 1851. The work was started from both ends simultaneously and was carried out in the main by mass peasant *corvées*, toiling with their bare hands or using those long-handled, small-bladed Russian shovels, moving some sixty million cubic yards of earth, mostly in those primitive two-man wooden stretchers which are favoured above wheelbarrows in Russia even today. Much of the labour was provided by local landowners, some of whom came along with their own serfs and set up temporary homes; most, however, was supplied under contract by middle-men conjured up by the occasion who made themselves fortunes by swindling both the Government and their employees. Most interestingly, the drive came from General Kleinmikhel, one of the Tsar's few trusted friends, who though technically illiterate was put in charge of all transportation in Russia. Kleinmikhel, a brute, and a corrupt brute at that, was singled out by Herzen as the very type of sycophantic, ignorant bully. He had inexhaustible vitality and in the name of the Emperor he drove all those under him to the limit of endurance and beyond: it was he who had performed the miracle of the rebuilding of the Winter Palace within a year after the great fire – regardless of the cost in human life. The railway cost innumerable lives. There were frequent revolts among the forced labourers, and the revolts were put down with shootings and savage floggings by a special corps of railway police.

It was after watching the Kleinmikhel system in action that Whistler wrote to his father-in-law in America:

In a country like this success is almost the sole criteria [*sic*] of merit – much credit following success, and a single failure obliterates all merit – this intimidates the many while it inspires a sort of desperate energy in the few and makes them firm believers in the catholic principle that the end justifies the means. Not only is the will of the Emperor the law of laws, but the very whim of the Emperor is the law of these few – indeed I might say all – for it is quite apparent in the perfect submission of the many as it is in the energy of the few.[8]

It is reasonable to see in Kleinmikhel the prototype of a Lazar Kaganovich, who, as Stalin's right-hand, was responsible for the development of the Soviet transportation system, using almost identical methods in the period of the first Five-Year Plan eighty years later, and with the same absolute obedience to Stalin's commands.

The line was built. When it was finished it was the longest railway in the world. It was cut through virgin forest, raised on causeways through treacherous swamps. It was beautifully landscaped, with innumerable fine bridges and deep cuttings through the Valdai hills, and also the most splendidly constructed. Long before the official opening by the Tsar, accompanied by the whole imperial family in their gleaming royal coach, the line had been used for the transport of troops. But such was the lack of cohesion and drive that although gifted planners had sketched out a formidable railway network in detail, and although it had been proved in the teeth of the sceptics that the locomotives and rolling stock of the day were capable of operating in the Russian extremes of climate, and although Nicholas and his generals had grasped the strategic advantages of railway transport, there was no immediate follow-through. A line from St Petersburg to Warsaw was started in 1852, but that was all; and when the Crimean War broke out in 1854 there were still only plans for railways to the south: the troops which could be shuttled about so easily between Moscow and St Petersburg had to march the whole way from Moscow, nearly a thousand miles, on shocking roads, a third of them dying of disease in transit.

The decisive factor in the slow development of Russian railways, as of the modernisation of Russian industry generally, was lack of money. The capital available was hopelessly inadequate to develop and sustain a great military power in the industrial age. Worse, the available capital was misapplied by Kankrin, who was quite generous with state loans for essentially non-productive purposes – e.g. the development of the great estates, to keep the landowners, seen as bulwarks of the *status quo*, in the style to which they were accustomed – but reluctant to finance state enterprise in industry or to grant loans to private manufacturers. The lack of capital itself was the outcome of the serf system. The nobility were exempt from direct taxation. By far the larger portion of the state revenue was derived from the poll tax on the peasants, who were kept in such penury that their yield was small.

5

Very little work has been done by recent historians to demonstrate the organic connection between the approaches to the use of industrial and agricultural manpower between post-revolutionary and pre-revolutionary governments. The most cursory study of industry and agriculture under the three Alexanders and the first Nicholas throws a flood of illumination on Soviet policies, including the institution of forced labour, the traditional background of which has been obscured by the Witte and Stolypin reforms under the second Nicholas and the expressed, but unrealised, aspirations of Lenin and the early Bolsheviks.

When Nicholas came to the throne in 1825 the population of the Empire was very rapidly expanding. Between 1811 and 1863 it was all but doubled, from 41 million to over 74 million. There are no precise figures for the beginning of Nicholas's reign, but at the time of the Crimean War there were 42 million serfs and state peasants, nearly two million 'revision souls' in the towns and more than a hundred thousand serfs employed as factory workers. The mass of the serfs were village peasants working the land, peasants employed in domestic service, or peasants working seasonally, and to a lesser degree full-time, in factories and mines. Rather more than half of these were the personal property of individual landowners; the lesser half, chiefly in the poor lands of Moscow, and in Siberia, belonged to the Crown.

But this world of serfs also comprehended a great number of individuals who would have appeared to the outsider as free men. The service owed by the serfs to their masters could be rendered in a number of ways. They could be taken into the household as servants and there on occasion rise to positions of responsibility and of power over others: as stewards, as architects and builders on princely estates, as skilled craftsmen of all kinds, as actors and musicians. If they remained on the land they could live in the traditional quasi-feudal manner (*barshchina*), working so many days a week on their master's estate and on their own acres for the rest of the time; or they could make money payments (*obrok*) instead of work. In the wide steppe-lands of eastern central Russia, where labour was scarce and the land to be cultivated vast, the landowners preferred labour services to money payments; but in the more densely populated areas of old Muscovy they did better up to a point out of money payments, and serfs were encouraged to set themselves up as independent craftsmen, as traders and entrepreneurs in the name of their masters, to whom they had to pay agreed percentages of their profits. Some of these merchant serfs did so well that they became rouble millionaires; but they still belonged to their master, unless he would allow them to buy themselves into freedom. Perhaps the most wretched category of all were the factory serfs and those assigned to *corvée* work on the construction of roads, canals and railways. Even Russians who knew their country well were sometimes shocked by the depths of degradation revealed by thousands of these unfortunates, particularly those who came from such remote and poverty-stricken areas as parts of Byelorussia. Thus Valerian Panaev, Melnikov's chief assistant on the Moscow–St Petersburg railway, wrote of the peasants who came from the Smolensk region to do navvying work:

These were the most unhappy people in all the Russian land, who less resembled people than working cattle, from whom inhuman strength was demanded in their labours, one might say, without any reward . . . When I saw these people for the first time at the works, I was struck by the following: each person, before passing me, bowed, so that his back came to a horizontal position; then, with mincing steps, he hastened up to me, seized the cloth end of my cape, kissed it with the words, 'I kiss you, *pan* colonel', and withdrew in the same position.[9]

Certain great landowning families displayed in the vast range of their affairs every aspect of the serf system in microcosm. One of the most spectacular of these were the Sheremetyevs, but there were others who equalled them in magnificence, and very many more who followed the same life-style adapted to their lesser resources.

The Sheremetyevs were a family of ancient line established long before the Romanov dynasty was launched. But their extreme wealth was more recent. Field-Marshal Boris Sheremetyev was one of Peter the Great's most devoted supporters, first in the struggle with the Regent Sophia, then in pushing through the Petrine reforms. He was rewarded extravagantly with grants of land and serfs in many parts of Russia. In 1743 his son Peter married the Princess Barbara Cherkassy, whose dowry almost doubled his possessions and included the remote village of Ivanovno to the north-east of Moscow, already known for its textiles. When Peter III, Catherine's wretched husband, released the nobility from all bonds of service in 1762, Count Peter Sheremetyev settled down to a life of amiable, highly cultured, but wholly selfish extravagance, which was continued by his successors. By the middle of the nineteenth century the reigning Sheremetyev owned more than two hundred thousand serfs and was deeply in debt, kept going by the sort of unproductive loans that Kankrin delighted to concede on the Tsar's behalf.

The debts went back a long way. Count Peter Sheremetyev and his son Nicholas were manic builders. All their money, and much more, went on the building and maintenance of palaces and the provision of extravagant entertainments in the grandest imaginable manner. Apart from their immense town palaces in St Petersburg and Moscow, the two most famous of these were Count Peter's palace of Kuskovo (1762–75) and Count Nicholas's palace at Ostankino (1799), both very close to Moscow.

These were intended not as places to live in but in effect as permanent architectural stage-sets for extravagant entertainments. Kuskovo, exquisite in the Palladian style, its construction supervised from start to finish by a serf architect, Alexei Mironov, besides its suite of connected reception rooms, its vast ballroom, its state bedroom modelled on the bedroom of Louis XIV at Versailles, its rococo garden pavilions, and its vast park, contained at one time three separate theatres (one of them in the open air), for opera, ballet and drama. The stage designers, the scene-painters, the actors, dancers and singers and musicians were all serfs. Barbara Cherkassy had brought with her dowry a number of gifted painter serfs from her own family estates. The Sheremetyevs themselves clearly went out of their way to develop latent artistic talent in their own serfs and to acquire others who showed talent. Some, like the builder-architect, Mironov, were very gifted indeed and in the West would have carved out independent careers. The leading soprano in Nicholas Sheremetyev's opera company at Ostankino (where the theatre with all its elaborate machinery is still intact), Parasha Kovaleva, was widely renowned: the daughter of a blacksmith serf on one of the Sheremetyev estates, she was picked out by her master at the age of eleven, trained as a musician under the best masters in Moscow, taught French and Italian. Besides winning fame as a singer, she was a great beauty, and in the end her master married her. It was somehow characteristic of the Sheremetyev world that after building up his famous opera company, giving the first performances of Gluck and Mozart in Russia and marrying his prima donna, Nicholas Sheremetyev suddenly became bored with playing impresario, disbanded his company, and returned his celebrated troupe to household and horticultural duties.[10]

He was already in deep water. Ostankino had been intended as a sumptuous centre for all the arts, and plans were sought from a number of foreign architects, including the gifted Italian Quarenghi. But this vision exceeded even the Sheremetyev means, and had to be abandoned. One of the causes was the extravagance of Peter Sheremetyev, whose great parties lasted for days on end. On gala days at Kuskovo there were sometimes as many as thirty thousand guests assembled. On one occasion nearly three thousand carriages converged on the palace and there were not enough horses in all Moscow to convey those who were invited.[11]

To find the equivalent of this sort of splendour in the West one has to look to the great Esterhazy establishment in Theresian Hungary where Haydn presided over the musicians, not a serf, but a salaried servant, bound by an elaborate contract into which he voluntarily entered. The wealth of the Esterhazys, however, was founded on a highly productive agriculture and a highly developed rural economy. It was limitless. The Sheremetyev wealth was founded on the labour and the *obrok* of serfs. This was limited to a degree. The agriculture was subsistence agriculture, the *obrok* low: two to three roubles per head per year. On the eve of the emancipation of the serfs the Sheremetyev income came to just over 700,000 roubles a year, of which nearly 600,000 came from *obrok* payments. From all their vast estates they received from the sale of agricultural produce only 18,400 roubles. In 1859 the servicing of their debts came to 736,000 roubles – more than their total income. In addition to this 344,000 roubles went on running expenses – a deficiency in one year of nearly 400,000 roubles, which could only be met by incurring still further debts.[12]

The Sheremetyevs, that is to say, had nothing whatever to show for their grandeur but grandeur itself. And in the nineteenth century beyond giving subsistence employment to their army of slaves, and founding a number of charities (e.g. the famous hospital in Moscow called after them), they contributed little to the national economy. They did not justify their existence as pioneers of advanced agriculture, and despite the employment of a corps of administrators, a sort of private bureaucracy, which would have been large enough to run the government of a small sovereign state in Western Europe, they proved incapable of the imaginative management of their immense possessions even in the most narrowly self-interested manner. In the two villages of Ivanovno and Voznesensk, united to form one great industrial complex, they possessed the headquarters of the Russian textile industry, the Russian Manchester, which employed thousands of the Sheremetyev serfs.

But these spectacular magnates did not profit by their potential wealth as, for example, the great English aristocrats profited by the coal beneath their fields. Instead, the development of the textile mills was given over to talented serfs who, as they prospered, paid great sums in *obrok* and, in due course, could afford to pay such a price for their freedom that their masters were unable to resist seizing the immediate, short-sighted advantage to pay off some of their debts. The geese that laid the golden eggs were thus killed off one after another, and great fortunes in textiles were made over the decades by representatives of a new merchant class, lately risen from serfdom – in this case the Grachevs, the Garelins, and others. The proceeds of these sales of freedom, together with the additional income from rents and sales of property, certainly helped to keep the landowners going in style. But it was a style achieved and sustained in an essentially hand-to-mouth manner by families who were consumers rather than producers and lacking, with certain notable exceptions, any sense of participation in building up national prosperity. It was quite a usual thing for grandees of all kinds, from imperial Grand Dukes downwards, to sell up their Russian estates and take their money, their wives and mistresses, their jewels, into palatial and voluntary exile in Mediterranean France or Italy. So hard-driven were the new industrialists to meet their redemption dues, that the lot of the serfs they themselves employed was if anything worse than before.

6

A basic flaw in the Russian industrial system as practised until the emancipation of the serfs in 1861 had been built into it by Peter the Great. Peter had seen Russian industry of whatever kind as an integral part of the military machine which he needed to establish Russia as a power. Iron was for guns, textiles were for uniforms, and so on. To achieve this end he set up a number of state factories, but preferred to farm out contracts to private entrepreneurs, like the Demidov family. Smaller industry was left to smaller men, outsiders – the serfs of large landowners, or schismatics and dissenters who were excluded from the main stream of Russian society and compensated for this by making money, starting often as street pedlars. Under the centralised autocracy with the nobility attached to the Crown, and the masses attached as serfs to the nobility, or to the Crown direct in those areas where landowners were few and far between (above all in the forest zone, with its poor soil, to the north of Moscow), there was no room for private enterprise to develop anywhere west of the Urals.

Thus there were no guilds of merchants, tradesmen and craftsmen to combine in pressure groups and build up middle-class power. Peter brought industry to Russia, but he did nothing to encourage the establishment of the relatively open society which was the pre-requisite for the organic growth of Western capitalism, operating through countless small enterprises in furious competition with one another. Peter's mills and factories, and the mills and factories of his favoured private entrepreneurs, were thus organised not as the materialisation of the personal dreams, ambitions and greed of countless individuals seeking to better themselves, or seized with the love of power or riches, or the sheer delight in making things work, but rather as extensions of the central government, as sources of supply for the central power. At a time when the highly productive workshops of the West were essentially family businesses the far fewer workshops in Russia were, for all practical purposes, civilian barracks. Thus there grew up a tradition of the large factory, employing hundreds, often thousands. And, although many of these were only seasonal workers, peasant serfs, working their fields in summer and migrating, sometimes hundreds of miles on foot, to do factory work in winter, they lived and worked in the factory towns under quasi-military discipline.

The wastefulness of this system, together with the slow transport of products by river and canal, had led to the swift decline of the Ural iron industry in the eighteenth century. And the convention of barrack labour, persisting into the nineteenth and twentieth centuries, and exploited by foreign concessionaries (as in the mining districts of the Donbas), was responsible for the great paradox of Russian industry. In this empty and backward country, where the proletariat formed such a minute fraction of the total population, organised industrial revolt could play a disproportionately large role simply because the workers were clustered together, enclaves of unskilled labourers isolated in rural oceans, and far more easily operated upon by revolutionary agitators than their fellows in Western Europe, for whom the factory was simply a place of work from which they returned to their own homes, however wretched, into the bosoms of their own families, however poor, when work was done.

Thus, as late as 1844, when Nicholas decided to set up a locomotive works at Alexandrovsk on the outskirts of St Petersburg (a plant established and run for eighteen years by American experts), there was no gentle natural growth: the whole concept sprang fully armed from the head of the state bureaucracy: by December 1845 the factory was built and 1600 skilled workmen were turning out ten passenger coaches a day and one locomotive a week. The American engineer in charge declared that it was the finest establishment in all Europe. So no doubt it was. But it was run under military discipline.[13]

It was the sort of discipline established earlier in the Urals, where, in the early years of Alexander's reign, in an effort to bring Ural iron production up to date, the entire area, centred on a number of purely industrial townships, was organised as a military command. By the Mining Statute of 1806, a special centralised mining administration was set up in St Petersburg as a department of the Ministry of Finance. Both private and state mines came under its control, and were divided into areas known as mining circuits and mining towns. Each circuit, with its complex of mines and factories, was run by a Captain of Mines, whose task was not only to set production targets under general direction from the centre and supervise the whole process of manufacture, but also to control the police and judicial officials within the circuits, as well as the powerful detachments of soldiers, who were responsible for maintaining security and order.[14] The mining circuits, in a word, were to all intents and purposes vast open concentration camps employing serf labour, largely seasonal, which drifted to and from the peasant villages each year under the authority of special passes. Perhaps less than three per cent of the total labour force in the mines were regular salaried employees. And of course, there was a perpetual influx of convicts. Some enterprises were staffed almost entirely by convicts. It was all one to the Captain of the Mines, who was virtual dictator of all the souls under his command.

It was not a system conducive to enterprise. Moreover, the fact that the privately worked mines and factories, profitable as they could be to their owners, were also subject to the Captain of Mines, induced in the minds of the great Russian entrepreneurs a fatal attitude of irresponsibility. They were forced by the state to provide hospitals, medical services, etc. (an advantage over the Western system of unbridled free enterprise which the Russians never tired of pointing out) but all were reduced to one level in the eyes of the centre, and they were dependent on the state for their freedom to operate.

In the general context of Russian conditions, where corporal punishment was the rule, where subsistence level of existence was abysmally low, where the workers were chattels, it could be said that the overriding interest of the central planners prevented the worst factory owners from driving their workers and their children as cruelly as the worst English ones – who provided no medical services, however sketchy. On the other hand, there was little or no chance, or inducement, for the best to set the sort of example of enlightened employment which was to become a feature of the West, active as a leavener, quickening public opinion, a perpetual spur to dulled consciences. From time to time the Tsar would sign a decree, limiting the hours of employment, forbidding such and such a form of child labour; but there were no Lord Shaftesburys in Imperial Russia, no Factory Acts pushed through by awakening public opinion in the teeth of doctrinaire *laissez-faire*.

And, until 1861, the serf system held sway. It was absolute. Individual landowners from time to time liberated their serfs: the father of the composer Rimsky-Korsakov was one of these, stricken by conscience. The novelist Turgenev was another. But these were individual actions frowned upon as dangerous eccentricity by the landowning classes as a whole. Thus Rimsky-Korsakov senior stood out a very long way among his contemporaries. A considerable hereditary landowner, he had been swindled out of his estate by friends in whom he put too much trust. He was then appointed to be civil Governor of Volhynia, the westernmost province bordering Congress Poland and largely inhabited by Poles. After the rigorous crushing of the 1830 Polish revolt this gentle and humane man found himself quite unable to lend his authority and name to the oppressive policies adopted by St Petersburg. He put in his resignation and retired to live quietly on what was left of his inheritance. By that time, however, he had come to the conclusion that the whole principle of serfdom was evil: he freed his domestics and serfs, one by one, some of them staying on as paid servants.[15] There were many others who felt like old Rimsky-Korsakov, and there were some who were ready to pay for their convictions. The wonder was that there were any of these at all: they had to face the stigma of betraying their class.

Individual gifted serfs, of course, might buy their own freedom at any time, provided they were prepared to pay enough for it. Others attracted the attention of their masters or their masters' friends, who helped them to make a career, and gave them their freedom as a gift. One of the most remarkable of these was A. V. Nikitenko, the son of a talented and favoured serf on one of the Sheremetyev estates. The young Nikitenko was taken up by the future Decembrists, Prince Eugene Obolensky and the poet Ryleyev, who was hanged. He survived the downfall of his protectors and emerged as one of the most interesting and enlightened officials in the Ministry of Education, functioning above all in the censorship office, where he was renowned for his unremitting efforts to protect the best writers of the day from the crasser excesses of his own ministry and the Third Section. With all this he was utterly powerless to persuade Count Dmitri Sheremetyev to give freedom to his own widowed mother and his brother, who remained serfs until they died.

'Here am I,' he wrote in his journal on 11 March 1841, 'a full citizen, even enjoying a certain fame and influence; and I cannot even bring about – what? – the independence of my mother and brother! A half-witted grandee has the right to refuse me; this is called law. My blood boils, and I understand how it is that people go to extremes.'[16]

The 'half-witted grandee' was the contemporary Sheremetyev, the inheritor of a great name, immense wealth, 200,000 slaves, vast lands and fabulous palaces. He was a man whose stake in the country was so great that the force of enlightened self-interest should, one would have thought, have spurred him into unceasing labours in the interest of national prosperity. But like so many, though not all, of his kind, he did next to nothing. His ex-serf, Nikitenko, on the other hand, while serving loyally, arduously and thanklessly to ameliorate conditions in a society in which he had no stake and which kept his family in bonds, was, without knowing it, voicing the accents of a future from which he would have shrunk in horror had he seen it.

CHAPTER FIVE

The Growth of the Mind

QUITE early in his reign, holding forth to Pushkin, Nicholas offered an insight into the philosophy behind his passion for autocratic rule. Russia, he carefully explained, did not yet exist as a whole: 'the elements comprising her are not yet harmonised . ... Take away the limitless, all-powerful will of the Monarch and at the least shock she would crumble.' That was only fourteen years after the defeat of Napoleon by the people of Russia in arms.

With at least a part of his mind Nicholas deplored this state of affairs, but he did nothing to remedy it: at no time in his thirty years of absolute rule did he seriously undertake any institutional reform. Worse, at no time did it occur to him that it was beyond the powers of any man to hold the vast realm together single-handed. Speransky and others too had perceived that the first requisites for a strong and effective autocratic system were the rule of law and the responsible delegation of authority within the framework of established law. Nicholas did not understand the meaning of law and, as already noted, he did not know how to bring forward men of ability and integrity, delegating to them defined areas of responsibility from national down to parochial level, their conduct regulated by a clear-cut statutory code.

This could not be thought of because Nicholas trusted nobody beyond a handful of familiars and could tolerate no autonomous or quasi-autonomous institutions: nobody, therefore, was truly responsible in the whole of that vast Empire. The senior officials, the heads of the great administrative areas, were bound neither by an established code nor by a common service loyalty. Their only restraining force was obedience to the will of the Emperor. The will of the Emperor was essentially arbitrary and capricious; and, in any case, the Emperor had no means of telling whether he was being obeyed or not.

The general effect of this situation, which did no more than carry traditional tendencies to something like a logical conclusion, was to produce a society quite irreparably fragmented, unified only in the person of the Tsar. The Tsar was Caesar, commander-in-chief, head of the Church, head of government – not only Prime Minister and Foreign Minister, but also effective head of each separate government department – chief of police, Little Father of all the serfs. He was everything, and because he was everything he was nothing. His instruments – army, police, bureaucracy, religious hierarchy – between them maintained the appearance of order, and when that order was violated, as it was violated with increasing frequency by outbreaks of peasant violence, the murdering of landlords and the burning of their houses, punishment was swift and savage. But there was no dynamic interdependence between government and people. Such creative forces as existed were unofficial and self-generating, owing little or nothing to the central government: they arose from a sense of common interest among various sections of society, inward-looking, which developed a series of virtually self-contained co-operatives, almost closed-shops, exclusive and separate from each other. The Church, the strong groupings of heretical schismatics or sectarians, the grand nobility, the small landowners, the merchants, the peasant serfs themselves, all inhabited overlapping but quite separate circles, all subject to the Imperial decree, some to the importunities of the tax-gatherer and the police. But beneath the incubus of officialdom they led almost secret existences, their backs turned firmly on St Petersburg.

This fragmentation inhibited wide-scale social mobility with its leavening and re-vitalising influence and concealed from the central government the real life of the country. It should not be thought that the Tsar was ignorant of the words and actions of his subjects. The Third Section was everywhere, and the archives (opened since the Revolution) have shown that its intelligence system was good and its reporting remarkably direct: when it found evidence that this or that aspect of Imperial policy was proving more than usually unpopular it said so, even though the personal conduct of the Tsar himself might be at issue. But what the Third Section could never do was explore the underlying reasons for unrest. This would have meant holding in question the very system which it was its duty to sustain. Any such questioning would have led those on the inside of the system to the conclusion, not to put too fine a point on it, that the autocracy was a fraud. Indeed, it was not an autocracy at all. It was a conspiracy of pretence. To put it another way, the autocracy was a concept, not a system. And the most fateful consequence of this confusion of idea with reality was that it blinded not only the Tsar himself and all loyal subjects from the highest to the lowest but also all the opponents of the regime, liberals, radical reformers and revolutionaries, who, in their way, were as far removed from understanding the reality as the silliest aide-de-camp at the Imperial court.

The Emperor had no clothes. He was powerless in all matters affecting the proper government of the Empire. He and he alone stood high. The peasant serf's only consolation was that the Tsar, standing high above all others, looked down equally upon all others. If the serfs had no rights *vis-à-vis* their masters, neither did their masters have rights *vis-à-vis* the crown. Peter the Great had seen to that when he abolished the privileges of the hereditary nobility and instituted his 'nobility of service', with its carefully graded table of fourteen ranks, or *Chins*. 'All the Romanovs,' said Pushkin (he was speaking to the Tsar's younger brother, the Grand Duke Michael) 'have been revolutionaries and levellers.' De Custine put it less kindly. He was writing of the two great occasions which took place each year when the Tsar opened his palaces – the Winter Palace at the new year; Tsarskoe Selo in the summer – to all his subjects: 'When the Tsar ostensibly opens his palace freely to the privileged peasants and the chosen bourgeoisie whom he permits the honour of paying him court twice a year, he does not say to the labourer and the merchant: "You are a man like me", but he does say to the grandee: "You are a slave like them, and I, your god, soar above you all equally." '[1]

And in case this observation by a Frenchman should be dismissed as the prejudice of an ignorant and superficial outsider, here are the thoughts of that frustrated reformer Count Speransky, as he approached his great, vain task of bringing Russia into the nineteenth century:

I should like someone to show the difference between the peasants' subservience to the landlords and the nobility's subservience to the monarch; I wish someone would point out that the authority the sovereign wields over the landlords is in no way different from the power the landlord has over his peasants. And thus, instead of the pompous division of the free Russian people into the most free classes of the nobility, merchants, etc., I find in Russia only two estates: the slaves of the sovereign and the slaves of the landlords. The former are called free in relation to the latter, but there are no free men in Russia except beggars and philosophers.[2]

And yet the Tsar was the prisoner of the nobility. He dared not move against them. Why, if his power was absolute, if he was truly an autocrat, was he afraid? The answer, quite simply, was that he feared the fate of so many of his forebears, of his own father, the Emperor Paul, the fate that seemed about to claim him on the very day of his accession: death at the hands of his own Guards. If the autocracy had once made sense, as in far away years it had, it made no sense now on the threshold of the industrial revolution. And the absurdity of the concept and of the Tsar's attitude towards it is perfectly summed up in Nicholas's own words on the subject of serfdom. Shortly before his death he uttered a lament. Time and time again, he said, he had tried to break through resistance to the emancipation of the serfs, time and time again he had been defeated by the vested interests of the landowners. And indeed he had set up no fewer than nine special commissions to find ways and means of abolishing serfdom. But how half-heartedly! In 1842, at the very height of his power, he declared to the Council of State: 'There is no doubt that serfdom in its present form is a flagrant evil which everyone realises; yet to attempt to remedy it now would be, of course, an evil even more disastrous.'³

This kind of sad fatuity held Russia in its grip. What sort of an autocrat was he that he stood helpless before the obstinacy of a ruling class which owed all its privileges to the Crown and over the members of which the Emperor was supposed to hold the power of life and death? He could put a man in chains, he could dismiss a faithful servant out of hand, he could prescribe in minute detail the arrangement of buttons on a uniform jacket, he could tear families apart and make his subjects tremble with a look. He could conclude a treaty or declare a war. He could veto any forward-looking or constructive policy or expedient. But when it came to commanding the acceptance of such a policy against the will of the landowners he was impotent.

In this, admittedly, the Tsar was in much the same position as the head of any European government of the day, in face of powerful interest groups of any kind. The difference was that Nicholas called himself an autocrat, thought of himself as an autocrat, spoke as an autocrat, and was confirmed in this charade by all his subjects, the disaffected no less than the loyal. It was as though monarch and subjects had entered into a conspiracy to deceive each other. And the consequences of this fundamental delusion, deception, or lie, were far-reaching. Both the defenders and the most articulate opponents of the *status quo* based their arguments on a false premise which ensured that their thinking would have no foundation in reality.

2

The supreme paradox of the leaden age of Nicholas, who forbade all change, was the enlargement of the mind. Under Alexander – in the Russia of Arakcheyev indeed – the golden age of poetry had been born. This was an aristocratic age, and although its understanding owed much to the revolutionary ferment and expanded to delight in the new sensibility, it was still eighteenth-century in attitude and tone and steeped in the culture of France, a tone which was carried into the early years of the reign of Nicholas but then gave way to a new, harsh spirit of alienation.

For some years before his death in 1837, and even while he was producing some of his greatest work, Pushkin himself was to be contemptuously rejected by a young and usually far from aristocratic generation whose spiritual home was Germany.

All the great figures of the golden age, its path made straight by the polymath of genius, M. V. Lomonosov (1711–65), the virtual creator of the modern Russian language, were either well born or accepted as equals by their well-born contemporaries, whose manners they adopted. It did not matter that Zhukovsky was the bastard of a Tula landowner and a Turkish slave-girl: he was brought up as his father's son and moved in St Petersburg drawing-rooms with no less assurance than Pushkin with his fierce ancestral pride (Pushkin, too, of course, besides tracing his nobility back six hundred years on his father's side, had received through his mother the blood of 'Peter the Great's Nigger', the Ethiopian General of Engineers, Abraham Hannibal). The members of the Arzamas society, all friends of Pushkin – Batyushkov, Vyazemsky and others, besides Zhukovsky: a sort of joke counterblast to the solemn literary club of arid official writers – all came from landowning families. So did their hero, Karamzin, who had been an essayist and story-teller before he became the great historian and publicist. Their family estates were scattered all over Russia, and their friends, supporters and hangers-on between them established what amounted to a concealed or shadow network of cultural vitality flung over the whole land of European Russia, and about which the autocrat knew nothing beyond what was reported to him by the Third Section.

Here is an aspect of nineteenth-century Russian provincial life that has not been thoroughly explored. So many talented men, to say nothing of the occasional genius, spent their childhood in those cool white manor houses dotted about the great plain. Almost always limited to a single storey, with wide-flung wings reaching out to each side of a central colonnaded porch surmounted by a pediment in the classical 'Catherine' style, with tall, cool rooms, these houses, teeming with servants, relatives and hangers-on, were the centres of whole communities of serfs. The worst, like the house of the young Turgenev, were veritable prisons in which master or mistress were sadistic despots; most were the homes of inveterate potterers and idlers whose cultural level was little higher than that of their serfs; but some were remote, almost missionary centres of culture and intellectual vitality, linked to one another with ties of friendship or blood. Kamenka, near Kiev, for example, was the family seat of the Davydov family, distinguished for its soldier-intellectuals, very much a centre for the Decembrist conspiracy, and Pushkin's most cherished haven. At Simbirsk, high above the Volga as it approaches its easternmost stretch, Karamzin was born and brought up (and after him both Lenin and Kerensky!). F. I. Tyutchev, E. A. Baratynsky, Pushkin's closest friend, the poet Baron Delvig, many more besides, shared the common background of aristocratic upbringing in rural isolation, the sort of background so perfectly rendered by S. T. Aksakov and by Tolstoy himself. They moved in and out of the world of the mind and the world of high society with unconscious ease.

The dramatist Griboyedov, famous for his satirical comedy, *Woe from Wit*, banned by the Imperial master he served, was an especially remarkable example of this ambivalence. He was a brilliant member of the foreign service, chosen for the most delicate missions. He was a cousin of General Paskevich, the Tsar's favourite. For a time he was secretary to General Yermolov in the Caucasian campaign. Then he was arrested and brought back to St Petersburg suspected (almost certainly justly) of involvement in the Decembrist affair, which he denied angrily, almost insolently. Cleared of this, he returned to the Caucasus, served at Paskevich's headquarters during the successful Persian War, was given the task of negotiating the Treaty of Turkmanchai which ended that war, and returned to St Petersburg to be received this time with a salute of guns from the fortress and with rich rewards. Now appointed Russian Minister to Persia, he fell in love with a sixteen-year-old Persian princess and married her. But, at Tabriz, he soon ran into trouble with the Persians. Some of the Tsar's demands of the Shah were unenforceable. Griboyedov warned St Petersburg of this, but went ahead just the same. The result was calamitous. Leaving his young bride under the protection of the British Minister at Tabriz, he journeyed to Teheran to talk personally with the Shah. In January 1831 a mob took the Russian legation by storm and massacred everyone inside – all but a solitary survivor – including Griboyedov, who died fighting, his body stripped and mutilated.

I include this brief sketch of the career of Griboyedov who died at thirty-six because, with all its ambivalence, it shows how highly critical intelligences accepted the Russia of Nicholas as a going concern. To those of the Emperor's subjects who were capable of seeing beyond their immediate masters to the state which bound each to all, Russia in the early years of the reign of Nicholas was the very image of stability. To most of them she was also land of hope and glory. Feelings of patriotism ran high and could flare up into violent chauvinism when affronted by greedy Persians, scheming Turks, turbulent Caucasian tribesmen, rebellious Poles. The revolutionary year of 1848 saw Russia passing without a visible tremor through the earthquake which threatened to swallow up half

Europe; and when in the following year Nicholas leapt to the rescue of the new young Emperor of Austria, despatching Paskevich with a powerful army to destroy the Hungarian rebels under Kossuth, no less a person than the young Count Leo Tolstoy seriously considered the idea of enlisting in the army of repression. A year or two later that same Tolstoy voluntarily joined the army in the Caucasus to fight a colonial war against Moslem tribesmen.

Tolstoy was of course himself an aristocrat, very consciously so. As such, coming of age with the publication of *Childhood* in 1852 (he was then twenty-four), he was something of a throwback to the beginning of the reign, standing proudly aloof among the new intelligentsia who could not claim descent from tenth-century Volkonskys.

But the point to be made is that in the first years of the reign of Nicholas, and to a lesser degree thereafter, the evident mood of the times was reflected not by the friends of the Decembrists mourning the banished and the dead, not by the new critics of the regime whose voices began to be heard soon after the death of Griboyedov, but rather by the career of Griboyedov himself. It was reflected in the manner of the life and death of Pushkin, gagged by the censors, forbidden to travel without police permission, compelled to accept his ludicrous position at court because the Tsar had a shallow eye for the shallow beauty of the wife who was to precipitate the duel in which he died. It was reflected in the fate of Pushkin's younger contemporary Lermontov, an officer of the Guards who was also a poet of genius and a Byronic *poseur*: expelled from the Guards and sent to a line regiment in the Caucasus for writing his savage poem about the death of Pushkin, banished a second time for fighting a duel, he was killed in yet another duel at twenty-seven, to leave behind a romantic legend, a record of unsurpassed bravery in action, some poetry and prose of the highest quality, and, in *A Hero of Our Time*, the first great Russian novel.

But already by the time of Lermontov's fatal duel in 1841 there had come a change. Pushkin and Griboyedov might detest the system and criticise it savagely; but it was their natural habitat. Lermontov, on the other hand, although he came of an old army family, was play-acting. He was neither one thing nor the other. He accepted the system but had no natural home in it, and he deeply resented the fact that he was not sufficiently well born to be accepted in the highest Petersburg society which Pushkin had taken for granted. He was a misfit who belonged neither to the old world nor the new. And his life and death reflected perfectly the empty inanity of the society over which Nicholas presided and which he encouraged in its silliness, even while half his mind was wrestling with the serious problems of the age of steam. He wrestled largely alone: it never occurred to him that he was driving not only the poets of the land but also its potential economists, engineers, managers and political leaders, to drink, to women, to cards, to duelling, to suicide.

They were playing cards with Namurov of the Horse Guards. The long winter night slipped by imperceptibly; it was five in the morning when they broke off to eat. Those who had won ate with a hearty appetite; the others stared abstractedly at empty plates. But champagne appeared; the talk became livelier, and soon everyone joined in.

In this opening passage of *The Queen of Spades*, Pushkin reflects absolutely the mood of St Petersburg: this was how gentlemen spent their nights, and of course they continued to do so for many years to come. Just as Onegin kills his friend Lensky in a duel, breaks the heart of Tatiana, repents too late – all without a word of self-justification – so Pushkin accepted the cruelty of life without a murmur of self-pity. Lermontov, also a great gambler and a duellist, who not only wrote with something of Pushkin's own marvellous transparency but also had his matter-of-factness – a matter-of-factness which was to be the basis of Russian realism for the rest of the century – and was more than ready to throw his life away, yet nevertheless injected a new element of self-dramatisation. Here is Maurice Baring's prose translation of Lermontov's 'Testament': a mortally wounded officer gives his last message to a friend:[4]

I want to be alone with you, my friend, just for a moment. They say I have not long to live and you will soon be going home on leave. Well look . . . but why? There is not a soul over there who will be greatly troubled about my fate.

And yet, if someone were to ask you, whoever it might be, tell them a bullet hit me in the chest and say that I died honourably 'for king and country', that our doctors are fools and that I send my best love to the old country.

My father and my mother you will scarcely find alive, and to tell the truth it would be a pity to make them unhappy, but if one of them should still be living, say that I am bad at writing, that they sent us to the front and that they need not wait for me.

We had a neighbour . . . as you will remember, and she – how long ago it is – we said goodbye! She will not ask after me. But no matter, tell her everything, do not spare her empty heart, let her have her cry, tears cost her nothing.

The technique is the technique of Pushkin; the content belongs to a new age. And it was an age which was to turn its back on poetry for nearly forty years, during which the great novelists on the one hand, the musicians on the other, gathered into themselves all that was most creative in the Russian spirit. The first part of Gogol's *Dead Souls* was published in 1842, the year after Lermontov's death. Dostoevsky's *Poor Folk* appeared in 1846; so did the first parts of S. T. Aksakov's *Family Chronicle*; Turgenev's *A Sportsman's Sketches* started coming out as a serial in the following year; and after another five years Tolstoy produced *Childhood*. The work of all these men was complicated by the necessity of waging perpetual guerrilla warfare with the censorship. But it was warfare with a difference.

When Pushkin was writing, the literary journalism of St Petersburg was the virtual monopoly of a group of venal hacks, the chief of whom, F. V. Bulgarin, was a paid police agent. It was Bulgarin who was responsible for the most crass of all Nicholas's excursions into active censorship, when the Tsar gave it as his own opinion that Pushkin's sombre Shakespearian drama, *Boris Godunov*, had better be re-written 'as an historical tale or novel in the manner of Walter Scott'.⁵ Co-editor of *The Northern Bee* with the equally venal Nicholas Grech, Bulgarin was one of those unscrupulous climbers whose ambitions are ludicrously disproportionate to their talents. Everybody knew that he was in the employ of the Third Section, and everybody knew that he used this position to destroy his rivals and embarrass his manifest superiors. He was one of those wretches whose pretensions first irritate, then amuse, then, by their sheer persistence, half-hypnotise the great with whom they aspire to mix and who first condescend to them, then use them, then come to rely upon them. Bulgarin and Grech for many years featured as a pair of unholy and damaging twins in the developing literary society of St Petersburg. Allied with them was a clever-smart feuilletonist and critic J. J. Senkowski, a professional cynic incapable of recognising either genius or decency, who knew only how to destroy. Men like these exist in all societies and were to persist in Russia. But after the 1840s they were never again to dominate the Russian literary scene absolutely, until their spirit found a new incarnation in the official literary establishment under Stalin. The new mood was established above all by Belinsky, later to be celebrated as the father of the Russian intelligentsia, in his own time the standard-bearer of political commitment.

3

This book is not concerned with literature as such, and it may be asked why a historical study of nineteenth- and early twentieth-century Russia should dwell upon the work of novelists and poets, let alone literary journalists. The answer is that in the profoundest sense the history of Russia, from the accession of Nicholas I to the declaration of war in 1914, was the product of an interplay between the autocracy and intelligentsia – the intelligentsia at first operating in a void, then harnessed to a revolutionary movement which at last destroyed it. It is possible to write a coherent historical study of nineteenth-century Britain without mentioning Matthew Arnold or John Stuart Mill, or even Charles Dickens, because the ideas they stood for were reflected to a greater or lesser degree in the actions of powerful and effective political movements. But imagine a land in which Arnold, Mill and Dickens, repressed by the censors and harried by the police, represented the *only* articulate force offering opposition to a dictatorial will. . . . So it was with Belinsky, Turgenev and many others – none of them regarded by authority as anything but subversive, but all of them making history. Widely different, even violently opposed in many of their ideas, these men, soon to be joined by women too, represented a phenomenon peculiar to Russia. The very name by which they came to be known, the intelligentsia, had no counterpart in any other land. For in Imperial Russia, as later in Soviet Russia, to think for oneself was by definition to be subversive. So that, as time went on, the intelligentsia was to become for all practical purposes an estate of the realm in which active and aggressive revolutionaries were in some degree united with men who detested the very idea of revolution, bound together by common opposition to the autocracy and by the refusal of the autocracy to admit the difference between a revolutionary bent on its destruction and a liberal seeking to reform it.

One of the products of this state of affairs was the subordination of the arts, literature of course above all, to politics, more particularly to the stimulation of criticism of the existing system and the shortcomings of the society that permitted it to flourish. And it was Belinsky who infected Russian literature with the social consciousness that was to distinguish it ever after. But he was not an isolated figure appearing out of the blue. The early 1830s saw the beginning of an extraordinary intellectual flowering, a springtime of the mind and spirit which showed every promise of almost infinite development. But summer never came.

The precise chronology of growth, the interplay of cause and effect, was complex in the extreme. Two sets of ardent spirits, both fiercely rejecting official Russia, found guidance in two very different sources: on the one hand in German idealistic philosophy in particular and the Western cultural and material achievement in general; on the other hand in a backward-looking invocation of the pure spirit of Slavdom, uncorrupted by the Petrine reforms – a belief that by revitalising antique Russian institutions and rediscovering the old Slav virtues, Russia could not only save herself and avoid the mistakes of the West but could also show the West how to redeem itself.

Thus there arose the opposition of the Westernisers and the Slavophiles which, however, was by no means absolute. Although extreme positions were stated by individuals in each camp no fixed battle-lines were drawn. Most of the Slavophiles conceded freely that there were lessons to be learnt from the West and believed that Western techniques must be called in aid to help Russia move out of her own backwardness and fit herself for her holy mission: it was not until much later that philosophical Slavophilism was overtaken by the chauvinistic crudities of the extreme Panslavs, who preached an apocalyptic confrontation between an almighty Russia and an effete West which must end in the total victory of Slavdom. Conversely, many of the Westernisers entertained understandable reservations about Western attitudes and institutions and as time went on, particularly after the failure of the 1848 revolutions, suffered severe disillusionment – as when Alexander Herzen himself found a last refuge in a quasi-mystical veneration of the hidden virtues of the Russian peasant.

In earlier days the opposition was religious and philosophical rather than political. The Slavophiles were aristocratic, conservative and Christian. Their founder and prophet, A. S. Khomyakov, was one of the most brilliant men of his day. An officer in the Horse Guards, he fought in the Turkish War of 1828–9 and then settled down as an enlightened and progressive landowner, philosopher, theologian and poet, who regarded it as his main task to recall his country to her special mission as the moral conscience of the world. Russia was great not because she was Russia: Khomyakov lacked the least taint of chauvinistic nationalism. She was great because the Orthodox Church was the repository of the true spirit of Christianity, uncorrupted by the formalistic, legalistic, essentially rationalistic breath of Rome. Only in pre-Petrine Russia had the pure spirit of Christianity been preserved from the crushing distortions of a quasi-secular institutionalism. That spirit had been driven underground by Peter, but not destroyed. It had to be resurrected. Standing in the way of this resurrection was the bureaucracy, which Khomyakov saw as an alien growth having no organic connection with the ancient Russia but simply imposed by Peter in accordance with the seventeenth-century Western ideal of secular absolutism.

It is thus interesting to note that Khomyakov from his very different standpoint came close to Conrad's concept of the Russian autocracy as 'a visitation . . . a curse from heaven falling in the darkness of the ages . . .'. But not a curse from heaven. . . . Khomyakov believed that the curse came from the West. He was a beautiful prose-writer, a poet too.

He could argue and debate better than any man alive. And in the Moscow drawing-rooms he met and argued with the best of good humour with men who disagreed with him. This deeply religious man made a friend of the atheist Herzen. He would have shone in any Western debating chamber. And he was a practical man of affairs. No sharper criticism of Nicholas need be made than the reflection that a man of Khomyakov's calibre was excluded from participation in the government of Russia: the very idea that he might be used never entered the Tsar's head.

A little older than Khomyakov, a sort of bridge linking the present with those aristocratic conservatives of goodwill who might have made something of Russia if Alexander I had given them the chance, was S. T. Aksakov, himself a landowner turned writer who achieved two things: in his *Family Chronicle* he founded and brought to perhaps its supreme peak that uniquely Russian style of autobiographical writing, lyrical, elegiac, yet scrupulously realistic and exact, which was to be picked up by the young Tolstoy in *Childhood, Boyhood* and *Youth*, and carried through decade after decade to its most recent flowering in the masterpiece of Konstantin Paustovsky.[6] He also painted the classical picture of the old Russian patriarchal society which was to lend substance to the dreams of the backward-looking Slavophiles.

His two sons, followers of Khomyakov, were to make their names as Slavophiles; so were the two Kireyevsky brothers, their contemporaries. But the time to consider these comes later, in the next reign, when the emphasis of the Slavophiles began to move away from religion towards nationalism and racialism.

In the thirties and the forties the Slavophiles, distinguished as their leaders individually were, carried far less influence than the Westernisers, who themselves revolved in two distinct but overlapping circles, both of them centred on the University of Moscow. St Petersburg, frozen in the shadow of Nicholas and his court, had nothing to offer – although, ironically, the interest in foreign ideas was fed by the action of two St Petersburg Ministers of Education, Prince K. A. Lieven and Count S. S. Uvarov, who sent selected students to study abroad in the hope that they would return and help to raise higher education in Russia out of the slough into which it had sunk.

There was nothing limited or hard-and-fast about these circles. They were simply discussion groups, one centred on Alexander Herzen and his friend and fellow-rebel, N. P. Ogarev, which was concerned above all with political action and found its main inspiration in Fourier and Saint-Simon. It was when this group was denounced to the police in 1834 that Herzen was banished to Vyatka province where, because of his education and his formidable connections, he was put to work in the Governor's office. Thus the young man who as a boy had stood looking over Moscow from the Sparrow Hills and vowed with Ogarev that he would dedicate his life to completing the work of the Decembrists, now found himself working on the inside of the bureaucratic machine which he was able to study and condemn in detail. On his return to Moscow six years later he found a new circle in full swing, called after a gifted young aristocrat, N. V. Stankevich, one of those invaluable men who make no direct personal contribution to politics or ideas, but know how to fire and sustain the minds of their contemporaries. Stankevich, who died very young, was more a philosopher than a politician. His ruling deity was Hegel. He found common ground with Michael Bakunin before that brilliant and erratic aristocrat embraced the dogma of destruction. One of his protégés was the young Belinsky, who for some time had been making a name in Moscow journalism and was now taken up by Herzen.

There was a further element in the explosive compound now being mixed in Moscow. This was a new school of journalism which owed nothing to the favour of Benckendorff and the court and everything to the drive and ambition of two energetic and enthusiastic members of the new middle class who could never have made careers for themselves in St Petersburg without falling into sycophancy: Nicholas Polevoy with his *Moscow Telegraph* and Nicholas Nadezhdin with the *Telescope*. Both in their indiscriminate and often half-baked onslaught on past Russian literary achievement in general and St Petersburg manners in particular helped to establish the climate in which the new young radicals could flourish. Belinsky started writing for *Telescope* when he came down from the university in 1832, but Nadezhdin's most celebrated achievement was to publish the *Philosophical Letter* of Peter Chaadayev, as a result of which his journal was closed down, he himself exiled and driven out of literature, and Chaadayev, at the Tsar's command, pronounced insane and placed under medical supervision.

4

Chaadayev belonged to none of the Moscow circles, nor was he in any sense a professional writer. Nineteen years older than Belinsky, seventeen years older than Herzen, he had pursued an aloof and lonely course; a friend of Pushkin's, a Hussar of the Guards, after the Decembrist tragedy he sought personal salvation in religion, combining an element of personal mysticism with a highly idiosyncratic leaning towards the Church of Rome, seen by him as the lofty and aspiring edifice which had sheltered, nurtured indeed, the diverse but unified culture of the West.

In 1830 Chaadayev composed in French a series of essays which he circulated among his friends, but not until six years later when the flooding ideas of the young radicals in Moscow had begun to burst their banks, was he persuaded to publish the first of these *Philosophical Letters* – and found in Nadezhdin an editor brave enough to share the risk. The impact was immediate and almost brutal. Others before Chaadayev had deplored the backwardness of Russia and sought to show how and why she had fallen so far behind the achievement of the West. But few since Peter the Great had insisted unequivocally on Russia's responsibility for her own condition, and none had linked the moral development of Western Christendom and the rule of law with Western material advancement.

Situated between the two great divisions of the world, between East and West, one elbow resting on China, the other on Germany, we should be able to unite in ourselves the two great principles of consciousness, imagination and reason, thus embracing in our own culture the histories of the whole world. But this is not at all the role that Providence has assigned to us. On the contrary, she seems not to take the slightest interest in our destiny. Denying us her beneficent influence on the human spirit, she has left us completely to ourselves. She has not wished to involve herself in our affairs, she has not wished to teach us. The experience of the ages has meant nothing to us; we have profited not at all from all the epochs and the generations which have gone before. To look at us, one would say that the general law governing humanity has been revoked on our account. Alone among all the peoples of the world we have given nothing to the world, we have learned nothing from the world. We have contributed nothing to the progress of the human mind, we have only disfigured it. There is something in our blood which rejects all true progress. It would seem that we have lived, still live, only to serve as a great lesson of some kind for a remote posterity which will know how to profit by it. Today we are nothing but a lacuna in the intellectual order.[7]

This extreme statement of Chaadayev's desolating consciousness of Russian inferiority, which he elaborated circumstantially throughout his essay, helped more than any single writing to bring to a head the dissatisfaction of thinking Russians with their inheritance which had first surfaced among the young Decembrists and had then been driven roughly underground. The *Philosophical Letter* appeared in the same year as Gogol's satirical masterpiece, *Revisor, The Government Inspector*, which held up for all to see the corruption and sycophancy in which the system was entangled. It was Nicholas himself who bestowed his official blessing on Gogol (later rescinded), much to the surprise of everybody, including the official censors, just as it was Nicholas himself who ordered that Chaadayev must be certified insane. To understand this apparent contradiction it is convenient to leap forward a hundred and twenty years.

After the death of Stalin in 1953, his successors, viewing with unease the abysmal state to which all the arts had been brought by Stalinist repression, began to urge novelists and dramatists to wake up and play their part in attacking, or satirising, 'negative' aspects of Soviet society instead of pretending that everything was for the best in the best possible of worlds. But it was quickly understood that criticism must be directed only to symptoms, never to causes. That is to say, a dramatist might write a play about the scandals arising from idle or corrupt officials, managers, bureaucrats; but there must be no suggestion at all that the system or the leadership could be held in any way to blame for the behaviour of such individuals. Thus, when Nicholas saw *The Government Inspector* and enjoyed it, what he saw was an attack on precisely the corruption and venality of the bureaucracy which he himself deplored. It did not occur to him that the attitudes which permitted a Khlestyakov to pose as a high official and get away with it were a reflection on him, personally, as autocrat, or on the long line of his forebears. Chaadayev, however, was quite different. Here Holy Russia incarnate was under attack. Worse, an alien world was held up as a model. For Chaadayev was not content to denounce his own countrymen nor did he confine himself, as others had done in the past and were increasingly to do in future, to contrasting the material backwardness of Russia with the material advancement of the West. This, within limits, was permissible – even to be encouraged. It was agreed that the West had better railways and that Russia must profit more from the technical skills of Britain, Germany and France. What was impermissible was to look to the West for spiritual enlightenment. Chaadayev did precisely this:

The peoples of Europe have a common physiognomy, a family resemblance. Despite their general division into Latins and Teutons, into southerners and northerners, it is plain to anyone who has studied their history that there is a common bond which unites them into one group. You know that not too long ago all Europe considered itself to be Christian, *and this term had its place in public law (droit)* [my italics]. Besides this general character, each of these peoples has its own character, but all that is only history and tradition. It is the patrimony of inherited ideas. There each individual is in full possession of the common heritage, and without difficulty or effort gathers to himself those notions which have been scattered throughout society, and profits from them. Do you want to know what these ideas are? They are the concepts of duty, justice, law and order.[8]

Nadezhdin was exiled for publishing Chaadayev and never returned to journalism. The *Telescope* was closed down. Polevoy soon found himself in trouble for a comparatively minor offence against the censorship. Unlike Nadezhdin he bowed to authority and degenerated into an obedient hack. But the work of these two was done. Chaadayev himself was fairly soon allowed back to Moscow. He wrote very little but never compromised and exerted a powerful moral influence – his strange, tall, gangling figure with a bald, high dome of a head so much at odds with the idea of a cavalry officer, moving serenely through the liberal Muscovite salons, deeply respected even by those who had no use for his mysticism, his devotion to Rome, and who never understood his burning passion for the rule of law. It has sometimes been said that he recanted when, in 1837, he wrote another essay: *Apology of a Madman*. But this was an apologia, not an apology. Nor was there anything new or surprising in his conclusion that the very barrenness of Russia's past gave her an immense advantage over all other nations: 'We come to every new idea with virgin minds.' Even in the offending *Philosophical Letter* he had touched on this idea, and in a letter to Turgenev, dated 1833, he had been more specific:

Like all peoples, we too are racing ahead today – in our own way if you like, but we are running, that is certain. I am sure that in a little while the great ideas, once they have reached us, will find it easier to realise themselves in our midst and to incarnate themselves in our people than anywhere else, because here they will find no deep-rooted prejudices, no old habits, no obstinate routines to fight. It seems to me that the European thinker should not be totally indifferent to the present state of his meditations among us.[9]

The great ideas were indeed arriving. Chaadayev would have thought they were the wrong ideas, or the right ideas distorted. He was very much an isolated figure. The religious-minded Slavophiles rejected absolutely his veneration for Rome and looked back to Byzantium: with their rejection of Rome they rejected, without comprehending, the concept of the rule of law which they equated with arid and hypocritical legalism. The Westernisers, agnostic or, more usually, atheist, regarded blankly his evocation of a universal Christianity with its roots in the West:

Remember that for fifteen centuries they spoke to God in the same language, lived under a single moral authority, and shared the same belief. Remember that for fifteen centuries, each year, on the same day, at the same hour, with the same words, they all together raised their voices towards the Supreme Being, to extol his glory. A wonderful concert, a thousand times more sublime than all the harmonies of the physical world![10]

The ideas when they began to reach the Moscow discussion circles were the ideas of the Western philosophers, above all the romantic Germans, who were in full revolt against the spiritual authority of Rome; and the Slavophiles themselves were far more in sympathy with the Western Protestants than with the Catholics. But Chaadayev's words were a pointer to the immediate future – and a prophecy.

The immediate future was to be ruled by Belinsky inside Russia and outside by Herzen, the expatriate revolutionary. Neither understood the core of Chaadayev's vision: the paramount need for law. Both were to initiate movements which, largely because of this failure of comprehension, were to encourage the awakening Russian mind to seize and ruinously distort 'the great ideas', turning them into agents of destruction.

It was V. G. Korolenko, one of the most gentle, honest, self-effacing and courageous of Russian liberals (he thought of himself as a revolutionary), who wrote at the turn of the century, when Belinsky had been dead for fifty years: 'My country is not Russia; my country is Russian literature.'[11] This was not a retreat from reality, from the world of action into the world of dreams. On the contrary, it was an affirmation, a declaration of allegiance, as on the part of a man standing up to be counted, to the one force in Imperial Russia which functioned not only as the conscience of the land but also as the spearhead of social reform. Those words might be echoed by Solzhenitsyn in our own time.

5

It was Belinsky who first, for better or for worse, gave to that affirmation substance.[12] He was not, as already indicated, an isolated figure appearing out of the blue. Very early on in his all too brief career (he was born in 1810 and he died, worn out with consumption and nervous exhaustion, at thirty-eight) he became a dominant one. His purely literary insights were his own, but his general ideas he owed very much to others, coming as he did from a poor family and being plunged into the hurricane of ideas from the West which swept through Moscow University in the early 1830s – where even a young and ardent professor of medieval history, T. N. Granovsky, could use his lectures to publicise, barely disguised, the ideas of Hegel and Fichte and their application to Russian conditions.

Belinsky's unique contribution was the overpowering intensity, directness and single-mindedness of his determination to seek the truth and speak it out. Unresting, violent, hectoring, often insufferable, constantly changing his ground in the light of yet another revelation, he drove himself to the limit and beyond, forced himself to write far too much in order to keep body and soul together (it is amazing that he managed this as long as he did), even then as often as not forgetting to eat, his feeble body shuddering with asthma, in the end spitting blood. And he drove others as hard as he drove himself, demanding, insisting, that they, with him, should purge themselves of all falsity, double-talk, evasiveness, hypocrisy, self-approval. He not only won their absolute devotion in life, but also ensured that for long decades after he was dead those who had once known him, like Turgenev, would for ever measure their own conduct in the light of his memory.

Belinsky infected Russian literature with the social and political consciousness which was to distinguish it, both for better and for worse, ever after. His position was unique. No literary critic in history has exercised a comparable influence not only in his own day but for generations to come. It is not too much to say that as a founding father of the Russian intelligentsia – this so furious and explosive anti-patriarch! – he was, though himself never politically engaged in the narrow sense of the term, also the hero of the radicals of almost every colour and therefore a founder of the revolutionary movement. But in spirit he was a liberator who moved from the philosophical acceptance of reality which stemmed from Hegel to a dynamic activism.

In fact he was a self-taught romantic who lacked an outer skin. Bakunin, brilliant, overflowing, irresponsible, could and did stimulate and mould his intellect. But Belinsky's final guide was the heart. His heart, his whole being, was lacerated by the cruelties which man inflicts on man – in the name of religion, in the name of government, in the name of property, in the name of matrimony, in the name of every institution, every ideology, every convention yet established or conceived. He was a feminist before his time because he could not bear to see the humiliation of women at the hands of men. He could not bear the spectacle of poverty, of men turned into drunkards by the squalor in which they were condemned to live, of the corrupt smile on the face of the girl driven to walk the streets. His articles and letters are catalogues of all the evils and wickednesses, arising mainly from inertia and complacency, which were to obsess successive generations of reformers in all lands throughout the nineteenth century and after. There was nothing selective in his vision of horror: he loaded his own back with all the sins of the world, and hated himself: 'I all but weep when I give an old soldier a kopek; I run from a beggar to whom I have given a kopek as though I have committed an evil deed and try to drown the sound of my own footsteps. This is life: to sit on the pavement in rags with an idiot expression collecting kopeks by day to spend on getting drunk by night. Men see it. But nobody cares.' Belinsky was consumed, devoured by care for others and for suffering humanity. It was this that drove him to question the decency of art. 'What do I care for the existence of the universal when the individual suffers? What do I care if genius on earth lives in heaven when the mass is wallowing in filth?' And so on and for ever: the first great cry against the vanity and selfishness of the dreamer who seeks the celestial city while his neighbour starves, which was to echo and re-echo through the Russian century. No Shakespeare, no Pushkin, so long as a single living soul must go barefoot, in rags!

So many who were to take up that cry knew next to nothing of Shakespeare or Pushkin and cared less, and the hearts of too many of them far from bleeding for the weak were consumed with envy and filled to the exclusion of all else by hatred of the strong – and the desire for power to humiliate the strong. Not Belinsky. His literary understanding was erratic and uncertain. But he had the authentic passion for poetry, and he was the first Russian critic to perceive the true stature of Pushkin, in almost every superficial aspect his antithesis, and to celebrate it. When he came to proclaim his conviction that it was better to be an inferior artist in the service of liberalism than a supreme poet who pays lip-service to reactionary ideas he was stating, with inadequate definition, a position entirely valid at the height of the Nicholas period (when, indeed, it was inconceivable that any sane individual with an artist's sensibility could decently insulate himself from the clamant needs of the time). What finally drove him to despair was his bitter disappointment when in 1846 Gogol published the farrago entitled *Selected Passages from Letters to my Friends*. This was the attempt of a man sick in mind to put himself right with God and the Tsar, to regenerate Russia and to save his own soul. It was in effect an abject and often ludicrous glorification of the autocracy, of Orthodoxy, of serfdom, of the alleged piety and spirituality of the Russian peasant finding fulfilment in the discipline of absolutism, and it came as a shock to many of Gogol's admirers.

Belinsky, like all other Russian radicals, had quite failed, reasonably enough, to understand that the man who was presented as a prince of satirists in *Dead Souls* and *The Government Inspector* and as a compassionate champion of the underdog in *The Overcoat* had not the faintest idea of what he had been doing: far from being an embattled rebel against the system, Gogol was irresponsible; in his thought, such as it was, a conventionally blinkered and frightened conservative, who happened to be possessed by an uncontrollable streak of almost surrealist fantasy owing nothing to reason. Thus poor Gogol's clumsy and desperate attempt to put himself right with God and the Tsar seemed to Belinsky, as to many others, an act of deliberate apostasy calling for violent condemnation. Hence his celebrated letter openly addressed to the novelist which was to have such enduring effects and also to distort the true image of Belinsky himself.

The effects were twofold. In the first place Belinsky denounced root and branch in a superb explosion of invective the whole concept carried to a ludicrous point by Gogol, but shared also by many Slavophiles, and later by Tolstoy – of the Russian peasant as an essentially religious creature, the unconscious and unselfconscious repository of a pure spirituality out of the reach of the more sophisticated. Religion in Russia, Belinsky insisted, was a confidence trick, an agglomeration of unworthy superstitions, and the Russian priesthood, universally drunken, always corrupt, was held in contempt by those who bowed before it. This over-simplification, this half-truth, was to blind later generations of Russian radicals to certain aspects of Russian reality which persist to this day. In the second place it drove Belinsky himself to his exaltation of the social reformer over the artist and his insistence that literature must be the handmaiden of politics.

Belinsky died before he could either qualify this idea or refine it. But it was this message that was taken up and pushed to extreme lengths in the next reign by the young Turks of the radical movement, N. G. Chernyshevsky, N. A. Dobrolyubov, and their followers. These men were not artists heroically harnessing their talents to politics; they were politicians compelled to present themselves as artists in a society where politicians could not practise openly. In time they came to believe in all sincerity that they were what they pretended to be.

The working of the great ferment which intoxicated a generation of ardent and often brilliant spirits forced into the closest community, in spite of their fundamentally contrasting views, by their desperate vulnerability was to continue with very little impact on the containing world. Not until Nicholas was dead and the myth of Russian power shattered by the Crimean War did the seismic forces generated by the Moscow circles begin to shake the earth.

CHAPTER SIX

The Imperial Mission

THE death of Nicholas in humiliation and defeat was a bitter end for a man who regarded himself, and was once accepted by the world, as one of the main pillars of the European order, an order which he was pledged to maintain. He had no designs on Europe. The role of Russia was to lend her strong arm to the maintenance of the *status quo* and the preservation of established governments from the forces of subversion. For Nicholas this role was a fixed idea. He could maintain order at home, while abroad his great, his incomparable, army was ready when required to intervene in the interests of stability throughout the Continent.

Alas, there was nobody to tell him that although inside Russia he could ban all change, even though this meant laying up grief for his successors, outside his own frontiers he could do no such thing and that any foreign policy which ignored the first principles of human mutability was bound to fail.

His chief adviser in the international field was the clever, unassuming, self-effacing little half-Jewish German, Count K. V. Nesselrode, most oddly brought up in the Anglican faith, who knew the chancellories of Europe inside out, was famed for his dinner parties, and got on well with everyone he met. Having steered Alexander through the Congress of Vienna and done his best to level out his erratic course thereafter, he now stood ready to place his vast experience at the new Tsar's disposal. Nesselrode knew very well that the simple certitudes which appeared to govern the attitude of Nicholas had little relevance to the dark and shifting complexities of dynastic rivalries, to say nothing of the unpredictable motions of mass opinion in the post-Napoleonic epoch. But he was not the man to instruct his master in the facts of political life, or indeed, of human nature. And although he was able to play a far more positive part than he cared to claim for himself ('I am simply my Imperial master's voice,' he would confide, in effect, to all and sundry), this part consisted in the main of enjoining caution at critical moments, of discreetly sowing ideas for the Tsar to discover as his own, and of skilful diplomatic manoeuvre to ensure that his country secured the maximum advantage from any given action by Nicholas, whether misguided or not. In a word, he did wonders in keeping a proud, violent and disturbingly emotional autocrat more or less on the rails.

No man was less well equipped than Nicholas for flexible diplomacy. No man was less capable of entering into the minds of his European contemporaries or understanding their fears. He knew, of course, that he could not lay down the law to London or Vienna; but he could not accept this limitation gracefully as an ineluctable fact of nature. It was so blindingly obvious to him (surely it must be no less obvious to a Metternich, a Canning, or a Palmerston) not only that he was correct in all his actions, but also that these actions were inspired infallibly by the noblest of motives. We remember his observation to his own Council of State: 'I cannot permit that any individual should dare defy my wishes once he knows what they are.' The spirit behind that declaration was never far beneath the surface in his dealings with the powers.

In his passionate need to be believed, he was eager to explain himself; but even in his efforts to justify himself the authoritarian tone, the apoplectic glint in those protruding eyes, too often came through. So that sometimes he appeared to parody himself, almost as though to say, 'I cannot permit that any Government should question my motives once I have indicated what they are.'

But alas, those motives were all too mixed. Nicholas was not only a pillar of the European order; he was also the heir to a great Empire which was still in the process of enlargement. And although he regarded his frontiers in the west as fixed for all time, in the south, on the borders of Persia and Turkey, there was no such stability. Here, the expansionist tradition was still active, the imperial idea a dynamic force, as it had been since Catherine had established Russia on the shores of the Black Sea at the expense of Turkey. Nicholas knew very well that what was known in the chancellories of Europe as the 'Eastern Question' had to be approached with extreme circumspection. The tensions set up by the slow decline of Ottoman power since the end of the seventeenth century, when it had been pushed back from the gates of Vienna, were such that any Russian move in the direction of Constantinople and the Straits, the Dardanelles, the connecting link between the Aegean and the Black Sea, via the Sea of Marmora and the Bosphorus, must provoke an international crisis. But although he knew this in his mind Nicholas found it always hard, sometimes impossible, to acknowledge it in his heart.

2

His career as the master of a great military power started off imposingly enough. The problem of Turkey in Europe, with him from the very moment of his accession, first presented itself in the guise of the Greek struggle for independence. Here an extremely ticklish situation was converted into an opportunity for joint action with Britain and France, which ended with a Turkish fleet being sent to the bottom by Admiral Codrington at Navarino and the assurance of Greece's future as an independent state.

Almost at once he scored another triumph. Even while the three powers had been concerting their attitude to Turkey in the summer of 1826, Persia had decided to take advantage of Russia's larger preoccupations by launching a campaign to recover parts of her old empire which had been lost to Russia in an earlier age – Georgia and the northern part of Azerbaijan, the Caspian province. At first she had made good progress. In the very moment of his coronation Nicholas had the humiliation of seeing the Persians penetrating almost to Tiflis. When the tide had been reversed, General Yermolov, one of the heroes of the 1812 campaign, was replaced by General Paskevich, an erratic, ruthless and much overrated commander, one of the Emperor's few trusted friends, who was later to become the scourge first of the Poles in revolt against Russia, then of the Hungarians in revolt against the Habsburgs. Now he quickly recovered the lost territories and took the war into the enemy camp, finishing up in 1827 by capturing Tabriz and Erevan, the capital of Persian Armenia.

It was a good start for Nicholas. Within two years of his accession he had broken a revolt against the Crown, entered into an advantageous, if fleeting, alliance with Britain and France against Turkey, assisted in the abasement of Turkish power, and now had Persia at his mercy. He was very correct. Some expected him to move on and occupy Teheran: Persia should become a vassal state. But Nicholas had no such plans: the Shah had indeed been guilty of wanton aggression, but the Shah was a fellow-monarch, and monarchs did not destroy one another. So Russia kept Erevan and Persian Armenia with its Christian population, but magnanimously returned Tabriz.

The trouble was that these easy victories gave Nicholas a false idea of his army's competence. So that when after Navarino Turkey repudiated the Treaty of Akkerman which had conceded to Russia all her demands it never crossed his mind that the war he proceeded to declare would be anything but a parade. He himself took the field.

For a time things seemed to go well against the Turks. Paskevich and his hard-bitten army, far away on the other side of the Caucasus, won a whole series of victories including the capture of Kars, the great fortress on the main trade route between Asia Minor and Transcaucasia, but Wittgenstein's main army soon found itself in trouble.

The Principalities of Moldavia and Wallachia, later to become the Kingdom of Roumania, were still under Turkish suzerainty but had been demilitarised under treaty agreement with Russia. The Turkish fortified line followed the Danube, which divided what is now Roumania from what is now Bulgaria (then a Turkish province). After an easy start, a quick march across the Principalities and the reduction of a number of Danube forts, the Russians found themselves in trouble. Nicholas was installed with a great deal of pomp at army headquarters and was soon to see for himself something of the sufferings of his troops.

It was high summer now, in arid country. The blazing summer heat with an accompanying water shortage murdered the troops, already wearied by their long march south over terrible roads. Those same terrible roads, together with the faulty organisation of the supply services, held up the provision of rations and ammunition. With all the vast resources of an empire and a standing army of over half a million men, Wittgenstein now found himself on Turkish soil far removed from base with less than a hundred thousand, and these heavily reduced by sickness. It was a measure of his desperation that Nicholas decided to send for the Imperial Guard, and the regiments of the Guard had to march nearly a thousand miles through the summer heat to reach the scene of battle.

At first Nicholas was slow to realise the very real dangers of the situation. He seems to have lived in a dream. All that was needed, he was sure, to give zest and enthusiasm to the troops was for him to show himself and hold a succession of grand reviews. With him, he had a positive galaxy of aides and equerries, all beautifully mounted, together with a host of servitors. Army headquarters was a miniature St Petersburg. Nesselrode was there and half the diplomatic corps, invited to witness the Imperial triumph. Ten thousand horses were required to transport this Imperial circus and its baggage – taking their oats from the starving regimental beasts.[1] At first Nicholas had allowed Wittgenstein, wise, but old and very cautious, to conduct the campaign while he, the Tsar, looked on approvingly. But now he convinced himself that he must intervene personally: bold and decisive action was all, and he alone could supply it! There must be no more hanging about. The stubborn fortresses of Varna, Shumla, Silistria, must all be invested and taken simultaneously, and he, the Tsar, moving swiftly from place to place, would supervise the operation and lend courage to the troops. Thus it was that the weak Russian forces were divided. The generals looked on appalled as, for example, 30,000 men were sent against Shumla where the Turks had 40,000 defensively disposed.

It was before Shumla that Nicholas suddenly lost his nerve. He had brought his beloved soldiers to this godforsaken land and now had to stand by and see them ravaged by disease, broken and torn by war, with no proper hospitals to care for them. The shock, the pain, the humiliation were too much.[2] He realised at last that he was simply getting in the way of his commanders, so he gave up, removed himself from the battlefield, and after some weeks in Odessa where the Tsaritsa came to join him, departed for St Petersburg. There, welcomed by joyous subjects who had been muttering at his long absence, he could tidily resume the task for which God had clearly made him: the superintendance of the affairs of the Empire coolly and from a great height.

It would be hard to imagine a more terrible blow for a man, an autocrat, who had thought of himself above all as a soldier. But Nicholas seemed completely unaffected. And when in the following year the successor to Wittgenstein, the Silesian General Diebitsch, turned the tide in the Balkans, while Paskevich in the east made his triumphant advance to Erzerum, Nicholas gloried in their victories as though they were his own, apparently no longer affected by thoughts of the cost in human suffering and blessedly forgetful of his own past ignominy.

Victory was indeed absolute. With the Russians at Adrianople poised to sweep down to Constantinople and the Straits, the Sultan hurried to make peace, and it was time for the Tsar to be a diplomat again. He was studiously modest in his demands. He wanted no more, he insisted, than Turkish recognition of the legitimate rights for which he had fought. In the teeth of considerable dissent from patriotic Russians who were outraged by the failure to seize Constantinople, Nicholas had demonstrated to the Western powers that he had meant what he said when insisting that he had no designs on Turkey and saw her survival as a European necessity. After a shaky start he had also demonstrated the continued force of the Imperial army.

It was the autumn of 1829. Nicholas had beaten his own mutineers, he had beaten the Persians, he had beaten the Turks, he had shown the world that he was magnanimous in victory, and was indeed more concerned with maintaining peace in Europe than in adding to his realm. He had shown his subjects that he knew his own mind. For a brief moment joy was unconfined. While St Petersburg embarked on a long sparkling winter of the gayest relaxation, the people of the vast plain looked to their new Tsar to concentrate now on the reforms so long overdue.

3

Things did not turn out like that at all. In the second half of 1830 there occurred a related series of events which were to bring luridly to the surface the true nature of Nicholas and demonstrate the strained artificiality of his Olympian magnanimity and calm. They were to show, too, that his proclaimed determination to preserve the concert of the powers, sincere enough as far as it went, counted for little or nothing beside his own self-regard. He, Nicholas, was ruler by divine right, and the same principle of legitimacy must apply to all other monarchs, or all would be lost. When the Paris revolution of July 1830 was followed by a revolt in Belgium against the House of Orange, Nicholas was outraged and full of the conviction that it was his duty to intervene. All over Europe there was very real alarm at the threatening noises emanating from the champions of order in St Petersburg. Russia, so incomparably the greatest power on the Continent, was on the rampage. Not even the most conservative elements could regard with equanimity the prospect of Cossack armies sweeping out of the east on the pretext of restoring order in lands that asked only to be left to work out their own destinies. The existence of such fears, let alone their reasonableness, never seems to have crossed the mind of Nicholas. He knew very well that he had no designs on Europe, what then had Europe to fear from him? By all means he rattled his sabre, but it was in a holy cause which had nothing to do with Russian nationalism; and when the cause was won the sabre would be sheathed. He was not politically illiterate, but he lacked to a remarkable degree a sense of the possible – and of what was good for Russia. Luckily for him, however, before he could commit himself irretrievably in western Europe, he was diverted by a crisis much nearer home.

The diversion was revolt in Poland.

Nicholas, absolute master of an expanding Empire, was also the constitutional monarch of four million Poles. It was a situation which this abhorrer of constitutions found, to say the least, distasteful. But it was a legacy of the erratic idealism of his revered brother, Alexander, and because of this, and because of his respect for his pledged word, Nicholas put up with it. The Poles had their Parliament: an institution born of the devil in his eyes, but he was determined to respect it. He sincerely believed that he did respect it, evidently unconscious of the effect produced by the fact that the Polish Council of Ministers conducted their business under the eyes of an official Russian delegate, appointed in bland defiance of the constitution so liberal on paper, who was virtual controller of the administration. The Poles had their own language. What more could they ask? Their own religion too. They enjoyed tax concessions and customs privileges. They even had their own army; and the Grand Duke Constantine, who commanded it, assured him of its loyalty, even though elements of that army had been in league with the Decembrists. But the Poles, he would lament, were never satisfied. Instead of being content with the rump of their country set up as an independent kingdom under a Russian Tsar, they were for ever demanding the return of all the lands taken by Catherine, which included Lithuania. This was absurd, but no attention need be paid. And so secure did Nicholas feel in Poland that in 1830, with revolutions breaking out in Paris and Brussels and threatening also some of the German lands, he took no special precautions in Warsaw. Indeed, he felt so secure that he was preparing to use Polish troops with the Russian army to put down the Belgian rebellion on the other side of Europe. In fact it was the general revolutionary excitement of 1830, and particularly the rumour that Poles were to be sent to quell the Belgians in their struggle against their Dutch overlords, which sparked off the revolt in Warsaw.

It had small beginnings. On 29 November a group of student cadets conspiring in total secrecy seized Constantine's residence, the Belvedere Palace, overlooking the Lazienski Park on the outskirts of Warsaw. Constantine himself managed to slip out at the back of the building, but his Prefect of Police and an army general were killed. This was the prelude to a period of chaos and bloodshed which lasted for over a year. It ended not only with the crushing of the Poles and the abolition of Alexander's constitution, but also with Nicholas and the Government of Russia branded indelibly in the eyes of liberal Europe with the mark of the beast.

The relationship between Russia and Poland has often been compared with the relationship between England and Ireland. This is a misleading comparison. The very similarity between the reckless, irresponsible, suicidal violence of the Poles and the Irish is itself misleading. For the Irish have been a subject people for close on a thousand years, their island home inevitably regarded as part and parcel of the British Isles. And their irresponsibility is the irresponsibility of an oppressed people treated for centuries as the lowest of the low. The Poles, on the other hand, are a people with a formidable past of the kind commonly thought of as glorious. That is to say they were a conquering people. At the summit of their glory, in the sixteenth century, their kingdom was one of the largest in Europe, extending from the Baltic almost to the Black Sea and including Lithuania and vast tracts of what came to be White Russia and the Ukraine. After the death of Ivan the Terrible a Polish army actually penetrated to Moscow and beyond. Thus conflict was inevitable. And the eventual ascendancy of Russia was determined partly by dynastic accidents but more particularly by the failure of the Poles to govern themselves effectively. For the irresponsibility of the Poles was not the irresponsibility of a subject people, but, on the contrary, the irresponsibility of a proud, arrogant and greedy nobility who treated their peasants very badly indeed and at the same time proved incapable of combining among themselves to develop a rational system of government.

Thus it was that Poland was so vulnerable when, in the eighteenth century, Catherine of Russia, Frederick of Prussia, and Joseph II of Austria came together to destroy her in the three successive partitions. These partitions were actions of the bleakest and most ruthless kind, perfect expressions of the political morality of the age. And when the map of Europe was re-drawn at the Congress of Vienna the newly established kingdom of Poland, with the Tsar of Russia as king, had to endure the bitterness of looking out across her narrow frontiers at rich lands torn from her east and west and south.

Short of general war in Europe, in which Poland itself would have suffered terribly, there was nothing that could help them. They could not hope to fight the Russians effectively without allies, and their nearest neighbours were Austria and Prussia, both masters of large areas of the old Poland. Would France and England be prepared to take on Russia, Austria and Prussia for the sake of Polish freedom and irredentism? The idea was absurd. But many Poles entertained it. So did many Englishmen and Frenchmen, burning with indignation at the bullying of a tiny people by the greatest power in the world.

Even before 1830 the Poles had provoked Nicholas in a number of ways to no very useful purpose, stimulating his worst suspicions by their gentle treatment of those of their compatriots who had been embroiled in the Decembrist conspiracy. But Constantine, who had come to identify himself with the Poles, or at least with the Polish army, spoke up for them, assured his brother of their basic loyalty. Even when the news of the student revolt came through, Nicholas, although he made fiery declarations in characteristically theatrical terms, at first did nothing. By quick action, by the swift intervention of loyal troops, the revolt could have been crushed almost immediately. But Constantine, though shattered to discover that his beloved Polish army harboured rebels, set his face firmly against shooting and sought to negotiate while feelings cooled. Nicholas himself, still very much in the dark as to what was happening (was it another Decembrist conspiracy involving a handful of officers? Was it a full scale army mutiny? Was it a popular revolution?), was also determined to honour his constitutional oath, and held his hand, hoping that wiser counsels would prevail and that the main part of the army and the civil authorities would remain loyal and contain the revolt.

This did not happen. The situation was soon out of hand. Drucki-Lubecki and Czartoryski, the great friend of Alexander I in youth, tried to check the avalanche. They put up a popular soldier, General Chlopicki, to gain the confidence of the rebels while they appealed to Poles not to fight each other. But it was too late. Chlopicki tried to hold the line by proclaiming himself dictator and sent a high-powered delegation to St Petersburg to plead with Nicholas. It was now that an element of surrealism entered the scene. While protesting his total loyalty Chlopicki assured Nicholas that all he, the Tsar, had to do to restore order in Poland was to return the Lithuanian provinces. At the same time his delegate in St Petersburg, having prostrated himself before the throne, hopefully suggested that Nicholas should show the way for the Poles to make amends: let the Poles march at once on Galicia and Poznania, the provinces held by Austria and Prussia respectively, and keep them. Let Russia, in a word, turn Poland loose against Russia's closest allies. . . . No wonder Nicholas wrote to Constantine: 'They are all more or less out of their minds: I can explain it in no other way.'[3]

More than two months went by before the Russians nerved themselves to take decisive action. But the Polish army had by that time organised itself; when the first major clash occurred in February, at Grochow across the Vistula from Warsaw, it was able to claim a victory. What should have been for the Poles immediate and crushing defeat, turned out to be a long-drawn-out campaign. One is reminded of the ignominious campaign of Soviet Russia against the Finns in 1939. Russia had to win. But she took a long time doing so. Some of the bravest rebels came from the Russian lands, where they were quickly put down and had afterwards to suffer terribly for their treason. The Russians themselves were not properly equipped for a winter war, and shivered and froze in the snow. With the spring came cholera. Diebitsch was struck down by the disease. He died. So did poor Constantine, tagging along broken-hearted behind the Russian forces. It was not until Paskevich, the hero of the Caucasus, was sent out to succeed Diebitsch that the Russians at last took hold, seized Warsaw, and soon brought about the end.

Poland was now treated like a conquered country. Whereas Nicholas had been slow to regard the Polish revolt as an act of war, once he moved in for the kill he was determined on total subjugation. There was a moment, at the height of the fighting, while Russian troops were heavily engaged and stricken with disease (in the battle of Ostroleka to the northeast of Warsaw towards the end of May 1831 each side suffered 6,000 casualties), when Nicholas seriously considered pulling out of Western

Poland altogether. 'We can affirm,' he wrote in a draft memorandum, 'that Russian honour has been amply satisfied by the conquest of the Kingdom, but that Russia has no interest in possessing a province whose ingratitude has been so flagrant: that her real interests dictate fixing of the frontiers at the Vistula and the Narew, that she abandons the rest as being unworthy of belonging to her, leaving to her allies the care of making what use they like of it.'[4]

But this mood of defeatism did not last. With Paskevich in Warsaw, Nicholas regained his confidence and his sense of dynastic duty. He was not, after all, the man to shirk the burden of responsibility laid upon his shoulders by a Higher Power. The Poles, alas, would not simply disappear. They had to be governed, and governed they would be by a Russian Tsar now happily released from his constitutional oath.

The Congress Kingdom remained. But there was no longer a Governor to succeed poor Constantine. Instead Paskevich was made Prince of Warsaw and appointed Viceroy. The constitution was replaced by a so-called Organic Statute, providing for limited self-government – which was in fact a dead letter. Paskevich was dictator. It was characteristic of Nicholas that he should have trusted this man almost above all others. A competent soldier, he was nevertheless liable to hesitate in a crisis; but he knew how to strike when he was sure that he could win. He had intrigued against his superiors, and he was loathed by his subordinates, who instantly aroused his jealousy by the least sign of real ability. But in some curious way he was aware of his own failings, which gave him a certain air of honesty in a corrupt environment. Nicholas, it is hardly too much to say, almost looked up to him (indeed, they were very much alike) and addressed him as 'My Colonel Father'. To an English traveller journeying from St Petersburg to Warsaw he recommended the Viceroy as *'homme froid, distrait, rêveur, mais un grand homme'*.[5] One of his affectations was to move about always escorted by a detachment of his celebrated regiment of 'Mussulmen' – horsemen recruited from the subject races he himself had conquered in the Caucasus and Transcaucasia, magnificently mounted and exotic in their national dress, a breath of barbaric Asia in the heart of Catholic Poland.

It was not Paskevich but Nicholas, however, who fixed the terms of the surrender. A delegation of twelve Polish magnates, headed by Prince Radziwill, were summoned to the Winter Palace to make public obeisance and express their gratitude to the Emperor for the continued existence of the kingdom. The colours of the defeated and disbanded Polish regiments were hung as trophies from the pillars of Our Lady of Kazan in St Petersburg, side by side with the standards and the eagles taken from Napoleon's invading army. The ringleaders of the revolt and the senior officers of the Polish army were sent into exile deep into Russia and Siberia, their estates confiscated, together with the estates of over two thousand Poles who had fled the country. The children of the émigrés and deportees, together with the orphans of army officers, were sent to Russian military schools and brought up at the Emperor's expense, as Russians. A systematic campaign was mounted to erase the least traces of Polish nationalism. Whole libraries were confiscated by illiterate police agents. The educational system, local government, all books and periodicals, were russified. Even the Catholic Church had to surrender its lands and revenues, its clergy becoming salaried employees of the state. Much later, when Nicholas was writing urgently to warn Frederick William IV of Prussia never to compromise with revolutionaries, he cited as an example of appropriate behaviour the Russian subjugation of Poland. Russia, he declared, had redeemed the errors of Alexander I with her blood. '*The Poles*,' he went on to say, '*must be made happy in spite of themselves*, by taking from them the power to do themselves harm, by treating them like blind children, who take into their hands toys which might hurt them and others too.'[6] It was the Polish campaign and Nicholas's subsequent behaviour towards the Poles which more than anything else established the Tsar in Western liberal eyes as a blood-stained tyrant to be hated and feared. But Nicholas was not alone, and what the West never understood, indeed has not understood to this day, is the extraordinary position occupied by Poland in Russian eyes. The extremely intelligent Austrian Ambassador to St Petersburg, Count Karl de Fiquelmont, approached close to the heart of the matter when he reported to Metternich in 1830: 'Here they have the profound feeling that Russia has become strong and powerful only by the fall of Poland, and should the Polish provinces one day escape from her, then she would become again only an Asiatic power. This feeling is the basis of all measures taken. . . .'[7]

Pushkin, an ardent spirit if ever there was one, generous of heart, romantic in temperament, himself at odds with the autocracy and all it stood for, put it another way. In two poems 'To the Slanderers of Russia' and 'The Anniversary of Borodino', he inveighed with searing bitterness against those foreigners who protested against Russian treatment of the Poles. What had occurred, he said, was simply one more chapter in an age-long dispute between Slavs. Now the Poles had been uppermost, now the Russians. It was a quarrel which concerned the outside world not at all. Foreigners should mind their own business. If they did not, then either they were filled with envious hatred of Russian power, or they felt guilty because it had been Russia, not they, who had shown the greatest heroism in resisting Napoleon. And he finished by declaring that if any outsider dared try to translate threats into action, then all Russia would rise up, 'bristling with steel'.

Not every Russian felt so sure of Russian virtue in this context. But Pushkin was close to the general feeling about the Poles, and it is plain that this feeling went far deeper than the natural irritation, disdain, or even guilt experienced by the subjects of a great imperial power in face of the defiance of a small but awkward neighbour. We echo de Fiquelmont: 'Here they have the profound feeling that Russia has become strong and powerful only by the fall of Poland . . .' And Pushkin: 'Who will prevail in the unequal struggle, the haughty Pole, or the loyal Russian? Will the Slav streams flow together in the Russian sea? Or will that sea dry up?'

It is not too much to say that it was only by virtue of her mastery of Poland that Russia could feel European. For long, Poland had been the barrier, barring the way to Europe when Muscovy emerged from Tartar domination. Catholic, arrogant, devious, very pleased with themselves, shallow, facile and showy: this is how the Poles appeared in the eyes of the Russian boyars. But they belonged to the West and at the zenith of their power pushed Russia east, even farther from the West.

4

The alarms of 1830 slowly died away. It was too late now for Nicholas to do anything about the Belgian revolt. Indeed he had been saved by the Polish crisis from exposing himself there quite recklessly. Now, suddenly, events outside his control were to deal him a new hand that was very much like a straight flush producing a resounding diplomatic victory.

It was Turkey again. After the conclusion of the Greek affair in 1826 it was generally assumed that the Eastern Question would remain quiescent, at least for some years. This was not to be. Mohammed Ali, the Sultan Mahmoud's viceroy in Egypt, who had sent his son Ibrahim with powerful forces to help his sovereign put down the Greeks, considered that he was ill used. He was deeply resentful because insufficiently rewarded for his help at a critical time. He was incomparably the most able man in the Ottoman Empire. With blood and fire he had secured Egypt, massacring the Mamelukes; he had recovered Mecca; he had annexed the Sudan. Now he wanted all Syria for himself. When the Sultan refused, Ali decided to play for the highest stakes. Ibrahim advanced into Asia Minor and won an overwhelming victory over the Sultan at Konya in Anatolia. This was in December 1832. With the rebel forces poised to descend on Constantinople itself the Sultan was driven to beg for immediate assistance from any foreign power prepared to give it.

Russia obliged. It was a splendid moment for Nicholas when Mahmoud appealed to him, the hereditary foe, for aid. In no time at all the Russian Black Sea fleet appeared off Constantinople. Troops followed the navy. Count Orlov, the Emperor's emissary, followed the troops and arrived to negotiate a formal treaty with the Porte. Mohammed Ali, unable to face the prospect of war with Russia, backed down, but was granted such favourable terms that his power was greater than before he started.

In July, Count Orlov, triumphant, signed at Unkiar Skelessi a treaty of alliance between Turkey and Russia which provided that Russia would give military aid to Turkey if and when requested to do so, while Turkey for her part would close the Straits to all foreign warships.

This, for the time being, was all that Nicholas desired. No foreign power apart from Russia herself had any conceivable interest in attacking Turkey, so that Russian commitment involved no risk at all. On the other hand, the closing of the Straits against foreign warships removed a possible threat to Russia's Black Sea ports. Britain saw what was, at least for the time being, an essentially defensive manoeuvre as a stage in the reduction of Turkey to satellite status. But there was nothing she could do about it, except send Lord Ponsonby to Constantinople with the general brief of weaning the Sultan away from dependence on Russia. Ponsonby was the first of those British representatives in Constantinople to develop that wildly exaggerated Russophobia, seeing a Russian agent under every bed, which was in years to come to make it virtually impossible for the British public to regard Russian activities in the Middle East with any detachment or even common sense. It should be said in fairness, however, that these exaggerated suspicions were inflamed by the almost melodramatic clumsiness of such Russian agents as there were, and also by the increasing ambiguities of the Tsar's own motives – ambiguities which multiplied until, looking back, it is clear that he himself did not know whether he wanted to dismember Turkey or not.

In 1833, however, Nicholas had achieved his aim and felt more secure on his southern borders than had seemed possible at the beginning of his reign. There remained the task of mending fences with his natural allies, Austria and Prussia. Nicholas from a great height made it known that he was prepared at last to come in person to Bohemia to meet his brother monarchs in a conference that Metternich, whom he had never met, had been urging for the past two years. They met at Münchengrätz, 'a small, filthy town' in the words of Princess Metternich, north-east of Prague. There they sought to recapture the spirit of the Holy Alliance. It was the hunting season, September 1833. The Tsar of Russia, the Emperor of

Austria and the Crown Prince of Prussia went deer shooting by day while Metternich and Nesselrode, to say nothing of the Tsar's head of secret police, Count Benckendorff, held long conversations, very largely, it was reported, about their amatory adventures.

Benckendorff was there as the upholder of law and order and the scourge of revolution: he went home with an agreement that the Russian and the Austrian police would work harmoniously together to make Europe fit for autocracy.

He was also a man to talk business with. The Münchengrätz Convention established a conservative alliance binding for another twenty years. The Ottoman Empire was to be preserved; if its collapse at any time seemed imminent the high contracting powers would take joint action in the matter of partition. The existing partition of Poland was guaranteed and, what was more, joint action was promised by all in case of rebellion in any part. Finally, the three governments each agreed to go to the help of any sovereign who appealed for aid in combating liberal insurgency.

5

For some years after Münchengrätz the European pattern – on the one hand the 'northern' three monarchies, on the other England and France – remained undisturbed. But all the time as an imperial power Russia was constantly on the move, probing and pushing forward in relatively soft areas around her immense periphery far from the glare of the spotlight that shone unwinkingly on Constantinople and the Straits.

Her main military activity was in the Caucasus. After the ending of the Persian War the Russian lines of communication between Stavropol, Tiflis and Baku were constantly threatened by unsubdued tribesmen operating in high mountain country, to the west of Circassia overlooking the Black Sea, and to the east in Daghestan rising up from the Caspian shore. The river valleys, above all the Kuban and the Terek, had long been controlled by Cossack settlers who, in exchange for their freedom from oppressive central control, organised themselves as fighting outposts in defence of a fluid frontier. Paskevich had been preparing a major operation against the Circassians when he was taken away first to fight the invading Persians, then to break the Polish revolt. But towards the end of the 1830s a serious attempt was made with sea landings and a determined push into the mountains from the north, both operations followed up by the building of a formidable ring of forts, to drive the tribesmen in upon themselves and squeeze them into submission. Things did not go as well as hoped. The Circassians were very brave. They were encouraged, moreover, by the knowledge that in Daghestan, on the eastern side of the Caucasian massif, the imperial forces were facing a really dangerous threat in the form of a holy war conducted by a guerrilla tactician of genius who was also a venerated spiritual leader; the Imam Shamil, indeed, at one time threatened to undermine the whole Russian position in the Caucasus.

Here the fighting was long and severe, and Shamil was not in fact destroyed until after the Crimean War. For nearly two decades the fighting in Circassia and, above all, Daghestan, demanded a sustained Russian military effort. This theatre offered a superb training ground – admittedly in a rather specialised form of warfare – for the fostering of initiative, imagination and self-reliance among officers. But it was never intelligently exploited. The Russian army of the Caucasus led its own separate existence, constantly fighting. It gave the bored and disaffected the chance to escape from the bureaucratic blight which afflicted Russia proper. It gave adventure to those who sought it; oblivion to those who wanted to forget their pasts; the restoration of honour for those in disgrace or under a cloud. And the fighting was by no means always minor. The action which had ended with the death of Shamil's predecessor had involved a sharp offensive on the part of 10,000 troops operating in high mountains. In campaign after campaign that followed it was quite usual for the Russians to suffer casualties running into thousands.

From the beginning to the end of this long-drawn-out war of conquest the exoticism of the Caucasian landscape, its high mountains raising their everlasting snows above the sub-tropical richness of the river valleys and the coastal rivers, caught the imagination of the Russians. For them it was more than the land where the lemon trees bloom; it was a land of rushing mighty torrents, high passes, jagged peaks; a land of virile and hot-blooded tribesmen – Georgian Christians who were also men of war holding their own for centuries under their own kings and queens; haughty and vengeful Moslems with an ancient culture compounded of romantic savagery and high chivalry; marvellous Circassian women, prized above all others by the Turkish slavers; pride, glory, quick-tempered honour. It was a land which affected even the Russian Cossack settlers and turned stolid Russian peasants into dashing freebooters; a land alive with bears and wolves where a man could quickly prove himself against the elements, a world away from Benckendorff and the dreary, venal clerks, the peasant slaves, the sycophantic courtiers of the great Russian plain. Pushkin with *A Captive of the Caucasus*, Lermontov with *A Hero of Our Time*, Tolstoy with *The Cossacks, The Raid, The Wood-felling, Hadji Murad*, were all caught by this magic. The young Tolstoy himself fought with the army in one of the campaigns against Shamil.

People have wondered why the Russian campaigns in the Caucasus should have inspired so much more great literature than the analogous British campaigns against the tribesmen of the Indian north-west frontier. Apart from the accident of literary genius, the reason surely was that for the Russian romantic the Caucasian experience was a revelatory entry into a world not only of supreme and magical natural beauty but also of unimaginable freedom – an escape from an all-embracing system from which they were alienated in their hearts.

There was less literary excitement about the other main points of imperial expansion. The first, east of the Caspian and south, was a movement which brought Russian power fairly irresistibly into the open steppelands of what is now Kazakhstan and up to the more closely organised pastoral lands of Turkestan: this thrust was not to develop its full weight until much later; it was a thrust, moreover, in the general direction of India, which was to arouse in London the profoundest misgivings; the Russians had reciprocal apprehensions of the British descending from Afghanistan towards Khiva and Bokhara.

The third growing-point was far away on the borders of China, where a recklessly chauvinistic and energetic governor-general of Eastern Siberia, Count N. N. Muraviev, sailed up the Amur river (for which he was allowed to call himself Count Muraviev-Amursky), circumnavigated Sakhalin Island, which he seized in the name of the Tsar, and, on the eve of the Crimean War, founded the settlement (later to be the city) of Nikolaevsk.

The fourth point was in the far north-east, where the Russians in 1744 had crossed from Kamchatka to Alaska over the Bering Straits named after the Russian arctic explorer.

Nicholas in St Petersburg looked out over this remote, persistent empire-building and found it good. The frontiers of Imperial Russia were being quietly pushed forward to keep at arm's length all foreigners – British, Chinese, Canadians, Americans – who might be tempted to infiltrate the empty spaces. It did not matter that Russia was already so vast that it was beyond the powers of any central government to administer it properly; it did not matter that her people were so thin on the ground that it seemed absurd to spread them even more thinly; it did not matter, any more than it had mattered under earlier monarchs, that this ceaseless enlargement of frontiers meant neglecting the infinitely rich natural resources of the lands nearer home. All that mattered was that Russia was great, and the only way to sustain her greatness was to push the foreigner even farther away from her heart.

6

The European powers, especially England, and to a lesser degree Austria, viewed this process with alarm. Where would it end and what did it mean? It appeared to make no sense at all unless as part of a purposeful drive towards limitless territorial aggrandisement on the part of a people who already possessed more land than they knew what to do with.

Nowadays it is customary to ridicule those nineteenth-century British diplomatists and politicians who were obsessed by their vision of the Russian menace to Britain's imperial position. And indeed, this obsession was in some respects poorly founded and the conclusions drawn from it exaggerated even when they were not false. But Western statesmen were not alone in questioning the restless, probing, uneasily menacing drive of successive Romanovs to the limits of the permissible, and sometimes beyond. It was a patriotic Russian, the enlightened conservative ex-serf Nikitenko, who at the time of the Crimean War declared that Russia had nobody but herself to blame for catastrophe after frightening Europe into fits with thirty years of restless plunging, backed by menacing noises.[8] Even before that, in 1838, one of the most able Russian diplomatists, Baron Brunnow, at that time senior diplomatic adviser to Nesselrode, prepared a review of imperial foreign policy, which was also a warning, for the instruction of the Tsarevich, the future Alexander II. He was careful to hark back to the days of Catherine: under Nicholas, of course, such things happened no more. But Alexander understood well enough the implicit criticism of his father:

The policy of the Russian court in the reign of Catherine unfortunately justifies only too well the suspicions concerning the intentions of our government which are spread abroad today. The English always remember that countries taken under the protection of Russia have all ended by losing their independence; that Russia extended her protection to Poland in order to bring about her partition, that she freed the Georgian tribes from Ottoman dominion only to subjugate them herself; that she recognised the independence of the Crimea in order to annex it to her Empire. Examples from the past, therefore, reflect on the present, and the noble motives of our policy today are denied because memories of distant events are still alive in the minds of foreign governments alarmed by and envious of our might.[9]

It could not have been put more exactly. Brunnow was writing at a moment when British suspicions of Russian intentions had been aggravated on two counts. In the previous year St Petersburg had been actively encouraging the new Shah of Persia to march against Afghanistan in order to win back Herat, which had belonged to the old Persian Empire, desisting only when it became clear that Britain was prepared to fight to keep the Shah (and Russian influence) away from her North-West Frontier. And in 1839, as the stability of the Ottoman Empire was once more threatened by renewed conflict between the Sultan and Mohammed Ali, Palmerston was annoyed and apprehensive when, without reference to London, Nicholas and the Emperor Franz of Austria met at Teplitz in Bohemia to affirm their support for the Sultan in accordance with Unkiar Skelessi and Münchengrätz. But within a year the situation had changed quite dramatically: England, Russia, Austria and Prussia were working closely together to thwart Mohammed Ali – and not only Mohammed Ali, but also Britain's official ally, France, who at one time seemed on the point of declaring war on the rest of Europe, so determined was she to push the claims of her protégé, the Egyptian Pasha. And it was Brunnow himself who, on two special missions to London, had the satisfaction of carrying the most complex and delicate negotiations to a happy end.

Mohammed Ali, not content with the terms he had won at the end of the first crisis in 1833, was now demanding hereditary sovereignty over Egypt and Syria and appeared to be dreaming of establishing a new Arab Empire. France supported him against the Sultan and Russia, while the Sultan wooed British support with important trade concessions – to say nothing of the lease of Aden. A long and indeterminate sequence of diplomatic manoeuvrings and multilateral intrigues was brought to a sudden end when the Sultan lost patience, invaded Syria, and was soundly beaten by Ibrahim Pasha at Nezhib.

It was now, in June 1839, that swift action had to be taken both to save the Sultan and avoid a dangerous collision between the powers. Nicholas and Nesselrode saw clearly what had already been dimly perceived, namely that so long as Britain had a legitimate interest in the Levant Russia could not hope to dominate Turkey as she had dreamed of doing; further, that the Sultan could not be effectively sustained against Egypt and Syria without the help of British naval power. Russia must therefore reach an accommodation with Britain, and in so doing work towards a coveted end: the break-up of the Anglo-French alliance, which Nicholas regarded as a focus of revolutionary activity and thought. Palmerston on his side saw the chance to deprive Russia of her special position *vis-à-vis* Turkey and the Straits accorded by the Treaty of Unkiar Skelessi after her victory in 1833, and reach a binding agreement over the matter of the Straits which would remove the Porte from its subservience to St Petersburg, while respecting the future security of Russia.

So, in an atmosphere of excursions and alarms, the wheels were set in motion. The upshot was a formal agreement signed in the summer of 1840 by Britain and the Northern Powers, taking no account of France, under which the new allies agreed to act together to sustain the Sultan. British and Austrian naval forces would operate off Syria and Egypt. The powers would unite to protect the Bosphorus and Dardanelles for this unique occasion. Mohammed Ali would be offered the hereditary ruler-ship of Egypt and possession of southern Syria during his lifetime.

The rest was something of an anti-climax. Mohammed Ali's days of conquest were also over. The Syrians rose against his rule. British and Austrian forces landed in the Lebanon and Acre was bombarded into submission by a joint British, Austrian and Turkish force. Ibrahim Pasha was finished and so were Mohammed Ali's dreams of empire. But the Sultan was dead and never saw his victory. Russia had been required to take no active part in the whole operation; but her great power loomed menacingly in the background.

The chance for a general settlement now lay to hand, and Britain and Russia seized it. There could be no such settlement without France, so Nicholas had to overcome his abhorrence of Louis-Philippe and France had to rise above her fury against England. Once more Palmerston pre-sided, and at the London Convention of 1841 it was finally agreed that so long as Turkey was at peace no foreign power would be allowed to send her warships into the Dardanelles and the Bosphorus. Russia was thus protected no less effectively than she had been by Unkiar Skelessi; but Turkey was no longer her satellite. The Black Sea was still vulnerable should Turkey, allied with any hostile power, go to war with Russia. But this was the sort of contingency which no conceivable agreement could provide for. Nicholas accepted this imperfection in 1841. But it went against the grain. Emotional and impatient as he was, with a passion for minute and detailed regulation and a deep-seated fear of the impalp-able and indeterminate, he did not profit by the lessons of the Mohammed Ali crisis and the London Convention. He was still driven to regulate the future as well as the present. This would have been tiresome enough if he had been able to make up his mind, and stick to it, about the precise outlines of the future. But this he could not do.

CHAPTER SEVEN

The Slow Drift to Disaster

I

THE London Convention was a first-class example of what could be achieved by cool and skilled diplomacy in circumstances that were heavily adverse. For even while these negotiations were in train Palmerston was continuing his considered policy of countering to the best of his ability all Russian activity which by any stretch of the imagination might seem to be pushing the influence of St Petersburg beyond existing frontiers. And the popular mood in England was still violently, almost rabidly, anti-Russian. Palmerston himself, usually regarded as the champion of liberalism and the scourge of reaction, was constantly under fire for his 'appeasement' of St Petersburg. Early in 1835 when Peel decided to send that notorious reactionary Lord Londonderry (Castlereagh's half-brother) as Ambassador to St Petersburg, he was attacked in *The Times* on the grounds that the noble marquis had 'disqualified himself . . . by his want of sympathy with the known feelings of Englishmen in favour of the oppressed liberties and trampled rights of Poland'. The article went on to characterise St Petersburg in a memorable phrase as the seat of 'the most subtle and insidious Court of Europe'.[1] Peel had to give way. And five years later the public mood was little changed.

Nevertheless it was in 1840 that the time was considered suitable for a visit of the young Tsarevich, Alexander, to England. And four years after that Nicholas himself took the plunge and made on Victoria the strong and uneasy impression recorded in an earlier chapter. And it was this visit, which went off very well indeed, that was to lay up a store of trouble for the future. It arose from the Tsar's obsessional concern with the imminent demise of the Turkish Empire. He could not leave the subject alone. He could not rest until he had made the powers, above all Britain, appreciate the dangers inherent in the collapse of Turkey and enter with him into the business of working out a cut-and-dried plan of action. The action he required was agreement on a contingency plan whereby the powers would amicably share out among themselves in advance the Ottoman possessions, thus obviating all future misunderstanding. The more Nicholas talked about this, the more he insisted in his declamatory manner that he had no designs on Turkey and wished to sustain her so long as this was possible, the livelier became the suspicions of the powers – above all of Britain with her congenital reluctance to entertain hypothetical questions or, indeed, to take thought for a tomorrow that, even if it came, would be very different from all expectations.

Nicholas had opened the subject with Austria as early as 1833, at the time of the first Mohammed Ali crisis, and long before he had realised the critical importance of the role that Britain was bound to play. He would do all he could to help the Sultan, he assured de Fiquelmont, the Austrian Ambassador, but it would not be enough. 'I lack the power to give life to a corpse, and the Turkish Empire is dead. It will perhaps be possible for us to check the present crisis. But even if we succeed in doing so, I have no confidence in the maintenance of this ancient body; it is breaking down on all sides; a little sooner, or a little later, it will collapse.'[2]

Here is the first statement of the theme which was to sound again and again, with appropriate variations, for the next twenty years. No sooner was the Straits Convention safely signed than he was back at his old obsessive worrying. In the following year an abortive rising in Serbia reminded him, if he needed reminding, of the instability of the Turkish position in the Balkans and of his own self-imposed obligations as protector of the Orthodox Christians under Moslem rule. At the same time he was far from happy about his own cherished Northern Alliance, which was not quite the force it had appeared to be at the time of Münchengrätz. In Vienna the shrewd, cautious old Franz I had died in 1835, to be succeeded by Ferdinand, a gentle, sweet-tempered imbecile. And in Berlin the death of Frederick William III in 1840 had deprived Nicholas of a staunch and obedient ally of approved reactionary temper. His son Frederick William IV, the Tsaritsa's brother, was a doubtful quantity. He believed in the divine right of kings, was possessed, indeed, by a high dynastic romanticism: so far so good. But he also appeared to think that flirting with liberal ideas was a seemly occupation for a mid-nineteenth-century ruler, and this filled Nicholas with profound misgivings – later to turn to anger and contempt. Added to this was the return of Peel to power in England, Palmerston's replacement at the Foreign Office by Aberdeen, and the consequent conviction on the part of Nicholas that the British had once again begun to suspect him of nourishing aggressive designs on Turkey. He was feeling very unsettled indeed, and he started to behave in a very unsettling way. He suggested to Austria, out of the blue, that she might take Constantinople.[3]

De Fiquelmont, to whom Nicholas made this offer, could not believe his ears, nor could Metternich when the news reached him in Vienna. Here, Nicholas had said, was perfect proof that he himself had no designs on Turkey. But Turkey was falling apart, and if the powers were not prepared the ensuing conflict of interest would be catastrophic. 'Is it not better to anticipate events and assume the direction of them?' How reprehensible to wait until disaster struck. What would Russia do with Constantinople? Its possession, even as a gift from the powers, would alter the whole character of her empire. It was Austria, with her immediate interest in the Balkans, which should be its natural ruler:

'I shall never cross the Danube and everything between the river and the Adriatic ought to be yours ... This combination is the only one which can save us from a frightful upheaval; it has preoccupied me daily for a long time; I find no other which can take its place.'[4]

The one thing about which he was adamant was that no power other than Austria should have Constantinople:

'I do not want the re-establishment of a Byzantine empire; I will never permit it. I do not want the French or the English, either together or separately, to occupy Constantinople or give it material protection. I shall resist these combinations with all my forces.'[5]

Of course it came to nothing. Metternich, better than anyone, knew how to deprive even the sharpest diplomatic initiative of its momentum, so that it died a natural death. But what was he to make of this unpredictable monarch who insisted that his only desire was to defuse a potentially inflammable situation and now suggested as an appropriate solution a course of action which would inevitably precipitate a general war?

The powers were right to feel uneasy about Nicholas, not because, as they sometimes thought, he was intent on breaking up the Ottoman Empire under cover of fair words, but because as a compulsive meddler, as an autocrat who could not be content until he could 'anticipate events and assume direction of them', he could not leave well alone. None of them believed that the Turkish Empire was in imminent danger of collapse. Conditions beneath the Crescent were admittedly in many respects a disgrace and a scandal, but at least an independent Turkey not dominated by any single power served the purpose of keeping under heavy restraint a turbulent and indeed barbaric corner of Europe, besides acting as a buffer between the great imperial powers. Even if Nicholas was to be believed in his fervent assurances that he wanted to preserve Turkey for as long as possible, this perpetual harping on the perils lurking in a hypothetical future was, to say the least, unsettling. The trouble was that Nicholas had worked himself up into such a state that he was no longer capable of taking an objective view. As he himself put it in conversation one day:

'Nesselrode and I do not agree: he thinks that Turkey is on the point of collapse: I think she has collapsed already.'

What was the reason for this blindness? Apart from the Tsar's profound need to see himself as master of events, one can only conclude that deep in his soul he felt guilty of sins of omission when it came to fulfilling the Romanov destiny, first proclaimed by Catherine the Great as protector of the Christians. He may indeed have abandoned Catherine's more spectacular goal, possession of Constantinople. But as head of the Orthodox Church he was failing in his duty to his co-religionists under Moslem rule. In a word, with at least half of his mind he was *willing* the Ottoman Empire to fall apart and thus felt a particular responsibility for the new order which must take its place.

In 1844, getting no charge out of Metternich, he decided to address himself to England. He was in a mood of very considerable frustration.

None of this mood showed when he arrived in London that summer, in all his towering magnificence. As we have seen, the very young Queen found him the very picture of handsomeness, but others, who had seen him in earlier days, were struck by a marked deterioration in his physique: he was still tall and magnificently commanding, but his features had coarsened and there was a suggestion of paunchiness. He was only forty-eight, but he was feeling the self-imposed strains of his absolutism, to say nothing of his determination to organise a Europe which steadfastly refused to be organised.

The British, poor man, he found quite delightfully helpful. Closeted with Peel and Aberdeen he was a world away from Metternich's smilingly polite, repressive negatives. All was gravely genial and easy-going. Your Imperial Majesty is anxious to sustain the Porte for as long as it may be possible? It gives us the greatest pleasure to affirm our perfect accord. Your Imperial Majesty has no designs on Constantinople or any part of the Ottoman Empire? It is gracious of Your Imperial Majesty to offer such an assurance, but no such suspicion could conceivably arise. Your Imperial Majesty would like to establish the principle that Her Britannic Majesty's Government will enter into immediate consultations with Your Imperial Majesty as to the proper disposition of the Sultan's territories should the unhappy necessity arise? Indeed, Your Imperial Majesty may rest assured.

That was as far as Nicholas got. There were no useful discussions of the kind he so passionately desired about the shape the ultimate carve-up should take. But he believed that what he now had was a binding written agreement that if it became clear that Turkey must soon collapse Russia and Britain would proceed together in advance to reach agreement on a new order which would take full account of their treaty rights.

As far as England was concerned, the subsequent exchange of letters was not much more than a provisional declaration of intent, and a fairly vague one at that.[6] It could be in no way binding on future governments.

It has frequently been asserted that Nicholas went home convinced that Britain was in fact formally committed – and that his subsequent disillusionment excused his conduct on the eve of the Crimean War. Certainly the British were, as always, evasive; certainly they remained suspicious of the Tsar's designs; certainly, even if they had believed every word he said, they would have been incapable, for better or for worse, of committing themselves, and their successors, to specific action in a hypothetical future. Nicholas may not have understood all this. The fact remains that the picture of the Tsar's own attitude is false. For little more than a year after his English journey, the apparent results of which (we are asked to believe) he found highly satisfactory, he returned to the charge with Metternich. And what had he to say to him now in the light of his vaunted understanding with London? Once again that Austria must have Constantinople and all European Turkey. 'If the English, French, or any other forces wish to seize Constantinople, I shall chase them away, and I do not believe in the chances of expulsion, for I shall be on the spot before either of these forces. Once in Constantinople, I shall not withdraw.'[7]

Nicholas then categorically stated that he had said all this to Aberdeen in London. This was a very odd statement to make. Certainly Count Colloredo, who was then the new Austrian Ambassador to St Petersburg, was convinced of the Emperor's bad faith in the whole matter affecting Austria and Turkey. He believed that what the Tsar had in mind was the provision of a pretext for moving against Turkey when the time was ripe without laying himself open to the charge of self-aggrandisement. But, once in possession of Constantinople, he would find ways and means of setting up a new state owing everything to him and effectively controlled by him.

I have made a good deal of these exchanges because they are vital for an appreciation of the attitude of the powers eight years later on the eve of the Crimean War. It is not necessary to agree with Count Colloredo or with the active Russophobes in England that Nicholas was playing a deep and devious game designed to precipitate the break up of the Turkish Empire and win Constantinople for himself. It is, on the other hand, essential to realise that he was in fact engaged in a double game, at best playing off one power against the other – but in the interest of what? The overriding impression, as one contemplates the quite remarkable vagaries of Nicholas's Turkish policy over nearly thirty years, is that he himself never made up his mind as to precisely what he wanted. He was indeed genuinely worried by Turkey's weakness and apprehensive of the power struggle which might be precipitated by her dissolution; he believed Russia to have a historic-religious role to play and felt that he was betraying the holy cause by shrinking from decisive action. The peace of Europe he was determined to preserve; but when it came to the Balkans, even if he himself refrained from grabbing, he saw it at least as Russia's due to preside over the division of the spoils (the British could take Egypt if they wanted, he had grandly announced to de Fiquelmont, and they and the French could divide the Aegean islands between themselves). The overriding impression, that is to say, is less of calculated deceit than of a rather trivial duplicity, less of duplicity than of a fundamental silliness – that silliness already encountered in the Emperor's dealings with his own subjects, his irrepressible meddling, his consistent inability, remarkable in a monarch usually regarded as a pillar of conservatism, to leave well alone. There was also an element of megalomania.

2

Nicholas was now in his fiftieth year and beginning to be worn down with disillusionment. He had, he decided, no friends. He still liked the new king of Prussia as a person, but politically, with his flirtation with liberal ideas, Frederick William IV was a lost soul. His loathing for Louis-Philippe was undiminished. He trusted England no more than England trusted him. He was inclined to turn his back on Europe and let it stew in its own juice. There were problems enough at home. Kiselev, in the teeth of bitter opposition, had been able to take action to improve the lot of the state peasants, but all attempts to persuade the nobility to tackle the problem of serfdom with an open mind had failed: there was no open mind. Industry was developing, and so was international trade. In the first twenty years of the reign the factory work-force had more than doubled, from 200,000 to nearly half a million. And a new class of capitalists was taking over from the nobility. The railway age had dawned. There were even new hard-surfaced highways. There were steamers on the Volga. The growth of international trade was bringing Russia into greater contact with the wretched outer world at the very time when Nicholas wanted to shut it out. The export of wheat was going ahead by leaps and bounds. The economy depended on it, which meant that it depended on foreigners. This was undesirable but the whole uneasy process could be managed if only he, the Tsar, could keep his health, and oversee every detail of the activity of his realm.

It was impossible for him to remain unaffected by the adulation with which he was surrounded. In our own age we have viewed with dazed incomprehension the flattery of Stalin as the universal genius, the great leader, the teacher; but the men who led the Soviet Union in Stalin-worship were in the direct line of descent from the administrators who led Imperial Russia in worship of the Tsar. It was not a phantasist, it was the German-born Minister of Finance, Count Kankrin, who solemnly suggested that the very name of Russia should be changed. 'Everything: glory, power, prosperity and enlightenment,' he declared, 'we owe to the Romanov family; and, out of gratitude, we should change our general tribal name of Slavs to the name of the creator of the empire and of its well-being. Russia should be called *Petrovia*, and we *Petrovians*; or the empire should be named *Romanovia*, and we – *Romanovites*.'[8] Even the excesses of the Pan-slavs, the professional publicists Pogodin and Shevyrev, the gifted poet Tyutchev, with their exaltation of all things Russian, their expressed contempt for an ugly and corrupt West, diseased and moribund, their glorification of the quickening and purging power of the Russian spirit (and the Russian sword) made their contribution to the Tsar's increasing self-worship. Paradoxically, the more he was disgusted with the venality and selfishness of his countrymen, the more proudly he was possessed by the sense of his own lonely destiny. He may well have raised his eyebrows at Tyutchev's patriotic extravagance:

Seven inland seas and seven great rivers!...
From the Nile to the Neva, from the Elbe to China –
From the Volga to the Euphrates, from the Ganges to the Danube...
This is the Russian Tsardom...

but the mood of euphoria affected him all the same. As the 1840s progressed he became more, not less, detached from reality. He was governing now through more useless creatures than ever before. Even the faithful Kankrin who had done so much for the Empire's finances was forced into resignation in 1844 because Nicholas refused to listen to his overwhelming case for suspending the Caucasian campaign of conquest which was bankrupting the state. He was replaced by a nonentity: 'I shall be my own Minister of Finance,' Nicholas fatuously remarked, and there was not a soul to murmur that he was mad. Benckendorff was dead, a man who was at least literate and kindly, and the new head of the Third Section was a majestic and blondly handsome oaf, Prince Orlov, whose sole claim to regard was that he had rallied the loyal troops to break the Decembrist revolt – and from then on he had been trusted by Nicholas and used by him on special missions where all he had to do was carry out instructions to the letter. He was perfect of his kind, a god-like figure in drawing-rooms, a man to strike terror into all his subordinates, but a man who, notoriously, behaved face to face with Nicholas like a third-form schoolboy face to face with his headmaster.[9] And it was this man with whom the Emperor spent more time than with any other, sharing his carriage on those innumerable compulsive journeys across the length and breadth of Russia, from barracks to barracks, from school to school. Perhaps the climax of this process was the dismissal of Uvarov as Minister of Education in 1849 and his replacement by a sycophant to end all sycophants, Prince Shirinsky-Shikhmatov, a sort of joke figure compared with whom Uvarov was a paladin of enlightenment with a will of iron. Shikhmatov was one of those men who achieve immortality by a phrase. It was he who proudly announced to a subordinate: 'You should know that I have neither a mind nor a will of my own – I am merely a blind tool of the Emperor's will.'[10]

3

This, admittedly, was at a moment when Nicholas had the bit between his teeth. In 1848 Europe had exploded into revolution. Louis-Philippe was driven off the throne of France; in Vienna Metternich fell, the Imperial family had to run for their lives; and while the students of Vienna fought for civil liberties, Italians, Hungarians, Bohemians and Poles fought for their national independence. In Berlin Frederick William IV was forced to concede a constitution; in Dresden the composer Richard Wagner joined hands with the Russian anarchist Bakunin in proclaiming the dawn of a new age. Even in London the Government watched with unnecessary apprehension the preparation for the great Chartist demonstration of 11 April.

'There is a general fight going on all over the Continent,' wrote Palmerston, 'between governors and governed, between law and disorder, between those who have and those who want to have, between honest men and rogues.'[11]

Karl Marx, then just thirty years old and heard of by nobody, put it another way. Only a few weeks before the Paris revolution he had published the text of his *Communist Manifesto*. It began:

'A spectre is haunting Europe – the spectre of communism. All the powers of old Europe have entered into a holy alliance to exorcise this spectre: Pope and Tsar, Metternich and Guizot, French radicals and German police spies . . .'

And it finished: 'Let the ruling classes tremble at a communist revolution. The proletarians have nothing to lose but their chains. They have a world to win.

'Workers of all lands, unite.'

The diagnosis was not quite correct. Certainly the have-nots (equated by Palmerston with rogues) played their part in the general turbulence. But it was not the major part. In so far as the 1848 revolutions had to do with social reform, including constitutional reform, they were in the main led by students and intellectuals demanding civil liberties. In Vienna, for example, it was not until these were out on the streets in violent conflict with the authorities that Marx's proletariat came pouring out of their tenements and hovels. But almost everywhere the complicating factor was the new spirit of popular nationalism. This naturally counted for most in the Habsburg Empire, where Italians, Hungarians and Slavs rose against the Teutonic overlord. But the French upheaval was also in large measure a nationalistic demonstration on the part of an impatient people thirsty for renewed prestige and glory of a kind which their rulers were unable to provide.

Nicholas, it goes without saying, had no sense at all of what was going on. Of the new spirit of nationalism he had no conception and could not recognise it for what it was. The Poles in his eyes were not nationalists: the women of Warsaw who still wore mourning for their murdered land were not patriots; they were simply ill-intentioned subjects too wicked or too ignorant to recognise the supreme God and bow to him. Nationalism, of course, was blowing a strong wind in Russia; but here it was the nationalism of a people seeking to establish its own identity: it celebrated the autocracy. What Nicholas saw when he looked out from the Winter Palace was a Europe threatened with anarchy. Even now, twenty-three years after his own accession, he did not feel safe.

When the news of the deposition of Louis-Philippe reached St Petersburg Nicholas was torn between satisfaction at the humiliation of the detested usurper and alarm at the victory of the mob. Diplomatic relations with France were broken off as a matter of course. Nicholas was no longer in the war-like mood of his early years. Nevertheless, he did in fact order the immediate concentration of some 350,000 troops on his western frontier to be ready to march to the Rhine. No more came of this than had come of that earlier mobilisation against Belgium in 1829. Then the Polish revolt had come between Nicholas and his projected march to the west. Now it was quite a different sort of revolt in Prussia. 'Oh, my poor brother! my poor William!' the Tsaritsa exclaimed in horror when the news came that Frederick William in Berlin was also assailed by a revolutionary mob – and was giving way to its demands without a fight. 'Who cares about your brother,' Nicholas retorted in effect, 'when the whole of Europe is crumbling and Russia herself may go under?'

He was never to subdue his wrath against his brother-in-law. In one of many letters to Frederick William he wrote: 'Through your caprice

Prussia has come to renounce the traditions which have been her strength, her glory, her prosperity for centuries past . . . The old Prussia has *ceased to be* . . . Our age-old unity has vanished with it. Russia cannot come to the aid of a power . . . which must henceforth struggle with all the obstacles of constitutional forms.'[12]

The peace and quiet remained, scarcely a ripple broke its surface. Within Russia's 'stout, high wall' (to use Zhukovsky's phrase) emergency measures were taken to close the gateways to the West – and to keep them closed. Nicholas was in a mood of such desperation that for a moment he turned to England. 'What remains standing in Europe?' he demanded in a personal appeal to Queen Victoria. 'Great Britain and Russia!' Surely they should join forces to fight revolution wherever it showed its head? The Queen did not respond.[13]

Nicholas feared his own shadow, but there was really nothing to fear. The proletariat scarcely existed in Russia – and the warning was clear to all those who would recklessly let it grow through the rapid expansion of industry and the liberation of the serfs. The intelligentsia were still far too weak and fragmented either to form a coherent secret opposition or to command popular support. But Nicholas had the fresh memory of Chaadayev's despairing attack on all that was sacred in Russia. And even though Chaadayev himself had been chastened and now, released from his confinement as a madman, was showing himself harmlessly in St Petersburg society, in the salon of the Tsar's own sister-in-law, the Grand Duchess Helen, a centre of subversive infection which was hard to police. Worse still was the underground circulation of Belinsky's letter to Gogol and, above all, the discovery of what looked like an actively dangerous conspiracy in the shape of the Petrashevsky Circle.

Something had to be done. Under Prince Menshikov the Tsar put on a permanent footing a standing censorship committee with virtually unlimited powers which superseded the statutory censorship of the Ministry of Education. All criticism of government and administrative institutions, even at the lowest level, was forbidden. But even this was not enough. Soon all praise was forbidden too – on the grounds that it was *lèse-majesté* for the Tsar's subjects to comment on government activities even with approval. It was a growing madness, with new restrictions added whenever they came into the heads of the Tsar and his committee. Thus in 1851 all musical scores had to be submitted to the censor in case the notation concealed cipher messages. Harriet Beecher Stowe and Nathaniel Hawthorne were among the foreign writers placed on the index of banned authors. Belinsky's death in 1848 saved him from certain arrest and banishment, if not imprisonment. In 1849 the long and largely barren investigation into the Petrashevsky Circle was concluded. It revealed no active conspiracy but only the existence of the first socialist discussion group, its members including writers and officers of the Guard, teachers and businessmen, civil servants and university students. But fifteen of the thirty-nine accused were sentenced to death. Though reprieved in the end they were given savage punishments. Dostoevsky, whose offence had been to read aloud Belinsky's letter, was sent to hard labour in Siberia and after that condemned to a spell in the ranks. He survived, as we know, to glorify the holy mission of his country, which set it above all others. By now Gogol himself, once the admired of Nicholas, had been turned into what would nowadays in the Soviet Union be called an unperson – and the novelist Ivan Turgenev quite early in his career was put under house-arrest on his country estate for publishing a respectful obituary when Gogol died in 1852.

The only possible danger to the stability of the realm was posed by peasant unrest. Even this was not serious, though locally alarming. The activities of the special commissions enquiring into the problems of serf-dom had given rise to rumours about impending liberation, rumours of the kind that ran like the wind through Imperial Russia; there was also resistance to the emergency recruiting called for by the need to strengthen the army against subversion from without (it was at this time that Nicholas published his hysterical manifesto, quoted earlier, of militant challenge to the world); there was cholera; the weather had ruined the winter sowings over large areas. Many knowledgeable Russians were convinced that the Emperor was allowing himself to be far too much preoccupied with a chimerical threat from abroad. It was not imported ideas he had to fear, appealing only to the few, but rather the age-old spectre of a spontaneous peasant revolt.

In fact Nicholas feared both. He decided that it was time to get the nobility firmly on his side. There had been a good deal of grumbling in that quarter. The established nobles very much resented the dilution of their ranks by the promotion of what they saw as potential undesirables from the higher ranks of the civil service. They were also affronted by so much official talk about the emancipation of the serfs. In the middle of April 1849 Nicholas delivered himself of one of those theatrical declarations in which rhetoric took the place of sense. To a deputation of nobles in St Petersburg, he declared: 'Gentlemen, I have no police. I do not like them. You are my police.'14 He went on to explain that he made them responsible for the good behaviour of all those in their charge – their serfs, that is to say. And he solemnly affirmed to them the sacred principle of their ownership of the land. What went on in the mind of this monarch who commanded the most powerful police force in the world and made a confidant of its chief? What went on in the minds of those who listened with unquestioning acquiescence to what they knew to be a lie, thus forming with their master a conspiracy of nonsense?

4

It was in the following year that Nicholas achieved a sort of apotheosis. The Holy Alliance came true. The Habsburg monarchy had been firmly re-established in the name of the young Emperor Franz Joseph, but Hungary still resisted. Partly through inefficiency, partly because they found it almost impossibly hard to fight with sufficient ruthlessness against their late comrades and fellow-officers of the Hungarian regiments, the Austrian generals had failed to crush the Hungarians as they had crushed the Czechs, the Italians and the revolutionary Viennese. After a great deal of hesitation Franz Joseph appealed to Nicholas for aid. Nicholas himself was in two minds, even though he was now presented with the perfect pretext for marching to the support of legitimacy and also for putting Austria under a heavy obligation. What helped to make up his mind was the knowledge that among the rebel Hungarian commanders were two very distinguished Polish generals who had escaped his vengeance in 1831. With a flourish he sent in 200,000 men under the inevitable Paskevich. The Hungarians could not hope to stand against this massive assault from the rear. Kossuth fled to Turkey, handing over supreme command to the gifted rebel general Görgey, who contrived to spite the Austrians by making his surrender to the Russians, so that Paskevich could send off yet another of his famous signals to the Tsar: 'Hungary lies at Your Majesty's feet!' He also infuriated the Austrians by taking Görgey under his personal protection while Nicholas, the scourge of rebel Poles, made matters worse by urging Franz Joseph to show clemency towards rebel Hungarians.

This was the Tsar's finest hour. For once his talk about his God-given role as champion of legitimacy had been translated into effective action. He had indeed triumphantly proved himself as 'the greatest earthly potentate', and he proceeded to behave as such, alienating almost all Europe in the process.

5

In the aftermath of revolution and successful counter-revolution the times were nervous and disturbed. There was not a statesman in Europe who was not convinced that Russia, which had stood like a rock, apparently unaffected by the recent turmoil, was irresistible. Nicholas shared this view.

He should have been warned by a number of happenings. The British reaction, which went as far as a challenging show of force, to his peremptory demands to the Sultan to surrender the Polish refugees who had fled from Hungary to Turkey; the Austrian coolness towards his enthusiastic offer to go to war with Turkey, if necessary, in support of Vienna's sharp and successful insistence that Omer Pasha should abandon his ruthless punitive campaign against insurgent Montenegro; above all the very evident determination of Louis Napoleon to win prestige for himself and restore France to her proper status as a major power by fishing in troubled waters and presenting himself as the champion of oppressed nationalities. Prussia was fearful of French ambitions in the Rhineland; Austria was afraid of what Napoleon might do in Italy. England was uneasily aware of a new and disturbing influence in the power balance. The Sultan could see that Europe was at sixes and sevens, offering Turkey the chance to escape from her dependence on Russia. Only Nicholas, who still thought in simple terms of revolutionaries versus authority, seemed oblivious of the deep sea-change. He soon got used to Louis Napoleon as President of the French Republic, but his assumption of the Imperial Crown was another matter. Once more the Tsar of Russia found himself unable to address a fellow-monarch as 'mon Frère'. And Napoleon now was playing politics in Turkey.

For centuries the Holy Places in Jerusalem and Bethlehem, under Turkish sovereignty, had been tended by monks of both the Catholic and the Orthodox persuasion. Latins and Greeks, their introverted lives pent-up in small and stuffy enclaves in the Moslem wilderness, their existence dominated by niceties of ritual and precedence, were not unnaturally given to quarrelling among themselves. In the 1840s their differences had found more than usually sharp expression: they made off with each other's treasured ornaments, trampled on each other's altar cloths, even came to blows. Louis Napoleon, on the look-out for pretexts to assert himself, saw the chance to put himself forward as the champion of the Latins, thus bringing himself as head of state into collision with the Tsar, the champion of the Greeks, who also regarded himself as the protector of all the Christians in the Ottoman Empire. In the course of 1852 Nicholas discovered that the Sultan had been conceding rights to the French which he regarded as his own assured due. With Louis Napoleon crowned Emperor, it was time to put a stop to his intrigues in Turkey and, once again, to bring the Sultan to heel.

6

It is certain that the last thing Nicholas wanted was a European war. It is almost certain that he did not consciously desire war with Turkey. War could have been avoided if Napoleon had not been on the make, if England had acted more intelligently and decisively, if Austria had spoken with a clearer voice. Perhaps. But certainly it could have been avoided if Nicholas had been single-minded in his proclaimed, his repeatedly proclaimed, determination to preserve the Ottoman Empire in being for as long as was possible. He was also increasingly a man possessed with a crusading urge. Any account of the origins of the Crimean War which bases itself on a simple record of the diplomatic exchanges which led up to it is incomplete, indeed meaningless, because it leaves out of account the Russian Emperor's mood, his attitude of mind, his tone of voice, all expressive of a man who could not bring himself to believe that he was simply a ruler among other rulers, even though in his cooler moments he knew that this was so.

Proof of the good and peaceful intentions of Nicholas has again and again been discovered in the generosity he displayed in his hypothetical partitioning of Turkey. He asked for nothing for himself but control of the Principalities and Bulgaria. All the rest was to be divided among the powers – in different ways at different moments. What is rather astonishingly overlooked is the highly possessive manner in which he spoke of the partitioning: he might not demand much for Russia, but it was he, Nicholas, who was as it were giving the rest away. Thus it was again in January 1853 as it had been during the Tsar's visit to London, and afterwards, in 1844.

The timing was interesting. At a ball in St Petersburg he had the first of a long series of conversations with Lord Seymour, the British Ambassador. It was the old story of the imminent collapse of the Ottoman Empire. But now the note was more urgently struck than it had been nine years earlier. There could well, he said, be war over the matter of the Holy Places, or even over Turkey's atrocious treatment of the Montenegrins. Turkey could not survive such a war. But even without war, the end could not be far away. As on so many occasions in so many different contexts, Nicholas seemed self-hypnotised by his own rhetoric: 'We have on our hands a sick man, a man who is seriously ill.' And again: 'The Bear is dying; you may give him musk, but even musk will not keep him long alive.'[15]

Seymour was not at first seriously alarmed. The Tsar, he thought, was a congenital worrier who needed reassurance. By all means Turkey was in an unhealthy condition, but she was surely far from collapse, and the powers in concert should have no difficulty in sustaining her and underpinning her existence. Nicholas concurred, but without enthusiasm; and soon he was worrying again, now making new suggestions for the division of the spoils.

The Principalities were already 'in fact an independent state under my protection', and the interest of the oppressed Christians (who, of course, were also Slavs) in the Balkans generally would best be served by giving Bulgaria and Serbia the same sort of government. England could take Egypt, and Cyprus, too, if she cared to. France, in disgrace, was to get nothing. As for Constantinople, which Nicholas had earlier offered to Austria, neither Russia nor any of the powers should hold it: perhaps it had better be a free city, but Russia might be forced to occupy it temporarily until the dust had settled. Austria, he declared, in an astonishing aside, was fully in accord with these ideas. Nothing could have been farther from the truth; but Nicholas was to remain blind to the Austrian reality for some time to come: he took it for granted that he carried the young Franz Joseph with him, indeed that his intervention in the matter of Hungary must inevitably bind Austria to him with bonds of undying gratitude. 'Austria will astonish the world with the magnitude of her ingratitude,' Schwarzenberg is supposed to have remarked in response to an objection that by accepting Russian help against the Hungarians he was putting himself and his Emperor under an intolerable obligation to the Tsar. He almost certainly said nothing of the kind, but the apocryphal saying was a true enough reflection of reality, as Nicholas was soon, belatedly, to discover to his very great cost.

Meanwhile, even as the conversations between Seymour and the Tsar were continuing in St Petersburg, Nicholas was acting. In February he sent Prince Menshikov to Constantinople to force a resolution of the Holy Places dispute in Russia's favour. At first Menshikov was successful in reminding the Sultan that he had more to fear from Russia than from France, even though the French fleet in the Mediterranean had shown itself very much a force to be reckoned with. He acted with arrogance and high-handedness, forcing the Grand Vizier to resign by publicly insulting him. And he was materially assisted by the British Ambassador, Lord Stratford de Redcliffe, a man who exercised great influence in Constantinople and who is usually presented as an intriguing and unscrupulous enemy of Russia. Certainly Stratford was a dangerous opponent when his enmity was roused; but in the early spring of 1853 he used all his influence to smooth over the new crisis by urging acceptance of Menshikov's demands. And in fact by early May an agreement was reached and signed by Menshikov and the French Ambassador. The French gave way and all seemed to be set fair – until, suddenly, Menshikov came up with a new demand: this time for a treaty between Russia and Turkey guaranteeing the right of the Russian Government to protect the Orthodox subjects of the Ottoman Empire.

This carried the crisis on to a higher level. The Sultan rejected what he saw as a direct infringement of Turkish sovereignty, and now Stratford supported him. Three weeks later on 21 May, Menshikov returned in dudgeon to St Petersburg. England was now alarmed and on 2 June an Anglo-French naval force arrived in Besika Bay outside the Dardanelles. It should have been clear by now to Nicholas that his last demand, affecting as it did the integrity of Turkey and opening the way, had it been accepted, to direct armed Russian intervention in Turkish affairs, would not be tolerated by the other powers. He did not abate it. Instead, on 2 July, he ordered his troops to cross the Pruth and occupy the Principalities.

The diplomatic activity which followed was feverish, complex, muddled to a degree but, in the last resort, irrelevant. A course had been set. Nicholas, while still proclaiming his desire to keep the Ottoman Empire in being, had made a demand which undermined the integrity of that Empire. He did not want to go to war, but his prophecy that war would come had a self-fulfilling quality. All the parties hoped that something would happen to inhibit the war. All the parties toiled away, above all in Vienna, to produce new formulae. In August it was Turkey who rejected the first formula, seeing in it a Franco-Russian plot. In September it was England: Nicholas had recently met Franz Joseph at Olmütz and shown himself most reasonable; so now what was suspected in London was an Austro-Russian plot. The British fleet was sent through the Dardanelles at last, and the French fleet followed. On 8 October war was declared on Russia by a Turkey conscious of the naval backing of the maritime powers. A fortnight later Turkish troops under Omer Pasha had crossed the Danube.

CHAPTER EIGHT

The Crimean Fiasco

I

THE fighting at first was limited to the Danube basin and the Caucasus, and it went on the whole in favour of Russia. But on 30 November came the dramatic shock of the naval battle at Sinope in which Admiral Nakhimov caught the Turkish fleet in harbour and destroyed it. The British Press worked itself up into a frenzy about what was called a 'massacre': it was nothing of the kind, rather a bold and brilliantly conceived naval action in which an antiquated Russian fleet managed to sink a no less antiquated Turkish one. But it meant that for the moment Russia was master of the Black Sea unless something was done to reduce her. So, in January 1854, the British and French at last brought themselves to sail through the Bosporus and six weeks later demanded the evacuation of the Principalities within two months.

The interesting thing is that even before this ultimatum Paskevich, as commander-in-chief, was himself urging on the Emperor the need for evacuation. The Russian army could do no good there, he insisted. Orlov had been despatched to Vienna in one more desperate attempt to secure at least the promise of Austrian neutrality, and had failed. This meant that the Russians in the Principalities were threatened on their extended right flank by the powerful army of an Austria whose intentions were very far from clear. But Nicholas was stubborn. When the Anglo-French ultimatum was received on 27 February, he ignored it, and on 28 March Britain and France declared war.

Nicholas, in spite of Paskevich's apprehension, was determined to press on and cross the Danube. He still could not believe that Austria would turn against him. In October he had written to Franz Joseph: 'My hope is in God and in the justice of the cause I am defending, the cause of Christendom. The fanaticism that now dominates the unhappy Turks makes it almost a crusade, in which Russia defends Christianity while France and England are guilty of the infamy of fighting for the Crescent.

Is it conceivable that Russia should have no allies in the holy cause she is defending?'[1] However righteous in the eyes of an exclusively Christian God, the Tsar's plea was not one calculated to strike an answering chord in the heart of a Habsburg. For centuries the Austrian Habsburgs had borne the weight of the Turkish thrust into Europe, and on certain critical occasions, indeed for a great deal of the time, the Christian kings of France had done all they could to help the Turks destroy the Christian Habsburgs. Their successors were unable to believe in Nicholas as a crusader. He wanted his way in Turkey, and that was fair enough. There was no need to wrap it up in talk about a holy war. And if the Tsar of Russia's ambitions conflicted with what Austria took to be her own interest in the Balkans, then the Tsar must be discouraged and if necessary stopped. There was in fact a sharp division of opinion in Vienna, which Nicholas never seemed to grasp. The war party urged a fighting alliance with England and France: a military victory would put an end to Russian activities in the Balkans for a long time to come. The conservative generals, however, viewed the dissolution of the alliance with Russia as unthinkable. And there was a complicating factor in Louis Napoleon: the more completely he was committed in the East the less the danger of his intervention at Austria's cost in Italy. So Franz Joseph confined himself to a single demand. Austria would remain neutral only if Nicholas would give 'a most definite and solemn undertaking that Russia would stay on the defensive on the left bank of the Danube – or, if forced by military exigency to cross that river, would not depart in the least degree from the letter and spirit of existing treaties' – i.e. would make no new claims on Turkey.[2]

Nicholas had never been spoken to like this before. He had convinced himself, erroneously, that in demanding a protectorate over Christians in Turkey he was exercising his rights under Catherine's Treaty of Kutchuk Kainardji. Franz Joseph's cold demand brought out in him all the dark, wounded, self-pitying pride which clouded his vision, exacerbated by a sense of outrage at the unthinkable: that he was being challenged by a young monarch who might almost have been his grandson and whose throne he had so lately saved.

'Is there not something hatefully superfluous,' he wrote, 'in permitting oneself to doubt his [the Tsar's] word, once given, or in asking him to reaffirm it? . . . Are you truly to make the Turks' cause your own? Emperor Apostolical, does your conscience permit it? If it be so, well and good; then Russia alone shall raise the Holy Cross and follow its commandments. If you were to range yourself with the Crescent against me, then I say to you, that would be a parricidal war.'[3]

This brooding, minatory, almost hieratic diction is a strange echo from the very distant past. Ivan the Terrible had addressed Elizabeth of England in very similar tones when reproving her for the evasive and off-hand rejection of his solemn overtures. Ivan was a Russian, Nicholas was almost wholly German; but both in their different ways were men possessed and shaped by the hopeless immensity and backwardness of the land they tried to rule. Both were autocrats, almost religious in their absolutism, deeply affronted and crying out in regal anguish from the heart. Such diction in a private letter (one of many such), from one nineteenth-century monarch to another had nothing to do with diplomacy, but rather with a sort of mania: absolutism seeking to punish the doubter with excommunication. Even though Nicholas did not want war, even though the incident that actually precipitated war was absurd, it is hard, perhaps impossible, to see how a man in this frame of mind, who was also obsessed with his need, his *duty*, to preside, even though most generously, over the dismemberment of Turkey, would not have been compulsively driven, sooner or later, to push too far.

Absolutism had gone to his head. He might, and did, see the need to work as an equal with the powers. But he was still the man, now operating on an international scale, who had once in youth told his army command that the slightest disobedience would be punished without mercy. He was also a man ever-ready to suspect the motives of others, incapable of trust, who nevertheless expected to be believed and trusted by all others.

There was a revealing incident concerning the gentle and venerated teacher and poet, V. A. Zhukovsky. Zhukovsky was a court familiar who did more than any man to fight the inanities of the censorship and the prejudices of Nicholas. Pushkin and many others owed him an immeasurable debt. He occupied a position of great trust. When Nicholas, as Grand Duke, married his German bride, the Princess Charlotte, Zhukovsky was chosen to be her Russian tutor. Later, Nicholas himself had appointed him tutor to his son and heir, the future Alexander II. One day Zhukovsky went to the Emperor in deep distress. He was upset and horrified by a violent attack made by Benckendorff in person on the work and character of a brilliant young protégé, I. V. Kireyevsky (later to win fame as a prominent Slavophile), who was alleged to hold the autocracy itself in question. Zhukovsky declared to Nicholas that he personally would vouch for Kireyevsky's integrity and loyalty. But Nicholas turned those preposterous eyes on to this extremely faithful and devoted servant, and said: 'And who will vouch for you?'[4]

This was the man who found it intolerable that any living soul should doubt the nobility and rectitude of his intentions towards Turkey – even though those intentions, as expressed, had so often changed.

And so the muddled process continued. In April Austria and Prussia agreed on an alliance of neutrality. In May Nicholas pushed forward to take Silistria and cross the Danube. The assault failed. A week later, on 3 June, it was Austria's turn to demand formally the evacuation of the Principalities, and almost at once she concluded a convention with Turkey permitting her to move in when the Russians moved out. At this very moment the British and the French were going into action, landing 60,000 troops between them at Varna on the Black Sea while a British squadron sailed deep into the Baltic, appearing off Kronstadt at the sea gates of St Petersburg. It was an extraordinary situation and a humiliating one for Nicholas. Gorchakov's army in the Principalities was threatened by the Anglo-French forces in the Varna bridgehead to the east, by Omer Pasha along the Danube to the south, by the might of Austria from Galicia in the west. The army of the Caucasus was deeply engaged already. The Tsar, the Tsaritsa and their children were actually in residence at Peterhof, with its dream palaces and fountains and cascades overlooking the sea, when the British squadron, under Admiral Napier, sailed by, in full view. The Russian fleet would not come out to fight, and Napier felt incapable of attacking it in harbour. He confined himself to assaulting and destroying certain island bases in conjunction with the French. The direct naval threat was removed; but not the longer-term danger. Two hundred thousand of the Tsar's best troops, including all the regiments of the Guards, were pinned down for the rest of the war in Finland and around St Petersburg. It was not only that the Russians feared a major Allied landing in the north. Had such an assault been made Sweden would have joined in too.

Thus it was that at last, on 8 August, Nicholas had to give way and evacuate the Principalities, which he had come to regard as part of Russia for all practical and strategic purposes. Austria occupied Wallachia without firing a shot, still formally neutral. Was there now any need for war? The diplomats sprang into immediate action. France, Britain, Austria agreed on four points to be put to Russia: the status of the Principalities, Serbia as well, to be worked out and guaranteed by all the powers; freedom of navigation on the Danube; abandonment by Russia of its claim to a protectorate over the Orthodox subjects of the Sultan; revision of the Straits Convention 'in the interests of the balance of power in Europe'.

On 26 August Russia rejected these terms; the sticking point was the fourth. The war continued. After much discussion of possibilities between France and Britain, the decision was taken to invade the Crimea, above all to seize the great naval base at Sevastopol. The landings started at Eupatoria on 14 September. They were unopposed. Twenty-seven thousand British, twenty-five thousand Frenchmen, some six or seven thousand

Turks were safely got ashore, sixty thousand in all. The Russians had just that number, too. They were commanded by Prince Menshikov, the one-time cavalry soldier who had been put in charge of the navy. As a commanding general he was inept. But there was a great shortage of good generals. Most of the veterans of 1812 were dead. Paskevich was in supreme command; Gorchakov was conducting the long and painful evacuation of the Principalities, harassed and slowed down by refugees, his men half-starved and dying in thousands from exhaustion and disease. Wrangel, Andronnikov and Bebutov were active and successful in the Caucasus. Menshikov was very much on his own, and when he met the invaders on the river Alma on 20 September, although he occupied a most commanding position on the heights above the river, he was out-manoeuvred, outnumbered and outgunned. He failed, losing nearly 6,000 men out of 33,000, while the Allies lost 3,000 out of 57,000.

2

It could have been the end. Sevastopol, the vital Black Sea base, was wide open, its defences rudimentary from the landward side. The Allies did not know this. Instead of pushing on and turning the Russian defeat into a rout they rested, then two days later decided to defer the assault on the fortress, instead to march round it, east and then south, seize Balaclava harbour to use as a supply base, and attack Sevastopol from the south instead of from the west. Thus opportunity was lost and the long-drawn-out agony of the Crimean War began.

Menshikov was still on his own. He took his main forces away from Sevastopol and deployed them along the river Belbek, north-east of the fortress. The defence of Sevastopol itself was left to Admirals Nakhimov and Vladimir Kornilov, commanding an assortment of units from the army and the fleet. Nakhimov had been the hero of the brilliant action at Sinope. He was now to show a genius for organisation. He was also a great leader. He had at his disposal a General Totleben, a gifted and determined engineer. It was Nakhimov who provided the inspiration; but it was Totleben who designed and built against time the formidable system of fortifications, a series of bastions linked by immense earth ramparts, which was to hold the Allies at bay for so long.

These men, their lives confined to a tiny enclave at the southernmost tip of the remote Crimean peninsula, inhabited a world of their own. Why, people ask, was it possible for Russia with her great continental army of half a million men, operating on internal lines of communication, to suffer defeat at the hands of a relatively small invading force thousands of miles from home and occupying an insignificant bridgehead on the extreme periphery of a vast empire?

In fact only a part of the Tsar's great army was ever deployed in the Crimea. The shape of Russia on the map, ominous and overwhelming when viewed from western Europe, has a very different aspect when viewed from the inside. To the Russian general staff it is nothing but frontier, an infinity of frontier, most of it exposed and highly vulnerable. To them the vast land area which intimidates the West is more a liability than an asset, standing for the immense distances over which men and supplies must be moved on inadequate roads; at best a defensive trap for the invader. It is the frontier that counts, a frontier which may be breached at far more points than can be properly defended. Thus Nicholas, faced with invasion by Turkey, France and Britain, was forced to divide his available forces into a number of virtually self-contained armies. And the problem was magnified by fear of attack from Austria, even (though remotely) from Prussia, and from a Sweden which was pledged to march if Austria did so.

Paskevich had been correct in his insistence on the early evacuation of the Principalities; but it was the only sensible decision he was to take throughout the war. For it was Paskevich's overrating of the Austrian danger and consistent underrating of the importance of the Crimean theatre which gave the British and the French, later augmented by 35,000 Piedmontese, their chance.

In the first place, like Menshikov (but unlike Gorchakov) he was convinced that the Allies would not attempt a landing before the spring of 1854; further, that there was no threat to the Crimea: the Allies would attempt a landing in Circassia to support the Turkish forces operating in the Caucasus. Then, when proved wrong, for a critical period he persuaded the Tsar to refuse urgently needed reinforcements for the army in the Crimea: there were 60,000 men there, and they could hold on indefinitely in face of any force the Allies might bring against them. Obviously considerable forces had to stand guard against the opening of a Baltic front in the north and Austrian intervention in the west. But Paskevich's obsessive fears led to an absurd distortion. While Menshikov with his 60,000 was being driven back at Sevastopol, 200,000 men stood idle in Finland, and in Poland 200,000 more watched Austria. Add to these the fighting army in the Caucasus and strong garrisons at other danger spots (in August 1854 a British naval force did in fact carry out a destructive raid on the Kola Peninsula in the Arctic, and in September an Anglo-French force, half a world away, attacked the garrison in Petropavlovsk in Kamchatka), and the wonder is that the Russians in the Crimea held out until reinforcements at last began to arrive.

They could never have done so but for the ineptitude of the Allied commanders. But the notorious failures on the Allied side were matched and surpassed by the failures of the Russians. The Allies, when all is said, to a considerable extent corrected their errors, and did in the end achieve what they set out to do, though far from home in a hostile land. The Russians failed absolutely. And a major factor in this difference was the lack of a free press to expose the true state of affairs. There were good and gifted individuals on the Russian side. There was even a Russian equivalent of Florence Nightingale – not a woman, but a devoted surgeon, N. I. Pirogov, who also became a legend among the troops – who performed prodigies of organisation single-handed, and had to help him a devoted band of volunteer nurses sent out by that unquenchable fighter for good causes, the Grand Duchess Helen. But neither Nicholas nor Paskevich ever brought themselves to understand the true state of affairs.

There was no independent newspaper correspondent to tell the truth and rouse public opinion. There was no public opinion. There was the Tsar's command. And the Tsar thought in terms of his immaculate parade-ground army moving into action with piston-like precision. It was not like that at all.

When Prince Gorchakov's headquarters made its slow, painful retreat from the Danube and established itself at Kishinev one of the junior staff officers was his young kinsman, Leo Tolstoy, then just twenty-five. On a trip to Odessa, under blockade by the British fleet, Tolstoy encountered some English and French prisoners and was overwhelmed by the sturdiness of their bearing and appearance. 'The air and manner of these men gives me, why I don't know, a sinking certainty that they are far superior to our soldiers,' he wrote in his diary.[5] Soon, disgusted by the luxury and brilliance of headquarters life, he applied for a transfer to the Crimean front, and on his way he encountered French and British wounded. 'Every soldier among them is proud of his position and has a sense of his value. He feels that he is a positive asset to his army. He has good weapons and knows how to use them, he is young, he has ideas about politics and art and this gives him a feeling of dignity.'

Lord Cardigan, lapped in the comforts of his yacht in Balaclava harbour while his men faced the onset of winter in tents (tents which were soon to be blown down and torn to ribbons by the early winter gales), would have been hard put to it to recognise his own troops from the young Tolstoy's description. But in fact both the British and the French were bigger and stronger and mentally more alert than the Russian conscripts, who were serfs in uniform. 'Senseless training, useless weapons, ill treatment, universal procrastination, ignorance, appalling hygiene and food, stifle the last spark of pride in a man and even give him, by comparison, too high an opinion of the enemy.'[6]

That was Tolstoy's first view of the Russian troops in the Crimea. Very soon he found himself where the action was, actually under bombardment in Sevastopol. Then he began to feel differently about his own side. 'My little soldiers are very nice,' he wrote, 'I feel quite gay with them.'[7] He was half attracted, half terrified by the danger. And it was perhaps the first time that he had ever seen the peasant conscripts as human beings. But his earlier harsh judgement was close enough to the truth.

For the Russian army, cavalry and infantry alike, was trained for nothing at all but close formation drill on the parade ground: the cavalry was superb when it came to dressage. Nicholas himself once observed delightedly to one of his colonels after a parade: 'You have led before me a whole regiment of riding masters!'[8] They could charge, as a set piece; but the light cavalry, the hussars and the uhlans (or lancers) were not taught even the elements of their trade, skirmishing, reconnaissance and scouting. Nor were they good at marching. In a land of such vast distances it was almost incredible that the recognised day's march was ten or eleven miles a day, always at a walk, with trotting strictly barred. When it was a question of forced marching, in which they were never trained, to cover sixteen miles in a day was regarded as a superhuman achievement. The care of horses was complicated by old wives' superstitions. At the end of a day's march the horses were held for two hours, still saddled and blanketed, unwatered, to keep them from catching cold.[9] German military observers who commented on these practices found them incomprehensible. But nobody who was with the Soviet army during the Second World War would be surprised. The Russian peasant conscript even then had not the faintest idea of how to look after the horses on which his transport relied.[10] There is no reason to suppose that the serf conscript under Nicholas knew any better. The rules, devised by stupid men for even more stupid troops, had to be simple and iron hard. Otherwise the horses would have been ridden to death in no time at all. As things were, it was usually their fate to be starved to death when the fodder they carried was all consumed and the surrounding countryside could provide no more. Only the Cossacks, who lived on horseback, bred a hardier sort of mount and travelled light, showed themselves as an effective cavalry army in any but set-piece battles. This effectiveness was, however, reduced by absence of discipline.

As for the infantry in their drab masses, on paper so overwhelming, these, as already remarked, were peasant serfs in uniform, detailed for army service by their owners; long-service troops that is to say, drilled and savagely beaten into unquestioning obedience. There were no reserves of short-service troops to leaven the mass. Their officers, almost all sons of the nobility (very often inferior and poverty-stricken nobility) were themselves trained to unthinking obedience: only a very few had attended one of the cadet schools which were the Tsar's pride. Most idled away their time drinking and gambling; and these included men of high intelligence who, in other lands, would at this time have been taking a serious interest in problems of training and strategy. There was good reason for this: the least display of initiative, even of an enquiring intelligence, was frowned on by the senior commanders who, as a rule, owed their promotion to family connections.

The armament and equipment of the infantry soldier was as inadequate as his training. Weapons which served well enough against mountain tribesmen and even Turks were useless in face of the British and the French rifles, which could far outrange the Russian muskets as well as achieve a more rapid rate of fire. The infantryman was not trained to use his weapons properly: there was little or no target practice with live ammunition. Reliance was placed on the bayonet; and, indeed, when it came to hand-to-hand fighting the long Russian bayonets were formidable. It is hardly too much to say that in the early stages of the war the Russian musket was seen not as a firearm at all, but rather as a bayonet-holder in battle and as an ornament on parade. Little or no effort was made to teach the men to cherish their muskets. Barrels and bolts were rarely if ever oiled. To brighten the barrels for parade purposes the men used files and emery paper, so that the metal was rubbed dangerously thin, causing frequent bursting of the barrel. The stocks were weakened so that the ramrods fitted loosely in their slots, to produce an imposing rattle when the muskets were slapped about on parade.[11]

It is not necessary to dwell on the deficiencies of the British army under Lord Raglan and the ineptitudes of the high command: they were to become a national disgrace, never to be forgotten. It is, however, worth bearing in mind that the British army was by tradition neglected by governments and starved of funds. The Russian army, on the contrary, was the be-all and end-all of the Emperor's existence, to which everything was sacrificed.

Why, it has often been asked, if cavalry and infantry were so poor, did the Russian gunners and engineers do so well? There need be no mystery about this. Brains and initiative could be, and were, actively discouraged among infantrymen and cavalrymen; but for gunnery a degree of education is essential, and the same goes for many of the activities of field engineers – who also have to work on their own and employ initiative in solving each problem as it arises. Even the crassest general staff officer was aware of this, and had to tolerate the necessary intelligence, with the result that the intelligent naturally gravitated into these two arms. It was to the gunners with their cannon and the engineers with their fortifications and their mines that Sevastopol owed its ability to keep going for so long.

Sustained by the endurance of the peasant soldiers, leavened somewhat by the fleet sailors now serving on land, these gunners and engineers could have held out indefinitely, forcing the Allies to retire (as they would have had to do before a second winter), had they received even reasonable support from St Petersburg, or if, indeed Menshikov had not failed so abjectly in his manoeuvring outside the great fortress. But Menshikov, always inadequate, was soon a broken man.

Already after the humiliation on the Alma he had started turning inward upon himself. This useless and unpleasantly arrogant man was a perfect expression of the Tsar's own failure to surround himself with good lieutenants and advisers. Like Kleinmikhel, he was a sycophant of the bullying sort, but far more vainglorious and far less capable. A cavalry officer put in charge of the navy, which he allowed to fall into neglect; a Governor of Finland who became notorious for his brutalities; the close of his arid career was in itself an echo of his Imperial master's. He was approaching seventy, not a great age in a society which, whether under Romanov or Soviet rule, has always found it insuperably difficult to retire its run-down and discredited veterans, but old enough to be seized with a too easy sense of hopelessness. Always aloof from his subordinates, to say nothing of his troops, he was reaching the stage when he could communicate with nobody. When he started his flank march which was to bring him to a commanding position north-east of Sevastopol, he told nobody what he was doing. Without a word of his intentions to Admirals Nakhimov and Vladimir Kornilov in Sevastopol, he gave the order to march and simply vanished with his army, leaving the Sevastopol defenders to believe that he had abandoned them to their fate. At the same time he quite overlooked the need to put out scouts to see what the enemy was doing, and was thus taken by surprise when he discovered that the Allies, instead of attacking immediately, were conducting their own flank march to bring them round the fortress to Balaclava harbour. He knew nothing about this until an Allied column stumbled into the end of his own baggage train and destroyed it. He was thus lucky that his own ineptitude was matched by that of the Allied commanders, who also forgot about scouts. If either side had been the first to realise what the other was doing, it would have had an overwhelming advantage in a probably decisive battle.

This was on 25 September, five days after Alma. Totleben in Sevastopol used the breathing space resulting from the Allied re-deployment to build up the landward defences with one of those tremendous bursts of energy, so quickly exhausted, so formidable for a time, characteristic of Russian activity of every kind. He rejected the admirable but all too leisurely copy-book plans for elaborate stonework defences and put all the available troops to throwing up improvised earthworks in a sort of inspired military *corvée*. So when the Allies were firmly established round their new base at Balaclava, they discovered to their great suprise that what a month earlier had seemed a vulnerable defence system was now impregnable, with earth and timber bastions joined by a screen of tall earthen walls, the key to the whole being Malakhov Hill.

3

By the end of September it was clear that the Allies had settled down to lay siege, and it was Menshikov's job to throw them into the sea before they could build up too formidable a force from the little fjord-like harbour at Balaclava.

He had reinforcements at last, some of them useless for his purposes, but enough to bring his army up to 100,000 men. At first he was ready to let the Allies spend themselves on a major assault on the fortress, which opened with a tremendous bombardment on 17 October. It turned out to be a risky decision. The French were beaten back and their guns silenced; the great cannon in the fortress outranged the naval guns of the Allied fleet, which was forced to stand off. But the British assault was luckier. With direct hits on the magazines the third bastion was virtually annihil-ated. Had the bombardment been followed up with an assault the fortifica-tions would have been breached and the defence of the remaining bastions made impossible. Even though assault never came, the whole defence was breaking down. The gunners had expended almost all their ammunition, and Menshikov could no longer postpone action. On 24 October he sent one of his divisions to attack the British in front of Balaclava, not to drive them into the sea, but to ease the pressure on Sevastopol. To some extent the move succeeded. Four redoubts manned by Turkish troops were cap-tured, and Liprandi's divisional artillery, newly established on the heights overlooking the harbour, were then accorded the uncovenanted bonus of virtually destroying the legendary Light Brigade which charged in error into the heart of the Russian position and was shattered by point-blank gunfire on the long sad ride back down the valley.

But although Balaclava was good for Russian morale it was not a great victory. The Allies learnt their lesson from it, and strengthened their position at a point of critical weakness. Menshikov had to try again, and in this last ill-fated action he was able to deploy three infantry divisions and a considerable force of cavalry. This was the battle of Inkerman, on 5 November.

From the Russian point of view Inkerman was a model of how not to fight a battle. Nobody knew the terrain. In spite of the fact that Menshikov had two divisions of light cavalry eating their heads off, no reconnaissance was made, and there were no proper maps. Regardless of this, Menshikov devised an unnecessarily complex plan of attack. It was the sort of plan guaranteed to go wrong even in peacetime manoeuvres. It called for the synchronisation of two separate approach marches, a diversionary demonstration at divisional strength, and a synchronised sortie from Sevastopol itself. When the two attacking columns joined forces, their commanders, Generals Soimonov and Pavlov, were to put themselves at the disposal of a senior general, who would co-ordinate the final attack. The senior general was Dannenberg, a man who had notoriously failed in the Danube campaign. To make catastrophe doubly sure, the whole operation was to be supervised by Menshikov himself from rear headquarters. In the circumstances it was the plan of a madman.

And yet it was nearly a Russian triumph. Everything went wrong, as it was bound to go wrong when commanders and troops of the quality then available are required to march and make a junction on the battlefield itself. There were the inevitable delays and muddles. Nothing was properly synchronised. But with all this the Russians managed to achieve surprise, largely because the advance was concealed by unexpected fog. Instead of the crushing blow intended, it degenerated into a sort of serial fight which had a repetitive nightmare quality. There seemed no end to the waves of attackers. But the British were saved by the French, who had been the target of the Liprandi division's planned diversionary attack. The trouble was that Liprandi did not know how to make his feint look like the real thing, and the French commander, Bosquet, seeing it for what it was, had the sense and the courage, the decency too, to despatch the greater part of his own command to the aid of the British.

The day was lost for the Russians, even though the Allies did not know it, conscious as they were of the overwhelming strength of the enemy forces: they fully expected a renewed attack next day. But in fact their resistance had torn the heart out of the Russians. Dannenberg and Gorchakov lost their nerve. They still had vast reserves immediately under their command, and the Allies could not have stood against them. But they threw in their hands, and sounded the retreat. They had lost nearly 12,000 men, including half a dozen generals, out of some 42,000 actually engaged; the Allies had lost some 4,000 out of the 8,000 or 9,000 engaged.

4

For Menshikov it was the end. It should have been clear to Nicholas and Paskevich that this disastrous man would never fight again. He went about declaring that Russia's only hope was for storms and gales to break the sea communications of the Allies. It was this mood which the young Tolstoy commented on so scathingly as he arrived in Sevastopol after Inkerman. In fact his hopes were nearly to come true. Already some of the British generals were advocating an end to the campaign, while just a week after Inkerman came a terrible storm which raged for two days and a night, blowing the British tents away and exposing the troops first to slashing rain, then to bitter cold. The supply roads from the harbour were virtually washed away and the British troops had to act as their own pack animals. This was the beginning of the terrible winter of disease, exhaustion and death. For some months the Allied armies, even the French in their comparatively warm wooden huts, were virtually extinguished as a fighting force. All they could do was hang on and pray that the Russians would not mount a major attack. Menshikov obliged. His new Chief of Staff, Prince Vasilchikov, fretted and fumed against this inactivity. The Tsar in St Petersburg, nearly fifteen hundred miles away, bombarded him with demands for action while, as he saw it, dangerously exposing his frontiers by sending ever more reinforcements to the Crimea. But Menshikov would not stir. In fact the reinforcements were less imposing in reality than they were on paper. At least a third of them died of disease in the course of their long march over unmade roads. For there was still no railway south of Moscow.

It was indeed the condition of the reinforcements when they arrived, the deficient supply position and the appalling fate of the thousands of wounded after Inkerman which had finally reduced Menshikov to the apathy of despair. There were no hospitals. Every building, every cellar, in the town of Sevastopol itself was filled with the wounded. Pirogov and his devoted team of surgeons toiled like men possessed, operating and amputating round the clock in shocking conditions, often almost knee-deep in mud. The sufferings of those who survived to be evacuated to base hospitals were beyond imagining. The conventional Russian waggon is a sort of wooden trough on four wheels, unsprung, the sides sloping sharply outwards. There was room for just one stretcher-case to lie on the narrow plank floor; two others, one on each side, were wedged insecurely between him and the sloping sides. The unfortunates were crushed together and shaken to pieces in all weathers, often without food for many days.

Nicholas knew nothing about this. 'For God's sake lose no time, it is precious . . . ,' he cried out across the vast, frozen winter landscape to his old favourite, who seemed paralysed.[12] It was clear that the garrison was in good heart. Its immediate commanders encouraged frequent sorties, often at company strength, to surprise the enemy in his bleak hibernation and capture prisoners. The French sappers were kept well back by Russian countermining of the most determined and imaginative kind. But there was no longer an effective central command. All this Nicholas knew. He himself as winter approached was possessed with a positive mania of energy, and yet was not far from breaking-point. The man who had once gone out into the streets of St Petersburg to help the fire-fighters, who had stood up to the cholera rioters and whipped them back into their hovels, was now directing the war in the Crimea almost, it seemed to him, single-handed. His nerves were screaming. All through the autumn every defeat had been the personal humiliation of a man who did not know defeat, every flicker of good news a personal triumph. He could not hide his tears, whether of chagrin or short-lived joy. He was unable to face the return to the public life of St Petersburg. Instead, he immured himself with the Empress in the solitary gloom of his father's old palace at Gatchina. There the Empress fell ill and nearly died. Nicholas lived only for her, not eating, not sleeping, watching always at her bedside. He was on the edge of moral abdication.

Then, suddenly, he pulled himself together and returned to the Winter Palace, determined again to command. Now the reports and battle orders of every separate unit commander in the Crimea came to him directly; and in his own handwriting he issued precise and detailed orders for the composition, assignment, deployment of each separate unit.[13] He was desperate now to get the Allies out of the Crimea before he had to face the long-feared Austrian invasion from the west. For on 2 December Austria had at last come off the fence, abandoned her neutrality, and concluded an alliance with Britain and France. It never occurred to Nicholas that there was anything incongruous in the spectacle of a head of state dealing with a world in arms against him while regulating in the minutest detail the operations of a far-off army of whose conditions he had no true idea. It never occurred to him that his lack of trust in the men on the spot was bound to stifle boldness and initiative. First he had committed the Nakhimovs, the Totlebens to the supervision of an untalented favourite, seen as an extension of himself. Now, when that favourite had failed, he had nobody but himself. He had destroyed his beloved army in the field as he had destroyed the totality of life throughout his Empire during all his reign.

5

That reign was now about to end, in gloom and a sense of outrage and betrayal – betrayal by Menshikov, who was belatedly retired to be replaced by Gorchakov, commander of the Danube army; betrayal by Franz Joseph in Vienna; outrage when Sardinia joined the Allied coalition at the far-sighted instance of Cavour, seeking a voice at the peace conference for his royal master (35,000 Piedmontese were sent uncomprehendingly across half Europe to the Crimea to achieve this consummation). For even before Gorchakov could take up his new command Nicholas was dead. His death came to his people with a shock of incredulous surprise; but in fact he seemed to have courted it. On 12 February he attended the wedding of the daughter of Count Kleinmikhel in bitter weather wearing only the scarlet uniform of the Horse Guards with buckskin breeches and silk stockings beneath the high boots. That evening he developed a cold, made light of it, dined alone with Count Kiselev who refused at first because he himself had influenza, and went to bed early. But next day he was up again to attend a routine review at the Riding School. That night he too went down with influenza. Within twenty-four hours he was dead. He was fifty-nine. He was conscious most of the time and died well, dictating telegrams of farewell to Moscow, to Warsaw and to the Prussian King, urging him to remember the alliance. The Empress wanted to bring his mistress, Barbara Nelidova, to him to say farewell; but Nicholas said it would not do. He thought of his heir. There was to be no repetition of December 1825: all the regiments of the Guards were brought flocking into the great halls of the Winter Palace to swear allegiance to the new Emperor, Alexander II, the moment Nicholas was dead.

6

The war continued. The very fact that Nicholas died leaving the conflict unresolved underlined symbolically the continuing influence of his cata-strophic policies. His son Alexander, now thirty-seven years old, was not given a clean sheet, and the reforms he had been brooding on could not begin until the war was lost or won. There seemed to be a chance of peace. But there were many months of fighting to be gone through yet, and before the end was reached in the spring and summer of 1855 the defence of Sevastopol achieved a level of sustained heroism rarely equalled, per-haps never excelled. Gorchakov had been full of optimism to begin with; six more weeks he gave the war, assuring the troops in his first order of the day that they had the worst behind them. The defenders on the ground knew better, and Gorchakov himself within ten days had swung from bombastic optimism to something like defeatism. But he was a better man than Menshikov. He really cared for his troops, and showed himself among them. Though by no means a talented commander he knew how to recognise talent in others and was not afraid to give it a clear run. In a word, he brought a new atmosphere to the whole army, which was now some 300,000 strong, above all to the beleaguered fortress. And the war between the engineers became an epic within an epic, with the Russians again and again taking new strong points into the fortified system to counter the French and the British – above all the French – who advanced their own works with brilliant attack and imagination. It was a war in which new bastions, redoubts and lunettes, new batteries and parallels, sprang into being overnight, each side countering the other with their mines and countermines, their saps, their raids. Some of the sorties were major actions. In March, for example, 5,000 men were sent to destroy the latest French works, which had been pushed forward dangerously close to the ramparts, and the Russians thought their achievement well worth the loss of a thousand men.

But, of course, the Allied assaults were on an altogether bigger scale, as when no fewer than five divisions attacked the Malakhov after a tremendous preliminary bombardment, the Russians losing 2,500 the French almost 3,000, the British 500. And this almost successful assault was soon followed up by a still greater and more costly action only a fort-night later.

This determined Franco-British attempt to finish off the war was co-ordinated by Pélissier and Lord Raglan. It failed, in spite of an intense preliminary bombardment and the sacrificial refusal of the Allies to accept repulse on repulse as defeat. The fire from brilliantly sited Russian can-non, sweeping the attackers with grape-shot at almost point-blank range and pursuing them back to their trenches after each abortive assault was now unendurable. But it was a measure of the determination of the attackers and the stubbornness of the defenders that the Russians lost almost 5,000 men, the French over 3,000, the British some 1,600 more.

This day, 18 June, was a turning point. While the new Tsar in his letter of congratulation to Gorchakov was exulting in the repulse and declaring that now, obviously, there could be no more talk of abandoning the fort-ress, Gorchakov himself did not see how his troops could hold out much longer, and although the arrival of fresh reinforcements gave him new heart, this did not last more than a day or two. It was soon plain to every responsible commander on the Russian side that evacuation was the only way. They did not realise that there was despair also on the Allied side.

In August, with the Tsar and his emissaries constantly urging an offensive to relieve the fortress, and with the arrival of still further reinforcements, Gorchakov decided that since he could not evacuate with honour, that since he was losing men all the time by disease and shell-fire, he had better make a virtue of necessity and stake his army on one throw. He would mount a major attack on the very strong Allied positions on the Chernaya river. It would be make or break.

He believed it would be break. No general ever went into battle at a point of his own choosing more certain of defeat. His plan was opposed by his best commanders, including Totleben. He himself wrote to St Petersburg that he expected defeat: his position had been hopeless, he said, from the moment he had taken over from Menshikov; it was hopeless still. His plan, indeed, underlined the hopelessness. It was a plan without point. Even if the 30,000 Russian troops engaged had managed to storm the fortified heights there was no provision for a follow-through, and the attackers would have been vulnerable to immediate counter-attack by the Allied reserves. As things were, Gorchakov's immediate orders were so muddled that the plan, such as it was, went wrong. The attack was thrown back with a minimum of loss to the French and the Piedmontese on the heights – less than 2,000. The Russian losses were eleven generals and 8,000 men. That was on 16 August. From this moment the Allies were able to concentrate all their efforts on the reduction of the fortress itself, no longer fearing attack from outside. From this moment Gorchakov concentrated all his thoughts on inevitable evacuation.

The final bombardment of Sevastopol began on 18 August. It was to last twenty days. For nearly three weeks the great redoubts were battered slowly to pieces by bombardment without end. For three weeks the defenders fought back, their numbers diminished day by day, hour by hour; their fire-power diminished by direct hits on their guns, still more by the inexorable drying up of their ammunition supply. On the eve of the final assault only eight of the sixty-three heavy pieces in the Malakhov were still in action. The defenders were driven to lie out in shallow trenches in front of the ruined ramparts to hold the enemy off with small-arms fire. For days past they had been steadily reduced at the rate of some 2,500 a day.

Now, beaten down, exhausted, waiting for reliefs and reinforcements which never came, they looked forward to total extinction. In fact they were still to celebrate their finest hour, performing marvels of valour when the assault at last came, pulling themselves together in scenes of chaos and confusion to beat off all but one of twelve separate Allied stormings. The confusion was cleverly engineered by the French, who by repeated false alarms heralded by sharp and intense bombardments, by misleading rocket signals, time and time again convinced the defenders that the moment had come. Then there would be a lull. So that when the real assault came the defenders, driven into their dugouts by the too familiar bombardment, took it as another false alarm.

The real thing, when it came, was a sudden lengthening of the French gunners' range and a spectacular charge of 10,000 Frenchmen led in person by General MacMahon across forty yards of open ground to the Kornilov bastion on the Malakhov Hill. At the same time many thousands more stormed the second bastion and the ramparts and the batteries. The British, with the third bastion as their objective, were late off the mark.

When the day was ended it looked as though the Russians had achieved a great victory. The British were thrown back. The French attacking the fifth bastion were thrown back. The second bastion was cleared. General Pelissier was convinced that he would have his work cut out to defend his solitary foothold, the Kornilov bastion, against an overwhelming Russian counter-attack. The Russians themselves gloried in victory. They had lost 13,000 men in the fighting that day. But the Allies had lost at least 10,000 and were back where they started – except for their hold on the shambles which had been the Kornilov bastion.

Only Gorchakov knew better. He could never, he knew, retake the Kornilov and with the Allies installed there Totleben's whole great complex was indefensible. He must get out, and he did so. His withdrawal was the most effective operation in a not very dazzling career. The Allies, collecting themselves against counter-attack, had not the least idea of what was going on behind the Russian lines. At five o'clock, even before the fighting had died down, the order for general evacuation had gone out. At seven the withdrawal had begun, under cover of intensive fire from the fortifications designed to mislead the enemy. The evacuation was made possible because for months past Gorchakov had been preparing for just this eventuality. In secrecy, under the noses of the Allies, his engineers had constructed a floating bridge a third of a mile long across the inlet. The plank roadway was supported by huge floating baulks of timber, all of them brought from the Ukraine across the treeless Crimea by thousands of waggons plodding their laborious way on those unmade roads in the confusion of reinforcements on the march, endless waggon-trains of ammunition, food and fodder, and the grim procession of wounded moving back to the base hospitals. The building of this bridge was one of the most remarkable feats of the war. It saved an army from annihilation. All through the night the defenders streamed across the bridge, taking with them many of their guns. Others crossed the bay in steamers and small boats. Even the wounded were got away. The magazines were blown up; most of the city was burned down.

The war had been about Sevastopol and command of the Black Sea. With the fall of Sevastopol it was effectively over. There was still fierce fighting in Transcaucasia, and the battle for Kars went on until November, when General Muraviev brought about its fall. With better generalship the Russians should have captured Kars much earlier and gone on to take Erzerum and break the Turkish hold on eastern Anatolia. Once again in this theatre the Russian troops won the almost awed respect of their opponents. Once again their generals let them down.

But at least the capture of Kars gave point to the realisation that although Sevastopol had fallen and been destroyed, and although the Russian Black Sea fleet was no more, the Imperial army had suffered defeat on only one front. Russia had not been invaded in depth and the bulk of her great army still stood intact. The maritime powers had achieved their main purpose, which was to neutralise Russian power in the Black Sea. Russia no longer had a Black Sea fleet to fight for, so the question of the Straits was for the time being academic. It was while both sides were considering how best to make peace that Austria decided that the moment had come for her to reap the harvest sown by others. On 15 December she delivered an ultimatum which made two demands additional to the so-familiar Four Points: she was to receive southern Bessarabia from Russia, which would thus surrender control of the Danube, and the Allies (including, of course, Austria, which had not fought) were to have the right to stipulate further points at the formal peace conference.

On 15 January 1856, the new Tsar in Council decided that he could not take on Austria as well as France, Britain and Sardinia. He gave in. The war was at an end.

CHAPTER NINE

The New Tsar

I

NOBODY knew much about the new Tsar. He turned out to be one of those rulers, so satisfying to historical determinists, who are shaped by the events they appear to master. He was gentle in manner, not bad looking, but a little flabby (he started putting on weight before he was twenty), and with a drooping moustache half-concealing a weak mouth and chin. He had fine eyes, dark blue; and he knew how to charm but not how to reassure. He was, indeed, an unpredictable mixture of stubbornness and feebleness, boldness and timidity, enlightenment and obscurantism. He was to preside over an epoch of radical change, now initiating change, now resisting it; but, even though he is celebrated in history as the Tsar-Liberator, he left no personal stamp on the age; he gave it no colour. He could, and did, assert himself and fight hard to secure the emancipation of the serfs, the reform of the judiciary, the revival of local government after centuries of neglect; but to these remarkable achievements he brought a curiously negative approach. He insisted and he decreed; but the creative drive came from others.

His reign was also distinguished on the one hand by expansionist imperialism in the grand manner, on the other by an artistic flowering of marvellous richness; but he did little to encourage either, and his conquering generals were almost as complete and irresponsible in their individualism as the great writers and musicians. There was no hard centre to the reign. There was no discernible pattern. In the end everything turned sour. The reforms, spectacular as they were, lost their impetus; the incomplete was never completed; the virtue drained away into desert sand. The imperial drive added little or nothing to the country's resources, sapped its wealth, and ended in a diplomatic humiliation scarcely less bitter than the military defeat with which his reign had opened. Nothing could diminish the glory of artistic achievement; but this owed nothing to the Tsar and was hindered and obstructed by the censorship. The powerful movement of political and moral ideas, on the other hand, was to degenerate into an exaltation of revolutionary violence and terror which reached its first climax with the assassination of Alexander himself.

It has been said that no future monarch was given a better chance to equip himself for high destiny. In the sense that Nicholas put himself out to prepare the Tsarevich for the throne and later to induct him into the processes of government, this may be true; for the father did not repeat the error of so many of his predecessors, who excluded the heir from the mysteries of power because they feared the development of a rival force, or shrank from exposing their own uncertainties and inadequacies. But the very fact of having Nicholas for a father was enough to inhibit harmonious growth in any but the strongest character. Alexander was not very strong. He was not as strong as his younger brother Constantine, who quietly developed into a convinced radical in reaction against his father's policies, but was at the same time steady enough to keep his own counsel when there was nothing to be gained by demonstrative protest.

Alexander was kindly, sensitive and easily moved to tears. From an early age he was full of short-lived enthusiasms but lacking in application. In the schoolroom he was quickly defeated when he ran into difficulties. Problems presented themselves to him not as challenges but as insurmountable obstacles; and his solution was to abandon the struggle and pretend the problem did not exist. Enthusiasm would be followed by periods of apparent apathy, disturbing to his tutors; and this alternation was to last his lifetime, disturbing his advisers. But to set against this he possessed, as so often in weak men, a quality of obstinacy which, once roused, made him immovable. He could, on occasion, even defy his father and make him give way. But the occasions were rare and unpredictable, linked in no coherent pattern.

His tutors were more enlightened and imaginative than the mood of the times would have led one to expect, the chief of these outstandingly so. This was V. A. Zhukovsky, poet, humanist, friend of Pushkin, who had been appointed Russian teacher to the young bride of Nicholas, the future Tsaritsa, who quickly grew to love and trust him. It was she, the Empress, who insisted that Zhukovsky was the only man to supervise the studies of the infant Tsarevich. Nicholas yielded with a very bad grace, and on several occasions behaved abominably towards poor Zhukovsky. But he never brought himself to dismiss the poet, who exercised a liberal influence over his young pupil until he came to manhood – not only directly, but also through his mother in the long and careful letters he addressed to her.

It was an extraordinary situation for this tolerant, enquiring, deeply humane man, who could have made a name for himself in any Western capital. He had had so many friends and acquaintances in and around the Decembrist circles that it is a wonder that he had survived into Nicholas's reign. Alexander had been seven years old on that terrible December day, old enough to remember something of the tension and alarm in the Winter Palace as his father went out to face the mutiny on the Senate Square. Zhukovsky called at tea-time that day to pay his respects to the Tsaritsa in her new apartments in the Winter Palace and found Alexander and his sisters playing in the room with their mother 'absolutely calm, although her face bore traces of the day's terrible anxiety'.[1] Zhukovsky himself, although he did not then know the full story of the events of that day, must have suffered profound apprehension. Who among his friends was directly involved? Who would be found guilty 'by association'? What fate might lie in store for him? Loyal he was to the autocracy, but highly critical of some of its aspects and widely known to be the friend, indeed the protector, of some of the radical critics of the regime. But he had his own protector in the Tsaritsa, who at that time could do what she liked with Nicholas, and he was loved by Alexander, who responded to him as to nobody else.

Within the framework of the system Zhukovsky was very brave indeed. He had no use for violence as a means of change; but his heart could bleed for those whose convictions drove them to violence. Picked out by Alexander I on the strength of a patriotic poem which became famous throughout Russia, he had soon proved himself to be a most gifted teacher. And he held his own in face of court intrigues by his unassailable sincerity and honesty. As the reign wore on and Nicholas revealed himself ever more certainly for what he was, Zhukovsky made it his special concern to open his young pupil's mind to the best thought both inside and outside Russia and to counteract the stultifying effect of the Tsar's determination to turn his heir into a soldier like himself. There was one point at which Tsar and tutor came together: the Tsarevich must on no account be spoiled or pampered and all manifestations of arrogance or conceit must be jumped on promptly. For Nicholas this meant that his son must sleep, as he himself did, on a hard, narrow bed set up like a fakir's couch in the midst of the gilded extravagances of the Winter Palace or Tsarskoe Selo. It meant military discipline and hard driving at the desk. It meant school-room food. For Zhukovsky it meant constant and persuasive reminders of Alexander's burden of responsibility to all in the vast realm that would be one day his to command, of the debt owed by his privileged position to the misfortunes of others, above all to instil in him a distrust of militarism and a hatred of war. The boy himself shrank from violence and was easily moved to pity by the sight of misery. He had none of his father's attachment to the military ethos, but his head could be turned all too easily by parade-ground display. When he visited Berlin at the age of eleven his uncle, the King of Prussia, made him colonel of a regiment of uhlans, and he would not be parted from his fine new uniform. From earliest days Zhukovsky set his face against such vanities. There is a remarkable and courageous letter addressed from Dresden to the Empress in the summer of 1826. Zhukovsky had had to leave Russia to convalesce after an illness, and thus missed the fever and the splendours of the coronation ceremonies in Moscow. When, from a distance, he read about the part played in these festivities by the eight-year-old Alexander he was filled with dismay. The boy had appeared in uniform on horseback and been mobbed by ecstatic crowds. This was no way to bring up a child, and Zhukovsky, taking his life in his hands, decided to speak out:

Such an episode, Madame, is quite out of place in the beautiful poem on which we are working. I earnestly beg Your Majesty not to let it happen again for some time. Naturally the crowds were delighted to see that lovely child – but think of the impression it must have made on him . . . Is he not in danger of imagining himself a fully grown man? It is just as though an eight-year-old girl were to be taught all the arts of coquetry . . . Madame, forgive me . . . but an overdeveloped passion for the art of war – even if indulged in on the parade-ground – would cripple the soul and the mind. . . . He would end by seeing his people as an immense regiment and his country as a barracks. . . .[2]

The Tsaritsa knew very well that it was precisely in this light that Zhukovsky saw her own husband. But she kept her counsel and worked steadily and effectively to circumvent her husband's will.

It was only the passionate determination of the Tsaritsa, whom Nicholas still adored, who herself was divided from the world of Nicholas by a hopeless, if unacknowledged gulf, which kept Zhukovsky safe. For some of his teaching, if it had come to the Tsar's ears, would have been seen as nothing less than subversive. Here is an extract from a little homily on 'The Perfect Ruler' which Zhukovsky composed for the eleven-year-old Alexander:

Respect the law and let his example make others respect it; a law disregarded by the Tsar will not be kept by the people.

Love education and promote it; it is the finest and strongest support of all authority . . . An uneducated nation is a nation without dignity, and blind slaves can easily turn into savage rebels.

Let him have respect for his people's opinion . . . Let him love justice.

A sovereign's real strength lies in the well-being of his subjects and not in the numbers of his soldiers . . .[3]

It was not that Zhukovsky took refuge behind the petticoats of the

Tsaritsa. On her he depended. But when the occasion demanded he could and did stand up to Nicholas himself. In an earlier chapter we glimpsed him braving the Emperor's wrath on behalf of his Slavophile protégé, Kireyevsky. But he could speak up for himself and for others too – as when Nicholas sharply objected to his recommendation of a certain professor to teach geography and history to Alexander when he himself had to go abroad for a short time for his health. This was the historian Arseniev, who had been officially downgraded in the past for his outspoken criticism of corruption and serfdom. Nicholas insisted that he was a disloyal subject. But Zhukovsky replied:

'Sir, loyalty and flattery are not synonymous. There are countless grave defects in our juridical system, and none knows it better than Your Majesty. The Grand Duke is approaching an age when truth, however hard, should not be concealed from him.'[4]

It must have seemed to Nicholas at times that this gentle but disconcertingly plain-spoken tutor regarded it as part of his duty to educate the father as well as the son. It says something for the Tsar's fundamental honesty that he put up with this awkward but so transparently good man and sometimes gave in to him. It suggests that had there been others in and around the court to match Zhukovsky in courage as well as decency and speak their minds quietly but persistently, Nicholas might well have been changed in his courses.

2

Nicholas at least had the sense to realise that his heir should know something about the conditions in the country he would one day rule. He, Nicholas, had once travelled widely; his son must travel more widely still. And so it was that this strange man despatched the nineteen-year-old youth on a seven months' tour in the company not of one of his trusted favourites but of none other than Zhukovsky, about whose influence he had held deep reservations, and whose formal duties as tutor were now at an end. And the man chosen to plan the itinerary was that Professor Arseniev, the historian, whose appointment the Tsar had so bitterly resisted. With him, as A.D.C., went the young Count A. A. Kavelin, Alexander's exact contemporary. Nicholas's own contribution was to draw up a timetable in minute detail – as though Russian roads permitted precise timing! – prescribing who should be visited and what seen in every town.

The journey for Zhukovsky, now fifty-six and in poor health (the year was 1837), was purgatory. It was hurry, hurry, hurry all the way. 'Even in bed at night,' he wrote to the Tsaritsa, 'we feel as though we were still galloping.' But it was also rewarding. There was no time to enquire deeply into local conditions and the virtues and shortcomings of the men who ruled in the Emperor's name over the vast areas they travelled. But there was plenty of time for impressions. At every official halt the Tsarevich was almost swept off his feet by loyal demonstrations, hailed by a rejoicing people as the augury of a better future. Provincial governors laid on splendid banquets and conducted His Imperial Highness to view their prize exhibits – schools, fire-stations, factories, almshouses, prisons painted up and furbished for the occasion.

But they did not have things all their own way. Alexander was gratified by the warmth of his reception, but he was determined to see more. And he rejoiced Zhukovsky's heart and dismayed and exasperated the local officials by insisting on unscheduled stops, not once but many times, in godforsaken villages of whose existence they were barely conscious and whose inhabitants they regarded as something less than human. They were human to Alexander. While the officials exchanged despairing glances and railed at each other for mismanaging the tour, Alexander went into the wretched huts, chosen at random, and sat down on filthy stools in the dark and airless murk, seeing and feeling for himself the misery which encompassed so many millions of his loyal subjects. He received no words of complaint from them: none dared to speak. But he could see, and he could remember.

It went on like this, all over European Russia and finally over the Urals into Siberia: the first visit by any Romanov to Siberia. In the Urals he saw something of the barely touched mineral wealth which, properly exploited, could transform his future realm. He was dazzled by giant emeralds and loaded down with presents of Siberian gold and semi-precious stones. But he also insisted on visiting a number of convict settlements and watched the prisoners at work in chains. Many of them were murderers, he was told. Better they had been hanged than committed to a living death, he retorted. At Tobolsk he shocked officialdom by demanding to meet some of the exiled Decembrists and the wives who had followed them twelve years before. He was so shocked by the conditions under which some of them lived that he despatched a special courier back to his father in St Petersburg with an emotional letter begging him to grant them certain privileges and reliefs. Nicholas, whose hatred of the Decembrists was unabated, astonishingly agreed. His reply reached the Imperial party after they had left Siberia and were moving back up the valley of the Volga on the road from Simbirsk. 'Yesterday,' Zhukovsky wrote to the Empress, 'was one of the happiest days of my life. There on the road, under the open sky, His Imperial Highness, Kavelin and I embraced each other because of His Majesty's kindness in easing the bitter lot of those people at Tobolsk.'[5]

Nicholas conceded one other point. At Vyatka in the bleak north-eastern forest-land, Alexander encountered the young Alexander Herzen serving his term of exile in the shadow of the notoriously corrupt and sadistic governor, Tyufayev. Even before he reached Vyatka the Tsarevich had learnt of the Governor's reputation and when they met treated him so coolly that Tyufayev fell into confusion and the young Herzen was sent for to show the imperial party round. Afterwards Zhukovsky and Arseniev questioned Herzen closely and resolved to ask the Tsarevich to intercede for him. Alexander wrote to Nicholas, begging that this harmless and well-connected young man should be forgiven any indiscretions and allowed back to St Petersburg. Nicholas replied that this would not be fair to other exiles, but was prepared to allow him to settle in Vladimir, much closer to Moscow. At the same time the Tsarevich enquired more deeply into Tyufayev and had him dismissed. On such chances did the fate of Russians hang.[6]

The attitude of Nicholas towards Alexander is full of unexplained riddles. Here was his son and heir, already considered unsatisfactory from a military point of view, allowed to tour Russia with tutors whom the Emperor did not trust, and confirming his worst fears by begging mercy for his father's proved enemies. Instead of flying into a rage, Nicholas listened and, to a limited extent, gave way. Now, back in St Petersburg, it was time for the Tsarevich to see the outer world and also to seek a bride. And once again Zhukovsky was chosen to accompany him on his European tour. Already Alexander had infuriated his father by falling in love with a Polish girl and insisting that he wished to marry her, even if it meant giving up the throne. He had got over that, but Nicholas still had grave doubts about his mental and emotional stability – yet off he was sent to Germany with Zhukovsky and Kavelin. There, although he was told that he had complete freedom of choice, it was expected of him that he would in fact choose a Baden princess. He did nothing of the kind. Instead, after months of travel, interrupted to his father's further irrita-tion by illness and a consequent convalescent stay in Italy, he encountered by chance the fifteen-year-old Princess Marie of Hesse-Darmstadt, beauti-ful, highly intelligent, warm-hearted. Alexander was transported. Zhukov-sky was delighted. The news was sent happily off to St Petersburg. It came as a chilling shock when the courier came galloping back with the Tsar's reply. Such a marriage, Nicholas declared, was out of the question: the Tsarevich must break off his tour and come straight home.

It was now that Alexander showed his stubbornness. He went home dutifully enough and listened to his parents' arguments, but was unmoved. Under a cloud, he paid his delayed visit to London and danced with and charmed the young Queen Victoria. Back again in St Petersburg he faced his parents again, offered to renounce the throne if necessary, but would marry nobody else. Various reasons have been given for the Tsar's fury. The favourite scandal story is that Princess Marie was a bastard and Nicholas and Alexandra knew it. Another reason sometimes put forward is that the parents feared the existence of a congenital malformation which would make it impossible for the girl to have children: the first wife of the mad Emperor Paul had been a Hesse-Darmstadt, and she had died in childbirth after appalling suffering. Be that as it may, the opposition was real and almost violent: no Romanov might ever marry a Hesse-Darmstadt princess. But Alexander triumphed, and for a long time the influence of this warm-hearted and intelligent girl was to bring out the best in him and steady him in his enlightened views.

3

Alexander's marriage took place in 1840. Almost at once we find that Nicholas had put the long-drawn-out quarrel behind him, overcome his apprehensions as to his son's maturity, and started to go out of his way to bring him into the business of government. From now until the Emperor's death the Tsarevich was to act as his deputy during all his absences from St Petersburg. And in 1842 he was given a major appointment as chairman of the latest commission of enquiry into serfdom. Even more contradictory was Alexander's own conduct. Twenty-two years old, married to the girl he loved and who loved him, master of his own household in the Annichkov Palace in St Petersburg and the Alexander Palace at Tsarskoe Selo, he and his young bride built round them their own circle of friends, among whom all sorts of ideas were freely discussed, books read, music made. At the same time Alexander kept on the best of terms with his father's careerist, sycophantic favourites – the Adlerbergs, the Orlovs and the Shuvalovs – and appeared to accept absolutely the autocratic principle as pushed to its logical extreme of regimentation. There is no making the two sides meet: throughout his whole life Alexander was to push in his conduct a chronic dissociation of ideas to inexplicable extremes. There was no evident centre to his mind, no point of junction where opposed ideas met and fused and modified each other. Reaction and liberalism existed side by side, running as it were on parallel lines that never touched; sensibility with callousness; gentleness with harshness; enlightenment with obscurantism.

This had come out, as we have seen, already in childhood. Now, in the hopeless tangle over the problem of serfdom, it was more sharply manifest. Alexander had seen the state of the peasants at first hand. When his father instructed him to take his place on one of the secret committees of enquiry he found himself one of a small group of men of widely differing views. There was Count Orlov and his supporters, whose opposition to emancipation was determined and loud. On the other side there was Count Kiselev, now approaching sixty. He had devoted his whole life to the thankless cause of liberation, starting as a young man under Alexander I, for whom he wrote an outspoken and prophetic memorandum, continuing under Nicholas as Minister for the State Peasants, whose lot he worked hard and successfully to ameliorate. Kiselev stood for everything that Zhukovsky stood for. He was prepared to work until he dropped, again and again accepting the burdens of intensive committee work while knowing in his heart that the Tsar did not mean business. Alexander, knowing what he knew from his own travels, feeling as he did about the sufferings of the underdog, would surely have cleaved loyally to this splendid man. But not a bit of it. Time and again he showed himself a defender of the privileges of the landlords. It was not as though he had been allowed to forget what he had seen on his travels in European Russia. Among the documents in front of the committee was a report by one of his most able officials, Zablotsky-Desyatovsky, on the condition of the serfs in 1841. This account of the lives of peasant serfs and the callous attitude of the average landlord was so hair-raising that even Kiselev felt unable to show it to the Tsar, who could never have faced the truth he had asked the committee to uncover. But Alexander saw it, and recognised the truth because he himself had penetrated into those decayed and stinking huts.

The report was a powerful indictment.[7] Some Western historians maintain to this day that the serfs of Russia, with unhappy exceptions, were materially better off than free peasants and labourers elsewhere in Europe, including England. Certainly it should be remembered that Desyatovsky and his companions were reporting at the time of the 'hungry forties' and the Irish famine. Only ten years earlier Cobbett in England had collected together and published as a book his *Rural Rides*, with their dramatisation of the miseries of English agricultural labourers during the post-Napoleonic depression. There were to be further depressions to come. And in France the new post-revolutionary class of peasant proprietors was finding life very hard indeed. Certainly in Russia peasant serfs lucky enough to live on the estates of benevolent or progressive landlords were cushioned against destitution to a degree which many English labourers would have envied. But these were far from typical, and it is impossible to read Desyatovsky's report and still believe that the peasant serfs as a whole were favoured compared with their peers in other lands. Too often the landowners left the management of their estates to unjust stewards concerned only with extracting the last kopek for their masters, or to line their own pockets. Then the peasants were treated like animals.

'Their huts are built of aspen or birch, and sometimes the material is so rotten that they decay within five or six years.' When this happened there were no materials for proper repairs, which usually had to be no more than a patching up with dung and straw and clay. 'We saw hardly a single hut with a sound roof. Straw is usually needed for fuel and fodder, so that it cannot be spared for roofing.'

There were no chimneys in the huts. Smoke was let out of the open door regardless of the cold – though, of course, once the Russian stove was drawing it was virtually smokeless. There was nothing to eat but cabbage, onions, turnips and rye-bread; fish, if there was a river close by; meat not more than 'once or twice a year'. Salt was an expensive luxury.

No such thing as parish relief existed, nor any sort of poor law, however harsh. If the landowner did not feed his own serfs in bad years they were not fed at all.

'If the harvest fails they starve. In the Government of Tula in 1840 they kept themselves alive on bog-grass, acorns, straw and the bark of trees. In bad years they die like flies.'

This sort of Irish existence was permanent. In England there was heavy infant mortality and there were occasional deaths from malnutrition. Poverty could be grinding in bad periods, hunger acute. But, as a rule, the wretched labourers were not left to starve to death. In Russia they were. Of course, conditions varied: in the forested north the peasant huts were solider and warmer – but there was less to eat; in the south life was easier except in years (all too frequent) of summer drought, when all crops were burnt up. The Desyatovsky report was concerned mainly with central European Russia, the prosperous districts of Tula and Orel, Tolstoy and Turgenev country. And what made the lot of the Russian peasant exceptionally harsh was the climate. To cope with those extremes of cold and heat men and women need more to eat and sounder shelter than the peasants of more temperate lands. Cooped up in the gloom for months on end in winter, cut off from neighbours by mud and floods in spring and autumn, frantically overworked in the searing heat of the short summers, the lives of millions of Russians were lowering in the extreme. They sought escape in drink. Cheap and nasty spirits induced first forgetfulness, then oblivion, on every possible occasion.

How to reconcile this picture with the comfortable and cosy image of cluttered, rambling manor-houses where the serfs were treated as part of the family. Which is right? Both are right. There were plenty of land-owners who behaved abominably towards their house-serfs (Turgenev's terrible mother, for example, was still alive in 1841 and treating her servants with spectacular cruelty), but many more were regarded as part of the family. And if there was a difference between the trusted and beloved familiars of the type of Pushkin's nurses on the one hand and the uncouth houseboys on the other, well, that was reasonable. The fact that they usually had to sleep on door-mats, in cupboards, or under the table, was neither here nor there: they were warm, and Russians were (and still are) accustomed to sleeping in odd places. As for physical violence, this was the accepted thing: even Tolstoy as a young man was not above striking a servant in anger. But one may also see in Tolstoy (compare the lyrical passages about country life in *Childhood* and the vignettes of the peasant serfs in *A Landlord's Morning*) a failure to recognise the peasants, nameless in their hovels, as fully human. He might sleep with individual peasant girls, but as a class he gave them up as a bad job: the only hope, he saw, lay in getting hold of their children very young and opening their minds to better things. The parents of those children were the impenetrable creatures who had laughed at his offer of conditional freedom. Or, in the words of Desyatovsky's report: 'A peasant – always facing compulsion, desperate in his worries, on the edge of destitution – relies on cunning and deceit to see him through life's difficulties. He cheats systematically, and he teaches his children to cheat. To steal his master's property is right and natural in his eyes.'

Tolstoy saw this at Yasnaya Polyana when young. But it took him many years to reach the depth of understanding shown by these patiently investigating officials in the reign of Nicholas I. Desyatovsky saw how, embattled against the landowners with no trick too low to play on them, they were nevertheless endlessly kind to each other, the half-starving ever ready to help the starving with his last crust. And he saw as clearly as a Belinsky the absurdity of the claims that the Russian peasant possessed an innate spirituality which raised him above all others and was some-how nourished by his destitution. 'They have no religious knowledge ... They learn how and when to cross themselves but they have no idea why they do it. Without any education, they grow up like savages . . . Their understanding has twisted the teaching of Our Lord into an absurd myth-ology . . . A peasant will call God to witness while telling the most monstrous lie. The priests have next to no influence. Ignorant and rough themselves, they are despised by landowner and peasant alike.'

The committee which Zablotsky-Desyatovsky served was abortive, as were all Nicholas's committees on the serf problem. But the Tsarevich had learnt a great deal; and although he made no serious attempt to set himself up against the landowners, and indeed gave them the impression that he was on their side, he had seen enough to know that radical action could not be postponed much longer. And when to his insights into the degradation of untold millions of his future subjects was added the bleak exposure in the Crimean War of the deficiencies of the administration and the army, the writing on the wall showed large and clear. The most shameful thing was that the epic of Sevastopol had been sustained not by the ruling caste, but in spite of it, by peasant soldiers reared in those stinking huts and now ready to fight to the death because in the corporate loyalty of army life they had found a cause which carried them outside themselves and turned them into men, with, as their symbol, an imperial crown, divine and infinitely remote.

4

Before anything could be done in the way of major reform the war in the Crimea had to be ended. The new Tsar when he was sworn in in March 1855 was intent on victory: Sevastopol must be held and the enemy driven into the sea. Seven months passed before that dream faded, and it was not until February of the following year that the peace conference opened in Paris. But even in the shadow of the war the new reign opened with a blaze of hope. The censorship was eased at once, foreign travel was once more permitted, with the raising of countless restrictions life flowed back into the universities which had been dead since 1848. The intelligentsia of every colour, furious radicals and mild liberals, progressive Westernisers and conservative Slavophiles, for a time forgot their differences and united to hail the new dawn – and of course the new Tsar who alone could conjure the miracle of sunrise.

The peace conference, which ended with the signing of the Treaty of Paris on 30 March 1856, was a tidying-up operation. The effect of Russia's defeat was to neutralise the Eastern Question and reduce for the time being the fears inspired by the sheer size of her army. Russia could now be seen simply as one power among others, no longer overwhelming in her might; and so she was to remain for close on a hundred years.

The main upshot of the Treaty of Paris was that Alexander had to agree to the neutralisation of the Black Sea, which meant that neither Russia nor Turkey could keep warships there; to the final independence of the Principalities, which were soon to be joined in a single state, Roumania; to the loss (ultimately to Roumania) of southern Bessarabia. She was, that is to say, excluded from the Danube delta. It was the Black Sea arrangement which told most heavily on Alexander; to be forbidden to keep a naval force to protect Odessa and the Black Sea coast was a humiliation. The fact that Turkey could not keep her fleet in the Black Sea either did not affect the issue; for the Turks could maintain as many ships as they liked in the Aegean and bring them swiftly through the Straits in time of war. It was an arrangement that could not last, and Alexander was determined one day to put an end to it. He was ready to wait, however, until he had reformed his social system, his administration, and his army. What did endure was Russian distrust and hatred of Austria.

There was never again to be so much as a gleam of the old friendship between the two great monarchies, and for a long time to come Prussia, Bismarck's Prussia, was the main beneficiary of Russian goodwill at the expense first of Austria, then later, in 1870, of France. Thus it was thanks largely to his understanding with Russia that Bismarck was able to construct the unified Reich which was later to destroy her.

CHAPTER TEN

Revolution from Above

I

It was on 30 March 1856, as the peace was being concluded in Paris, that Alexander in Moscow called together the marshals of the nobility and addressed them in terms which marked the beginning of a new epoch. 'It is better,' he declared in the now celebrated phrase, 'to abolish serfdom from above than to wait until the serfs begin to liberate themselves from below.' He went on to explain carefully that he had no intention of taking precipitate action: there was no question of immediate abolition; the goal was indeed emancipation, but it must be achieved in easy stages. He asked his nobles to bend their own minds to the problem and to set up small committees among the landowners of their own districts to consider ways and means of reaching the desired end and to report on their findings.

Everybody listened respectfully and went home – and nothing happened. The landowners had not the least intention of devising the machinery for their own undoing. When pressed by the mild and liberal Count Lanskoy, a convinced abolitionist, a veteran of the days of Alexander I, and now, at sixty-eight, Minister of the Interior, they replied, boot-faced, that they had received no guidance from the Government and that it was not for them to take the initiative in suggesting general principles of policy. This display of passive resistance was the start of a long and bitter struggle between the abolitionists and their opponents.

On the face of it there was nothing new in the expressed determination of the monarch at the outset of his reign to do away with serfdom. From the accession of Catherine the Great almost a hundred years earlier, successive autocrats had one after another insisted that serfdom must go. Even Alexander's striking phrase about abolishing serfdom from above was borrowed from a memorandum prepared by one of his father's special committees of the 1840s. So it might seem that the landowners had some excuse for ignoring their monarch's appeal and believing that if they did nothing the matter would soon be forgotten and overlaid in the press of more urgent business.

But there was a difference. Now no business was more urgent. The more intelligent landowners and officials all over the land knew very well that the bankruptcy of the system had been humiliatingly exposed by the war that had just ended. And when even a Gorchakov could declare that serfdom was 'the root of all evil in Russia' it meant that change was in the air. There was also a new awareness of the inhumanity of the serf system, as well as its inefficiency. More and more individuals were beginning to see the peasants as human beings instead of as a species of cattle. Many had been unhappily aware of the squalor and degradation which crippled the lives of millions of their fellow-countrymen; now, in increasing numbers, they began to understand, perhaps sometimes to exaggerate, the potential splendour of the human qualities crushed almost out of existence by the burden of poverty and fear. This understanding had been quickened to quite an astonishing degree by the publication of Turgenev's *A Sportsman's Sketches*, in which peasant serfs were shown in their daily lives as complete human beings, with all the qualities, good and bad alike, of human beings everywhere and in every walk of life. Alexander himself was reported to have been deeply affected by these portraits offered not as propaganda but simply as a reflection of reality. He had seen some of the squalor and degradation on his grand tour of Russia; perhaps it took an artist of genius to illuminate for him the unquenchable humanity which somehow managed to survive that degradation. Quite evidently the mood of the country was changing. Very soon there were to be troubled landowners coming forward to declare that it was not only the peasants who were degraded by slavery but also they themselves, the slave-owners.

The majority of landowners had never heard of Turgenev. But even the backwoodsmen sensed impending change. There was no public discussion of emancipation, but plenty of private talk giving rise to all sorts of rumours. The whole countryside was full of rumour, and rumour had wings. Something was in fact brewing, and the peasants knew it; and by their response they made still more imperative the need for action. By the summer of 1856 rumour had crystallised out into a single almost universal conviction: that the new Tsar intended to give the serfs their freedom and their land when he went to Moscow to be crowned in the following year. A corollary of this was that the landowners would naturally do their level best to thwart the Tsar.

It was not only the dyed-in-the-wool reactionaries who were alarmed by this new and more purposeful wave of peasant unrest. Many comparatively enlightened men who were prepared to concede personal freedom to their serfs saw only ruin, not only for themselves but also for the country as a whole, if the peasants were given land as well as freedom. Such profound misgivings are conveyed most vividly in a letter addressed to the reform-minded Minister, Count Bludov, by, of all people, the novelist Leo Tolstoy, then twenty-eight and with sainthood still a very long way off. In a characteristic burst of enthusiasm he had decided to be in the van of liberation and worked out a scheme to free his own serfs at Yasnaya Polyana: in brief, they were to pay him rent for thirty years and then the land would be theirs. The young Tolstoy was shaken by the depth of the cynicism and the impenetrability of the suspicion with which his proposals were received – and rejected. It took him a little time to discover that one and all were convinced that within a very few months the Tsar would grant them their freedom and their land outright; that the young master knew this as well as they did; that therefore he was trying to cheat them by getting them to pay rent for land which would soon be theirs for nothing.

'Their obstinacy put me into such a rage that I could hardly control myself,' Tolstoy wrote in his diary.[1] He had come to hate those servile faces – some lumpish, some twisted like gargoyles, some with the fine broad features and blankly noble look of the storybook Russian peasant with his splendid beard and long, straight, centre-parted hair; some the fathers of girls he had enjoyed; but all sly, suspicious, covetous, cynically hostile, corrupted by centuries of servitude. Many years were to pass before Tolstoy started to proclaim the Russian peasant as the repository of all wisdom, goodness, spirituality. Now he was convinced that he was dangerous. So in his almost panic-stricken letter to Bludov, with whom he was acquainted, he imparted to him with the air of a discoverer information about the peasant mood which was no news at all ('When at one of my meetings they told me to give them all the land and I answered that then I should have to go barefoot, they simply laughed at me'), blamed the Government for not making its position clear, and above all insisted that he saw no sense in giving the peasants land as well as freedom. The important thing was personal freedom. And that must come quickly. 'Time is short . . . If the serfs are not free in six months, we are in for a holocaust. Everything is ripe for it. Only one criminal hand is needed to fan the flames of rebellion, and we shall all be consumed in the blaze.'[2]

It took five years, not six months, to achieve the liberation. The holocaust held off for another sixty years.

2

It is arguable that the manner of the liberation, when it came, was a major cause of that final holocaust. But it is hard to see how Alexander could have done much more. What happened, when the principle of granting land to the peasants with their personal freedom was finally accepted and the details worked out, was that too many peasants had too little land to live on, while the excessive redemption dues they had to pay drove many of them into hopeless debt. On the other side, the compensation received by the landowners was not enough; and very few of these, even when they so desired, could afford the capital investment needed to exploit and develop what remained of their estates.

'Too little and too late' – far from explaining anything, this favourite phrase of frustrated reformers is a mindless parrot-cry. Since perfection in human institutions is unattainable it follows that every attempted reform will either be too little or too much, too soon or too late – if not a combination of all four. It is possible to argue very cogently that the Emancipation Act of 1861, far from being too little and too late, was in fact too much, too soon – though not for the reasons advanced by the most active opponents of the reform. To close the mind to this possibility is to show inadequate comprehension of the sheer magnitude of the reform. It was a revolution.

On the eve of the Emancipation there were more than 48 million serfs, half of them privately owned, the other half state peasants. With their families they amounted to four-fifths of the total population. The peasant serfs with few exceptions were not only illiterate but also the most incompetent and backward agriculturalists in Europe, deprived of self-respect by centuries of oppression. They were managed, again with few exceptions, by stewards and overseers who were above all concerned with providing immediate cash with the least possible outlay for their masters as well as rich pickings for themselves. The smaller landowners who worked their own estates were often almost as illiterate as their own peasants. Productivity was wretchedly low and the estates were grossly overmanned. The peasant serfs lived in their huts in their own villages looking for leadership not to the master but to their own elders. As already observed, they regarded their masters less as the natural heads of a patriarchal community centred on the manor-house than as alien trespassers, invaders to whom they must pay tribute, invaders backed by the apparatus of colonial rule – the police and the bureaucracy. Only the house-serfs, the domestics, as a rule felt any sense of involvement with the master's family. For the villagers their only father was the Tsar himself, remote, ineffable, unconscious of their plight, cut off from them by detested and despised officials.

It is hard to imagine the scale of the upheaval involved in the liberation of a nation of slaves from one day to the next. With the best will in the world this whole complex of traditional existence could not be changed overnight simply by changing the status of the peasants, who had to go on living in the same huts in the same villages, in the same rigid social groups or communes, cohering round the same elders; in the shadow of the same masters; at the mercy of the same tax-collectors, bureaucrats, police. The same numbers were living off less than the same amount of land, cultivating it by the same primitive methods: the only differences lay in a partial redistribution of the land and the severing of traditional bonds of mutual responsibility between gentry and peasant. The sense of disorientation was acute, and it showed itself as often as not in the refusal of the liberated serfs to pay the redemption dues on the land they regarded as their own.

And this was only one side of the picture. The other showed hundreds of thousands of landowners, great and small, required to surrender their slaves with no compensation at all and at least a third of their land with compensation that was inadequate. The wonder is not that it took the reformers five years of often bitter struggle to force the Emancipation through, but that they succeeded in the end, and without creating a vast landless class of labourers. And it is indeed arguable that with the tide of feeling against serfdom as a national disgrace slowly rising, Alexander would have been wiser to rely on the growth of humanitarianism and the pressures of economic development to do his work for him. He could perhaps have offered material inducements and incentives to encourage voluntary liberation (already becoming more frequent) on the widest possible front; again, he could have drastically curtailed the serf-owner's rights over his slaves and compelled him to allow all who wished to buy their freedom to do so on favourable terms. Would the serfs in fact have risen in nation-wide revolt had Alexander gone about his task more slowly and selectively? It is impossible to tell. He did not try. Nor did it even occur to him to address the people as a whole, explaining his intentions, indicating the difficulties, proclaiming a happier future, but appealing for co-operation in a mighty task. He spoke only to his nobles.

The opponents of emancipation did not help to clarify the situation. There was no serious debate on the social and economic advantages and disadvantages of gradualism as opposed to instant action. This was because the opposition was moved by selfishness or fear, using passive resistance at first, then deliberate obstructionist tactics in committee, in blank opposition to the Emperor's will. At first the conservatives stood against the very idea of emancipation in any shape or form; forced from this position they fell back on furious rejection of the proposal to give the peasants land; forced from this position they were finally reduced to fighting every inch of the way to secure the best deal for themselves and the worst for their peasants. At no stage was the debate carried up to a high level; at no stage, that is to say, were the leading abolitionists, moved as they were by the highest motives, forced by their opponents to think through the possible consequences of a sudden liberation and to consider ways and means of meeting such consequences. All their energies and their minds were concentrated on the immediate and very strenuous task of defeating the opposition and securing emancipation as an end in itself. One of the more regrettable consequences of this over-simplification of the issue was that the moderate landowners of goodwill were squeezed between the extremists, their voices never heard.

What worried Alexander above all was not how to achieve a just settlement of the peasants (he was determined in principle that they should be given land with their freedom), but how to overcome the resistance of the nobility without alienating them from the Crown, how to take land from them without causing their ruin.

How could it have been otherwise? The nobility were his servants and he was their protector. He might inveigh against them for making his life difficult; but theirs was the language he spoke and understood. He has been criticised for calling in aid the very men who were most determinedly opposed to abolition in any shape or form. And indeed, when he set up his formal secret committee which met for the first time in January 1857 it might have seemed that he was weighing the scales against himself. The Tsar was nominal chairman, but his deputy and effective chairman was none other than Prince Orlov, now seventy-one, Nicholas's favoured confidant and Benckendorff's successor as head of the Third Section, and now, as President of the Council of State, the very image of the old regime firmly presiding over the councils of the new. The other most powerful members of the committee were also convinced reactionaries: the Princes Dolgoruky and Gagarin; the Minister of Justice, Panin; the somewhat sinister figure of Count M. N. Muraviev, whose cousin, Sergei Muraviev-Apostol, had been hanged as a Decembrist, who himself had been a peripheral Decembrist and survived. He had a sense of humour: 'I am one of the hanging Muravievs,' he used to boast, 'not one of the ones who get hanged.' So he was to outrage opinion with his atrocities against the Lithuanians after the failure of the second Polish rebellion in 1858.

To set against these formidable representatives of the old order were the elderly Count Lanskoy and General Rostovtsev, a very senior soldier who was regarded by some with suspicion because of the part he had played as a subaltern officer in warning Nicholas of the plans of his friends, the Decembrists (in fact he had behaved quite honourably, informing the conspirators of his intentions in advance). Rostovtsev was to work himself to death in the struggle to come. Together with one of Lanskoy's senior officials in the Ministry of the Interior, Nicholas Milyutin, he was to be the main architect of the Emancipation Act.

What could this little group of reformers hope to achieve in face of Orlov and his friends? If Alexander really wanted them to succeed, why did he not strengthen their hand? But in fact he did, in his oblique and opaque manner. At critical moments, again and again when the day seemed lost, the Tsar intervened.

It is not hard to imagine his state of mind, or indeed to sympathise with it. His mind told him that this great act must be done, and his heart moved with his mind when he contemplated the misery in which so many of his subjects lived. But in quite another sense his heart was not at all in step with his mind; all his instincts favoured courses offering the least possible disturbance to the *status quo*. He was sufficiently Russian, however, in spite of his almost wholly German ancestry, to think in terms of absolutes and extremes: he did not want to move, but since move he must he would make a virtue of it and go all the way. Caught up in this sort of confusion it was surely the most natural thing in the world for him to conscript into his committee precisely the men who most stoutly opposed its purpose. For in this way he at least postponed direct collision with the opposition. He would manoeuvre the great landowners into producing a blueprint for their own despoliation if he could; if he could not, he would at least involve them in reluctant acceptance of plans put forward by the reformers; if they stuck he would himself intervene, and be seen to intervene, but to limited effect, and by degrees, so that it would be hard for the opposition to rally itself for a decisive battle: Orlov and his friends would thus be forced on to the defensive and made to retreat by inches.

This, at least, is what happened. At no stage did Alexander indicate that he had lost heart: he applied the spur when it seemed necessary. On the other hand, at no stage did he throw himself into the struggle with any show of enthusiasm: the Emancipation had to be, he knew, but he did not like it. And he was very much the autocrat, watching from on high the opposing parties playing out their roles.

If he opened his mind at all it was only to his younger brother Constantine and his uncle Michael's widow, the Grand Duchess Helen. Constantine, an impassioned abolitionist (he was also, as Lord High Admiral, a very active naval reformer in his own right), he threw into the fight when the opposition was being especially obstructive. As for the

Grand Duchess Helen, it was in her drawing-room that the reformers met to restore their flagging spirits. And it was she who at last succeeded in bringing together Alexander and Nicholas Milyutin, whom he had never met and felt he could not afford to meet officially, even though he was Kiselev's nephew, Lanskoy's protégé, and Rostovtsev's right hand. But he could never bring himself to acknowledge the importance of Milyutin's contribution. When the struggle was over and the Emancipation Act had become law, one of his first actions was to throw to the wolves this man to whom he owed so much. He was sorry to do so, he said, but 'I must, because the nobility insist that you are one of the reds'.

He could be equally dismissive of the high nobility. When in the winter of 1860 Rostovtsev, worn out by his endeavours and by the unending intrigues against him, accompanied by a vicious whispering campaign of slander, fell ill and died with the final goal in sight, Alexander shocked and dismayed the reformers by appointing in his place, as President of the final Editing Commission, Rostovtsev's arch-opponent Panin. The Grand Duchess Helen was especially outraged. It had been Panin who had once publicly exclaimed that whoever had first put the idea of Emancipation into the Emperor's head deserved to be hanged, and he had kept up his opposition ever after. But to Helen Alexander said: 'You really don't know Panin. His principles consist in obeying my orders.'

Why then, it may be asked, had the Emperor allowed this man to lead the pack that hounded Rostovtsev to his death? We glimpse again the element of despotic fatuity which was so marked in Nicholas.

3

Alexander, in a word, was himself a despot in his soul. There were moments during the abolition struggle when a prophet might have declared that the Tsar had advanced too far along the path of co-operation with his people, or at least the well-born among them, ever to draw back. Many did believe just this, including Alexander Herzen, conducting his campaign against the autocracy far away in London. But this was an illusion. The autocrat in Alexander never slept. Unlike his father, he saw the necessity, or at least the desirability, of broadening the base of government, if only to put an end to the intolerable waste of talent and to modernise the economy. But government, as he saw it, was essentially the machine for executing the monarch's will: as soon as any of his subjects, no matter how exalted, started to question or to show any signs of developing ideas of their own, he put them sharply in their place.

The first moment of apparent release occurred in the winter of 1857-8, when for the first time a Tsar threw open a political issue to public debate. The nobility of Lithuania, responding at last to Alexander's appeal for suggestions, presented with due ceremony a plan for granting freedom without land. Alexander decided that it was time he made it clear once and for all that there was to be no liberation without land. In this sense he issued his celebrated rescript addressed to the Governor-General of Lithuania, General Nazimov, outlining his intention. A rescript was traditionally a private instruction from the Tsar to its recipient, but Alexander took everyone by surprise, first by circulating this rescript to other governors for guidance, then by publishing it for all the world to read. In this queer indirect manner he confided to his people for the first time what was in his mind. He meant business, he was saying in effect, and there could be no drawing back. He was publicly committed to the abolitionist cause. The opposition was thrown into confusion. But the intelligentsia went off their heads with delight. Even that dedicated foe of the régime, Chernyshevsky, so far forgot his hatred of the autocracy as to compare Alexander with Peter the Great. In London, Herzen brought out his celebrated article in *The Bell* which began and ended 'Thou hast conquered, O Galilean!'[3] The powerful editor and publicist, Michael Katkov, who was later to achieve distinction as an ardent supporter of reaction, led the cheers in his *Moskovsky Vedmosti* (*Moscow Gazette*).

This euphoria did not last long. It was on 20 January that the secret committee was transformed into the 'Main Committee on the Peasant Question', no longer secret, but the centre of the liveliest public discussion. But within four months Alexander had had enough of free comment in the Press. It was no doubt gratifying to be hailed as the supreme benefactor; but was it not also a little demeaning? Perhaps Nicholas had been right when he forbade public expressions of approval no less than public criticism on the ground that both were impertinent... Press comment, further, was getting out of hand. Be that as it may, the Main Committee issued a directive informing all editors that future discussion of the peasant question must be strictly confined to the outline of the official line.

Thus ended, after four months, the first Russian exercise in the free expression of opinion. This brief interlude, or thaw, the relaxation of rigid controls soon to be reversed, set a pattern which was to be repeated at intervals of varying length up to our own day. Most interesting and significant of all was the prohibition of public discussion outside the official terms of reference – outside, as we should say today, the party line. It was this reversal which was the cause of exaggerated disillusionment in Chernyshevsky and his fellow radicals. But within a year the same principle was being invoked with equal force against the conservatives, and it is ironical that the weapon which in years and decades to come was to be turned against reformers of every kind was in fact forged by Alexander and his ministerial supporters in the course of the first great struggle for reform. For when in the early autumn of 1859 the deputies from the provinces were called to St Petersburg to participate in what should have been the final stages of the great reform many of them not unnaturally sought to raise questions of principle. All were told unequivocally, not once but repeatedly, that they must know their place. It was not for them to question. Certainly their opinions were needed, but only when the Committee asked for them. Questions would be submitted and they would give their answers in writing. They could meet unofficially among themselves, not to discuss the general principles of emancipation, which were laid down for them in advance, but only as to how best to apply these principles to their own local conditions.

The deputies did not take this emasculation lying down. Their protests were loud and vehement. The opponents of reform were particularly noisy in declaring that the Committee itself was twisting the intentions of the Emperor (this was the harassing campaign that finally broke the health of poor Rostovtsev, who had to bear the brunt of it). There was even an appeal for the Tsar to set up an elective national assembly under his own presidency to work out and agree on the final measures to be taken. Nothing could have been better guaranteed to rouse the autocrat in Alexander. In the margin of one of the petitions he commented that it was becoming obvious that the petitioners and those who thought like them wished 'to establish in our country an oligarchic form of government.'[4] No elaboration was needed: this was the supreme offence against the autocracy. All those who had put forward petitions of any kind, whether conservative or liberal, were formally reprimanded. The deputies went home. The bureaucrats took over.

The point here is that had the voices of the majority in the provincial committees been allowed their full weight the abolitionists would have been routed. Any conceivable elective assembly would have come down heavily against any workable form of emancipation. The Emperor, in a word, was moving farther and faster than even the best intentioned landowners. And the sad paradox was that the embattled abolitionists, reformers to a man, the spearhead of what in any other land would have been a liberal party working for the amelioration of autocratic rule, were themselves in this way forced, whether they realised it or not, to support the autocratic principle in its full rigour. The drive to weaken the central bureaucracy, and with it the autocracy itself, came from the conservatives. The Tsar and the Tsar alone by the exercise of autocratic power could overcome reaction and lift the country into a new age.

No wonder Alexander was sometimes tired. No wonder, too, that the radicals among the intelligentsia grew desperate when faced with the formula which ran in effect: *autocracy is the root of all evil, but without autocracy there can be no reform.* How to break out of this dilemma? At first to the few, then to increasing numbers, there appeared to be only one answer: revolution.

4

Very few indeed were thinking of revolution in the spring of 1861 when the Emancipation Act became law. After so many years the actual liberation of the serfs came with a sense of anti-climax. So much had been expected, so much feared. The great drama had worked itself out, the great change been effected. Nobody was satisfied.

In the first place house-serfs had to wait two years before they were free. The peasants were saddled with redemption dues, set too high, for another fifty years to come; and the land on which these dues were to be paid was insufficient to sustain them and would diminish for each mouth as numbers grew. On top of his redemption dues, the peasant was still liable for the poll-tax, the idea behind this being that since the actual wealth of the country lay in the soil, those who worked the soil and were thus able to feed themselves should pay for the maintenance of the apparatus to which they owed their land and their security – the whole paraphernalia of the state, that is: bureaucracy, army, industrial development.

As for the landowners, they lost their serfs and a great part of their lands. Many of them, their serfs and lands already heavily mortgaged, were hard hit. Most found the compensation received from the state very far from adequate. Members of a traditionally improvident class of an improvident people, many spent what they had and then faced ruin. Others, the brighter ones, sold up and enrolled in the ranks of the enlarged bureaucracy or the new professions called into being by the post-Emancipation reforms. A very few of the most wealthy applied themselves to the introduction of modern farming methods with hired labour on their vast estates.

The entire operation was of a nature inconceivable in a society like our own in which constant change is accepted as inevitable and natural even by those who deplore it and no matter how regrettable for some – a society which, apart from occasionally violent upheavals when revolution from below is invited by a too rigid assertion of authority, has managed to transform itself by a more or less continuous process of organic growth. It was not simply that the Emancipation could not have been carried out as it was, peacefully, in any society other than an autocracy. It could not have been carried out in any society which set a high value on the rights of the individual or was seized with a conviction of the sacredness of private property.

Even so, the wonder is that there was not more violence. Of course there was some. But there was no suggestion of any move on the part of the nobility to depose the Tsar; nor was there any coherent peasant revolt. Peasants in scattered villages did indeed attack their landlords and burn their houses down. The conviction was widespread that the provisions of the Emancipation Act represented only a first instalment of a far more radical process – or, alternatively, that local landowners and officials had villainously suppressed the real act and substituted a fraudulent one. But violence on any organised scale was astonishingly rare. By far the most notorious case was the sad affair at Bezdna, on the estate of Count Musin Pushkin in the Government of Kazan. Here it was the troops who did the killing in the name of order. The Bezdna massacre offers a close-up view both of the mentality of the Russian peasant of the central plain a century ago – and also of the forces of law and order.

A young peasant serf called Petrov, who had learned to read, was readily accepted as a natural leader by his illiterate companions and elders. Nobody knows what he hoped to achieve, perhaps no more than a brief shiver of glory. Or perhaps he was out of his mind. But what he did was to invent a fantasy far-fetched even by the standards of contemporary rumour. He could assure his neighbours that all they believed about the betrayal of the Tsar's wishes by officials and landowners was indeed the truth. He, Petrov, had himself been in secret communication with the Tsar, who was preparing to strike back at those who had defrauded the people by presenting as the Act of Emancipation a document that was nothing but a forgery. At that very moment a special messenger from the Tsar was on his way to Bezdna bearing the Tsar's own manifesto written in his own hand for him, Petrov, to read out and publish to the multitude. But until the messenger arrived and handed over the precious document he, Petrov, stood in need of protection: evil men were plotting against his life. So he called on all the peasants from far and wide to gather round him and stand between him and the enemies of the Tsar.

Some five thousand responded to the call. They crowded the village and camped on the outskirts waiting for the messenger to come. But instead of the messenger came troops: Petrov was to be seized and taken away for spreading subversive rumours. The troops found themselves face to face with a solid phalanx of peasants barring access to Petrov's hut – unarmed except for staves and pitchforks, but in a mood of euphoric exaltation. It could not have lasted long. But instead of holding back his troops and leaving the peasants to cool off until they drifted home, as they soon inevitably would have done, to get food and look after their animals and crops, the commanding officer decided to force the issue. He gave the order to fire into the crowd ... By the time it was all over there were at least fifty dead and nearly twice as many wounded. And all over Russia the radical intelligentsia when they heard the news were convinced that nothing had changed: the Emancipation was indeed a fraud and a false dawn, and to co-operate with authority was betrayal.

This did not mean that there was a sudden upsurge of revolutionary activity. Nothing like that happened. There was a courageous demonstration at Kazan University, followed by disturbances at other centres. At the same time (the autumn of 1861) a number of very small groups started producing leaflets and broadsheets advocating revolution by violence. The first attempt at the creation of an active political party was the establishment in December 1861 of the secret organisation 'Land and Liberty' (*Zemlya i volya*) by an idealist in his twenties, N. A. Serno-Solovevich. None of these enterprises lasted very long, but all were forerunners pointing the way to an angry future. In May 1862 an epidemic of serious fires broke out in St Petersburg. Nobody knows to this day what lay behind them. But at the time it was easy enough for the word to go round that the radical students had turned incendiaries. And in this emotional climate the authorities decided to act firmly and decisively. Chernyshevsky, Serno-Solovevich and many others were arrested and sent away, while many students who were not revolutionary-minded at all were given a taste of life in the cells of the fortress of St Peter and St Paul. Alexander was out of the country at the time, and it has to be recorded in his favour that on his return he decided that reaction had gone too far and dismissed Admiral Putyatin, who had been ruling the students with the heaviest of hands from the Ministry of Education. But the damage had been done. The first of a new generation of revolutionary martyrs now sat in prison or in Siberia.

CHAPTER ELEVEN

Limits of Tolerance and Vision

I

THE conventional view of Alexander II is of a reforming monarch who drew back appalled by the radical and revolutionary forces he had unloosed and fell back into reaction. But the real pattern was far more complex. It may be questioned, indeed, if there was a pattern at all: the more one contemplates the twenty years between the Emancipation and the Tsar Liberator's death, the harder it is to trace a coherent line of development. Even during the great reforming years when every scrap of energy and talent was needed for the colossal task of dragging Russia into the nineteenth century Alexander squandered much of his substance on the drive to enlarge the frontiers of a realm crammed with unexploited riches and already too vast to be managed, while at the very end of his reign, after several attempts on his life, he was still capable of authorising a programme of reform. During all his twenty-five years as Tsar he was to display that inconsequence, that lack of a cutting edge, that alternation between enthusiasm and apathy, stubbornness and defeatism, vision and myopia, which in early days had so disconcerted his well-meaning tutors. He was consistent in only three particulars, and these were at odds: he seriously desired the good of his people and was ready to make radical changes in the interest of the common welfare; he was a convinced imperialist; and he was an autocrat in intention no less absolute than his father.

Unlike his father he had the sense to perceive that he could not personally supervise the entire activity of his realm. But he quite lacked the wisdom to draw the proper conclusions from this understanding. If he could not preside in person over everything, he needed the active assistance of the most able and devoted among his subjects. How to discover these men? There was only one way: they must be encouraged to emerge, natural leaders, in elective assemblies which would not only throw up the men he needed but would also provide a political training ground for high office. There was a moment in the early 1860s, with the creation of the zemstvos or local councils on district and provincial level, when it seemed possible that the Emperor had seen the light. But although some of the zemstvos were to do magnificent work on a purely local level, above all in the establishment and running of primary schools, fire services (especially important in a land of wooden houses), roads, rural medical services and the encouragement of improved agricultural practice, they lacked authority and were dominated by the landowners. Their performance varied sharply from district to district, province to province, according to the quality of the landowners. And they lacked executive power, depending for the enforcement of their regulations on the police, who took their orders from the Governor. The provincial Governor, indeed, was less of an absolute dictator than he had been under Nicholas, but he was still the object of sycophantic deference on the part of all those anxious to keep in with authority, and it called for great strength of character for zemstvo officials to resist his arbitrary interventions: since he was usually a retired general distinguished neither by intellect nor reforming ardour he stood as a rule for reaction even when benevolent.

The act which created the zemstvos was passed in 1864, and it was the severe limitation of the powers of the zemstvos and the Tsar's refusal to countenance the logical development of the zemstvo principle, an elective national assembly, which established the pattern destined to remain in force until, forty years later, and under violent pressure, Nicholas II conceded the first all-Russian Duma, or parliament. More than this, it made it inevitable that when a national assembly was at last established it would behave less as a responsible arm of government than as an instrument of revolution.

Alexander's solution to the problem of delegation was to strengthen the central bureaucracy. His ministers enjoyed more responsibility than their predecessors under Nicholas. They were also on the whole more able. But in so far as they operated independently, they themselves were minor autocrats, responsible only to the Tsar. Above all, they were chosen from the narrow court circle and the St Petersburg bureaucracy. No attempt was made to seek out and harness the hidden talent which undoubtedly existed among the landowning gentry who despised the place-seeking atmosphere of St Petersburg and preferred to live in Moscow, or on their own estates.

This deliberate exclusion of much-needed talent was not taken lying down. In the early 1860s there was a persistent but quite unco-ordinated effort by men of substance and goodwill to persuade Alexander to create the machinery which would allow them to participate without material reward in the business of government. Every such attempt was met with a flat rebuff.

Alexander had defined his attitude even during the struggle for Emancipation. Then, the nobility of Tver had insisted on putting forward their own ideas about problems arising from the projected upheaval, and for this display of insolence the Marshal of the Nobility of Tver had actually been exiled to Vyatka. This was in keeping with the determination to limit public discussion of the proposed Emancipation to matters arising from the local application of the imperially determined policy. The Tver landowners, however, refused to be intimidated. Very soon after the Emancipation Act had been promulgated they were so dismayed by the turbulence of the peasants and the wrangling between landowners, peasants and bureaucrats over the distribution of land and details of redemption and compensation that an imposing group of them, thirteen in all, including the far from revolutionary brother of the anarchist Bakunin, composed an address to the Emperor which appeared to him in its radical humanity as little short of a challenge. The address put forward the view that the problems were so complex, so intimately affecting so many in every walk of life, that there was only one way in which they could be tackled peaceably and constructively: the establishment by the Emperor of an assembly of elected deputies, regardless of rank. It was further suggested that since all the subjects of the Emperor were now free men, all must be equal in the eyes of the Crown, sharing equally in the privileges and the duties of full citizenship. Above all, it was clearly wrong that the whole burden of taxation should fall upon the labourer while nobility and gentry went almost scot free: 'Sir, we consider it a mortal sin to enjoy such benefits at the expense of others. It is indeed an unjust order of things when a poor man must pay a rouble while a rich man does not pay a kopek. This might well have been tolerated in the days of serfdom. But now we are being turned into parasites and drones. . . . We humbly beg Your Imperial Majesty to permit us to assume responsibility for certain taxes. . . .'[1]

The signatories of this notable declaration – which exposes an aspect of pre-revolutionary Russian society insufficiently explored even to this day – all of them men of substance and high standing, soon discovered that although they might think of themselves as over-privileged, on one matter they stood on a level with the lowest in the land: they were not free to speak. All thirteen were seized at the Tsar's command and briefly imprisoned in the fortress of St Peter and St Paul.[2] Alexander, instead of thanking God that among his loyal subjects some were eager to share in the regeneration of the country, was angered. Nor were the nobles of Tver the only offenders. Demands for a general assembly came in to St Petersburg from many other provinces, though none so radical. The new Minister of the Interior, Count P. A. Valuyev, who had succeeded old Count Lanskoy, issued a circular laying down once more in general terms the principle already established in the matter of the Emancipation: any assemblies of the nobility must confine their resolutions and recommendations to matters directly affecting their own local needs; on no account were they to put forward views or recommendations on matters affecting the government of the country as a whole. That was in March 1862. It was a slap in the face for all those outside the court and the bureaucracy who aspired to participate at their own expense in the better government of Russia.

A heavy fatality lay over the reforming years of the 1860s. The first years of that decade marked a turning point in more ways than one. They saw not merely the alienation of the intelligentsia but also the emasculation of reforms consequent upon the Emancipation, which, for a breathless moment, had seemed to portend the establishment of some form of representative government. But it was still far from the end of the struggle. Valuyev's voice was heard again in the hot debate that raged in the special commission charged with drafting the local government reform. Here he was arguing not with outsiders but with his fellow officials and ministers, some of whom wanted to give the zemstvos greater power and autonomy than either the Tsar or Valuyev felt was proper. 'To give the zemstvos a voice in matters common to the whole empire would be to break up the unitary executive power of the empire and distribute it among forty or fifty bodies. This would expose the social order and the entire imperial structure to perils which must be evident to all.'

Perhaps the final word was uttered by Alexander himself in January 1865. After the zemstvo act had been passed the assembled nobility of Moscow province voted overwhelmingly (236 to 36) in favour of an address to the Tsar formally pleading for the convocation of a general assembly of elected persons of the Russian land for the consideration of needs common to the whole state. Such an assembly, which the nobility would choose from the best people in their midst, they saw as the logical completion of the great government reforms. Once more the Tsar replied in anger and seized the opportunity to make his will clear in a formal rescript of extreme chilliness addressed to Valuyev. The business of reform, he declared, was a matter for the Tsar and nobody but the Tsar. No group or class of persons was entitled to speak on behalf of others. The Tsar and the Tsar alone, he said in effect, could (through his ministers) order matters for the common good. All attempts by others to influence the course of events could only make it harder for him to achieve his desired ends: 'in no case can they assist the realisation of the purpose to which they may be directed.'[3]

Alexander was not alone in the passion with which he held to this view. Paradoxically, he was supported not only by the Valuyevs, but also by many of the most determined reformers among his ministers and officials.

Indeed Valuyev himself was very far from being the monster he was made out to be by the radical intelligentsia. He was a smooth, sleek functionary with mutton-chop whiskers, a subtle line in flattery, a sharp understanding of the necessity for reform in all areas of government, but quite lacking in the devotion to principle which had distinguished his predecessor, Count Lanskoy. He would never have dreamed of openly contradicting his master, but he was not above secret intrigue to thwart his sovereign's purposes when these seemed likely to weaken the power of the bureaucracy. He wanted to be loved and respected, and with all his cynicism he prided himself on understanding and appreciating the idealism of those, especially the young, whose impractical but warm-hearted demands it was his sad duty to oppose. Korolenko in his autobiography has given a superb and very funny picture of Valuyev in action, as he sets himself to charm an assembly of university students into believing that he is on their side.[4] It is not too much to say that Valuyev was the first of what in Russia was an entirely new breed of politician. Among his predecessors had been a few enlightened nobles who devoted themselves to the public service; but many more had been sergeant-majors in field-marshal's uniform. Valuyev himself was, quite simply, a politician on the make, using the same techniques to win the confidence of his Emperor that his Western contemporaries were employing to win the confidence of the electorate at large. Only in this sense was he a monster.

But it was not only the Tsar and Valuyev who were set against any form of national assembly. Indeed there was a bizarre and undeclared alliance between the greatest and most powerful landowners on the one hand and the most ardently reforming bureaucrats on the other. The great magnates, rich enough in their various ways to survive without lethal injury the loss of all their serfs and much of their land, opposed any form of devolution which might diminish their still great influence in the country and give a voice to their lesser neighbours. The reforming bureaucrats were convinced that any national assembly would be dominated by the landowners who would stand in the way of further reforms. Rightly or wrongly they did not set much store by the spirit shown by the nobility of Tver when they pleaded to be allowed to pay taxes. Obviously such public spirit was not dominant, but the fact that it existed anywhere foreshadowed one of those profound changes of mood which in other countries have led to great consequences. In Russia it was aborted. The nobility in increasing numbers had become convinced that they owed an active duty to society. This conviction was due in part to the selective infiltration of ideas preached by the growing intelligentsia, in part to the Tsar's own example in seeking to transform the very basis of society, in part to the genuinely felt need among paternally-minded landowners to find a new role for themselves now that they no longer functioned automatically as an unofficial magistracy over communities of serfs. They were snubbed, rebuffed, threatened.

I dwell at what may seem to be inordinate length on this subdued and muffled conflict in the matter of a national assembly because it marked a climacteric, a turning point, in the development of Imperial Russia. Nobody would pretend that any conceivable kind of national assembly convened in the 1860s would have emerged as a fully-fledged parliament. The suffrage would have had to be rigidly limited, its powers most strictly circumscribed, and the autocratic powers of the Tsar would not have been diminished. The Tsar, moreover, knew that he needed advice in the formulation of his policies and assistance in fulfilling them. By setting up a national assembly he would have profited from local and specialised knowledge, to say nothing of brains, now going to waste; he would have provided a forum in which opposing interests and ideologies could have openly debated, knocking the corners off each other and bringing the problems of the day to the understanding of an ever wider public; he would have provided a school for political leaders in which men of ideas and ambition could test their ideas and measure their talents against reality.

It was not as though the idea of creating a national assembly was unheard-of *lèse-majesté*. Nicholas had regarded it as such, but Alexander I had once dreamed of it and Alexander II had on several occasions declared that he would be only too pleased to inaugurate a constituent assembly if only it would not lead inevitably to the collapse of authority and the ruin of the Empire. He was sustained in this simple belief by men who should have known better. Not only by the Valuyevs, who were naturally opposed to any threatened dilution of the powers of the central bureaucracy, but also by serious and enlightened thinkers and reformers whose disinterestedness and public spirit was beyond question.

Thus one of the chief brains behind the Emancipation Act, Nicholas Milyutin, and one of the most enlightened Slavophiles, Yuri Samarin, both argued strongly against a national assembly. Why? Milyutin, who had been slandered by reactionaries as a 'red' and suffered much as a result, should have welcomed above all others any possible step towards a broadening of the base of government; Samarin, who had been in serious trouble with the Tsar for deploring the excessive German influence in government, should have welcomed any move to reduce the supremacy of the court and the bureaucracy, both dominated by men of more or less direct Teutonic descent.

The grounds on which they based their opposition to a national assembly had nothing to do with considerations of this kind. It was the old, old Russian story of the better being the enemy of the good. Curtail the power of the autocracy in any way, they argued, and you put in its place a privileged group which will inevitably harden into a self-perpetuating oligarchy. Almost three hundred years earlier, in the Time of Troubles, the boyars had regarded this as the supreme evil to be avoided at all costs and thus, turning their backs on the chance to achieve self-government, had chosen to elect a new Tsar beneath whose sway they would attain equality in submission.[5] Now these highly intelligent thinkers of the mid-nineteenth century felt the same way. The day must come, they were convinced, when the people would be ripe to take a share of the government, but this must be postponed until the whole nation was sufficiently educated to play its part in the choosing of a truly representative assembly. They did not ask how such education was to be achieved unless by the gradual broadening of a governing class with a correspondingly gradual broadening of privileges and *duties*. The feeling for authoritarian rule ran very deep and displayed itself in many differing ways. In the summer of 1861, for example, among the various revolutionary manifestos which made their appearance in that year, we find pamphlets by two of the wilder dreamers, N. V. Shelgunov and M. Mikhailov, preaching total rejection of the existing system while carrying to an extreme degree the Slavophile rejection of all Western values. They too thought in authoritarian terms. The hereditary Tsar was to be replaced by an elected Tsar, 'a simple mortal, a man of the soil who understands the life of the people and is chosen by the people'.[6] Later in the century the eccentric philosopher Leontiev was to dream of a Tsar who would put himself at the head of the socialist movement and lead it.

It is not suggested that all intelligent Russians thought along these lines: far from it, but many did, and the feeling behind the thought was widespread and still is, so that in our own day the novelist Alexander Solzhenitsyn, who suffered so appallingly under tyranny, can still voice ideas not dissimilar to those that troubled so many under Alexander II. Solzhenitsyn, turning from contemplation of the excesses of Western democracy, looks back on Russian history to reach the interesting conclusion that until the advent of Peter the Great the Russian authoritarian order had a strong moral foundation, which made it not only viable but also capable of growth. Perhaps, he goes on to say, the Russian way must continue to be authoritarian.

Everything depends on *what sort* of authoritarian order lies in store for us in the future. It is not authoritarianism itself that is intolerable, but the ideological lies that are daily foisted upon us. Not so much authoritarianism as arbitrariness and illegality, the sheer illegality of having an overlord in each district, each province and each sphere, often ignorant and brutal, whose will alone decides all things. An authoritarian order does not necessarily mean that laws are unnecessary or that they exist only on paper, or that they should not reflect the notions and the will of the population. . . .[7]

2

There was to be no national assembly. The Tsar was to be the source of all reforms, and these were to be worked out in detail and applied by his own appointees. Some of the reforms were radical, far-reaching, and enduring; some of the appointees were men of character and ability. Apart from the institution of the zemstvos, the greatest and most enduring reforms were in the judicial system and the army. Russia at last received an independent judiciary based on the separation of powers and operating on a system which was an amalgam of English and French practice, but with the French predominating. It never seems to have occurred to Alexander that by introducing trial by jury in criminal cases and making judges irremovable he was compromising the autocratic principle. He was not, however, alone in innocence: the radical intelligentsia, who should have exploited the new situation, also failed to comprehend its full signi-ficance, even though the reforms called into being with surprising rapidity a legal profession which attracted many gifted and independent minds for which society had hitherto found no employment. The army reforms were conceived and executed with remarkable vision and persistence over more than a decade by General Dmitri Milyutin, the elder brother of Nicholas Milyutin, a career soldier who rose by sheer brilliance to be Minister of Defence in 1862. He had fought in the Crimea. As a staff officer in St Petersburg not long before his promotion to minister he had won the expressed admiration of Bismarck, then in the middle of his spell at the Prussian Embassy which gave him so profound an insight into Russian affairs.

Milyutin's first great act was to rid the army of the cruellest and most humiliating forms of corporal punishment (for example, running the gauntlet until the sufferer fell dead of exhaustion and pain). This was in 1863. He next reduced the length of service from twenty-five to sixteen years. He raised the status of the general staff, created the office of chief-of-staff, hastened the development of armaments, improved the army medical services beyond measure, pressed successfully for the construction of strategic railways, organised the whole realm into self-contained mili-tary districts. But his supreme battle, which lasted from 1863 to 1874, was for the institution of universal conscription, until then (since the abolition of serfdom had put an end to the landowners' power of detailing men for service) limited to peasants and labourers. The Conscription Act of 1 January 1874 was a triumph over the vested interests of the privileged, who resisted with a bitterness than can be imagined: for the scions of noble houses to be on a level with peasants! But put on a level they were. All young men became liable for service at the age of twenty, with certain compassionate exceptions which had nothing to do with class, though they affected mainly the poor with parents or grandparents to support. Each military district had to provide a stated quota of conscripts every year, and these were chosen by ballot. The basic terms of service were six years with the colours, nine on the reserve and five in the militia. The length of service with the colours was progressively reduced in inverse proportion to educational qualifications. Only those with no education at all served the full six years; primary education brought the term down to four years, partial secondary to three, full secondary to two, university to six months. In this way the gentry were clearly favoured, but as education rapidly developed boys from poor homes had increasing opportunities to achieve some sort of secondary education, the cleverest to go on to university. The important thing was that the army was transformed by a wholly new mood of professionalism. It was characteristic of the emotional complex of contradictions which surrounded the Alexandrine reforms that highly intelligent and enlightened soldiers, such as Prince Baryatinsky, the conqueror of the Caucasus, put up the most stubborn resistance to changes which could only work to their advantage.

There were other excellent men besides Milyutin, many of them young: Dmitri Milyutin himself was only forty-five, his brother Nicholas forty-three. Count M. K. Reutern, forty-one in 1861, an ardent reformer and a financial wizard, became Minister of Finance and succeeded in effecting unified financial control over all the ministries and presenting the first comprehensive budget; Baron N. A. Korff, not yet thirty, took over from Bludov as head of the Second Section of the Imperial Chancery, responsible for legislative drafting, while Bludov himself, a committed reformer, became President of both the Imperial Council and the Council of Ministers (he was now a veteran in his seventies). All these men looked to the future and Reutern and Korff in particular had fought hard against Valuyev for the enlargement of the responsibilities and authority of the zemstvos. But the most impressive of all the new men was A. V. Golovnin, who, in his early forties, brought air and light into the Ministry of Education.

The situation in the Ministry of Education illustrates as vividly as anything else the strange, almost incoherent unpredictability, the inconsequence, it is hardly too much to say, of the reforming drive.

In 1853, on the eve of the Crimean War, the ineffable Shirinsky-

Shikhmatov had been succeeded by an altogether more human, but far from strong, figure, A. S. Norov, who took many of his ideas from the ex-serf Nikitenko, and managed to win some respect from the better university professors. For the schools, however, he did all too little, and once the war was over the reforming movement was led from outside the establishment by N. I. Pirogov, the surgeon who had worn himself out in his efforts to create some sort of a useful medical service in the Crimea. How this remarkable man found the energy to lead a crusade for classless education with a heavy emphasis on a wide cultural background and the development of personality rather than learning by rote, it is hard to understand. But he did so, at forty-six launching out on a second career, fighting reaction all the way, only to be defeated by the intrigues of his enemies before the completion of what was to be his great monument, the creation of Odessa University.

Pirogov was a casualty of the 1861 backlash, and although in 1862 he was rehabilitated by Golovnin and put in charge of a group of Russian students detailed to study abroad in preparation for taking up appointments in Russian universities, his best work was done. It was continued, however, by another remarkable but less spectacular talent, K. D. Ushinsky, an official of the Ministry of Education who was also influenced by Nikitenko and at thirty-six, in 1860, was made editor of the ministry's journal, which he transformed into a periodical of great influence, open to the discussion of new ideas. Inspired by the vision of providing education for a whole people freed from slavery, he believed like Pirogov in a system which would turn pupils into whole men. Both reformers had a proper appreciation of the place of science in the curriculum, but both believed passionately in the regenerative power of the humanities – Pirogov placing his main emphasis on the classics, Ushinsky on the study of the Russian language.

The ideas of both these men, and others like them, were upheld, codified, and put into official practice by Golovnin, who appeared at the very moment when all seemed lost. The decent but inadequate Norov had been succeeded as a direct result of the summer disturbances of 1861 by Admiral Putyatin, a politically-minded sailor of considerable distinction who had no ideas about education other than to clamp down on rebellious students (he was soon to find his proper vocation as a tough negotiator in the interest of Russian expansionism in the Far East). Some of the best university professors resigned in protest and Alexander himself was persuaded that a more flexible approach was needed. Golovnin, himself a university professor, was given his chance, which he took with both hands. His great monuments were the University Statute of 1863, giving more autonomy to the universities than they had ever possessed or even seriously dreamed of; the secondary education statute of 1864 and the elementary education statute of 1865 which between them went a very long way towards establishing equal education for all as well as secularising village schools which the Holy Synod had regarded as its province.

An illuminating sidelight on the atmosphere inside the Ministry of Education under Golovnin is provided by a brush between Golovnin and Valuyev at the Ministry of the Interior over the educational experiment of Count Leo Tolstoy at Yasnaya Polyana. In 1862, acting on information received, Valuyev ordered a discreet enquiry into the activities of Tolstoy (already an admired and distinguished writer, but with *War and Peace* still ahead of him). The enquiry was set up and the report rendered to the Ministry of Education, which accepted it and passed it on to Valuyev with the comment that Count Tolstoy's educational activities could only command respect and that the Ministry of Education regarded it as its duty to help him and encourage him, even though it did not share all his ideas. 'To establish a simple, easy and independent relationship between master and pupil; cultivate mutual affection and trust; free lessons from constraint and learning by rote; transform the school into a kind of family in which the teacher acts as parent: what could be more desirable and profitable for all?'[8]

It was characteristic of Tolstoy not only that he was unaware that ministry officials were thinking about education along humane and enlightened lines and working hard to put their ideas into practice, but also that he totally rejected any philosophy of education which differed a hairsbreadth from his own uncompromising precepts. It was characteristic of the radical political rebels among the intelligentsia (whom Tolstoy also despised) that instead of welcoming the efforts of Golovnin and the most liberal of his subordinates they saw them simply as the enemy, as part of the official system they were determined to destroy. The revolutionary movement was being born at the very moment when devoted reformers were making a very real impact on the system. It was characteristic of Russia that with all her backwardness she could on occasion show herself ahead of the rest of the world.

3

The founding fathers of the Russian revolutionary movement had achieved their full stature outside Russia, condemned to eternal exile, as individual fighters in the cause of international socialism. The dominant figures were the two friends Michael Bakunin and Alexander Herzen, both aristocrats, but wildly different in temperament and mentality. It was Bakunin who became the very prototype of the revolutionary in Western eyes, flamboyant, courageous, apocalyptic, irresponsible, impossible to pin down and categorise. His direct influence on Russian radical thought had been at its strongest among the Moscow circles of the 1830s, before he went abroad and adopted his extreme positions. During the 1848 upheavals all over Europe his name became a byword. At the least manifestation of anti-authoritarian activity Bakunin would appear, a sort of one-man storm-troop, lending encouragement, preaching extreme and violent action, his huge and exhibitionist figure always in the forefront of the fray. Now he would be in Prague preaching defiance of Vienna to the Bohemians, but improving the hour by insisting that the only way to salvation lay in a union of all the Slavs under Russian leadership; now he would be in Dresden with the youthful Richard Wagner noisily demonstrating against the Saxon king and proposing that the revolutionaries should seize the Sistine madonna and march with it held aloft as a talisman, an icon at which no man would dare shoot. Handed over by the Austrian authorities to the Tsar, he was consigned to the fortress of St Peter and St Paul, then condemned to Siberian exile. It was in 1859 that he made his spectacular escape to America via Japan and became a living legend.

But there was no coherence in his views. An anarchist who believed in the total destruction of all existing systems before the new world could be planned, let alone built, he was also a socialist; a socialist, he also proclaimed the imminence of a bloody peasant uprising in Russia. It was amazing that he was able to co-operate with Karl Marx, the systematiser, for as long as five minutes, but co-operate he did, until the disagreements between the two men ended with the wrecking of the First International. In his last years, at Geneva, this passionate eccentric nourished the belief that he was the guide and inspiration of the new generation of Russian revolutionaries with whom, in fact, he was completely out of touch and whom he did not understand. And the final folly of this giant in decline was his support for the unspeakable Nechayev (to be encountered briefly in due course), the destructive psychopath with a minuscule following who, descending on Geneva, managed to convince Bakunin that he controlled a vast revolutionary organisation which was preparing for the day. Bakunin in his heart of hearts knew better, but his final disillusionment which he postponed beyond the eleventh hour had almost an element of high tragedy. This was in the early 1870s. Life had passed him by. The young Russians had long ceased looking to him for guidance (he was incapable of guiding anyone sensibly, and had always been incapable: he could only exhort to violence), but so great was the impact of his personality, so romantic his giant stature, so volcanic his nature, that he was vested with a glamour which never died, and was, in this sense, a continuing inspiration.

Alexander Herzen was also condemned to live abroad from 1848 onwards.[9] He had gone to Paris in 1847 when, after returning to Moscow from his provincial banishment, he had inherited a considerable fortune at his father's death. Arriving in the West on the very eve of the great revolutionary upheaval, intoxicated not only by the spectacle of Europe rising up to cast off its chains but also, for the moment, by the variety and richness of European society, he proclaimed in ringing tones his conviction of the imminent liberation of mankind. His disappointment when in country after country the revolution simply petered out was absolute. He was also stranded high and dry, unable to return to Russia, unwanted in France or Germany. The spectacle of a smug and prosperous bourgeoisie establishing itself on the ruins of the popular revolt, together with his entirely Russian revulsion from the prudential hypocrisies of a philistine society, convinced him that there could be no salvation in Europe even while Russia lay prostrate under Nicholas in his last most reactionary phase. But he pulled himself together and set about composing his two masterpieces, *From the Other Shore*, inspired directly by the failure of the revolution, and *My Past and Thoughts*. In 1853 he brought his wandering to an end and came to rest in London, to embark on the establishment of the first Russian opposition journals ever to be published abroad – the opening shots in a long and desultory bombardment which continues to this day. He was thus ready after the death of Nicholas to welcome and exploit from afar the immediate promise of reform. In 1857 he founded his celebrated paper *The Bell* (*Kolokol*) which was smuggled into Russia in large quantities. For the next four years *The Bell* was effectively the voice of the Russian conscience. They were the years of struggle and ferment which ended with the Emancipation Act of 1861; and *The Bell* did far more than influence and enlighten and clarify the thoughts of the radicals and reformers of every colour. It was also read by ministers and high officials, even, it was believed, by the Tsar himself. This was not so paradoxical as it sounds, because Herzen, although filled with socialistic ideas, was essentially a humanitarian pragmatist; he was a reformer who became a reluctant revolutionary only when convinced by events that radical reform depended on the overthrow of the system. He had none of Bakunin's destructive zest; indeed, he shrank from violence. He was a thinker and a dreamer, enough of a man of action to have become a liberal politician in the West. When he believed that Alexander was seriously intent on reform he was ready to back him with all his personal authority and to give praise where praise was due. At the same time he was unresting in his condemnation of injustice, corruption and all abuses of authority. So that it is scarcely an exaggeration to say that in a certain sense *The Bell* became an adjunct of government. Time and time again it would be found that abuses and excesses denounced in its pages stirred high authority into investigative and remedial action.

For a short time even the most extreme of the younger radicals, a new generation, were ready to put themselves to school under Herzen. They, too, were at first ready to credit Alexander with the genuine will to reform. But as the struggle for Emancipation dragged on, and as the Tsar clamped down on open discussion, their mood was soured. Even before the terms of the Emancipation Act became known they were asking themselves how they had ever allowed themselves to believe that genuine reform was possible under the autocracy. Poor Herzen now appeared to them as a worn-out liberal, no longer relevant to the age, and the estrangement between the grand old exile and the new standard-bearers of the enlightenment was increased when Herzen himself attacked them in *The Bell* for playing into the hands of the autocracy with their uncompromising extremism. He still remained for a time a venerated figure among the moderates, but in 1863 his courageous championship of the rebel Poles lost him the sympathy of all those right-thinking Russian liberals whose dreams of the millennium did not include a free Poland. Herzen's day was over. He himself lost his sense of direction: scorned by the 'new men', alienated from the moderates, wholly disillusioned with the West, this gifted and highly-tuned intellectual who, at one time, might have seemed the natural bridge between Russian and Western thinking, relapsed, like so many others, into quasi-mystical veneration of the Russian peasant as the future light of the world. As Turgenev put it, he was driven to 'seeking salvation in a sheepskin coat'.

The new men were quite other. The most influential were N. G. Chernyshevsky and N. A. Dobrolyubov, briefly referred to in an earlier chapter as the heirs and perverters of Belinsky's teaching of the need to subordinate art to politics. There was a considerable difference in the ages of these two: Chernyshevsky was twenty-seven when Alexander came to the throne, Dobrolyubov only nineteen. But together they made an indelible impression on the development of Russian revolutionary thinking.

Both were sons of Orthodox priests, like so many of the revolutionaries of years to come. With their seminarist's background they carried an inborn puritanism into their atheistical rejection of religion.[10] Both first welcomed the promise of the Alexandrine reforms, only to turn more sharply against the autocracy as the struggle for Emancipation dragged on and the Tsar decided that public discussion had gone far enough. Their main organ was the remarkable review, *The Contemporary (Sovremmenik)* run by N. A. Nekrasov, an original poet who was above all an editor of genius and a stubborn and accomplished adversary of the censorship, and to whose gifts for tactical compromise a whole generation of Russian writers and their readers owed a debt impossible to measure – the sort of debt owed a century later by Solzhenitsyn and so many others to another poet, Konstantin Tvardovsky, editor of the twentieth-century echo of *The Contemporary, New World (Novy Mir)*.

The Contemporary was Pushkin's old journal, which had survived under inoffensive and mediocre editors until 1846 when Nekrasov, at twenty-five, took charge, nursed it through the black reactionary years after the 1848 upheavals and, with Alexander's accession, stood ready to push the most radical ideas. He was the last person one would have expected to play a hero's role in the struggle for the good. A byword for extravagant and louche private life, he was one of the first Russian intellectual Bohemians, with a passion for gambling and drinking that would have been a credit to a young officer in the Guards. And, in the end, the strain of weakness in him conquered. In 1866, when the notorious hangman Count M. N. Muraviev was put in charge of the investigation into Karakozov's attempt on the life of the Tsar and sought to implicate the whole company of radicals, Nekrasov could not save *The Contemporary* from extinction, but he managed to save himself by composing a fulsome ode to Muraviev as the saviour of the realm.

With all this, he was possessed by a genuine humanitarian passion, a hatred of oppression, compassion for suffering, and a persistent determination to take under his wing all good fighters in the cause of reform. He also loved literature. His own poetry did not receive the recognition it deserved until long after his death, but he was wonderfully free from jealousy and seized upon, nourished and sustained the least sign of literary talent in others. He had a very fine eye. His was the honour of discovering the young Turgenev in 1847 and the still younger Tolstoy in 1852. *A Sportsman's Sketches* was first published in *The Contemporary*, and so were *Childhood, Boyhood* and *Youth*. But towards the end of the 1850s the tone of his review was changing as Chernyshevsky and Dobrolyubov developed their dour campaign to turn literature into the handmaiden of politics. Turgenev was half-revolted, half-fascinated by them. Tolstoy despised them. In the end Nekrasov, whom nobody took seriously as an artist (he was their editor, their paymaster, their shield against the censorship) but who loved literature and understood it, presided over a journal devoted to its destruction. It was in the pages of *The Contemporary* that, month after month, Dobrolyubov, implacable in his youthful arrogance, produced that extraordinary series of articles about contemporary masterpieces – Turgenev's *On the Eve*, Goncharov's *Oblomov*, Ostrovsky's *Storm*, etc. – which treated great works of literature as so much cannon-fodder in the fight against the autocracy, elaborating the political ideas they contained, or which he read into them, ignoring their artistry.

Dobrolyubov, it is hard to realise, died in 1861 at twenty-five. Chernyshevsky lived much longer, most of the time in exile. He was arrested in the post-Emancipation disturbances of 1862, spent two years in the fortress of St Peter and St Paul, and was then packed off to Siberia, first to prison, then to almost lifelong banishment in the far north-east. Gentle, mild-mannered, steel-spectacled, he bore himself with undeviating dignity, without a trace of heroics, clasping martyrdom to his breast. He was the most unlikely figure to have been the true father of Bolshevism, a posthumous child; but so he was. It was in the fortress that he managed to write his most famous work, the almost unreadable novel *What is to be done?* which celebrated the advent of a new type of revolutionary, hard, ruthless, totally dedicated, cunning, unforgiving. And the question he asked was to be argued and debated for another forty years, until Lenin, deliberately invoking Chernyshevsky, wrote his own polemic under that same title – and himself provided the terrible answer.

4

It was an artist, not a pamphleteer, who was the first to isolate, examine, and try to understand the nature of the ultimately dominant and successful element in the Russian revolutionary movement, even as it was being born. That artist was Turgenev. As already observed, he detested Chernyshevsky and Dobrolyubov. ('You are a snake!' he exclaimed to Chernyshevsky one day, 'but Dobrolyubov is a rattlesnake.') At the same time they were on the side of the angels, and they were young. Tolstoy, who twenty years later, after writing *War and Peace* and *Anna Karenina*, was to deny the validity of art with all the authority of his incomparable reputation, reacted so violently against Dobrolyubov and Chernyshevsky that at a time when the whole of intellectual Russia could think of nothing but the politics of reform, he put himself forward as the champion of art for art's sake. Turgenev, who was so supremely an artist (and on his death-bed in 1883 was to write to Tolstoy, 'great writer of the Russian land', begging him to return to art), found himself driven to sympathise with, at least to try to understand, these angry, bigoted young men, whose life-denying doctrines afflicted him almost physically. Out of this tension in the spring of 1861 the novel *Fathers and Sons* was born, with its epoch-making study of the scientific revolutionary Bazarov, the newest of the new men. Bazarov's cold and immovable convictions that nothing in this world is valid unless it can be weighed and measured, that humanitarian ideals are nothing but self-indulgent sentimentality, that vaguely aspiring liberalism is beneath contempt, that the whole fabric of society must be rejected and destroyed in order that later generations may build anew on scientific lines, threw intellectual Russia into a tumult and brought down on Turgenev's head a storm the echoes of which were to pursue him for the rest of his life – and, indeed, beyond the grave. Bazarov, who believed that the least new chemical discovery was worth more than all the art in the world, who sought to reduce social analysis to the level of a biologist dissecting frogs, became a portent and a symbol. It was for him that Turgenev invented the term 'nihilist', which was soon to become a stigma or a battle-cry. Poor Turgenev hardly knew which way to turn. Some moderates praised him for exposing the ruthless savagery of the new radicals; others attacked him for displaying them in a far too sympathetic light. Most of the new radicals themselves refused to recognise themselves in Bazarov, whose total scepticism seemed to deny their idealism, and were bitter in their reproaches for what they insisted was an ugly caricature.

But so fast were things moving that there were still newer new men, who seized the label 'nihilist' to stick proudly in their hats. The first of these was D. I. Pisarev, who was only twenty-two when *Fathers and Sons* was published and who wrote not for *The Contemporary* but for a rival journal called *The Russian Word* (*Russkoe Slovo*). With so many others, he was to be arrested later in that tempestuous year, imprisoned for four years and then, in 1868, drowned in a bathing accident. Pisarev was not a plebeian or a priest's son like so many of his radical contemporaries, but the son of a well-to-do landowner. For all his mordant nihilism and his carrying of the doctrine of art as politics to new extremes, there was something engaging about him and a relative flexibility of outlook and sharpness of perception which, had he lived, would have made him a figure very much to be reckoned with – perhaps the sort of pragmatical and level-headed guide whom the generations of revolutionaries to come so sorely lacked. At twenty-two he was proud, he declared, to be thought of as a nihilist, and proud to model himself upon Bazarov. And, indeed, there was a quality about him, absent in the Chernyshevskys and the Dobrolyubovs, which seemed to justify Turgenev's own troubled striving to understand the dedicated young, whose methods he questioned and whose manners he abhorred.

The picture that emerges of the state of intellectual Russia at the beginning of the 1860s is thus confused to a degree. It is also seething with life. Gone are the days when to a handful of aristocratic reformers were painfully added a zest of clever, impoverished students. The new bourgeoisie was gathering strength and numbers. The artistic and cultural life of the great cities too was developing an autonomy of its own. And there was already an important cultural element which, while critical of the autocracy, was still more critical of the radical young. The conservative reformers, symbolised by the journalist Michael Katkov, who now published both Turgenev and Tolstoy in his *Russian Herald (Russky Vestnik)*, had developed their own vested interest in the *status quo*. And the sense of a Russian identity, which had been precipitated thirty years earlier by Chaadayev's self-lacerating exposure of the nation's failings and crystallised out into the contradictory ideals of the Westernisers and the Slavophiles, was beginning to harden on the one hand into a total rejection of everything the system stood for and on the other into a growing nationalism which found an early and pure expression first in Tolstoy's *War and Peace,* then in the marvellous and sudden flowering of the great composers, only to degenerate into an increasingly strident Russian chauvinism which reached a climax in the war with Turkey in 1877.

The publication of *Fathers and Sons* thus did more than dramatise a new stage in the fight against the autocracy as such: it marked the parting of the ways between reform and revolution. From now on to be a radical demanded increasingly the preaching of violent change. It was the beginning of a long process whereby in ever growing numbers liberals who detested violence and recoiled from the excesses of the revolutionaries found themselves nevertheless shamed by feelings of guilt into tolerating, if not actively supporting, such excesses: the revolutionaries were wrongheaded by all means, their methods were deplorable, but, when all was said, they were on the side of the angels, and they were courageous, dedicated, single-minded unto death. How to condemn them? It was an attitude which was to persist until the final cataclysm. What was a wellintentioned, reform-minded individual to do? He was rejected by the autocracy which denied him all useful participation in responsible government, except on the local zemstvo level. Was he in his turn to condemn the zeal of those who preached revolution because there was no other way? And while the body of liberalism was weakened on one side by reluctant sympathy with the revolutionaries, on the other it was eroded by the defection of many who were driven to rationalise their acceptance of the system by equating it in the last resort with the spirit of Holy Russia.

Such was Russia. Such were the times. In these years, the first half of the sixties, all the main lines of future revolutionary thought were being more or less ineffectively projected, spun out of a void as it were, to be gathered up in years to come. They ranged from the idealistic populism which sought salvation in the Russian peasant (educated for the job, of course, by urban intellectuals), as first outlined in the programme of a young government official, Serno-Solovevich, whose secret society, 'Land and Liberty', was broken up by his arrest in 1862, to the 'Russian Jacobinism' of 'Young Russia', with its echoes of the hanged Decembrist

Pestel. Until 1866 Alexander kept his head and refused to be stampeded into systematic repressive action against the universities, as his conservative advisers demanded. But this kind of restraint was not enough. By presiding over the arrest, imprisonment and banishment of all individuals caught in the act of subversion, or even suspected of it, instead of shrugging them off, the autocrat ensured a steady supply of martyrs and, in consequence, a steady supply of disciples of these martyrs driven to desperate acts in protest.

It was the first desperate act, the unsuccessful attempt on Alexander's life made by the ex-student Karakozov in 1866, which turned the balance. In face of deliberate regicide the Tsar was forced to concede that those who had counselled repressive action had been right. And popular opinion supported him in a sharp wave of reaction against the intelligentsia as a whole. The spearheads of the reaction were the Tsar's old friend, Count Peter Shuvalov, who was appointed head of the Third Section, Count Dmitri Tolstoy, who replaced the liberal Golovnin at the Ministry of Education, and General F. F. Trepov, who took over from Prince Suvorov as Governor-General of St Petersburg. It was this Trepov who won for himself so vile a reputation that when, sixteen years later, he was shot at and wounded by the terrorist Vera Zasulich, the jury refused to convict her.

The reaction in fact was not by any means savagely repressive. Compared with the situation under Nicholas it was very mild. Even Count Tolstoy who came to be detested as the very pattern of an obscurantist bully was very far from being that. Certainly he feared ideas and regarded Golovnin's universities, not without reason, as forcing-houses of dangerous and subversive thinking. He put it down to the new fad for the natural sciences (Bazarov's frogs) and reorganised the curriculum of both senior schools and the universities to exclude the sciences and emphasise the classics. But he still believed, not passionately (he was cold and dry by temperament) but with reasoned conviction, in the importance of education in a backward country, lavished infinite pains on it, worked hard at his job, and increased the number of schools remarkably, above all primary schools.[11]

But what under Nicholas would have been full of promise, under Alexander was a retrograde step. The radical intelligentsia were in no mood to move backwards, or even to mark time. By attacking a Tolstoy as though he were the devil himself they succeeded only in strengthening the hands of men like Count Shuvalov, who now had a finger in every pie and was able both to frighten the Tolstoys into increased rigidity and to hamper the efforts of non-doctrinaire reformers whose liberalism he detested – such as General Milyutin, then engaged on his great work of army reform. And it was not only the radicals who assisted the reactionaries in their opposition to orderly reform. Already moderate liberals with the best intentions in the world were beginning to display that fatal particularism, quarrelsomeness, divisiveness, that hopeless inability to sink small differences in order to secure unity of action on matters of primary importance which, in the decades to come, was to be the distinguishing and ruinous feature of all Russian movements towards reform – and of the revolutionary parties too, until, in Lenin, there came a man strong and determined enough to impose his own particularism on his quarrelling colleagues and destroy all those who opposed him.

CHAPTER TWELVE

Peace Abroad; Prosperity at Home

I

THE era of the great reforms marked the high-water mark of the Russian autocracy as a creative force. There were to be no more revolutions from above. For the next fifty years the dynasty was to conduct a holding action, only spasmodically intervening in a drama played out by forces beyond its control: the bureaucracy itself; imperially-minded soldiers; the rising class of capitalist entrepreneurs; nationalist or Panslav journalists and agitators; alienated reformers; revolutionaries dedicated to destructions – all these forces, and more besides, interacting against the background of a sullen peasantry and a rapidly increasing proletariat.

Alexander II was the most intelligent of all the Romanovs, the most truly humane as well. But his intelligence was not strong enough to force him to question the role of the dynasty in a rapidly changing and increasingly complex world. Even had he understood his limitations, to say nothing of the limitations of the Russian economy, the tasks that faced him would have been too much for the strongest of autocrats. The great reforms themselves would have been a life-work for one man. Add to these the imperative necessity of bringing Russia into the steel and railway age and of restoring her to her proper position among the powers, and the task was gargantuan. But the one thing Alexander seemed incapable of doing was to give the Empire a breathing space in which to contemplate its internal problems, sort them out, recover solvency and determine a system of priorities for future development while marking time as a great power. Everything had to be done at once, and nothing was done properly.

The Crimean War, while exposing the rottenness of the system, had at the same time demonstrated that Russia was invulnerable to invasion. There was nothing in the world to stop her turning in on herself and concentrating all her efforts and resources on self-improvement. But Alexander could not rest. Even in his youthful days he had combined his real concern for the well-being of the Russian people with a spirit of wild adventurism. It had been he who, in 1851, had persuaded his father to give official backing to Count Muraviev-Amursky's raising of the Russian flag on the Chinese border at the mouth of the Amur river. Now when the desperate need was for retrenchment, consolidation and the swift development by all means of the resources of metropolitan Russia, he embarked, or allowed his diplomats and soldiers to embark, on a series of conquests in Asia which added vast tracks of sparsely inhabited wilderness to the empty immensities of south-eastern Siberia and in central Asia over a million square miles inhabited by Moslems. In the process he alienated the Chinese, alarmed the European powers, strained the economy to the danger point, and left his country well set on the path which, as the years went on, led to the Russians being outnumbered by their subject nationalities.

There were only two other men whose functions enabled them to view the whole field presided over by the Tsar, and even these were kept on a short leash. They were the men who provided the money and the army, the Minister of Finance, Count Reutern, whose great achievement was to centralise all departmental finances so that at least a comprehensive budget could be worked out, and the Minister of Defence, General Dmitri Milyutin. For the rest Alexander sought to keep everything under his hand, and under his alone: he was as firmly opposed to cabinet government as his father had been. And, paradoxically, it was precisely this ideal of personal rule which made it possible for the explosive and restless adventurers in the field of empire-building to operate almost as sovereign warlords. If, that is to say, Count Muraviev-Amursky as Governor-General of Eastern Siberia, or General Kaufman, the brilliantly able but aggressive conqueror and Governor-General of Turkestan, had been accountable to a full cabinet of departmental ministers, they would have been compelled to justify all their actions and think twice about most of them. But they were responsible only to the Tsar. The Tsar was far too busy to know what they were doing at any given time. They acted first, and reported afterwards. And Alexander, for all his intelligence and humanity, could only be flattered by the splendid trophies they repeatedly laid at his feet.

He was a martyr, of course; a martyr to an idea. Humane but not just; stubborn but not strong: he was a natural victim of the fates. The chest weakness that had nearly killed him in his youth persisted all his life: he was racked and ravaged by asthmatic coughing. He persisted in attending court balls even when he had to fight for his breath. This, he was convinced, was the cross a Tsar must carry, must expect to carry. And indeed, if it had not been asthma it would have been something else. He was the last man to stand alone, but he had no real friends. In youth he had depended too much on his tutor, Zhukovsky; in the first years of his reign he could confide in the veteran liberal, Kiselev. But although he enjoyed playing cards and gossiping with some of his contemporaries there were no real intimates among them. Even Count Peter Shuvalov had to be careful what he said and was finally demoted for not guarding his tongue.

What Shuvalov had spoken about too freely was the Tsar's extraordinary liaison with Princess Catherine Dolgoruky. This is not a book about the private lives of emperors. It was not necessary to discuss the mistresses of Nicholas: he kept them firmly in their place. It is necessary to refer to Catherine Dolgoruky because Alexander's relationship with her not only illuminates his own character but also had a direct bearing on the character and conduct of his successor, Alexander III.

Alexander was forty-seven in 1865 when he fell head over heels in love with Catherine, who was precisely thirty years younger. She was also his own ward. She belonged to a family as old as the Romanovs, its destinies bound up with the dynasty. Her father, Prince Michael, had died prematurely after a wildly extravagant life, leaving colossal debts. Alexander took over guardianship of the children. The two girls were sent to the Smolny, the celebrated boarding-school for the daughters of the nobility founded by Catherine the Great and attached to the splendid convent orphanage established by the Empress Elizabeth, overlooking the great bend in the river Neva. It became clear that Alexander was taking a very lively interest in Catherine even when she was still at school. Already at fifteen by all accounts she was developing into a beauty of quite a stunning kind – dazzlingly blonde, but with very dark eyes. She was also disconcertingly grown-up: self-contained, grave, aloof, enigmatic in a word, fascinatingly so for those attracted by riddles, tiresomely so for those who were not. The secret of this particular riddle has never been discovered to this day.

Alexander, like his father, had enjoyed a number of mistresses: his marriage had long gone stale, and the court as a whole were on his side: they found the once adored Tsaritsa a contradictory mixture of cold formality and subversive attitudes. But the Dolgoruky affair was something else and was viewed with almost universal disapproval. Catherine may have behaved with absolute discretion, but she was so wrapped away that nobody had the least idea of what she thought and felt, or of her aims and ambitions, if any. For all practical purposes she became Alexander's only confidante, this child who might have been a younger daughter – living first in one or other of half a dozen villas, at Tsarskoe Selo, at Peterhof, at Yalta, later in her own apartments in the Winter Place itself. Alexander had declared to her, though nobody knew this, that he regarded her as his bride before God, and God blessed the exalted union with three children. (The whole family was brought into the Winter Palace in the panic after the bomb attempt on the Tsar in 1880.) Catherine may indeed have been saint-like in the renunciation of worldly show, but it was obvious that the brilliant world would put the worst possible construction on her relationship and regard her as a sinister influence. This judgement seemed to be confirmed when some years later the Tsaritsa died and Alexander married the girl within four months. It was, of course, a morganatic marriage, but Alexander was determined to have Catherine crowned Empress very soon. This would have happened had he himself lived only a little longer.

The whole affair was damaging to a degree, damaging to both the country and the Crown. Those who might have thought twice before openly opposing the Tsar's liberal policies could now present themselves as the loyalest of the loyal, working only to counteract the malign influence of the Dolgoruky. At the same time, the spectacle of the autocrat abasing himself before a chit of a girl deeply undermined the respect in which he had been held. It also built up trouble for the future. His son and successor, the future Alexander III, bitterly resented his mother's humiliation, to say nothing of the manner in which his father had lowered the Crown in the eyes of the world. In reacting against the personal conduct of his father he also reacted against his liberal policies and listened the more readily to the fulminations of his tutor, the formidable and disastrous K. P. Pobedonostsev, against the spirit of the age.

Alexander II, as observed, was not strong enough to stand alone. In the early 1860s he found no way of converting his fading passion for his wife into deep and comforting companionship. He needed to be worshipped and he was tired of easy affairs. But there had been one firm, rewarding focus to his life: this was in the person of his son and heir, the Grand Duke Nicholas, who seemed to have the makings of an intelligent, perceptive and enlightened monarch. Nicholas, alas, adored by his brothers as well as by his parents, died of meningitis in the very moment of his betrothal to the Danish Princess Dagmar, the sister of the legendarily beautiful, legendarily stupid future Queen Alexandra of England. His father was shattered. There was an atmosphere of high emotionalism about the whole tragedy. On his death-bed Nicholas begged his younger brother to marry Dagmar in his place. The twenty-year-old Alexander pledged himself to do so with dismay in his heart: he was in love with another girl. It is easy to imagine the fraught intensity of the emotions enveloping the Imperial household. For a time the Tsar was at the end of his tether. Estranged from his wife, he could find no comfort in the only home he knew, the family apartments cosily encapsulated in the vast and frozen splendours of the Winter Palace. The son on whom he had pinned all his hopes was suddenly dead, and the new heir, decent and honest enough, was dull and unresponsive. Poor Alexander existed in a sort of shining void between his working office and the cell-like bedroom with its camp-bed, the predilection for which he inherited from his father and shared with his contemporary Franz Joseph in Vienna. And it was this void that was miraculously filled by the astonishingly beautiful, docile, gravely worshipping, wholly determined creature who had been casting some sort of a spell over him for so long. She and she alone could give him new life. It seems very odd indeed that Alexander's contemporaries quite missed the obvious connection between the trauma created by the death of Nicholas in Nice at twenty-two and the maturing in that same year, 1865, of Alexander's obsessive passion for the girl who might have been his daughter. Those contemporaries, all the same, were quite right to question the Tsar's judgement, his command of himself, his command of affairs. The irrelevance of this private life, which intruded far too markedly into his public life, to the immense problem he was required to solve could not have been more absolute.

2

This lack of judgement, of instinctive balance, had already manifested itself in a number of ways, not least in the wholly disproportionate expenditure of energy and resources on imperial expansion. After the Crimean War there was nothing Alexander could do to make Russia's weight felt in Europe until she had overhauled her own domestic arrangements, including the army, and until the passage of time brought about changes in the European balance. He understood this quite well, and made no attempt to force matters. What he did not see was that by encouraging easy victories in colonial wars he was wasting the very substance his ministers were toiling to build up. And when it came to his waiting game in Europe he missed the significance of what was going on in Prussia, so long taken for granted as Russia's only dependable friend. The Prussian Ambassador to St Petersburg from 1859 to 1861 was a remarkable Junker called Count Otto von Bismarck Schönhausen, who, as Chancellor some years later, was to become the supreme agent of change. During his stay in St Petersburg Bismarck, a few years older than Alexander, made an acute and profound study of Russian manners and conditions. One result of this was that when, in 1864, he was ready for the opening move in his great campaign to win for Prussia the mastery of Germany, breaking Austrian hegemony and driving her to seek compensation in the Balkans, he knew just how to use Russia to serve his own ends while still retaining her as a friend. Russia, in a word, was used by Bismarck in his successful campaign to upset the balance of Europe by creating a powerful German Empire under the Hohenzollerns. Alexander was so filled with resentment against Vienna, after the Austrian 'betrayal' during the Crimean War, that he failed to perceive the potential dangers of this situation, which was to lead in due course to the destruction of the old European order and the end of Romanovs, Habsburgs and Hohenzollerns too.

Alexander had not been pleased with Prussia's attitude during the Crimean War: strict neutrality was less than was expected of an ally. But he was aware of Prussia's weakness, and at least King Frederick William, unlike that much stronger and false friend Franz Joseph of Austria, had held to his neutrality. Something of the old warmth in the relationship between the two countries was quickly restored. And when, in 1859, Austria, at Solferino, was humiliated by the combined armies of Louis Napoleon and Victor Emmanuel of Sardinia, Franz Joseph's sense of outrage at Prussia's refusal to march to his assistance was matched by Alexander's enjoyment at the Austrian humiliation.

Three years later, and with Bismarck now in the saddle and beginning to force the pace, Russia had a still better reason to be grateful to Prussia and to cleave to her. In 1863 Poland exploded once again, and Russia soon found herself universally vilified, threatened even from some quarters, with Prussia as her only supporter and friend.

This was the final act in the destruction of Poland, and it ended with wholesale slaughter on both sides, with the deportation to Siberia of at least a hundred thousand Poles, and with the very name of Poland wiped off the map: the small kingdom of Poland established at the Congress of Vienna ceased to exist, reduced to the status of a province of Russia, the Vistula Region.

The trouble had taken a long time building up. After the suppression of the 1830 revolt Poland, under the iron rule of Paskevich and the ruthless policy of russification, became as quiet as the grave. But when Alexander came to the throne he was determined to give the Poles another chance, believing that they would respond eagerly to his liberal approach. Paskevich was succeeded by Prince Michael Gorchakov, the last commander-in-chief in the Crimea, a kind and good man who got on well with all those Polish aristocrats – and they were numerous – who, some from good motives, some from base, were prepared to make the best of life in the shadow of St Petersburg. Political prisoners were set free, civil justice took the place of military courts-martial, Polish was once more taught and spoken in the schools. But this comparative liberalism soon led to demands for more. Early in 1861 the aristocracy and intelligentsia were swept by a new wave of nationalism. Children were taught to hate the

Russians in those very schools where Polish was once more allowed. Instead of pressing steadily and reasonably for more far-reaching concessions, and enjoying responsibly the concessions already secured, the Poles allowed themselves to indulge in impossible dreams. Their talk grew wilder, with renewed demands for total independence and the return to Poland of all the lands taken by Catherine. It seemed that the only immediate answer was brute force. Poor Gorchakov died of heart failure – or a broken heart. Alexander, urged on by Bismarck and the new Prussian King, William I, sent out a military strong-man, General N. O. Sukhozanet, who instituted something like a reign of terror, placed the whole country under martial law and inflicted notable brutalities on women and children as well as men.

Alexander, who still hoped to conquer without violence, was revolted by this behaviour when it was reported to him. In the late spring of 1862 Sukhozanet was recalled and the Tsar's brother Constantine, the staunchest of liberalisers, was appointed viceroy. Constantine, who had already played so active a part in the fight for Emancipation, was a very brave man. He was shot at and wounded. But he resisted his brother's order to return, he stayed on and kept his wife with him. More, he appeared in person before an immense and hostile throng, appealing for reason and an end to bloodshed. In the teeth of the advice of his generals he restored all the concessions and privileges taken away by Sukhozanet, freed the peasants from their vassalage to the landlords and appointed many Poles to administrative posts. It was all to no avail. Once the fighting started, it took fifteen months to restore order. There were no set battles as there had been in the 1830 revolt, because there was now no regular Polish army to lead the rebellion. It was a matter of interminable and often atrocious guerrilla fighting with little or no quarter given on either side. Russian troops, prominent among them Cossacks and terrifying Mongols on their shaggy ponies, slew without mercy; and the horror was compounded by the murderous activities of Polish peasants, who massacred the wives and children of the rebels. The insurgents killed Russian women and children too. And yet there was also heroism on a grand romantic scale; and where there was no fighting Russian authority still behaved with a leniency and generosity unimaginable by the standards of today. Korolenko, whose mother was a Pole married to a half-Polonised Ukrainian, a provincial judge in the service of the Crown, gives a moving insight into the muddle and confusion, the terror and the nobility, the degradation and the high romanticism of those dreadful months.[1] Apollo Korzeniowski, the father of the novelist Joseph Conrad, was an extreme and reckless Polish nationalist, a writer, a revolutionary with a devoted following. He would have been at the very head of the 1863 revolt had he not been arrested in 1861 and sent off with his wife and the four-year-old Joseph into exile in the northern forest. His wife was delicate. Consumption set in. The Governor of Vologda who was responsible for their safekeeping arranged for their transfer, on parole, not under guard, to the better climate of Chernigov in the Ukraine, much nearer home. The Governor of Kiev, under whose jurisdiction they now came, took pity on Evelina Korzeniowski and allowed her to take her son for a long stay on the estate of her brother, one of those sober and influential Poles who, while hating Russian rule, believed that no good could come of violent insurrection. Thus at the very height of the conflict high-ranking Russian officials could behave with remarkable humanity to the family of a rebel leader.[2] Thus too Alexander himself, after three months of carnage, could under Western pressure publicly promise a general amnesty at Easter 1863 on condition that the rebels laid down their arms. The Poles replied that they could put no trust in the honour of a Russian Tsar, and the fighting dragged on for another savage year.

It was a year made more bitter by the behaviour of the European powers, above all France and Britain, who ignored or were ignorant of Alexander's hesitations and almost desperate pleadings, saw only the gaoler's hand, or a dark and mighty giant looming with terrifying immensity over a gallant and defiant David. By demonstrative and insincere admonitions they encouraged the suicidal resistance of the Poles and outraged Russian pride. The Poles had appealed to Louis Napoleon, ever assiduous in putting himself forward as the champion of freedom for small nations. Had he not, when all was said, gone to war with Austria on behalf of Italian nationhood? He had done nothing of the kind: he had given his backing to Cavour to win glory for himself and Nice and Savoy for France. There were no pickings to be had for France in eastern Europe. Napoleon felt obliged to make martial noises, if only to satisfy his own public opinion. But he had no intention of embroiling himself in another war with Russia. France and Austria, England too, had missed their chance of crippling Russia for generations to come when they had made peace after the fall of Sevastopol. Austria now, scarcely less than Prussia, had an interest in preserving the *status quo* in Poland regardless of the strained relations between Vienna and St Petersburg. The Poles had also appealed to England, the land of the free, only to receive a dusty answer. London was liberal with notes of protest and much noisy condemnation of Russian brutality. But nothing was achieved. 'A war in the centre of Europe,' declared Disraeli, 'on the pretext of restoring Poland is a general war and a long one. The map of Europe will be much changed when it is concluded, but I doubt whether the name of Poland will appear on it.'[3]

Anyone could have told Alexander and Gorchakov that nobody would fight for Poland, but it is a commentary on the difficulty which even quite intelligent statesmen experience when under stress in distinguishing what may be from what cannot be that St Petersburg for a time seriously feared a declaration of war by France and Britain. The Admiralty in St Petersburg, with impressive secrecy and despatch, sent off a considerable fleet, each ship sailing separately under sealed orders, to Halifax, Nova Scotia, seen as an initial jumping-off ground to attack British shipping in the Atlantic should Britain declare war.[4]

The results of all this uproar were a confirmation of mutual hostility and suspicion between Russia and Britain, the reversal of the rapprochement between Russia and France, a strengthening of the ties between Russia and Prussia – the new bond sealed with the blood of those Polish insurgents who had fled to Prussia and were formally delivered by Bismarck into the hands of the Russians.

There was still another result: the insurrection itself and the moral support (if that is the correct term) offered the Poles by the European powers closed the ranks of the Russians as nothing else could have done, not only in face of the outside world but in face of the radical critics of the system, few as these were inside and outside Russia. Alexander Herzen, raising a lonely voice of protest in London, came to be regarded as a traitor by many who had sympathised with his general line. It was now that the famous radical journalist, Michael Katkov, was converted overnight into a champion of reaction and went on to become the first chauvinist Russian intellectual, wielding immense influence in the decades to come. Even the excesses inflicted upon the defeated Poles by the 'hanging Muraviev', now Governor of Lithuania, went unchallenged in public, though many Russians deplored his atrocities in private. At the same time the upsurge of chauvinist emotion created a favourable climate for imperialist adventures where these could be undertaken without immediate collision with the European powers.

3

The field for adventure was wide. It extended all along Russia's immense, indeterminate Asian frontier from the Pacific to the Caspian. It was irresistible.

Russia, in fact, had never stopped moving. The Crimean War had put a check to Nicholas's modest and carefully regulated expansionism. But even while the Treaty of Paris was being negotiated the conquest of the Caucasus was resumed. In 1859 after a heroic struggle against overwhelming odds Shamil, with the tiny remnant of his tribesmen, was finally encircled and surrendered to the Viceroy of the Caucasus, who received him with full military honours. This was now Prince Baryatinsky, who, as a field commander six years earlier, had been impressed by the courage of the young Count Leo Tolstoy and urged him to apply for a regular commission. This splendid man conveyed the defeated chieftain to St Petersburg, where he was presented to the Tsar, and afterwards established in some comfort – but far from his rugged homeland – in the rolling landscape of the muddy Russian heartland. Thirteen years later he was permitted to visit Mecca, and there he died.

The remainder of the Caucasian peoples, who could now be cleaned up with comparative ease, received less consideration. The unfortunate Circassians were subjected to treatment which was to be a very mild foretaste of Stalin's behaviour in the Caucasus and elsewhere (it was also, of course, an aftertaste of the techniques employed by pre-Romanov Tsars in the Novgorod region and elsewhere to reduce possible centres of resistance to autocratic rule): they were given ten weeks to decide whether they would go quietly to new lands assigned to them in the vast Russian plain or emigrate to Turkey. Nearly half a million of them, driven from their mountain fastnesses, chose emigration. By the spring of 1864 all was quiet and the whole of Caucasia and Transcaucasia was finally absorbed into the Russian imperium. It was not a happy settlement, but the transportation or enforced emigration of the Moslem tribes broke the heart of the resistance, and the Christian Georgians and Armenians were happy to receive Russian protection, as the lesser evil, from Turkey and Persia.

Prince Baryatinsky, for all his vice-regal splendour, was sickened and humiliated by the policies he was required to carry out. He was in some ways years ahead of his time. He wrote to Alexander recommending a line of policy which might have been inspired by Lord Lugard. Obviously, he said, a skeleton garrison must be maintained, but the first duty of Russian power was to help with men, material and money in the reconstruction of a devastated land. Further, local administrators must be educated in tribal customs and modes of thought, in their special needs as well, so that they would be able to work with and for, not against, the native population. All this would inevitably cost money, but it would be money well spent – and it certainly must be spent if Russia were to live up to her name as a civilising influence.

To Alexander it must have seemed that this honest soldier had gone off his head. What were colonies for if not to deliver their riches to the imperial power? He replied fairly sharply: 'the Prince will understand that the Caucasus is but one part of Russia, and Russia has the right to expect that the Caucasus should diminish and not increase national expenditure at a time of severe national stringency.'[5]

Russia was indeed hard up at the end of the Crimean War: there was not even the cash to finance desperately needed railways, mines, factories, let alone to rehabilitate a conquered land. But Alexander's insistence that Russia 'had the right' to expect the newly subject peoples to contribute to the wealth of the conqueror went deeper than that. And the attitude of the Russian officials sent to administer the new lands was the despair of Baryatinsky, who shortly afterwards resigned. He was succeeded by the Tsar's younger brother, the Grand Duke Michael, and to him Baryatinsky left a kind of testament which showed that he stood head and shoulders above all but a handful of his own Russian contemporaries in his understanding of the national susceptibilities of 'lesser breeds' and on a level with the most enlightened administrators of his age:

'In my opinion the main danger lies in the adoption of an unintelligently hostile attitude towards alien peoples and the unthinking imposition of our own usages and customs . . . This sort of attitude and behaviour can all too easily work down to the lowest level of officialdom, affecting the smallest and most trivial details of everyday activity . . . Ask yourself how such overbearing arrogance can hope to win the loyalty and devotion of any subject people?'[6]

Baryatinsky was writing in 1860, less than three years after the Indian Mutiny. And he went on to advocate principles of colonial administration which amounted to a system of indirect rule through native chieftains, a system incomprehensible to an autocrat and a bureaucracy who found themselves incapable of delegating responsibility for effective local government of their own people even to the most loyal and talented Russians of ancient family. How could Russian bureaucrats be expected to win the loyalty and respect of conquered peoples when they treated their own people like slaves?

4

The conquest of the Caucasus had been a cleaning up of unfinished business, necessary if only for the firm establishment of the frontier with Persia and Turkey. Alexander had no choice but to complete the task his father had left undone. But the Caucasus was far from being the only theatre of expansion, and Russian activity in Asia, above all Turkestan and along the Chinese border, was by no means so easy to justify.

It was inevitable that St Petersburg should find itself deeply concerned with the future of Japan. In the wake of the American Admiral Perry who, with his notorious show of force, had compelled the Japanese to open the ports of their secret land to foreign trade, other powers had clustered round to extract concessions, and it was natural enough for the government of Russia to join in the hunt. A treaty signed in the last year of Nicholas's reign had formalised a division of the Kurile Islands, opened certain Japanese ports to Russian trade, and established, in very vague terms, a joint Russo-Japanese sphere of interest in Sakhalin – which had only very recently been discovered to be an island, quite detached from the great Eurasian land-mass.

What, however, did cause the powers, above all England, very acute anxiety was the extraordinary persistence and depth of Russian penetration into China on the one hand and in the general direction of Afghanistan and India on the other. By all normal diplomatic and strategic standards there was not the least need for this sort of imperial activity if all Russia needed, as her new Foreign Minister, Prince Alexander Gorchakov, resoundingly declared, was nothing but 'peace abroad and prosperity at home'. Indeed, there was every reason for restraint in empire-building on the part of a power, virtually bankrupt, which was incapable of effective government over its existing realm and which could expect no immediate return remotely commensurate with the energy, manpower and resources expended in enlarging it. To the outside eye this steady and apparently purposeful expansion suggested the existence of a master-plan. Where would the Russians stop? What was the point of pushing ever onwards into the wilderness unless in obedience to a deep scheme of conquest at the expense of the Western position in Asia? There was no master-plan and there was indeed no immediate point. The causes of the Russian imperial drive in the nineteenth century were complex, but among the most important, not at all understood in the West, was the chance it gave to ambitious and enterprising individuals to escape from the bureaucratic frustrations of life in metropolitan Russia. Men whose talents should have been harnessed to the building of prosperity at home found scope for their individualism only on the frontier, as far away from the central authority as they could get.

This applied even to professional diplomats who had ideas of their own. Thus the very gifted and imperially-minded Count N. P. Ignatiev found scope for his talents as an intriguer, liar and dissembler first by seeking to open up to Russian influence the barbaric khanates of Turkestan, an activity which took him on missions to Khiva and Bokhara, then to China where he crowned the military and diplomatic manoeuvres of half a decade by concluding the Treaty of Peking, which gave Russia the vast area, now known as the Maritime Province, between the Amur and Ussuri rivers and her Pacific base of Vladivostok, Lord of the East.

Ignatiev, of course, was nominally and in fact the Tsar's emissary. But once away from St Petersburg he enjoyed a freedom of action undreamt of by his colleagues at the centre, and indeed he worked on the Chinese with great skill. The Chinese were in dire straits and very hard-pressed indeed by the British and the French who, in the Opium War and thereafter, were treating the world to a display of the ugliest side of commercial imperialism. Between 1858 and 1860 Russian envoys exploited the situation with a bleakly smiling ruthlessness which, a century later, was to characterise Soviet activities in eastern Europe – now threatening, now flattering and coaxing, now unveiling the flash of steel, now promising support against the British and the French, now working with them against the Chinese; by the Treaties of Aigun and Peking they had in a very short time obtained all they required.

It was the diplomat Ignatiev who negotiated the Treaty of Peking, as it was he who first penetrated deep into Turkestan. But the annexationist drive came from more simple-minded men. In the Far East the hero was Count Muraviev-Amursky, who as Governor-General of Eastern Siberia enjoyed an autonomy unapproached by any of his colleagues closer to home. Muraviev-Amursky was a sort of Russian Cecil Rhodes. He was convinced that Russia had a great future in south-east Asia, and as early as 1847 persuaded Nicholas to authorise the exploration of the lower Amur river in the teeth of opposition from the conventionally-minded Nesselrode, who saw no point in upsetting either the Chinese or the European powers by pursuing a forward policy in an area which could be of no conceivable use to Russia for as far ahead as he could see. Muraviev-Amursky won his point and started in person what was to be a series of voyages of exploration, finally, in 1851, establishing a Russian post at the mouth of the Amur (later to be the city of Nikolaevsk). It was thanks largely to the intervention of the Tsarevich Alexander, fired by the spirit of adventure, that Nicholas was persuaded to agree. Everything followed from that. Muraviev-Amursky was driven not merely by dreams of empire but also by an obsessional suspicion of the British. He saw British spies everywhere, though in fact what London was interested in was nothing more romantic or glorious than opening up the Chinese trade.

For better or worse, with the foundation of Vladivostok Russia became a Pacific power, and it was only a matter of time before it was seen to be desirable to put increased pressure on Japan. It was now the turn of Ignatiev again, as head of the Asiatic Department of the Ministry of Foreign Affairs. And the upshot of many years of negotiation interspersed with intimidation was the securing of the whole of Sakhalin Island by Russia and the recognition of Japanese sovereignty over the whole of the Kurile chain by the Treaty of St Petersburg in 1875. By that time the Kurile Islands were of less importance to Russia than had once seemed likely.

In the eighteenth century Russian fur-hunters had pursued their drive into the wilds of Siberia and beyond, establishing themselves in the Aleutian and Kurile Islands and on the mainland of the North American Continent. In 1797 a United American Company had been formed, modelled on the British East India Company, renamed in 1799 the Russian-American Company, with its headquarters on the island of Sitka, off Alaska. In the fullness of time, and while the great struggle with Napoleon was being fought out, Russian settlers occupied Alaska and set up trading-posts on the Pacific coast of North America as far south as Fort Ross, a little to the north of San Francisco Bay. That was in 1812, and in the same year the Russian commander went so far as to despatch an exploratory expedition to the Hawaiian Islands. It was not until 1817 that Alexander I disowned the spirited adventurer who was trying to secure these island in his name, and it was not until half a century later that his nephew Alexander II began to wonder whether he was not over-extending himself a little by holding on to Alaska. The chief value of that frozen province had lain in the fur of the sea-otter, but the Russian fur-hunters had virtually exterminated this harmless and attractive beast: there was no more revenue to be had. In 1867, with the American Civil War intervening, St Petersburg agreed to sell Alaska to Washington, and did so for 7 million dollars. Oil and early-warning systems remained hidden in the future.

5

It was in Turkestan, however, that Russia's colonial activity appeared most clearly to impinge on the immediate interests of the Western powers. In particular, as though baulked for the time being in her Mediterranean aspirations, she appeared to be developing a careful and systematic plan of conquest and annexation which would bring her to the Hindu Kush and threaten the British position in India.

In fact there was no such plan, even if sixty years earlier Tsar Paul had conceived the lunatic idea of joining forces with Napoleon in a land campaign against the British in India. The furious Russian activity in Turkestan during the 1860s was a natural consequence of the slow south-ward drift which had led to the absorption of the steppes of what is now Kazakhstan, with their hordes of nomad pastoralists. To the south of Kazakhstan the Russian adventurers found themselves faced with the descendants of an ancient and legendary culture tightly organised into three separate khanates, Kokand, Bokhara, Khiva, and on their flank, between the Aral Sea and the Caspian, a tough breed of stockbreeding nomads, the Turcomans. The Russians were actively concerned with what went on in these hidden lands, from which raiders would issue to prey upon the Kazakh shepherds and their herds, or carry off prisoners from outlying Cossack posts; in which, it was also furiously believed, British agents infiltrated from Afghanistan and Persia constantly schemed and intrigued for Russia's undoing.

Under Nicholas, before the Crimean War, there had been some fairly ineffective probing of this vast region. But it was the Indian Mutiny of 1857 which convinced Ignatiev that now was the moment to take advantage of British weakness and move deeper into central Asia. His missions to Khiva and Bokhara in 1858 were enough to show that if Russia wanted to control the khanates she would have to fight them and subdue them first. The need to control them appeared in a more urgent light only a year or two later, when Russia found herself desperate for raw cotton, her normal supplies from America curtailed by the Civil War. To secure and develop the potentially enormous source of supply in Turkestan was the final impulsion behind the long series of campaigns which started in 1864 and did not end until the defeat and massacre of the Turcomans in 1881.

The subjugation of Turkestan involved much arduous campaigning in punishing territory, both desert and mountain. The enemy was cruel and barbaric and fought hard. The romance of the place names, Samarkand, Bokhara; the mysterious river valleys of the Oxus (Amu-Darya) and the Jaxartes (Syr-Darya); the great mosques and the memories of Genghis Khan; all this, together with a ready-made national hero in General Kaufman, would have been material for a national epic. But in fact, although the spirit of Russian nationalism was developing fast, there was no public response to the Turkestan conquest to compare with the excitement over the opening up of the Caucasus. It may simply have been that there was no Pushkin to fire the imagination, no young Tolstoy or Lermontov to fight under Kaufman or Skobolev and live to tell the tale. It seems more likely, however, that the public mood was changing: the conquest of Turkestan was not a romance but a job to be done, a particular aspect of the White Man's Burden. And feelings about the conquest in the highest circles were very mixed.

Alexander took pleasure in extending the bounds of his inheritance, although he must have wondered before he died how it was that he, the liberator, the peace-maker, should have extended the Russian Empire east and south farther than his father's wildest dreams, to the tune of more than a million square miles: it was in January 1881, a month before Alexander's death, that the dashing Skobolev captured Geok-Tepe and ordered the massacre of the entire male population and the rounding up and killing of any who fled.

Ignatiev as a forward-looking diplomat and Dmitri Milyutin at the Ministry of Defence were the moving spirits behind the campaign of conquest, but they had, at least to begin with, a fairly strong antagonist in Reutern, as Minister of Finance, who insisted that wars, even colonial wars, were a luxury which a bankrupt country could not afford.

It was Prince Gorchakov, cousin of the Crimean Commander-in-Chief (and of the novelist, Tolstoy), who, as Foreign Minister, had to bear the weight of foreign disapproval. It worried him greatly. He was a vain little man of narrow views, but at least he understood that his country's primary task, apart from the domestic reforms which were not his concern, was to re-establish herself as a force to be reckoned with in Europe pending the eventual revision of the Treaty of Paris. To that end he sought to avoid unnecessary friction with the powers and to reassure them as best he could when friction arose. After the Polish insurrection he was hard put to it to explain away the upsurge of Russian nationalism which made possible the forward policies of Ignatiev and Milyutin. Now, in 1864, with Kaufman going hell for leather deep into Turkestan, he was moved to issue his famous circular to the powers. Intended as a gesture of conciliation, it treated those hoary and experienced sinners, Britain and France, to a kindergarten course in the meaning of imperialism: 'The position of Russia is similar to that of any other civilised country with half-savage, half-nomadic tribes for neighbours,' he started off and went on to argue that in the interests of security and the pursuit of trade such neighbours must be subjected to 'a certain authority'. But, alas, no sooner done than the benevolent overlords find their new frontiers threatened by yet another wave of barbarians, who must also be subdued, and so on again and again. Periodical punitive expeditions are not enough: when the conquering power withdraws her retreat is ascribed to weakness. Therefore a state must either abandon her civilising mission and leave her frontiers open to repeated attacks, or else move on even deeper. 'Such has been the pattern in all colonial history.' It was, he concluded, 'a process in which physical necessity supersedes ambition, and the hardest thing is to know where to stop . . .'[7]

Poor Gorchakov could tell nothing to Britain and France that they did not know already. But at least he did not pretend that Russia regarded her new acquisitions as anything but colonies. He would have been surprised to the point of incredulity had he been told that scarcely more than a century later Russia would stand in the world as the last imperial power, enjoying undisputed sovereignty for good or ill over the lands and peoples subdued by successive Tsars, the Tsar Liberator above all.

6

The year of the Polish revolt marked the end of the first phase of Alexander's post-Crimean diplomacy. He had only one aim: to achieve the repeal of the clauses in the Treaty of Paris which excluded Russian power from the Black Sea. Prussian support in this aim gave him one more reason for cleaving closely to Berlin, but Prussia was not enough, and he tried hard and persistently to win over Louis Napoleon, basing his policy on their common hostility to Austria. Napoleon did not feel strongly about the Black Sea, but he was not prepared to risk serious friction with the British, who were adamant against change. It was during this period of Franco-Russian co-operation, however, that certain movements occurred in the Balkans which were to have a lasting effect. In 1858 there arose a powerful demand for the unification of the Principalities, Moldavia and Wallachia. This was supported by Napoleon as champion of small nations, opposed by Austria; the British attitude was divided; Russia had no strong views but wanted to please Paris and annoy Vienna. In 1859, as the outcome of an international conference in Paris, Alexander Cuza was chosen as the ruler of a formally established United Principalities, which was the kingdom of Roumania in everything but name. In 1858 the pro-Austrian Alexander Karageorgevic was overthrown in Serbia and succeeded by the then pro-Russian Obrenevic dynasty, which also had the backing of France. In the same year France and Russia succeeded in securing more territory for Montenegro after a local rising against the Turks. In March 1859 France and Russia concluded a secret treaty assuring Napoleon of Russia's benevolent neutrality when France went to war with Austria, a war which England was straining every nerve to prevent.

From Tsarskoe Selo and the Winter Palace these years of feverish diplomacy had a very purposeful look indeed, and when Austria was defeated at Solferino and was compelled to cede Lombardy to Victor Emmanuel, soon to be included in a united Italy, Alexander and Gorchakov could contemplate with satisfaction not only the reassertion of Russian influence in the Balkans, above all at Austria's expense, but also close bonds with a France which, deeply as Alexander deplored Napoleon's encouragement of Garibaldi and his red-shirts, had to all appearances consolidated her position as a very great power indeed. But St Petersburg was oblivious of a danger much nearer home.

The understanding with France could not survive Napoleon's encouragement of the Polish revolt in 1863. And with the Polish affair came the first move in a new process which was to end by turning the old European balance upside down.

Russia, France, Britain, might think they were making European policy. They were wrong. The only man in all Europe who had a clear idea of where he wanted to go and how to get there was Bismarck, who became Prime Minister, or Chancellor, of Prussia in 1862 and who was already determined to put an end to Austrian hegemony in Germany, then to make Prussia supreme. As early as 1859, during his stint at the Embassy in St Petersburg, in a letter to Schleinitz, his Minister in Berlin, he began to open his mind: 'I regard the federal relationship in Germany as a sickness of which Prussia will sooner or later have to be cured, *ferro et igne*'.[8] In 1862, newly created Chancellor, he made the speech later to be famous, prophesying war: 'Germany does not look to Prussia's liberalism, but to her power . . . The great questions of the time will be decided, not by speeches and resolutions of majorities . . . but by iron and blood.'[9] In that year also, just before he assumed the premiership, he had gone to London and astonished Disraeli (who still had five years to go before becoming Prime Minister himself) with his candour:

I shall soon be compelled to undertake the conduct of the Prussian Government. My first care will be to reorganise the army, with or without the help of the *Landtag*. . . . As soon as the army shall have been brought to such a condition as to inspire respect, I shall seize the best pretext to declare war on Austria, dissolve the German Diet, subdue the minor States, and give national unity to Germany under Prussia's leadership. I have come here to say this to the Queen's Ministers.[10]

This was the man whose first major move, to bind Russia more closely to him, was to initiate that repellent treaty, foreshadowing even more vile agreements seventy-five years later, whereby Russia and Prussia should concert their border actions against the Poles and Prussia would hand over to the Tsar rebels found on her territory. Alexander and Gorchakov may be forgiven for not taking Bismarck seriously at that time. Nobody expected he would last long. The extravagant amorality of his ideas were already giving offence to liberal Prussians and also to the King, his master. But when, a year later, he contrived to jockey Austria into going to war with Denmark at Prussia's side in order to wrest Schleswig-Holstein from the Danish Crown, the Tsar and his ministers should have asked themselves some serious questions. They did not like the Prussian action. Alexander had the closest ties with Denmark. But he allowed it to happen because his support for Denmark might have led to the establishment of a Scandinavian bloc under the leadership of Sweden. And a stronger Sweden in alliance with Britain could have been a threat to the Russian position in the Baltic.

He chose Prussia. This meant that for the next critical six years he had surrendered the initiative to the only political genius of the age, who was to turn Prussia, in the shape of a united Germany, into the strongest military power in the world. For Prussia used Austria to subdue Denmark, then with brilliant opportunism exploited an Austrian indiscretion to ensure that Russian hatred of Austria should not die down: this was when France and Italy proposed that Austria should take the Principalities (Roumania) for herself, in exchange for the cession of Venetia. Austria quite properly declined, knowing that this would lead to war with Russia; but not before she had discussed the matter at some length. Bismarck, finding what was going on, informed the Russians. So that when the time came for him to pick his quarrel with Austria (over the aftermath of the Schleswig-Holstein affair), Alexander was in a black mood and stood by to watch with enjoyment the humiliation of Austria by von Moltke at Königgrätz. All this was emotionally understandable, though by now Alexander and Gorchakov should have been deeply troubled about the rapid growth of Prussian power. No doubt it still seemed to them that Berlin was bound to St Petersburg with bands of steel. A friendly, even a firmly neutral, Prussia was in effect a guarantee of her western frontier. Austria, on the other hand, besides proving herself ungrateful and doubly treacherous, was the potential antagonist in the Balkans. But what did the Russians make of it when, instead of crushing Austria after defeating her so absolutely in the field, Bismarck restrained his triumphant colleagues, prevented the imposition of crippling terms on Vienna, and made it quite plain that he proposed to transform the defeated foe into an ally? He not only left Austria strong: by excluding her from Germany he positively turned her towards the Balkans – and thus towards Russia. He believed he was clever and powerful enough to keep the peace between the two powers – as he put it years later, to hold the two heraldic beasts by their collars and keep them from getting at each other's throats. And so he was. Those who came after him lacked his skill, his understanding, above all his conception of war as a swift and terrible means to a strictly limited end.

His last war, whether deliberately planned or a swift response to an unforeseen opportunity, ended in the destruction of Napoleon and the Second Empire, the occupation of Paris, and the crowning of the Prussian king at Versailles as Emperor of Germany. He knew he could count on Russian neutrality, he knew that Austria would refrain from going to the help of France for fear of 300,000 Russians falling on her rear. To Alexander it brought a coveted prize. With France prostrate, with Austria friendless and alone, with the moral support of an all-conquering Prussian army, Russia could safely denounce the Black Sea clauses of the Treaty of Paris. And so she did. Britain was in no position to stand alone against the restoration of Russian naval power. She sought to make the best of a bad job, and at a conference of the powers held in London in 1871 the affair was regularised. Russia and Turkey should in future have the right to keep naval forces in the Black Sea and the Sultan might permit the passage through the Straits in peacetime of friendly and allied powers.

Thus it might be argued that by the exercise of discreet and skilful diplomacy over a period of fifteen years Alexander and Gorchakov had achieved without bloodshed the main aim of their European policy. So much for the short term. In the long term, however, by their steady assistance in facilitating the creation of Bismarckian Germany, which meant Hohenzollern Germany (for Bismarck could not live for ever), they were active in paving the way for the destruction of Imperial Russia. More immediately to the point, they had demonstrated once again the Russian propensity for fishing in troubled waters which had been so marked a feature of previous reigns and which had been the despair of the most intelligent and far-seeing officials under Nicholas. A conservative autocrat whose imperative interest was to preserve the principle of legitimacy in Europe and who was genuinely anxious to keep the peace had, nevertheless, lent his support first to the adventurer Napoleon III, then to the militarist dynamism of Bismarck's Prussia, the two forces both hellbent on changing the face of Europe. All to humiliate a fellow dynast in Vienna and to secure the revision of a treaty which Britain alone was determined to uphold. A wiser monarch, a cleverer and more perceptive diplomat, would have used all his influence to preserve the continental balance while addressing himself to London, seeking to demonstrate that Britain had nothing to fear in the Mediterranean or in Asia from a Russia which had all the space she needed, and more besides.

CHAPTER THIRTEEN

Aspects of Self-Love

I

It is usual, and fairly natural, to think of the 1870s in Russia as a period of revolutionary convulsion; and indeed towards the end of the decade even level-headed government officials such as Dmitri Milyutin were driven close to despair by the wave of terrorism which culminated in the murder of Alexander in 1881. But in fact the numbers directly involved were very small, and although the way was being prepared for the convulsions of 1905 and 1917, it is all too easy to overestimate in the light of hindsight the part played in the national consciousness by the revolutionary intelligentsia in the post-Emancipation years. The prime factors of the 1870s, as of the late 1860s, were not the destroyer with the bomb, or even the fanatical and disciplined conspirator, but on the one hand the accelerated development of the Empire's material resources and on the other the crystallisation of self-conscious nationalism.

After the reforms of the 1860s important material advances were made. For example, there was a notable though belated spurt in railway construction. At the time of the Crimean War Russia had only 650 miles of railway track; but twenty years later there were getting on for 12,000 miles. The war, of course, had shown the urgent need for strategic railways, but Reutern and others also saw that a transport network was needed to link together the producing centres, the great inland markets, and the ports. Under Nicholas it had been taken for granted that railway construction was a matter for the state. But now the state decided to call private developers in aid, and the men were there. Outstanding individuals in a new generation of gifted entrepreneurs were prepared to stake everything in their determination to make their fortunes and, at the same time, throw themselves into the act of creation for the sheer pleasure and excitement of making things work in a land where creation was frowned upon and very few things worked. Many of these were Baltic Germans, some were Jews – Meck, Derviz, Bloch. They parcelled out the vast spaces between them and soon had highly efficient lines running all over western and southern Russia and as far east as the Urals.

These private companies owed a great deal to the imagination and energy of Reutern, who encouraged the foundation of private banks and joint stock companies and also made it easy for small foreign depositors to invest in Russia – a revolutionary proceeding in itself, since hitherto foreign participation had been severely limited to government loans and to such foreign merchants, businessmen and entrepreneurs who were prepared to live and work in Russia under the eye of the central government. In a word, without fanfare, the Russian economy was becoming increasingly entangled with the West. The railways played a big part in this, quite apart from their borrowings. Thus, for example, the repeal in Britain of the Corn Laws in 1846 had opened up for foreign suppliers an important market for grain. Russia had been slow to exploit this, partly for political reasons, but more especially because of transport difficulties. With the new railways grain could be carried from the remote expanses of the rich Black Earth zone not only to feed the Russian cities but also to the ports for export, above all to Odessa, which throve exceedingly. Thus between 1860 and 1880 the export of grain went up from some 1.5 million tons a year to nearly 5 million tons. This was achieved at a time when there was a spectacular flight from the land on the part of the less prosperous nobility, who had found it hard to make ends meet after the Emancipation, and now gave up to find jobs in the army, the bureaucracy, the swiftly developing professions from medicine to law. It was achieved also at the expense of the provinces themselves, the very producers of the grain, who had to pay higher prices or see their local produce trundled off to new and more profitable markets. And before the century was out a new hazard made itself felt: in years of drought (which recur with terrible regularity in those broad, rich lands) the export of grain to fill the treasury in St Petersburg continued unabated. The peasants who had produced the grain were left to starve.

Other rates of growth were slower. The Ural iron industry suddenly declined with the flight of serf labour immediately after the Emancipation, and the newly discovered coal and iron complex in the Donetz basin and in the Western Ukraine round Krivoy Rog faltered in its development for a very characteristic reason. At the very moment, in 1869, when the Welsh ironmaster, John Hughes, was granted his charter to form the New Russia Company to mine coal and iron and manufacture steel in the Donetz basin, the new railways were putting in their demands for almost unlimited steel for the manufacture of rails, etc. But the Government, instead of seizing a heaven-sent chance to develop what would now be called a heavy industrial base with the aid of foreign capital, preferred to favour the Putilov works in St Petersburg and a lesser and more recently founded mill at Bryansk, not far from Moscow. And these in their turn found it cheaper to import their ore and coal from abroad. So the treasure of the Donetz basin was neglected for another twenty years. Then, towards the end of the century, it was to be exploited too fast and too late, serving as a breeding ground for revolution. It was Yuzovka, named after Hughes (later to be called Stalino, later still, Donetsk), that was to become the centre of a great industrial region run chiefly by a whole constellation of foreign concessionaires. And here, in 1906, nearly fifty years after its foundation, the boy Nikita Khrushchev was taken by his poor peasant parents to make a living. Khrushchev was to develop into one of those rough, bullying Party watch-dogs used by Stalin to destroy the Bolshevik intellectuals – men who had received their education amid the grim squalor of the Russian industrial revolution, who were to make mincemeat of the early dreamers with their university backgrounds and sometimes passionate ideals.

Lenin himself, for example, was born a few months after the start of the Franco-Prussian War, a few more months after the foundation of Yuzovka. He was born at Simbirsk, a pleasantly situated provincial capital standing high on the west bank of the middle Volga. As Vladimir Ilyich Ulyanov, he was the second son of an able, respected and quite gifted inspector and director of schools (a younger contemporary of Matthew Arnold), who was to be promoted State Councillor, and thus into the upper ranks of the service nobility – the military equivalent was Major-General. The infant Ulyanov, our Lenin, was born, that is to say, into the sort of family that represented the new post-reform Russia at its best – a comfortable and respectable, highly literate household, the parents critical of the regime, but deeply patriotic and in no way destructive in their criticism. It is worth remembering that from the 1870s onward we shall be contemplating the Russia in which Lenin grew up and was formed, contentedly accepting it at first, in childhood and early adolescence, intent on university and a conventional career, until, in his eighteenth year, he set out to destroy it: his elder brother had involved himself in an amateurish plot to assassinate Alexander III, for which he was hanged in 1887.

2

It was a Russia of considerable promise in the social sphere and miraculous achievement in the arts. In the 1860s Turgenev had published *On the Eve, Fathers and Sons, First Love* and *Smoke*. Dostoevsky had published

Memoirs from Underground, Crime and Punishment, The Gambler and *The Idiot*; while in December 1869 the final volume of Tolstoy's *War and Peace* came out. All these writers, and others too, were to produce further masterpieces in the 1870s, when the astonishing torrent of artistic vitality was reinforced by the musicians, above all Mussorgsky, Borodin, Rimsky-Korsakov, Tchaikovsky. Very importantly the writers and musicians found a public, as well as rich patrons, not only among the more active-minded nobility, but also among quite a new, rapidly growing class, sandwiched between the landowners and the peasants, between the courtiers and the shopkeepers. It was a class of younger landowners who had sold up their estates: cultivated civil servants, lawyers, doctors, army officers (of course) and the new entrepreneurs. It was, for example, the widow of one of the first railway tycoons, Nadezhda von Meck (but she had aristocratic blood in her veins), who for so long kept Tchaikovsky going with regular subsidies and safe havens, always refusing to meet him, but conducting with him for nearly fifteen years an elaborate and revealing correspondence.

There is no word for these people. They were indeed a middle class, but they were a middle class lacking any sense of corporate identity. Instead of forming a compact and powerful interest group which fought its way into power by hard work and an eye for the main chance, using its wealth to accumulate still more while enriching the state treasury in the process, the Russian middle class was fragmented, almost a species of wreckage thrown up by the Alexandrine reforms, partaking neither of the bourgeois virtues nor the bourgeois vices. Peripheral. The sort of society which was to increase in numbers but not in influence for half a century to come, to be depicted in its last stages by Anton Chekhov, himself a part of it (though his grandfather had been a serf who had bought his own freedom and his father a clerk with the mentality of the serf). Consider for a moment *The Three Sisters* – here is a middle-class milieu of schoolteachers and garrison officers in a dusty provincial town. But it is a middle class lost and remote from any purposeful social role, whether beneficial or pernicious. It exists in limbo.

It would be convenient to use the term 'intelligentsia' to cover all thinking Russians, and certainly the term was first used as a label for all those educated individuals who had an active role to play in society – whether as officials, army officers, lawyers, schoolteachers, or whatever. But very soon, even in the 1870s, the word was pre-empted by extreme radicals, or revolutionaries, dedicated to the overthrow of the dynasty and all established institutions: only the true-blue fanatic, the man or woman who understood the supreme, the quasi-mystical necessity of throwing the baby out with the bathwater, was worthy of the name *intelligent* (hard 'g'). This led to the peculiar situation in which a Nechayev qualified while the great chemist Mendeleyev did not. Even so, this is no sillier than current Soviet practice: for nowadays, seeking to defuse the word, the Soviet authorities have decreed that the term 'intelligentsia' must apply to all white-collar workers – thus, as a distinguished American scholar has pointed out, bringing about the happy brotherhood of the chief of the K.G.B. and his most vigorous adversary, Andrei Sakhavov, and others.

It is a tiresome word. I shall try to avoid it henceforth, referring instead to revolutionaries, radicals, liberals, moderates, conservatives, even occasionally, in moments of unusual unity, to the educated classes.

What the educated classes were above all preoccupied with in the 1860s and '70s was the search for national identity. This had started, as we have seen, with the early debates between the Slavophiles and the Westernisers. As the century advanced radicals and conservatives alike were caught up in that remarkable cult – the worship of the peasant. Besides holding back the material development of the country – the clinging to the village commune, regarded by the conservatives as a cement of great strength, by the radicals as a primitive form of socialism to be developed and not cast aside – this manifested itself in a number of ways, not least the great cultural renaissance. For it was to have a very direct bearing on Russia's finest gift to the world: the injection into the arts, above all in the novel and in opera, of that famous spirit of realism which in its origin was an inverted romanticism. It calls for a leap of the imagination to see how this followed from the search for national identity which was first dramatised by Chaadayev.

The Russia of Chaadayev had indeed given nothing to the world. It was the Russia of courtiers, bureaucrats, landowners, soldiers, illiterate priests, crude and grasping merchants, battening on the great mass of their fellow men and women, who were slaves. It was presided over by a Tsargod living the life of an anchorite in a welter of conspicuous extravagance which outdazzled the court at Versailles. It is easy to understand how the thinking Russian of the day must have found it inconceivable, intolerable even, that there could be no good in this vast land of his ancestors. If the ruling caste had failed this could only mean that it had cut itself off from the people, the source of all national vitality. And the people, exploited, ground down, had turned in on themselves, suffering in silence, but hugging to their breasts the primitive virtues uncorrupted by the meretricious and predatory greed of the great world. Or, to put it another way, the new and newly self-conscious educated classes had to believe in something, and the only thing they could believe in was the great unknown and untried, the Russian peasant, who had stood remote and aloof, outside the tides of history, and must one day come into his own and show not only his oppressors but also the tired and shabby Western world that, through suffering (suffering which could not be meaningless, which must one day prove itself justified), he had kept intact the virtues, the honour indeed, surrendered by the bourgeois of the West in return for material comforts.

Thus it was that even a Chernyshevsky could, for a time, see Russia's salvation in the village commune. This herald of the iron-faced revolutionary, who preached the need of a conspiratorial revolutionary élite partaking of the nature of supermen, had in fact nothing but contempt for the peasant. In his own words, 'The mass of the population knows nothing and cares about nothing except its material advantages. And this indifference of the mass is the main factor which makes possible the very idea of changes in political life . . . the mass is simply the raw material for diplomatic and political experiments. Whoever rules it tells it what to do and it obeys.'[1] But this same man, confronted with the mystique of the commune (as distinct from the individual peasant in the flesh), could contradict himself absurdly: 'the sacred and beneficial custom bequeathed to us by our past, the precious heirloom which alone richly recompenses us for all the past misery: may we never dare infringe on the communal holding of land.'[2]

The obeisance of the older Herzen to the peasant was more genuine, though no less irrelevant. Here it was more a case of a sophisticated, Westernising radical turning his back on the philistinism of Western bourgeois society and glorifying Russian peasant backwardness as the hope of the world.

An aspect of Western life which filled Herzen with particular and furious displeasure was faith in the rule of law. And, curiously, in his blazing contempt for the hypocrisies implicit in the whole Western confusion between the ideal and the real in the matter of abstract justice and equity, Herzen was closer to the Tsars than to any Western liberal or radical. He was, in a word, very Russian.

Like so many Russians he did not understand what law was about. Even in those countries where the rule of law is held in instinctive respect exaggerated legalism is regarded with some degree of unease, distrust or contempt. In Russia the law itself, the very principle of law, is and always has been widely regarded with suspicion, often with a contempt that has nothing to do with the pretensions, the greed, the pettifoggery of lawyers. It stems partly from the traditional understanding that the Tsar himself can be the only maker of laws and, at the same time, stands above all laws, partly from an aspect of the anarchic spirit to which the deliberate cult of autocracy was developed as an antidote: the Tsar was elevated above all men in order to hold all men together, be it with benevolence or savagery; and the undisputed will of this one man was considered to be restraint enough. On the other hand, the elevation of an elaborate code of laws into a series of binding contracts, necessarily spelt out in more or less rigid detail, implied the coming together of all men *to bind themselves,* a voluntary surrender of personal sovereignty which went against the Russian grain. The law, further, must stand for inflexibility and unforgivingness. It excludes the quickening warmth of human grace and impulse. It exalts hypocrisy, because the law-givers and the judges are men like other men, not free from human frailty, and yet, by virtue of their office, present themselves as being free from human frailty. Finally, it was understood very well by most Russians, and long before Engels and Marx, that laws are not immaculately conceived in abstract virtue but are made by the strong largely to protect their own privileges and possessions – a fact of nature more easily hidden in the West than in Russia, if only because in Russia the law, what there was of it, was the instrument of the autocracy itself, so that a university professor, a field-marshal, a high official, was no less vulnerable, no less liable to find himself on the wrong side of the law, than the poorest peasant. In the West, on the other hand, the unceasing aspiration of all but the desperately poor and the outcast towards respectability, towards gentility, then towards a measure of material prosperity, then towards the freedom of the green pastures of the landed gentry, ensured that all but the wicked or the irredeemable in rural and city slums had a vested interest in the law.

Herzen in his celebrated letter to the historian Michelet, expresses to perfection a profound Russian attitude. Here the son of an aristocrat, who inherited a considerable private fortune, and who even when in exile and preaching international socialism saw nothing out of the way in enlisting the support of the Rothschilds in proving his own financial claims, is closer to the peasant than to his own kind.

The peasant who has been acquitted by the court trudges home no more elated than if he had been condemned. In either case the decision seems to him the result of capricious tyranny or chance.

In the same way, when he is summoned as a witness he stubbornly professes to know nothing, even in face of incontestable fact. Being found guilty by a law-court does not disgrace a man in the eyes of the Russian peasant. Exiles and convicts go by the name of *unfortunates* with him.[3]

Speaking of the birth of the great literary movement of liberation, he elaborates this thought:

Between the peasantry and literature there looms the monster of official Russia. 'Russia the deception, Russia the pestilence', as you call her. This Russia extends from the Emperor, passing from gendarme to gendarme, from official to official, down to the lowest policeman in the remotest corner of the Empire. Every step of the ladder, as in Dante, gains a new power for evil, a new degree of corruption and cruelty. This living pyramid of crimes, abuses and bribery, built up of policemen, scoundrels, heartless German officials everlastingly greedy, ignorant judges everlastingly drunk, aristocrats everlastingly base: all this is held together by a community of interest in plunder and gain, and supported by six hundred thousand animated machines with bayonets. The peasant is never defiled by contact with the government of aggression; he endures its existence – only in that is he to blame.'⁴

Only in that . . .? But of course the judges were not all drunken, nor were the aristocrats all base or the officials, German or otherwise, all greedy. Many of them were, the majority no doubt; but many were not. Herzen knew this, none better. The son of an eccentric and immensely rich nobleman of ancient lineage, he was technically a bastard: although his father had gone through a proper form of marriage in Germany with the girl who was to become Herzen's mother, he failed to take the necessary step of repeating the ceremony in Russia. But the young Herzen was brought up in affluence, accustomed to the frequent presence in his guardian uncle's household of men close to the Tsar and occupying exalted positions – among them the jolly and ill-fated hero of 1812 and Governor of St Petersburg, Miloradovich, shot by one of the Decembrists whom Herzen was to idolise. As one of the earliest student rebels he had unexampled opportunities for experiencing at first hand the best and worst aspects of authority. As time went on, disgust at the worst and contempt for the small-mindedness, hypocrisy and absence of moral courage among the well-meaning blinded him to the best and transformed him into an agent of destruction.

He was a classic example of those Russians, and these include the finest, who seem to find difficulty not only in distinguishing between the evils endemic to humanity and those arising from a particular and local society but even in realising that such a distinction exists. The faintest recognition of the existence of original sin, as distinct from the sins of the regime, would have been of inestimable assistance to the Russian radicals in clarifying their views and refining their policies. Herzen was especially well placed to make a conceptual break-through of this kind. Sickened and outraged by the Tsarist system, he looked for salvation in the West and was sickened and outraged by what he saw there. Is it too much to expect that he might have started putting two and two together and asking himself whether he might not be on the wrong tack in his wholesale condemnation of all things Russian when he found himself driven to condemn, no less vehemently, all things Western? Might it not have occurred to him that human nature had something to do with the evils which he ascribed to political systems which, after all, were the products of human beings?

Instead, still addressing Michelet, defending Russia from his criticisms while conceding that Russia was sunk in unrelieved iniquity, with that depressingly masochistic breast-beating (boasting, one might almost say) which was to be so marked a feature of Russian criticism for decades to come, he continues:

> Can we honestly be contented with your threadbare morality, un-christian and inhuman, existing only in rhetorical exercises and speeches for the prosecution? What respect can be inspired in us by your Roman-barbaric system of law, that hollow, clumsy edifice, without light or air, repaired in the Middle Ages, whitewashed by the newly enfranchised petty-bourgeoisie? I admit that the daily brigandage in the Russian law courts is even worse, but it does not follow from this that you have justice in your laws or your courts.

Indeed it does not. Here again we catch the echo:

> We are held by too many chains to fasten fresh ones about us of our own free will. In this respect we stand precisely on a level with our peasants. We submit to brute force. We are slaves because we have no possibility of being free; but we accept nothing from our foes.
> Russia will never be Protestant, Russia will never be *juste milieu*.[5]

This kind of apocalyptic nonsense produced by a man of acute intelligence, perceptiveness and courage was itself to help forge the chains which bind the Russia of our own day. The nonsense went very deep. It could be argued that Herzen was writing in 1851 at the peak of the Nicholas reaction in Russia and at the moment of greatest disillusionment after the failure of the 1848 revolutions. So he was. But the mood persisted. And it was in this mood that he finally rejected official Russia even in the moment when the reform movement was making headway, and, obsessed with the imperfections of the Western system, was driven back like so many others to seek salvation in the peasant and in the peasant commune.

3

The search for national identity which so frequently led to the discovery of special virtue in the peasant masses was to manifest itself in more constructive ways. For a critical period it affected even Leo Tolstoy, who sat down to write *War and Peace* in 1863. For this tremendous novel, a celebration of life itself by a man who was later so painfully to turn away from life, unable to bear the clarity of his own vision of its complexity and mystery, was also a hymn to Russia. In its pages Russian nationhood was for the first time given features and structure: until then this nationhood had existed only in the declarations of the autocrat and his ministers and satraps.

What almost every imaginative writer of the age had in common was the desire to discover the people of Russia, including themselves, and present them as they were. For they did not know who they were. In the absence of a spontaneously organised society, how could they possibly know? The court and the great nobles, the men who should have been the country's natural leaders, hardly spoke their own language: they spoke French. The churchmen, champions of orthodoxy, had nothing to say about human values, whether spiritual or ethical, concerning themselves exclusively with the maintenance of the secular *status quo* and the ritual gestures designed to ensure a safe passage for the soul into the hereafter. The effective drive within the ruling bureaucracy came overwhelmingly from men of more or less German descent who were regarded almost universally as humourless, pedantic, rigid, and indecently hard-working. How to isolate the quality of Russianness, define it, and make it tell? We recall Herzen on the Russian intelligentsia: 'we stand precisely on a level with our peasants. We submit to brute force.' In the shadow of brute force all are equal. 'We are slaves because we have no possibility of being free; but we accept nothing from our foes.' In a society of slaves there is no communal responsibility, though there must be communal sympathy. The writers of Western Europe were never irredeemably at odds with the very substance and fabric of the society of which they formed a part; it was their own society, vile as it might seem to them in certain aspects. Society and themselves they took for granted: they did not have to ask who they were, as Frenchmen, as Englishmen: they thought they knew. Even the great satirists of the West were far less concerned than a Goncharov or a Saltykov-Schedrin with the shortcomings of their own societies than with human wickedness and folly regardless of particular circumstance and place.

The Russian novelists on the other hand, to generalise extremely, could take no society for granted. They had to find out who the Russians were, and it was this quest, pursued in a land almost wholly devoid of social, of communal, achievement, which gave rise to the sort of realism which we have come to think of as peculiarly Russian, unblinking, uninhibited, unashamed, in a certain sense formless.

And yet a remarkable thing about all these Russians, with certain shining exceptions, is that with all the marvellous directness of their vision, unclouded, undistorted, by the received ideas of a long-established society pressing in on them, they could not stay the course. Russian achievement was null; Western achievement was a mockery because it fell so far short of its pretensions. Russia had never pretended. Only the autocrat had pretended. Therefore the great human potential of the Russian people remained virgin and untapped, like the minerals beneath Russian soil. Instead of asking why the West had failed to live up to its great pretensions in spite of much heroic struggle, instead of reflecting that it might be a condition of life that the ideal must for ever be a dream to be striven for – that, indeed, the very triumph of an ideal must be its undoing – they turned their faces from the concept of amelioration and pinned their faith to revolution. And conservative Russians were in this respect no less revolutionary than the political radicals: from the early Slavophiles onwards, through Dostoevsky to the imperialist Panslavs, they believed in the holy mission of a reborn Russia to cleanse the corrupt and tainted world.

Thus it was that even the loftiest Russian thinkers of the second half of the nineteenth and the first decades of the twentieth centuries, with the rarest exceptions, such as V. S. Solovyev, thought in national not universal terms: or, when they thought in universal terms, it was only to impose national solutions on the world at large. Russian nationalism now, as in centuries past, expressed itself in orthodoxy. Some of the most radical pre-revolutionary thinkers fled back into the orthodoxy of the true Church. Others sought to establish a secular orthodoxy no less rigid, and finally succeeded. Nearly all dreamed of imposing Russian solutions upon the world at large.

4

The strange mixture of Russian nationalism and open-minded seeking was not confined to problems of a political and social kind. It went much deeper. And it may be illuminated from an unexpected angle by the activities of a circle far removed from politics – that group of mid-century musicians known as the Five: Balakirev, Cui, Mussorgsky, Borodin and Rimsky-Korsakov, together with their prophet, the critic Vladimir Stasov.

It was in 1858 that the first Russian composer of genius, Michael Glinka, got bored with writing music and went to live abroad on the rents from his inherited estates. But there was a laying-on of hands. And the chosen successor to the prophet's mantle was another well-to-do dilettante, the young Balakirev from Nizhni Novgorod, half Russian, half

Tartar, whose own compositions, apart from two or three anthology pieces, were no great shakes, but who exercised an overwhelmingly powerful influence over the group of young composers referred to above. These formed a strange mixture, ranging in talent from the genius, Modeste Mussorgsky, to the pedestrian César Cui, who was better as a publicist than as a composer. Cui indeed was hardly a Russian: his father, a French officer in Napoleon's *grande armée*, had settled in Vilna after a spell as prisoner-of-war, and Cui himself was a gifted military engineer who achieved the rank of general and wrote a standard work on fortification. The other three were entirely Russian. Borodin was a distinguished chemist who could spare all too little time for music from his work in the army medical school; Mussorgsky was an officer in the Preobazensky Guards. The only truly professional musician among them was Rimsky-Korsakov, who himself started life as a midshipman in the Imperial navy and became a naval bandmaster before getting himself transferred to civilian employment in the St Petersburg conservatoire, newly founded by the Grand Duchess Helen, who had a finger in every hopeful pie.

Poor Rimsky-Korsakov has come in for rough handling by mid-twentieth-century Western critics for his emasculation of the works of certain colleagues, above all for his version of *Boris Godunov* which held the stage for so long, and still keeps cropping up. Without in the least condoning Rimsky's failure to understand the power and originality of the rough corners he sought to smooth out, he nevertheless deserves more sympathy than he is ever likely to receive. For what he thought he was doing, and what badly needed doing, was reacting against the teaching of Balakirev which he believed, quite rightly, had perniciously affected the work of both Mussorgsky and Borodin by encouraging their amateurism as a divine Russian quality and hindering them from achieving a serious professionalism.

Here is Rimsky's portrait of Balakirev, brilliant, swift, instinctive, leisured, well-to-do. The young composers (Mussorgsky was still only twenty-one) needed a guide:

This guide was Balakirev, who had acquired everything by his astonishing, many-sided talent and experience, quite without labour and without system [he owed it in fact to a music-loving friend of his father's, who kept an exceptionally good serf-orchestra], and therefore had no idea of any system.... Having himself gone through no preparatory school, Balakirev thought it unnecessary for others as well. There was no need of training: one must begin to compose outright, to create and learn through one's own work of creation. Whatever would be unfinished and unskilful in the early work of his comrades and pupils he himself would finish; he would set everything to rights, completing it in case of need, and the composition would be ready to be issued for performance or publication.[6]

Here is Balakirev the teacher:

Under the influence of Schumann's compositions, melodic creative gifts were then looked upon with disfavour. The majority of melodies and themes were regarded as the weaker part of music.... In the majority of cases a piece was critically judged in accordance with the separate elements: the first four bars were said to be excellent, the next eight weak, the melody immediately following good for nothing, the transition from it to the next phrase fine, and so forth. A composition was never considered as a whole in its aesthetic significance ...[7]

No wonder the young Russians left so much of their work unfinished. No wonder Rimsky-Korsakov revolted and, at twenty-seven, decided to put himself to school.

What he was really reacting against – and it was the same with Tchaikovsky, who stood quite apart from the Five – was not only the wilful, if inspired, amateurism preached by Balakirev but also the exaltation of Russian music over all other music. Goodness knows, both Rimsky and Tchaikovsky were Russian enough in their choice of subjects for operas, in their spontaneous use of Russian folk-music and modes. But each in his different way saw himself as part of the vast complex of European music.

The immense achievement of the Russians, above all Mussorgsky, was the injection into opera and song of that same realism which was already manifesting itself in literature. And the true father of this element was not Glinka but his younger contemporary, yet another landowner, Dargomizhsky, whose *Stone Guest* was a landmark. Of Dargomizhsky, Stasov was to write:

He created an opera that is absolutely unique in the history of music. In it was embodied and expressed everything that the great reformer Gluck had striven for a century before – but in a framework even broader and deeper than Gluck's. Here there are no Greek gods and heroes, no classical subjects and characters. Gone are all the conventions and formal practices which had grown like an ugly excrescence on European music . . . In keeping with the demands of common sense and operatic realism, *The Stone Guest* consists entirely of declamatory recitative, of musical speech which pours from the lips of the characters in an irregular unsymmetrical stream, just as it does in everyday conversation and in drama. Yet despite the closeness of this recitative to human speech with all its twists and turns, its form is musical, artistic and poetic. This was an experiment in a new musical genre, the like of which had never been heard or seen before.'[8]

Making allowances for the gross exaggeration of Dargomizhsky's musical stature, there is a good deal of truth in this. But who would guess from the foregoing that by the time *The Stone Guest* was composed Richard Wagner in Germany was already halfway through his own colossal output?

And again:

The content of Mussorgsky's songs and his operas . . . is so rich, the characters so varied, that it would be impossible to examine them in detail here. They constitute an entire world, embodied in music with extraordinary genius, power and originality. Both individuals and masses of people pass before us in a multitude of scenes encompassing the widest possible range of human feeling and experience. Tsars and simpletons, muzhiks, boyars and monks, old peasant women and princesses, sextons and police officers, young ladies, functionaries and nurses, *streltsi* and Old Believers, innkeepers and seminarists, and a host of others form a rich national gallery, the like of which is not to be found in any other opera anywhere.[9]

Stasov might have been summing up the whole tremendous contribution of Russian realism in literature as well as music. He himself knew that the driving force was the search for national identity, which also moved the political and social reformers. But instead of recognising this for what it was, Stasov, in company with so many others, sought to transform into a supreme and original virtue an investigation, a pilgrimage almost, forced upon the Russians by their own past failure to achieve a coherent and constructive society; and in so doing, he, with so many others, found it necessary to spurn the Western achievement; indeed, to deny it.

'Another important distinguishing feature of our school is its constant search for national character . . . This began with Glinka and has continued uninterruptedly until the present time. No such striving is to be found in any other European school of composition.'[10]

And hand in hand with this attitude goes the rejection of professionalism, already so perversely displayed by Balakirev: 'none of our great musicians, from Glinka on, have ever put much faith in academic training. They have never regarded it with the servility and superstitious awe with which it is regarded, even nowadays, in many parts of Europe. It would be ridiculous to deny the value of learning in any field, including music, but the new Russian musicians look learning boldly in the eye.

They respect it, they avail themselves of its blessings, but they do not exaggerate its importance or genuflect before it . . .'

Stasov knew very well that every European composer of stature had begun to compose in extreme youth and had battled on in the teeth of academic disapproval, yet he could write: 'Our composers, unlike the Germans, did not waste endless years on the grammar of music; they learned it quickly and easily, like any other grammar. But this did not prevent them from learning it solidly and thoroughly.'[11]

On this sort of nonsense Stasov could base a whole argument against the setting up of a conservatoire in St Petersburg, whose object was not to train the genius but to produce a solid body of technically accomplished and disciplined musicians of every kind.

And it was this attitude which caused Tchaikovsky, in spite of his own deep Russianness, to exorcise his gifted colleagues, less in anger than in despair, for their 'horrible presumptuousness and wholly amateur conviction of superiority over all other musicians in the universe'.

Balakirev and Stasov were extreme examples of a tendency all too general, which was nevertheless rejected by many Russian critics and musicians who found musical chauvinism of this kind so repugnant that they discounted Stasov's admirable qualities. It was precisely the tendency which was to manifest itself in the political sphere as Russian chauvinism and Panslavism with such unfortunate results. And it went very deep. We remember that remarkable episode in *War and Peace* when Natasha dances her Russian dance. 'Where and how and when,' asks Tolstoy, 'has this young Countess, educated by an émigré French governess, imbibed from the Russian air she breathed that spirit . . .?' For 'the spirit and the movements were those inimitable and unteachable Russian ones that "Uncle" had expected of her.' We are all too close to Professor Pogodin with his 'Russia, a miracle! The Russian people, a miracle! The Russian language, a miracle! The Russian stove . . . a miracle!'[12]

5

Something has happened. We are in the 1870s and a long way from the Winter Palace and the court. A long way from the peasant too. Imperceptibly in the last decade a new force has been growing and consolidating. Until the middle 1860s Russia was the autocracy ruling over the peasant masses through the bureaucracy with the connivance of the landowners – opposed by a numerically very small intelligentsia in full reaction against it. Now a new middle class of displaced landowners, rich merchants, lawyers, teachers and industrialists is taking shape and beginning to live a life of its own. It has its own publicists, like the right-wing journalist Katkov. It embraces artists and would-be artists and conservatively minded academics. It is beginning to develop a sense of Russianness. It deplores the excesses of the revolutionaries no less than the excesses of the autocracy. It has no representation in official government and can thus find no way of political expression. But it is prosperous and firmly based enough to create a quasi-independent climate of opinion.

One reason for this apparent digression into a specialised field far removed, it may seem, from the main current of Russian history is that the musicians formed a bridge between official Russia and the rebellious intelligentsia. They depended on the favour of court officials who controlled the opera houses and the concert halls – and the orchestras and singers! But for their moral support they needed the outsiders. The very existence of these musicians reflects the development of a public opinion to which the Tsar was forced to bow. This public opinion was nationalist in spirit and also profoundly ignorant of the forces operating in the outside world.

CHAPTER FOURTEEN

'How Great is Russia!'

I

FOR nearly twenty years since the Treaty of Paris there had been no great movement to disturb the uneasy peace in the Balkans or to inflame the Eastern Question. Alexander was satisfied. He did not share his father's obsessive concern with the future of the Ottoman Empire. He had plenty to occupy himself with elsewhere, and the 1871 revision of the Treaty of Paris which gave Russia the right to maintain a fleet in the Black Sea was all he needed for the time being. The principle was what mattered; the fleet would have to wait until Reutern could find the cash to pay for it.

But in the summer of 1875 the Balkans were shaken by rebellions among the Serbs of Bosnia and Hercegovina, driven to desperation by renewed excesses of Turkish misrule. In Serbia proper there was an immediate outcry. King Milan, who had no illusions about the outcome if he went to war with Turkey, was hard put to it to resist his people's demand for a national crusade. But for nearly a year he was able to hold back the war party, sustained in his determination by the European powers in concert. And for nearly a year the powers indulged themselves in a fever of diplomacy to keep Serbia from war, to mediate between Turkey and the rebels. All desired peace, but even while they put pressure on Turkey they were at loggerheads among themselves.

Alexander still, very naturally, sought the reduction of Turkish power and was full of contingency plans, to which he sought the agreement of Austria, for redrawing the map should war ensue. Austria was divided. Her official voice was now the voice of the somewhat flamboyant Hungarian aristocrat and one-time rebel against Habsburg rule, Julius Andrassy, who was above all concerned with enhancing the position of Hungary in the Dual Monarchy and who saw in Turkish overlordship in the Balkans an insurance not only against Russia but also against the growth of nationalist aspirations among the Monarchy's own Slav peoples.

On the other hand, the Emperor Franz Joseph coveted Bosnia and Herce-govina to compensate for the loss of his Italian provinces, a cause of deep personal bitterness. Bismarck in Berlin had no active interest in the Balkans. He was very much concerned with keeping on equal terms of friendship with both Russia and Austria, as symbolised by the rather shaky Three Emperors' League. He hoped, or pretended to hope, that if the worst came to the worst Russia and Austria would intervene in con-cert against Turkey and agree to an amicable partition of Turkey in Europe. He feared the outbreak of any conflict which might give France a chance to escape from her post-1870 isolation by entering into an alliance with either side. England, with Disraeli now Prime Minister and inclined to histrionics where Russia was concerned, was as always pathologically suspicious of Russian intentions, and more determined than ever, since the opening of the Suez Canal in 1869, to keep Russia out of the Medi-terranean. She struck war-like attitudes and was incensed when the Northern Powers seemed to be agreeing among themselves. When the three Emperors came out with the proposal known as the Berlin Memo-randum in May 1876 (a two months' armistice, reforms to be imposed on Turkey by the three powers in agreement), the Cabinet saw a plot, and Disraeli exploded with indignation at the 'insult' implicit in the conduct of the three powers in asking Britain 'to sanction them in putting the knife to the throat of Turkey, whether we like it or not'.[1]

The consequences of this dangerous quarrel were never to be worked out. Almost immediately the situation changed. In April an entirely new rebellion had broken out, this time among the Bulgarians, and the Turkish response was to burn down sixty villages and massacre in cold blood some fifteen thousand men, women and children. When the news reached London, distrust of Russia was wiped out by an explosion of revulsion against Turkey – revulsion that was sharpened by feelings of shocked guilt that Britain should for so long have championed such manifest barbarians: London, in a word, was effectively removed from the equa-tion. With this one act the Turks had deprived themselves of their main support and ensured that for some time to come no British Cabinet would dare go to war on their behalf.

The Bulgarian atrocities proved the last straw for Serbia, too. On 30 June 1876, King Milan, fearing for his throne, for his life indeed, sur-rendered to the popular demand for war. All over Russia the churches rallied the faithful to pray for Serbian victory, to exalt the Slav, the true, the Orthodox cause. Now it was the turn of Alexander to come under pressure to fight.

Russia had been speaking for some time with two voices. The British had some excuse for suspecting that Alexander was manoeuvring towards war and the subsequent dismemberment of Turkey. What they did not understand was that the Tsar no longer stood in undisputed control of his own foreign policy. There was a joker in the pack: Russian national- ism, for the moment finding expression in Panslavism and penetrating the highest ranks of the bureaucracy and the army. Thus Gorchakov, Milyutin, Reutern, Valuyev, and a few others at the very summit of affairs, were united in their desire to be good Europeans and to take no action that might upset the European concert. They also regarded Pan- slavism with distaste and alarm if not disdain – 'slavophile onanism'[2] was Valuyev's contemptuous verdict on the emotional tide which was sweeping the educated classes. But many of their immediate subordi- nates, some of them very senior officials, felt otherwise. They had no use for Europe, did not understand the ancient diplomatic game, thought only in terms of Russian, or Slav supremacy.

For Russian Panslavism, the ugly step-child of the philosophic Slavo- philes, was very quickly to degenerate into chauvinism: the glorification not of Russian virtues, real or imagined, but of Russian might.

By the end of the 1860s the older and gentler Slavophiles were either dead or withdrawn from the world, largely disillusioned. One of their great aims had been achieved with the Emancipation, but Alexander's refusal to countenance any representative institution in the form of a national assembly and the very strict limits placed on the power and authority of the provincial zemstvos meant that no progress could be made, or even hoped for, towards the establishment of communal responsibility and wide participation in government. The successors of the first Slavo- philes, including the two Aksakov sons, had moved away almost imper- ceptibly at first from the search for Russian identity and the mainsprings of ancient Russian virtue to a simple assertion of moral superiority. And from this, by an easy process of extension, arose in the hearts of many a conviction of the special mission of Slavdom, with Russia as the natural and pre-ordained leader and teacher of all the Slav peoples. For political reasons such thinking was not actively discouraged, and the Tsar tolerated the foundation of Slavonic Benevolent Committees, subsidised partly by the Ministry of Education, partly by private subscription, to support the cultural and religious activities of Slavs under Turkish rule.

This in itself was an important shift in emphasis which among other things was to lead to a revival of the Eastern Question in a dangerous form. Since the days of Catherine the Great one Russian monarch after another had regarded himself as the protector of Christians under Turkish rule. But now the monarch was under pressure from educated Russians who were beginning for the first time to think in terms of the champion- ship of fellow peoples, fellow Slavs, to be rescued from the oppressor. The publicist Pogodin and the newspaper editor Katkov, who had abandoned his early liberalism, appealed strongly to the growing spirit of nationalism. But the most articulate standard-bearers of the Panslav movement were N. Y. Danielevsky and General R. A. Fadeyev, who published seminal works in 1869 and 1870 respectively. Danielevsky was a racialist preaching a pseudo-scientific sociology designed to prove the superiority of the Slavs, much as Houston Stewart-Chamberlain was to preach on behalf of the Aryan Germans a little later. He did not deny the historical importance of the Latin and Teutonic cultures. It was simply that they had had their day; and the new 'cultural historical' element which was to pick up the torch was represented by the Slavs. General Fadeyev took such theoretical conclusions briskly for granted and was more down to earth. Russia was one with the rest of Slavdom, and to all Slavdom the West was implacably opposed. Russia therefore had to choose. The one thing she could not do was to stand for ever shivering on the threshold of Europe. She must either assume the leadership of all Slavdom, not stopping until she had reached the Adriatic, or else retire beyond the Dnieper. The choice was 'Slavdom or Asia'.[3]

It was a strange and formidable confluence of forces. The prophets of Panslavism could count on the support of patriotic Russians – the composer Tchaikovsky is a fair example – who had no imperial dreams but believed it was time for Russia to make herself felt in the world and assert her special virtues. Standing up to the Sultan even more than rushing to succour the Serbs was the aspect of affairs that most appealed to them. Thus the idealists and the chauvinists, the dreamers and the cynics, were brought together to create a movement which forced the hand of the Tsar and compelled him to stand forward as the champion of Russian nationalism.

Much later, in 1889, the great Christian philosopher Vladimir Solovyev, who strove tirelessly to separate the mystical spirit of the Orthodox Church, which he revered, from any form of Russian nationalism, was to write, looking back:

Worship of one's own people as the chief bearer of universal truth; then worship of the people as an elemental force, without regard to universal truth; finally worship of the national one-sidedness and historical anomalies which cut off the people from educated humanity – that is to say, worship of one's people with a direct negation of the very idea of universal truth – these are the three separate stages of our nationalism, represented in succession by the Slavophiles, by Katkov, and by the latest obscurantists. The first of these taught pure fantasies; the second was a realist, with imagination; the last are realists without any imagination but also without any shame.[4]

By the time Solovyev was writing Alexander II was dead and his son was presiding over a Russia ruthlessly determined to impose cultural and religious uniformity on the Empire in all its parts. But the spirit which blossomed into this aggressive chauvinism was already emerging with all sorts of variations in all sorts of men who had only one thing in common: the ineradicable conviction of the innate superiority of the Russian consciousness – from the soldier Dragomirov, who preached the superiority of the great Suvorov and his peculiarly Russian military genius to all the great captains of history, to the novelist Dostoevsky who embraced Orthodoxy for no other reason than that it was the faith of the Russian people, the elect of God, and therefore *must* be true.

2

On the eve of the Russo-Turkish War, Panslavism had not yet hardened into chauvinism. Chief among its exponents was the brilliant, altogether overweening Count Ignatiev, already encountered in these pages as a pioneer of Russian expansion in Central Asia and the Far East, now Ambassador in Constantinople. Handsome and bold, his compelling personality was harnessed to a quite exceptional talent for lying and intrigue. His whole career had been turned away from Europe and he had little understanding of the intricacies of the European power balance. What he did understand he did not like. He saw no reason for Gorchakov's careful (craven, it seemed to him) subordination of Russian ambitions to the maintenance of good relations with other, lesser powers. Indeed, all other powers were visibly lesser: why should mighty Russia defer to a ramshackle Austria-Hungary, a parvenu Germany, a crippled France? He rejected absolutely the legitimacy of Britain's interest in the Straits, 'the key to the house', Russia's house. He did not understand, as Alexander and Gorchakov reluctantly understood, that nothing could be done about Constantinople and the Straits in face of the sea-power of that remote, small, cold, evasively inimical island. In the interests of Panslavism he intrigued against all the world and against his own masters too, now trying in vain to inveigle Alexander into treating directly with the Sultan, now, through a disciple at the Russian consulate in Belgrade, urging the Serbs to fight, assuring them that this was indeed what St Petersburg desired, even though Gorchakov, for obvious reasons, had to pretend that what he wanted was peace. There was only one reason for any Russian to encourage Serbia to go to war: if the Tsar would not act against the Sultan, he must be goaded into fighting. And so it happened.

Even before war was declared money from private subscriptions had been pouring into Serbia, and with the money, a trickle of volunteers ready to fight when needed. Chief among these was one of the heroes of the Turkestan campaigns, General Cherneyev, ardently Panslav, who resigned from the army and slipped into Serbia secretly, against the Tsar's express wish, to take command of the Serbian forces. Once war was declared, the Panslav agitation took on the aspect of a quasi-religious movement with overtones of hysteria. Katkov in his newspaper urged patriotic Russians to volunteer to fight for their brother Slavs; zemstvos, churches, Panslav societies, drummed up funds, organised and sent out ambulances and complete hospitals. Even the Tsar's own household was seized by the frenzy. The Tsaritsa herself presided over Serbian relief organisations, and the Tsarevich, the future Alexander III, already at odds with his father, publicly advocated Russian intervention to save fellow Slavs from destruction.

It was a measure of the strength of the movement that Alexander, even while he was patiently negotiating with the other major powers of Europe to find ways and means of stopping the war, felt unable to forbid the flow of volunteers, which included serving officers from his own Guards regiments. The fact that many of these were moved less by Panslav ideals than by the search for adventure or oblivion was neither here nor there (we remember how in *Anna Karenina* Vronsky, suffering from toothache, went off to fight for the Serbs after Anna had killed herself). The movement existed and the autocrat bowed to it. It was a climacteric in the history of the dynasty, and it was recognised as such by at least some Russians. 'What has happened in Russia this summer,' one of the Aksakov brothers triumphantly proclaimed, 'is an unheard-of phenomenon in the history of any country: public opinion unsupported by the government and without any State organisation behind it has conducted a war in a foreign country.'[5]

3

It was not a successful war. The Serbs did badly. Their army of 130,000 was no match for the Turks, equipped with the latest armaments from Messrs Krupp. They blamed their Russian comrades for their defeats; the Russians blamed them. In Moscow and St Petersburg public opinion turned sour. There was less talk now of succouring the Serbs, far more of the holy mission against the Turk, with Constantinople as the goal. The Serbs, it was now suspected, were not proper Slavs: they were too close to Austria; they were corrupted by Jews. Popular sympathy swung to the Bulgarians, the latest victims of Turkish barbarism. Bulgaria, too, was closer to Russia and lay on the direct route to Constantinople. Whereas the ungrateful Serbs were accused, with reason, of favouring Vienna above St Petersburg and were already tainted with Western ideas, the honest Bulgars had no ideas whatsoever and were thus wide open to Russian influence and could look to no other champion than Russia. Pressure on Alexander to intervene directly and declare war on Turkey became ever more irresistible, and it coincided with the growing conviction on Alexander's part that disagreement among the powers was presenting him with an opportunity that should be seized.

War did not come until May 1877. The detailed story of the diplomatic manoeuvrings which led up to the Russian declaration is here relevant only in so far as it exposes the anxieties, the uncertainties, the divisions of the chancellories of Europe at a critical moment in the process which was to culminate less than forty years later in the 1914 holocaust. Alexander had no wish to go to war, but it was clear to him that if Turkey defeated Serbia he would have to take action to prevent her from profiting by her victory to re-impose her grip on the Balkans: in this he was at one with popular opinion. But he still hoped to act with the agreement of the powers, who themselves were manoeuvring for advantage in an indeterminate and rather bad-tempered manner. Each of them with the exception of Prussia was divided against itself. As time went on and all efforts failed it became even more clear that the main danger to Russia lay in direct collision with Austria. To insure against this contingency Alexander demanded unequivocal support from Prussia, but Bismarck, forced against his will to choose, knew that, much as he valued the continuance of warm relations with St Petersburg, the vitally important factor for Prussia was the preservation of the Habsburg Empire. He was forced to show his hand, assuring Alexander of his benevolent neutrality, but no more. It was not enough. Russia was expecting her reward for having massed 300,000 Russian troops on the Galician frontier to keep Austria neutral while Prussia conquered France in 1870.

All the same, knowing that Prussia would not intervene, that England could not, the Tsar could now concentrate all his powers on reaching an agreement with Austria as to what would happen in the event of war and the collapse of Turkey. A series of agreements was laboriously achieved. A military convention promised Austria's benevolent neutrality in return for her occupation of Bosnia and Hercegovina. Montenegro and the Sanjak of Novibazar were to be a neutral zone. Serbia and Montenegro could assist Russia with troops only outside their own territory. Austria was not to touch Roumania. Russia was to receive only southern Bessarabia. Nothing was said about Turkey in Asia, which was now very much in Alexander's sights. And nothing was said about Bulgaria. But it was agreed that 'no large compact state, Slav or other' would be formed in the Balkans. If Turkey collapsed, Constantinople might become a free city, while Greece might take Crete, the southern Epirus and Thessaly.[6]

It was an agreement that would not have appealed to the Panslavs, who rejected very sharply indeed any formal recognition of Austrian influence in the Balkans, including suzerainty over large numbers of their Slav brothers. But although it was a diplomatic triumph for Austria, who appeared to have got all she wanted without a war, it at least freed Alexander's hands. Once he had secured Roumanian agreement for safe passage of his troops, he could declare war, knowing that neither Britain nor Prussia would intervene. The rest was up to his generals. There were prizes to be had in Asian Turkey, and if Turkey did collapse, then the future of Constantinople could be settled from a position of strength.

And so it happened, but not at all in the way that Alexander had foreseen.

At first things went well. Inside Russia the situation was immediately transformed. From a country so at odds with its ruler that even the soberest members of the Government had been fearing the breakdown of public order, there arose a mood of patriotic euphoria which swamped all doubts, stifled all revolutionary activity and offered the spectacle of a united people embarked on a holy crusade. But the sober-minded still kept their heads. If war there had to be, it had better be quick, limited, decisive. If the fighting dragged on, they feared – and Gorchakov and Shuvalov were most urgent in their warnings – not only a long-drawn-out campaign, stalemate, a growing casualty list, leading to renewed disaffection at home, but also the intervention of other powers: for with Russia heavily pinned down by the Turks, other powers might be tempted to strike.

4

The Russian march on Turkey started off light-heartedly enough. If Alexander approached the testing time in a fitting mood of almost religious resolution, his soldiers and the great crowds who saw them off were bursting with patriotic enthusiasm. For most of these it was less a question of rescuing brother Slavs from cruel oppression than of demonstrating to the world that Russia would no longer be pushed around or stand by while her little Serb cousins were bullied – and of, at last, fulfilling Catherine's promise to take Constantinople. It was the tenth war against Turkey since 1676. It was to be, disastrously, the last. Twenty-two years earlier Nicholas's army had marched through the Principalities (now Roumania), crossed the Danube, and then withdrawn ignominiously to concentrate its force in the Crimea, fearful of being cut off and destroyed by the watching Austrian army in Galicia along its extended right flank. Now Austria was friendly. The Russians had nothing to fear as they streamed through the Roumanian bottleneck. The Danube was reached and crossed in June at the cost of some sharp fighting and heavy casualties, and the first weeks of the advance towards the Balkan mountains running from east to west across Bulgaria went so well that it looked as though Alexander would be in Constantinople before July was out. Simultaneously a major offensive was opened in Transcaucasia in the direction of Kars.

But after that first triumphant advance things started going wrong. All through the summer and into the autumn it looked as though Andrassy's prophecy that the Russians would bog themselves down was coming true. On the Transcaucasian front the Grand Duke Michael, one of Alexander's brothers, found his army imperilled by rebellious tribesmen descending from the mountains to attack his rear and cut off his supplies: he was forced to break off the advance on Kars and retire to regroup, while at the foot of the Balkan mountains the steady advance was checked in a wholly unexpected manner. One of the most able of the post-Crimean generals, Y. V. Gurko, had already driven the Turks back through the mountains and over the Shipka Pass, commanding Philippopolis and the comparatively easy countryside beyond Adrianople. Everything seemed set for the decisive stroke when the main body moving up towards the mountains found itself threatened from what had seemed an unimportant strongpoint, the reduction of which had seemed an almost routine operation. This was the fortress of Plevna, which commanded a vital cross-roads as well as an obstacle in the form of a tributary of the Danube. What had happened was that Osman Pasha with a fresh army had made a bold and swift march across the Balkan range, getting behind the Russian vanguard and occupying Plevna. So long as Plevna was held there could be no question of continuing the advance across the mountains. The fortress had to be taken. There was no other way to the south: the comparatively easy coastal route round the western shores of the Black Sea was barred this time to the Russians who, with no fleet of their own, would have been vulnerable to bombardment from the Turkish fleet.

The siege of Plevna was to last four months. By the time it was over it had become in the minds of many thinking Russians a grim symbol of everything that was unsatisfactory about their government and their country.

After three months of close siege and the loss of innumerable lives Alexander in his rear headquarters swallowed his pride by bringing neutral Roumania and neutral Serbia into a war from which he had been determined to exclude them, fearful of putting himself under subsequent obligation. He even went so far as to put Prince Carol of Roumania in command of a strong army which included Russian troops. And when even this did not avail, when the third main assault on Plevna, on 11 September, ended in disaster with the loss of 15,000 Russians and 3,000 Roumanians, he revised his thinking more radically still.

The Grand Duke Nicholas, Alexander's brother, now Commander-in-Chief in the field, had lost his nerve. He urged a general retreat back across the Danube, but Alexander's old stubbornness would have none of it. If Plevna could not be stormed it could be blockaded and starved into submission; and the man for the job was none other than the hero of Sevastopol, the veteran General Totleben, who was brought down post-haste from St Petersburg to direct strategic planning. As a result of a series of minor but critical and carefully organised and integrated engagements Plevna was completely cut off from the outside world and its fall was only a matter of time.

Osman Pasha held out, amazingly, from the end of October until 10 December. Then, after a last attempt at a break-out, he was forced to surrender with 2,000 officers and 44,000 men. He could have got away much earlier when he saw what Totleben was planning and used his force to fight another day. But he was under orders from the Porte to hold on at all costs. And he did. And those same men in Constantinople who were responsible for the loss of Osman and his fine army now in their timidity restricted the movement of still larger armies waiting to fall on the Russians on the southern approaches to the Shipka Pass. The Balkan range is not very high (the Shipka Pass itself, the Pass of Wild Roses, is little more than four thousand feet), but getting troops and their supplies, above all man-handling heavy guns, across that wild and desert country in the depths of winter was a formidable enterprise. The Russians surprised the Turks by forcing the crossing at several points east and west of the Shipka, coming round to destroy Suleiman Pasha's army as it waited for a frontal attack. Within a month of the fall of Plevna they had taken Sofia and Philippopolis and swept on to Adrianople, which fell on 20 January 1878 almost without resistance. The victory was complete. Constantinople lay wide open to the Russian army: all that was needed now was the will to take it.

5

But Constantinople was not taken. Eighteen months later, in July 1879, Bismarck in one of his false-candid conversations with Peter Saburov, the Russian Ambassador to Berlin who was completely under his spell, could airily insist that after Plevna the Russians should have reinforced their army with 50,000 men and pushed on to Constantinople, while 'assuring Europe on oath' that they would evacuate the city after the war. 'England,' he went on, 'rather than risk herself in a struggle with such a doubtful issue, would probably have modified her tone.'[7]

The 'probably' (if Saburov indeed reported the conversation correctly) was good. England had already formally declared that she could not remain neutral if Russian troops entered Constantinople, even temporarily. The British fleet had lain in readiness in Besika Bay outside the Dardanelles for six months past. The London Government, now including the level-headed Salisbury, who had no illusions about Turkey, was alarmed by the way in which, after Plevna, Russian nationalism with a Panslav flavour seemed to have infected even Gorchakov and the most European-minded of the St Petersburg officials. There was indeed a very real danger of war with England, a war, moreover, which could quickly spread. Furthermore, would Russian public opinion ever allow the Tsar to give up Constantinople once he had it in his grasp? And in any case, what was the point of seizing Constantinople only to give it up, except as a pledge for favourable terms of peace which could be secured without it? Above all there was the wretched condition of the army. The generals, including Alexander's brother the Grand Duke Nicholas, knew that the army in the winter of 1877–8 could not fight another war. Had the advance not been checked at Plevna, Russia would have been in Constantinople by July, her army relatively fresh, strong enough to frighten Austria, and with British public opinion still virulently anti-Turk. But Osman Pasha's tremendous stand had changed all that. The British forgot all about the Bulgarian atrocities in their admiration for the heroism of the Plevna garrison: Turkey appeared once more as a weak and inoffensive power standing up gallantly to Russian bullying. Further, the Russian troops, straggling down into Adrianople in mid-winter, were ravaged by disease, exhaustion, cold. Their comrades in Transcaucasia had also suffered. But they had won through at last to Kars and found a new and rather improbable hero in their commander General Loris-Melikov, who was soon to soar to the heights. The Turks still held Erzerum and Batum. The Russians must have rest.

In the mind of Alexander there was confusion. Here he stood with

Turkey prostrate – the great prize, the dream of his forebears, Constantinople, the Straits, 'the key to the house', was within his grasp – and did nothing. When first the Grand Duke Nicholas, then Totleben, refused to move on to Constantinople Alexander did not insist, nor did he demonstratively assume supreme command in the field, as he should have done had he been quite single-minded. He did not even take soundings among the powers. He simply let the matter drop while proceeding with all possible speed to a peace treaty arrived at without reference to the powers. He very soon knew that the British were in a fairly determined mood: on 13 February, alarmed by certain Russian moves that looked like the prelude to a breach of the armistice terms and an advance to Constantinople, they sent their fleet through the Dardanelles into the Sea of Marmora. It was against this threatening background that Alexander pushed through with a peace treaty which, in his more sober moments, he must have known he would be forced to modify.

The man he chose to negotiate the peace was the Panslav Count Ignatiev, who had done more than any man to get Russia into the war. And what counted most with Ignatiev was his contempt for Austria and his profound conviction that Russia could, and should, stand alone against the world and behave as though Turkey in Europe as in Asia concerned her and her alone. So he set out at San Stefano, only seven miles from Constantinople, to reach a settlement which took no account of Western susceptibilities, fears, or needs, a settlement calculated above all to weaken Austrian and strengthen Russian influence in the Balkans. There was to be no question of Bosnia-Hercegovina going to Austria, even although this meant leaving many afflicted Christians under Turkish rule. The kingdom of Montenegro was enlarged. Above all, by the creation of a very large Bulgaria which owed its existence to St Petersburg and must look to it for support, Ignatiev brought Russian power into the heart of the Balkans while barring the way to Austria.

It looked like a diplomatic triumph. In fact it was a snare. It is easy enough to understand Ignatiev's motives. He was consistently Panslav, or Russian chauvinist, in everything he did, sustained by an exaggerated notion of the respect in which Russia was held by the powers. It is less easy to understand what went on in Alexander's mind. Was he sick at heart because, faced with the opportunity to realise his ancestral dream, his nerve had failed? Did he seek to compensate for the critical failure to take Constantinople (the tacit admission, indeed, that when it came to the test he simply dare not take it) by throwing his weight about where he felt it was safe to do so? But in fact Ignatiev's course was very far from safe and soon had to be abandoned, reversed, indeed, in humiliating circumstances. Or did he really believe, as Ignatiev himself may well have done, that by facing the powers with a *fait accompli* which respected the integrity of Constantinople and the Straits he would put Russia in a position so strong that she could not be gainsaid? Or was the decision to employ Ignatiev and give him his head simply one more example of that strange lack of centrality which had distinguished Alexander's behaviour even in the schoolroom, even in his finest hour, the struggle to abolish serfdom, when he had given comfort to his opponents and nearly broken the hearts of his most active supporters?

Or was this unilateral treaty-making, in direct contradiction to past policy, yet one more example of that peculiarly Russian (as distinct from Alexandrine) quality of equivocation which even in our own day renders Russian motives more impenetrable than most – that quality referred to by Lord Salisbury quite soon after San Stefano had been abrogated by the Treaty of Berlin: 'The usual duality of Russian policy is again making itself apparent. In Turkey they are conducting themselves as if their one object was to go to war with England. Every trick which it is possible for imagination to conceive, every subtle misconstruction of the Treaty, is being used for the purpose of hindering the proper execution of the Treaty. But from Livadia [Alexander's favourite summer palace on the Black Sea] we get nothing but very properly phrased professions of an intention to abide by the Treaty'.[8]

And what, anyway, do we mean by this all too familiar 'duality'? Do we understand by it deliberate duplicity? Or an inability of the left hand to communicate with the right? Or a rather innocently greedy desire to have things both ways? Or simply an instinct to hedge, to reinsure?

All these elements enter into it, no doubt, and many more besides. We have already seen some of them in action. Certainly duplicity plays a very strong part in Russian diplomacy, but it is not at all easy to fathom the Russian attitude to lying, which is governed by an elaborate code of conventions understood by all Russians from the highest to the lowest but inaccessible to outsiders. How to tell the difference between the lie for fun and the lie for a very real purpose? What, for example, possessed Prince Gorchakov when at the Congress of Berlin he brazenly and quite obviously tried to cheat by substituting for a map showing the agreed Bulgarian frontier another map on which he had drawn quite a different line? Did he expect to be found out? If so what was the object? Or did he believe he could deceive so easily?

To carry the questioning to a more serious level, there is a remarkable passage in Saburov's memoirs which briskly makes nonsense of so many official protestations by Tsars, ministers and their apologists of the absence of any aggressive or predatory intentions on the part of the Imperial Government. Nobody could have been a more amiable or peace-loving official than Saburov. But in describing the early stages of the Russo-Turkish War he lets the cat out of the bag without, apparently, being aware of either the container or the animal. 'The original plan of campaign,' he writes, 'had been to go no further than the Balkans [he refers to the Balkan mountains], and to create a limited Bulgaria. The Tsar and Prince Gorchakov shrank from the consequences of a thorough campaign, and preferred to hold to *our traditional policy, that of eating the artichoke leaf by leaf* . . .'[9] (The italics are mine.)

Ignatiev, sent to justify himself and his Government to Vienna, was helpless. What could he do, faced with Andrassy in the worst of tempers? For it was this handsome, moody, gypsy-like egomaniac who had himself given the go-ahead to Russia in exchange for large assurances about Bosnia-Hercegovina and no empire-building on the Russian side. There was a moment when Andrassy was threatening war, apparently restrained only by his master, the Emperor Franz Joseph. Ignatiev should have been the last person to be sent to treat with him – unless out of malice by Gorchakov. The real business was being done far away in London, where Count Peter Shuvalov was winning golden opinions as a man of peace and sense.

This Shuvalov was the very antithesis of the dynamic, darting, brilliantly opportunist Ignatiev. Long ago he had been one of Alexander's closest companions in the days of his youth, an arrogant young blood, handsome, tall and fair, worrying to poor Zhukovsky who regarded him as a bad influence. All through the struggle for the abolition of serfdom Shuvalov exploited his friendship with the new monarch to rally aristocratic opinion against the Emancipation and fight to the last against giving the freed serfs land. He was quite unscrupulous in his harrying of the reformers. Poor Rostovtsev, who died worn out by his labours, Nicholas Milyutin and many others had good reason to curse his name.

But although he schemed and worked against Alexander's express desires, he did not lose favour. When Alexander decided in 1862 that the time had come to take a tough line against radicalism and subversion, and made Shuvalov head of the Third Section, he reformed it root and branch and made it more powerful than ever before. It was easy for him to magnify his own importance by exaggerating the threat to authority from dissidents and liberals of all kinds, and this he did. Very soon complaints came thick and fast: Shuvalov was interfering in the internal business of every ministry and turning himself into virtual ruler of the land. One of his most pernicious activities was to make life almost impossible for the other Milyutin, General Dmitri Milyutin, then engaged in fighting reaction as part of his great army reform. Alexander, although he depended on Milyutin and was himself as sharply aware of the need for army reform as he had been of the need to get rid of serfdom, let it happen.

Translated to the London embassy as a punishment not for obstructing his master's policies but for making indiscreet remarks about Catherine Dolgoruky, he unexpectedly appeared as a shining light of sweet reason. The aristocratic conservatism which at home had made him a champion of reaction, was translated into an exact appreciation of established diplomatic usage in general and of the exigencies of the European power balance in particular. Large, jovial, florid now, one of those dangerously cold fish who conceal their thoughts behind a broadly expansive manner, plastered with orders, he was the precise antithesis of Ignatiev, whom he despised. Both men were ambitious to a degree, but Shuvalov, a figure from the Congress of Vienna, contained his ambition behind perfect manners and a bland carelessness, whereas Ignatiev, dark, moody, edgy in spite of his great charm, belonged to a later generation of self-seeking idealists. Shuvalov did not seek, he took, and he had no stock in ideals, regarding Ignatiev's nationalistic and racial enthusiasms with disdain.

This was the man chosen by Alexander to surrender the gains laid at his feet by Ignatiev. Through the spring and early summer of 1878 Shuvalov quietly dismantled the San Stefano Treaty, reaching such closeness of accord with London that in the end Austria, frightened of her increasing isolation, had to get into step with England before the grand European assembly which was to be the Congress of Berlin. It was a remarkable performance. Shuvalov almost single-handedly laid the spectre of war between Britain and Russia. Britain, acting with a new decisiveness now that Lord Derby had left the foreign office ('Making a feather-bed walk is nothing to the difficulty of making an irresolute man look two inches into the future,' his successor, Lord Salisbury, was later to write of him[10]), completed a diplomatic *tour de force* by private treaty – breaking up the proposed big Bulgaria before it was born, assuring Bosnia-Hercegovina to Austria, winning her alliance with a second private treaty, and then, by yet another private agreement with the Turks, obtaining Cyprus as an eastern Mediterranean base in exchange for the promise of British protection against Russia.

The Berlin Congress, which opened in June 1878, was designed in Western eyes to formalise and elaborate the undoing of the San Stefano Treaty already achieved in secret, in Russian eyes to ease some of the terms insisted on by London. Alexander hoped to achieve this easement through the good offices of Bismarck, who was persuaded against his will to preside over the Congress in the role of 'honest broker'. Unfortunately Bismarck was quite unable to give his backing to the Russians without antagonising Austria, which he was not prepared to do – with the result that he came to be regarded in St Petersburg as the great betrayer, while Disraeli and Salisbury were for a time respected as honest foes.

Disraeli wrote of Shuvalov to Lady Bradford from Berlin on 26 June that he fought a losing battle 'with marvellous talent and temper. He is a first-rate parliamentary debater, never takes a note, and yet in his reply never misses a point.'[11] Shuvalov also had to carry the burden of his aged senior Gorchakov, who could be guaranteed to irritate and antagonise the very plenipotentiaries he was supposed to conciliate, working industriously to undo, undermine or circumvent every single point of agreement laboriously reached. Bismarck, who had not forgiven Gorchakov for the trick he had played three years earlier when he had pretended to the French that he, Gorchakov, had averted another German invasion, also favoured Shuvalov, who was quite clearly head and shoulders above all other Russian conservatives.

The Congress of Berlin was the last full-dress meeting of the plenipotentiaries of all the Continental powers – Britain, France, Russia, Germany, Turkey, Italy – to take place in the old Europe. When it ended Metternich's dream of the European concert was dead. The Congress achieved a purpose. That is to say, it undid San Stefano and prevented Russia from dominating the Balkans. It gave Bosnia-Hercegovina to Austria to occupy and administer, but not to own. It broke up the new state of Bulgaria into three parts: there was a new independent Bulgaria in the north, a Turkish protectorate, to be known as Eastern Rumelia in the south, while Macedonia remained a part of Turkey. It ensured the survival of Turkey for decades to come. It restored to Russia Bessarabia taken from her after the Crimean War. It confirmed Britain in the possession of Cyprus – which was supposed to be a triumph – and it also gave her a most dubious slogan, proclaimed by Disraeli on his triumphant return from Berlin: 'Peace with Honour'.

On the face of it Russia had not done badly. She had started the war with no particularly stipulated aim beyond the recovery of Bessarabia and the chastisement of Turkey. Even in the early days of the campaign she had not aspired to penetrate beyond the Balkan mountains. The Turks were now chastised; Bessarabia was secured; a small Bulgaria, nominally independent, in fact dependent on Russia, was firmly established. The bitterness lay in the public humiliation, in being forced by the powers to give up what had been won.

There were plenty of dragon's teeth sown at the Congress of Berlin. Above all, of course, Austria and Russia found themselves facing each other altogether too directly in the Balkans. In spite of Bismarck's skill in riding two horses, it tied Germany to Austria in face of Russia. It gave

England an altogether false idea of her strength in a world dominated in fact by conscript armies.

The Three Emperors' League had been killed by the Austro-Russian conflict after San Stefano. Bismarck managed to revive it for a time after the Congress of Berlin, but it could not survive. The Allies were no longer dynasts commanding, or appearing to command, their own peoples and able without a backward look to pledge themselves to one or other of their peers; allies now were the peoples themselves, only partly under command of rulers who increasingly found it necessary to stir up popular opinion for their own ends and, in consequence, were increasingly vulnerable to its moods.

Indeed, the moods were threatening enough even in 1878. While Shuvalov was patiently negotiating in London, Britain was swept by a new wave of Russophobia, and on the boards of a London music-hall patriotism became all of a sudden jingoism:

> We don't want to fight, but by jingo if we do,
> We've got the ships, we've got the men, we've got the money too!

This spirit was matched in Russia, though more solemnly and with less catchpenny vulgarity. To the newly fledged nationalists, as to the veteran Slavophiles and the ardent Panslavs, it was unthinkable that the Tsar of Russia should defer to the arbitrament of foreigners, above all in a matter affecting the future of her fellow Slavs and her manifest destiny on the Bosphorus. But under threat of a new war, the unthinkable had to be thought. 'Our trust in the Tsar cannot be undermined. He has given us his word that his holy work shall be carried through to the end, and his word cannot be broken!'[12] Thus Ivan Aksakov, going as far as any loyal patriot dared, or decently could go, to challenge the Tsar. But the word was indeed broken, the holy work broken off. Alexander, having conquered in a war he had not sought, was now under fire for surrendering gains he had not expected. And to what purpose? 'We have sacrificed 100,000 men and 100 millions of money for an illusion!'[13] Gorchakov exclaimed tragically to Disraeli. This was true, of course, but not in the way Gorchakov understood it, only in the way that it is true of nearly all wars. For what it was worth, Russia's position in the Balkans was stronger than it had been before; above all, in the teeth of stubborn British resistance, she had secured Batum to serve as a Black Sea outlet for Transcaucasia – one day to become supremely important as the port for Caucasian oil. She had indeed quarrelled with Germany, but she was soon to make this up, and even before the ink on the Treaty was dry the new-found respect for the British as honest foes was vanishing. Just as Salisbury found the Russians in Turkey behaving as though they were planning war with England, while offering pacific assurances, so the Russians became extremely worked up by the possible consequences of the British occupation of Cyprus and her new-found interest in Asia Minor, expressed above all in the establishment of extra consulates and commercial missions. Within a year of Berlin Dmitri Milyutin was going so far as to alert the German Emperor: 'England is organising and arming Asia Minor; officials, generals, and officers disguised as consuls flood the country; that means hostile intentions against our possessions in the Caucasus . . . The conflict in the east is at hand.'[14]

But the very fact that Milyutin was able to unburden himself in this way to William I told its own story. Tiresome the British might be, but now they were quite unable to contemplate fighting Russia for the simple reason that they had no ally, which meant in practice no army. Milyutin should have known this. For Bismarck was already weaning Austria away from England and tying her to Germany by the Dual Alliance of October 1879. And almost at once he was charming Saburov into believing that all along he had meant only the best for Russia. The great movement was on foot which was to develop into the changing, but inflexible, system of alliances and counter-alliances which led by a sort of chain reaction just thirty-five years later to the cataclysm – by a process in which the obsessive idiocies of the Eastern Question, British agents in Kurdistan, Russian agents in Afghanistan and all the rest of the fashionable nonsense of the era, played no part at all.

CHAPTER FIFTEEN

The Impact of Terror

I

IT was now, in 1878, with the end of the Turkish War, that the revolutionary movement quite suddenly became a very real threat to the established order. Until then the interested ministries had for one reason and another largely exaggerated the peril and made very heavy weather indeed in combating it. Now at least they had some reason to fear – individuals for their own lives, as well as for the safety of the realm.

The herald of the change – rather than the signal for it – was the attempt on the St Petersburg police chief, General F. F. Trepov, by a young woman called Vera Zasulich. Trepov had a fixed hour for receiving petitioners. Miss Zasulich, dowdy, with blunt, unfinished features, already at twenty-six a veteran revolutionary, simply joined the queue and when it came to her turn produced a pistol and fired at the general point blank. She was not a very good shot, and Trepov was only wounded. She was, of course, immediately seized (she stood passively waiting to be arrested), and the authorities decided to charge her under the criminal code, not as a political offender, and to try her openly. There was no question as to her guilt. The evidence was clear and overwhelming. There could be no doubt about the verdict.

But this was to reckon without the strange public mood. The jury had no intention of convicting Miss Zasulich. So they simply ignored the evidence and found her not guilty, confirming the gloomy prediction of those who had opposed Alexander's reforms of the judicial system only fourteen years before. The law-abiding public was also on her side. When the police moved in to arrest her again she was caught up by friendly hands and spirited away into the crowd outside the prison, where she had gone to collect her things. Very soon she was safe in Geneva.

The attempt on General Trepov was the opening shot in an extraordinary war waged against the most powerful state in the world by a handful of determined and devoted fanatics employing selective terror as a weapon. Within a matter of months Alexander's War Minister, Dmitri Milyutin, was recording in his diary that what he called 'the secret society's satanic plan for terrorising the whole administration'[1] was beginning to succeed. A little later the usually cool and confident Valuyev was to write: 'One feels the ground trembling: the whole edifice is threatened with collapse.'[2] After the most spectacular and very nearly successful attempt on the life of his brother, the Tsar, the Grand Duke Constantine, staunchly liberal as always and still steady of nerve, confessed: 'We are re-living the Terror, but with this difference: the Parisians during the revolution saw their enemies face to face. We neither see them nor do we know them.'[3] Had Constantine known then how few those enemies were he would have felt ashamed.

Within limits, nevertheless, the few were terribly effective, and there seemed then no reason to suppose that the limits were as narrow as in fact they were. What had particularly shaken Constantine was a lethal explosion in the Winter Palace on 5 February 1880. A skilled workman called Khalturin, an active member of what Dmitri Milyutin thought of as the 'secret society', had succeeded in accumulating over a hundred pounds of dynamite under his bunk in the basement. Although made ill by the fumes, he bided his time, and finally set a fuse to detonate the improvised bomb immediately below the room in which Alexander was due to dine. The device went off successfully, killing ten members of the palace guard and wounding thirty-three more, as well as twenty-three civilians. But the Tsar escaped because he had been briefly delayed in conversation on his way to the dining-room – though for a time in the confusion everyone believed that he and the Tsaritsa and their children were all dead. If the 'secret society' could penetrate into the very heart of the Winter Palace it must have seemed to Alexander and all around him that it was numerous, ubiquitous, inexorable. And even more alarming, demoralising indeed, was the hostility to the regime displayed by the educated classes as a whole, or at least implicit, in their passive sympathy for the terrorists.

It has often been said that the alienation of the educated classes in the last years of Alexander's reign was largely due to Russia's humiliation at the Congress of Berlin and her failure, after so much sacrifice, to secure Constantinople. This was part of the truth; but we have seen enough to understand that the sickness went much deeper. The attempt on Trepov on the contrary occurred at a moment of high euphoria, on 24 January 1878, four days after the fall of Adrianople, and Vera Zasulich was tried and acquitted to general applause long before the Congress of Berlin and the undoing of San Stefano. What had been happening all through the second half of the 1860s and the first half of the 1870s was the widening of the gulf between the Tsar and his advisers on the one hand and the more socially and politically conscious of his subjects on the other. These formed a new class, a sort of bourgeoisie but without the instincts of the Western bourgeoisie, which very rapidly expanded as the new professions and the industrial age made their specialised demands, while the university students multiplied in spite of the efforts of the upright but highly conservative Minister of Education, Count D. A. Tolstoy, and others to frustrate the higher education of children of the lower orders. The gulf was partly concealed by the excitements of the Serbo-Turkish, then the Russo-Turkish, War. But even in the early seventies there had been a great deal of sympathy on the part of humane and liberal-minded citizens, impeccable in their respectability, for the desperate idealism with which so many of the young were flinging themselves into their attempts to change things for the better.

Trepov was perhaps the most detested man in St Petersburg, a dandified sadist of vicious temper who delighted to put himself on show as a patron of opera and the arts in general. He had first become notorious for his ruthlessness in firing on civilian crowds during the Polish revolt of 1863. Counsel for Vera Zasulich's defence made out a formidable list of other acts of inhumanity (she had indeed decided to kill him when he had lost his temper with an imprisoned student in the fortress of St Peter and St Paul and had him flogged, quite illegally, almost to death). But what the decent citizens who cheered the acquittal were protesting against was not so much Trepov himself, to them quite simply vile beyond redemption, but a ruler, a Tsar, so lacking in judgement or common sensibility that he saw nothing strange in delivering the lives and destinies of all the citizens of his great capital into the hands of a sycophantic bully unfit for decent company of any kind.

How deep was this feeling that the Tsar had failed his people time would very soon show. It was one thing for law-abiding citizens to take pleasure in the humiliation of a Trepov, quite another for those same citizens to stand by and watch apparently unmoved, as they were shortly to do, while their Emperor was hunted down and finally killed. Alexander failed in so many ways. He talked about reform and yet reposed his trust in subaltern tyrants; he talked about fidelity and openly betrayed his wife and outraged public opinion with his infatuation for Catherine Dolgoruky; he talked about Russia's holy mission and stopped short of liberating from Moslem oppression the Christians on Russia's own doorstep; he talked about national unity and deliberately rejected the co-operation of the men and women whose loyalty he demanded. The Tsar whose reign had opened so brightly was in a very bad way. He had less than three more years to live, and not even his courage in face of repeated terrorist attempts could any more endear him to his people.

'We are living through terrible times,' wrote Tchaikovsky to Nadezhda von Meck in September 1878, as the revolutionary terror was beginning to get into its stride, 'and if one stops to think about the present, one is terrified. On one side a completely panic-stricken government . . . on the other side, ill-fated youths, thousands of them exiled without trial to lands where not even a crow flies; and between these two extremes the masses, indifferent to everything, waist-deep in the mire of their egotistic interests, watching everything without a sign of protest.'[4]

Professional musicians are not necessarily competent political observers. I quote Tchaikovsky as he approached the peak of his fame precisely because he was an intelligent onlooker, deeply patriotic, but not politically involved.

How deep was this reluctant fellow-feeling for the rebels and how dismissive the accompanying contempt for the government is most vividly illustrated by the record of a conversation with Dostoevsky taken from the diary of the celebrated editor and publisher, A. S. Suvorin.

Suvorin and Dostoevsky were both convinced upholders of the autocracy. Suvorin was a peasant's son who founded the most popular conservative newspaper and became a millionaire. He was later to be the patron and friend of Anton Chekhov, who had to suffer the harsh reproaches of the radical intelligentsia for consorting with so reactionary a figure, until he finally broke with his old friend over the Dreyfus case. Dostoevsky, who was just entering the last year of his own life, had come a long way from the days when he had been sentenced to death and sent to Siberia as a member of the Petrashevsky Circle. Now he preached the special holiness of Russia and her institutions, above all peasantry, autocracy, Orthodox Church. Now, in February 1880, a few weeks after the terrible explosion in the Winter Palace which had killed and maimed so many innocent victims, Suvorin calling upon him one day found him brooding over terrorism in general and the attitude of the public in particular. Why was it, he wondered aloud, that 'society' seemed to sympathise with these crimes, or at least was 'not too clear about how to look at them'? And he went on to indicate that he was far from clear himself. 'Suppose,' he said 'you, Suvorin, and I happened to overhear by chance one obvious conspirator whisper to another, "The Winter Palace will go up very soon. I've set the machine." Would we go to the Winter Palace to warn them? Would we go to the police, or get the constable on the corner to arrest these men? Would you do that?'

And Suvorin replied, 'No, I would not.'

'Nor would I,' said Dostoevsky. And he then went on to analyse the reasons for this remarkable inhibition. The reasons for reporting the projected outrage were weighty and solid, he said; the reasons against 'absolutely trivial'. There was at first, naturally enough, a shrinking from getting mixed up with the police, perhaps coming under suspicion for complicity. But what really mattered was the fear of being thought of as an informer: the newspapers might report that he, Dostoevsky, had identified the criminals. 'Is this my business? It is the job of the police. This is what they have to do, what they are paid for. The liberals would never forgive me. They would torment me, drive me to despair.'

And he went on, already almost in despair: 'Is this normal? Everything is abnormal in our society; that is how these things happen, and, when they do, nobody knows how to act – not only in the most difficult situations, but even in the simplest.'[5]

Here is Tchaikovsky again, writing from Paris in December 1879. 'So long as all of us – the citizens of Russia – are not called upon to take part in our country's government, there is no hope for a better future.'[6] This is all that need be said. The direct threat to the autocracy came not from the convinced revolutionaries on the one hand or from the increasingly hard-driven peasantry on the other. It came from the disorientated, disenfranchised, politically superfluous members of the new bourgeoisie, the men whose talents should have been enlisted for the business of government but who were cast out and as it were disowned. As Dostoevsky said in that remarkable conversation with Suvorin: 'Everything is abnormal in our society . . . nobody knows how to act – not only in the most difficult situations, but even in the simplest.' Nobody was given a real opportunity to learn how to act: apart from the limited field of the zemstvo, all, unless they became professional bureaucrats, were excluded from adult activity of every kind outside the arts, and the arts themselves were bound. For this the Tsar above all must take the blame. But the Russians, many of them, Dostoevsky included, connived in the offence by pretending that their own society whose deliberate crippling, or emasculation, they so justly deplored was still in some quite indefinable manner superior to all those societies from which Russia had so much to learn. Russia in the last resort was holy Russia. And yet the very men who insisted on her exalted role extended their tolerance, if not their support, to those revolutionaries who spoke with the voice of a fanatical sanitary inspector who will blindly tear down a great building to get at the drains.

In the deceptive light of hindsight the active revolutionaries of nineteenth-century Russia appear with a far greater prominence on the national stage than was ever theirs in real life. In real life they were a nuisance, often a sinister nuisance, sometimes – as especially between 1878 and 1881 – a damaging one. But as far as the busy life of the country was concerned, except when the bombs were going off, their activities were peripheral and obscure. The fact that they were helping the dynasty to commit suicide was apparent only to a few outside their ranks.

A major development in the late 1870s was the infection of many of those who were inspired above all by the desire to serve their fellow men with the virus of those who were inspired above all by hatred. This was observable most clearly in the remarkable influence wielded by Sergei Nechayev.

The detailed biography of this very odd fish need not detain us here. All that matters is that he made himself sufficiently a legend to serve Dostoevsky as the model for the diabolical Peter Verkhovensky in *The Possessed*, that he lied, postured, stole, deceived, murdered – not at the expense of the autocracy but at the expense of his fellow revolutionaries from Bakunin downwards; that in *Revolutionary Catechism* he composed a declaration of revolutionary frightfulness demanding total subordination of the revolutionary to the sole task of destruction and the total subordination of means to end (but why apologise for the means when the end itself is evil?); that rising from the humblest beginnings he managed by the time he was twenty-five to establish a legend of single-minded devotion to the cause which even subsequent knowledge of his vile actions could not destroy; that after only four years as a revolutionary, three of them spent abroad, he spent the remaining ten years heroically enduring the dungeon life of St Peter and St Paul. By the time he died, worn out and rotted with prison illnesses, he had managed to convince at least twenty of his warders that revolution was imminent, that he would then rise up out of prison and lead prisoners and warders triumphantly into the red dawn.[7] This terrible young man quite evidently had what is nowadays called charisma. Hitler had it too.

The immediate attraction of Nechayev – apart from his personal magnetism, which must have been of a very high order – was that in his actions he appeared to personify the ruthless, dedicated liberator of whom the gentle and almost saintly Chernyshevsky had only dreamed. He was able to pretend that he controlled a wide-flung network of revolutionary cells throughout the length and breadth of Russia, all necessarily kept conspiratorially secret from each other. He was so successful in persuading the now elderly Bakunin of this in Geneva that he obtained from him a document formally recognising him as the leader of the future, which he was able to exploit to the full on his return to Russia. On his second and longer stay in Switzerland he managed to lay his hands on half the special reserve fund for the prosecution of revolution, of which Herzen and Ogarev had been co-trustees, and all but persuaded Herzen's daughter Natalie into marriage, bringing her own considerable fortune as her dowry.[8] He also promised immediate revolution. It was scheduled for March 1871.

It was the conspiratorial and concrete aspects of Nechayev which attracted a certain mentality, notably the gifted student Tkachev, who developed a theory of the role of the conspiratorial élite which was to survive Nechayev's demise and surface again in Lenin's Bolshevism. It was the dedicated, harshly single-minded aspect which won the respect and veneration of so many youngsters who were not at all ruthless by nature and often felt ashamed at their lack of single-mindedness. They thought of Nechayev in prison and banished frivolous desires. Thus it was that the spirit of Nechayev lived on to inspire the terrorists, even though these knew by then that he was a proved liar and swindler and probably a common murderer too. What was important was the legend. And the legend was so strong that in 1880 the terrorist group seriously considered abandoning an elaborately and patiently prepared attempt to assassinate the Tsar in order to mount an immediate rescue operation to get him out of the fortress.

Who were these terrorists, the members of Milyutin's dread 'secret society'?

2

They had not started off by being terrorists. Indeed, certain of the most implacable members of what was never more than a very small group came from the ranks of convinced gradualists – young men and girls who were moved more by humane concern for the oppressed than by hatred of the oppressor. They were turned into killers only by the obdurate and unyielding response of the autocracy to all efforts to change the nature of society. They emerged from the ranks of what came to be known as the Populist movement, which started innocuously enough, inspired by Herzen's phrase about 'going to the people'.

The immediate prophet of Populism was an ex-artillery officer, a gifted mathematician, P. L. Lavrov, who in his fortieth year had joined Serno-Solovevich's 'Land and Liberty' organisation, suffered arrest and banishment in 1866 with so many others after Karakozov's failed attempt on the Tsar, and escaped to Switzerland in 1870. During his four years of exile in Vologda province he had composed a series of essays which he called *Historical Letters* and which somehow slipped past the censorship and achieved wide fame before they could be banned. Lavrov's message, which he was later to elaborate from Switzerland in his periodical *Forward!* (*Vperyod!*) was that the educated classes owed everything they had to the illiterate and toiling masses: it was their manifest duty, therefore, to repay their debt by sacrificing themselves to make a better world for these masses. The better world could be achieved only by revolution: the old system must be discarded and a new one put in its place. But the revolution must be made for the people by the people in the form of a truly popular uprising. For this the people were not ready: first they must be awakened, instructed, enlightened. This could take a long time, but it was the task that the present generation of radicals must take upon themselves.[9]

And so they did. Many hundreds of ardent and starry-eyed dreamers, together with angry and frustrated young men and women of all shades of reformist or revolutionary opinion, moved out into the countryside – into the factories too, but especially to the villages – dressed like peasants or labourers, thinking high and living low, to awaken the unfortunates, point out the nature of their plight, analyse the reasons for their degradation, and exhort them to concerted action. The most remarkable aspect of this pilgrimage of grace was its spontaneity: there was no central organisation. In the years 1873 and 1874 thousands of students were simultaneously moved to sacrificial action. Poor students and rich students, girls and boys, undergraduates and post-graduates – all turned their backs on their familiar lives and went out to preach the gospel of self-help through revolution.

Their own awakening was bitter. Most of them had never talked to a peasant in their lives. They were appalled and shattered by their reception at the hands of the noble savages they had come to liberate. They were jeered at, abused, sometimes beaten and stoned, reported to the police. They discovered that the Russian peasant, to generalise, was sly, suspicious, envious, venal and drunken. They were shocked to find that the most able and articulate lived for the day they would be rich enough to employ and exploit their weaker neighbours – as they had been exploited by serf-owners in the past. Hundreds of these innocents were in fact arrested – over sixteen hundred between 1873 and 1877 – and sat in prison for years awaiting trial. The moment was unfortunate for them because, with the approach of the Turkish wars, their contemporaries still at liberty and their sympathisers of older generations were diverted from thoughts of revolution and reform by the wave of nationalism and Panslavism which swept the country. Some of the most ardent rebels, including no less a figure than Zhelyabov, who was later to hang for his part in the killing of the Tsar, were caught up in this new hysteria.

It was no doubt because the authorities were convinced that the loyalty of all right-minded Russians to the Crown was assured by the euphoria of war that they mounted two great trials in 1877. The first, in the spring, involved fifty individuals from what was known as the Moscow Circle; the second, running from October 1877 to January 1878, brought together no fewer than 193 young men and women. The trials achieved nothing at all beyond the publicising of revolutionary ideas through the agency of brave and gifted counsel for the defence. Was this the Tsar's reward for initiating and sanctioning the great juridical reform? The prosecution was inept to the point of farce. Authority was made a laughing-stock. It had the last laugh all the same: a great many of the accused were acquitted, but most of these were picked up by the police and sent off to Siberia and elsewhere by virtue of the special police powers of 'administrative exile' which were to play so critical a part in suppressing the opposition both before and after the revolution.

3

It was the day after the trial of the 193 had ended that Vera Zasulich tried to kill General Trepov. I said earlier that her attempt was a herald rather than a signal because it was an individual act by a muddle-headed woman who often got things wrong. The 'secret society' was in fact not quite ready for this sort of action. It was defining its role as its members transformed themselves from propagandist followers of Lavrov into quasi-professional terrorists.

The 'secret society' was in fact a reincarnation, with teeth, of the old 'Land and Liberty' society. Its leaders were three members of a Lavrovist group known as the Tchaikovsky Circle after its leader, N. V. Tchaikovsky; they were two very gifted radicals, Mark and Olga Natanson, and a frighteningly single-minded young woman, Sophia Perovskaya, the daughter of a distinguished family of soldiers: her father was a general. The Tchaikovsky Circle itself disintegrated with the shattering of the going-to-the-people movement, when it became clear to the Natansons, Perovskaya and others that propaganda and education were not enough. They joined forces with other active souls who were closer to the ideas of Nechayev and Tkachev, the latter now preaching in Geneva in his own paper, *The Tocsin* (*Nabat*), the need for immediate revolution to be carried out by a disciplined conspiratorial élite while there was still time before the solid middle class grew powerful enough to act as a buffer between a degenerate and desperate aristocracy and a peasantry simmering on the edge of violence. The new allies were, above all, the twenty-three-year-old A. D. Mikhailov, who proved to be an incredibly ingenious and resourceful conspirator, smuggler, organiser of escapes and assassinations, together with a number of like-minded colleagues from Odessa and Kiev. The new 'Land and Liberty' was organised not only as a highly efficient command structure – it formed the basis of the first fully-fledged political opposition party in Russian history.

This had been founded after the mass arrests of 1873–4, with a central command controlling the organisers of provincial and urban groups. The central command, or 'basic circle', was compartmentalised into five sections: the administrative, which supervised policy and looked after underground members living with false papers; sections two to four, which were responsible for winning support from the intelligentsia, the factory workers and the peasantry; and the fifth section called the 'Disorganising Section' which was responsible for assassinations, prison rescues, intelligence work including the infiltration of official organisations, and counter-intelligence against police-spies, etc. As time went on it was section five, of course, which master-minded the terror campaign.

There was no terror for several years. At first the organisation concentrated its efforts on trying to recruit supporters among the peasantry by means a good deal more subtle than those used before. Even so, little headway was made in the countryside. Quite a new development, however, was the dawning of a new political consciousness among the factory workers. The first public demonstration of the existence of 'Land and Liberty' occurred when 200 workers gathered outside the Kazan Cathedral in St Petersburg in December 1876: they were addressed by a twenty-year-old graduate of the Mining Institute, G. V. Plekhanov, who was to play a crucial part in the development of Russian Marxism.

It was in fact his objection to the use of terror that, more than anything else, turned Plekhanov towards Marxism. Certainly when he joined 'Land and Liberty', like most of his fellow members, he thought in terms of agitation and propaganda, not of killing. And the killing even when it started was *ad hoc* and more a matter of vengeance against detested individuals than a deliberate attempt to frighten authority into submission. The murder of Trepov was to be revenge for the flogging of the student Bogolyubov, who had been arrested during the Plekhanov demonstration of 1876. A little later, on 1 February 1878, the Disorganising Section murdered a police spy who had infiltrated their ranks. Various other attempts on provincial police officials and prosecutors were sometimes successful, mostly not. And then, on 4 August 1878, came the most spectacular coup: the stabbing in broad daylight in a St Petersburg street of General N. V. Mezentsev, Shuvalov's successor as head of the Third Section. The killing was carried out in style by one of the foundation members of the Tchaikovsky Circle, an ex-artillery officer, Sergei Kravchinsky. It was the general's custom to walk a little, accompanied only by an aide. On that August day he was overtaken by a smart equipage, which pulled up alongside. Out jumped Kravchinsky, pierced the general with his sword, leapt back into his carriage and drove off like the wind – and clean out of the country.[10]

But still nearly a year was to pass before systematic terror, as distinct from revenge killings, was to become the fixed policy of any group. By that time the harshness of the regime's response to the murder of Mezentsev and others had driven the tougher members of 'Land and Liberty' to the conclusion that the only hope was to frighten the autocracy into surrender. The successor to Mezentsev was yet another military man of the bull-necked, bellowing kind, General Alexander Drenteln, who urged on the Tsar the most savage measures of repression and was quite incapable of telling a liberal from a radical, a radical from a revolutionary, an anarchist from a constitutionalist. There was to be a drive to sweep subversion off the face of the land. What amounted to martial law was imposed on the main centres of terrorist activity – and three heroes of the recent war were sent out with virtually dictatorial powers to rule over them: General Gurko to St Petersburg, General Loris-Melikov to Kharkov, and the indestructible General Totleben to Odessa. The regular governors of other centres were granted similar powers. Two of the new satraps, Gurko and Totleben, behaved as might be expected. Their nets swept broadly and clumsily; the determined conspirator as often as not escaped; the innocent enthusiast was caught. Only Loris-Melikov showed sense, moderation and discrimination.

All this was fuel for the extremists of 'Land and Liberty'. But even those among them who advocated systematic terrorism were still divided as to the immediate aim: was it to frighten the autocracy into conceding a constitution which would give the revolutionaries a chance to propagate their views? Or was it to bring the whole system down in ruins? But like so many of the burning questions which then, and after, took up so much of the revolutionaries' time, the difference was irrelevant: it did not matter why they acted; what mattered was how they acted.

The final decision was taken in the summer of 1879. In June there was a secret conference of 'Land and Liberty' at Voronezh which was dominated by Mikhailov and a comparatively new recruit, A. I. Zhelyabov, who was to play a critical and colourful part in the events of the next two years, and then to die on the scaffold. Zhelyabov was a classical example of a revolutionary created against his will by the regime. He was the son of an ex-serf of Odessa, gifted, handsome, a little detached and cold, but kind, ambitious, immensely attractive to women. He had been driven off course as a university student by official behaviour of a kind guaranteed to drive the most loyal subject to rebellion. Not in the least interested in revolution to begin with, he had been expelled, arrested, his projected career as a lawyer destroyed in advance, imprisoned – all as the outcome of a chapter of silly little accidents arising out of his kindly and honest championship of fellow students in trouble. He had, in a word, spoken out of turn at a moment when Count D. A. Tolstoy was determined to make an example of any student who spoke at all. Now he was at Voronezh, as determined in an easy and relaxed way to change the system as he had once been content to live within it. He was not one of the fire-eaters. He believed in selective assassination as a weapon, but he did not share the implacable fury of Sophia Perovskaya (whose lover he nevertheless soon became) or the conspiratorial excitement of Mikhailov. He stood, however, with both these and others against all those who objected on principle to terror, most notably Plekhanov and P. B. Axelrod who walked out of the meeting.[11]

This demonstration was not intended to be a final split, only a protest. But within a few weeks the anti-terrorists had formed a separate organisation called 'Black Partition' (*Chorny Peredyel*) with a view to concentrating on the peasantry. 'Land and Liberty' was dead. The terrorists took a new name, the 'People's Will' (*Narodnaya Volya*), dedicated to violent political change. And it was the executive committee of 'People's Will' which now formally condemned the Tsar to death and for the next two years directed its main efforts to carrying out this sentence.[12]

3

It is usual to dismiss as ignorant and uncomprehending the whole administrative apparatus of the 1870s. This is not fair. The Mezentsevs and the Drentelns were brutal and crass. Totleben in Odessa, though splendid as a siege general, thought all he had to do was pick up untidy-looking students and imprison or exile them and all would be well. There were plenty of others like him. But the remarkable thing was that under extreme pressure from an unknown, shadowy force avowedly dedicated to the task of murdering the Tsar, there were still men who had the sense to see that the active terrorists were in a small minority and that if they could be separated from the well-meaning liberals and reformers their effectiveness would be rapidly diminished. They not only saw this for themselves but were able to persuade the Tsar to accept their diagnosis and let them make policy, a policy of reconciliation.

The turning point came after the shock of Khalturin's attempt on the Winter Palace. Already there had been earlier attempts on the Tsar, one very elaborate one with three linked groups responsible for three separate and spaced attempts to blow up the Imperial railway coach on the journey from the Crimea to St Petersburg. But the Winter Palace outrage, with its fearful carnage, was something else again. Now the panic could be felt. St Petersburg was placed under curfew; many of the wealthier and more noble inhabitants quietly slipped away for safety to their country estates – an eccentric procedure in the depths of winter. Alexander himself insisted on bringing Catherine Dolgoruky and their three children into the Winter Palace itself, where the Empress lay mortally ill. The Grand Duke Constantine was haunted by nightmares of the French Revolution. Yet at this very moment, and for the first time in more than a decade, sanity reared its head. Very reluctantly Alexander decided that Drenteln's indiscriminate strong-arm methods were worse than useless – a police chief who was unable to prevent a major explosion in the very heart of the Winter Palace – and then could not catch the perpetrator! . . . It was time to listen to those who urged that the best way to put a stop to terrorists was to rob the criminals of popular sympathy by getting the people on his side. So he set up an organ known as the Supreme Executive Committee, endowed with virtually dictatorial powers to root out sedition, destroy terrorists and devise ways and means for meeting the genuine grievances of the people. The most interesting thing about this wholly new departure, which without reducing the Tsar's absolute authority certainly distanced him from the business of day-to-day decision-making, was that it was urged by the Tsarevich, now a large, slow, heavy, honest, devout, conservative, deeply orthodox paterfamilias of thirty-five, who himself had been got at by the highly conservative Katkov. And the man chosen to head the commission and to recommend its composition was General Michael Loris-Melikov, a man as far removed, one would have said, from the upholders of orthodoxy and conservatism as it was possible to imagine.

Melikov was not even a Russian. He was an Armenian – even though one of his forebears had bought himself a Georgian title. He neither had any of the connections with the antique Russian lines enjoyed by the most favoured courtiers, nor was he one of those Germans who were tolerated because of their industry and efficiency. He was efficient and industrious all the same. And in spite of his somewhat Levantine features, his rather fulsome charm (he flattered like a Disraeli), he had won the approval of Dmitri Milyutin for his vigorous and clever conduct of the late war in the Caucasus (it was he who had captured Kars) and, latterly, the respect of the liberals for his comparatively enlightened conduct as the anti-terrorist dictator of Kharkov. He was easy to work with, amiable but decisive and quick. And he was a bit of an intellectual – a friend of Nekrasov, the radical poet and editor of *The Contemporary* in its great days.

The task he took on was enough to make the toughest quail. He was to have supreme responsibility for the safety of the realm, including the Tsar's person, and for working out a more constructive way of dealing with subversion. He started off with coolness and skill, concentrating first on isolating and picking off the active terrorists – of whom he was rightly convinced there were very few. And he was helped by a remarkable piece of luck. In the very first week of his new job, while his appointment was still the subject of much ill-natured gossip, an attempt was made on his life by an obscure member of the 'People's Will', who was caught, tried and hanged inside forty-eight hours: so the new saviour of the realm was already beating Drenteln hands down at his own game.

And he continued to do so. Drenteln was removed, and Melikov himself now controlled the Third Section as part of the Ministry of Internal Affairs – to say nothing of all the provincial governors. More of the genuine terrorists were arrested than ever before, and for the first time a clear idea of their limitations and their strength emerged from confessions and depositions. Melikov felt strong and secure enough to embark on what he regarded as his real programme: the reconciliation between the monarch and his subjects – honest citizens alienated and driven to sympathise with the revolutionaries by the crass behaviour of bureaucrats who treated them all as suspect; loyal patriots persecuted by police officials and others steeped in corruption, the true enemies of the realm; peasants who had never had the Emancipation Act explained to them and still believed that landowners and officials stood between them and the proper execution of that Act; conscripts treated like vermin; students driven to distraction by the curbs, restrictions and exclusions of the Tolstoy system; zemstvo officials who were never allowed to get on with their job because of government interference – to say nothing of the steady curtailment of their agreed spheres of action. Melikov made out his case with so remarkable a combination of tact, reasonableness, flattery and firmness that Alexander dismissed Tolstoy from the Ministry of Education and also from the Procuratorship of the Holy Synod (effectively, the Ministry of Religion), from which vantage points he had dominated the entire cultural scene, and replaced him by one of Melikov's own men at the education ministry. Less happily, the new Procurator of the Holy Synod was K. P. Pobedonostsev. Melikov turned to this man, who would soon destroy him, partly because he did not realise the extent of his obscurantism, largely because of his powerful influence over the Tsarevich, whose tutor he had been and whose mentor he still was. For all his steel spectacles and his desiccated appearance, Pobedonostsev was a reactionary in the high romantic manner. He believed in the total incapacity of mankind to govern itself intelligently or even to behave in a reasonable and decently intelligent manner over any length of time. The justice of this viewpoint was unhappily compromised by an equally strong conviction that he, Pobedonostsev, was an exception to the rule and alone knew what was what. Since he was in no position to lay down the law to 130 million subjects of the Tsar he did the next best thing, seizing upon the Tsarevich as the future ruler and guiding him along the proper lines. More than any single man he was to be the evil genius of the dynasty – all through the reign of Alexander III and well into that of Nicholas II, working with a single-minded dedication for the upholding of suicidal policies that, in retrospect, makes the Rasputin affair look like slapstick. How odd that this man should have been brought forward by the little Armenian who was to come nearer than any other individual under the Tsars to curtailing the Imperial absolutism!

Not that Pobedonostsev was void, nor was he as mad as some of his utterances concerning the divine right of Tsars might suggest. He was intelligent indeed, and in fact supported Melikov at first. He had no desire to keep the people down, to oppress, to exploit. On the contrary, as a deeply religious man he desired their good. His ill-starred policies sprang from the bleak but bravely borne conviction that people must be protected from themselves and that this nursery activity was the first and last duty of the Crown.

This did not matter then. The terrorists were still active, but on a reduced scale. Khalturin was still at large, but his nerve had gone after the Winter Palace bomb. Alexander Mikhailov had himself been arrested in November 1879 as a result of an indiscretion of so elementary a kind that one is tempted to think that he had the death-wish on him. But he confessed to nothing, and died in prison four years later with the authorities never knowing that he had anything to do with the attempt on the Tsar. The torch was now being carried by Zhelyabov, that strange mixture of equivocation and ruthless, single-minded planning, working closely with Sophia Perovskaya, always fanatical, now the very image of an avenging angel. The Tsar was still the main target and these two went on laying their plans apparently oblivious of the political wind of change that was now blowing over their heads. Or were they all the more determined to strike hard and decisively before the Melikov reforms began to undermine the radical will for violent change?

These projected reforms now had the full backing of the Tsar. But Melikov himself was already coming under fire from the conservatives, who thought he was going too far; worse, that as an alien he was too easily identified with that other alien force which, as was well known, had been steadily working against the true interests of the Russian people – the power of Jewry. There had been a wave of anti-semitism during the Serbo-Turkish War: Jewish influence was held to be partly responsible for the poor showing put up by the Serbs. Later, Jewish profiteers were widely believed to have made a good thing out of Russia's own war, and also to have heavily influenced the unfavourable peace. There was still no official anti-semitism (that was to come in the next reign) but already many simple Russians were being persuaded of the truth of the ancient myth that unleavened bread was made with Christian blood obtained by ritual murder, and officialdom did nothing to discourage this belief.

Katkov was not an active anti-semite. But Katkov now was coming out in his newspaper, *Moscow News*, against the very reforms he himself had helped to initiate.

In this charged and unpleasant atmosphere Melikov, far from losing his head, took advantage of his new ascendancy over the Tsar to press on with larger reforms. He was not above cynical manoeuvring. In May 1880 the Tsaritsa Marie Alexandrovna died. Before that summer was out Alexander had shocked the court by marrying Catherine Dolgoruky. He intended to proclaim her Tsaritsa very soon, but for the time being he created for her the title Princess Yurevskaya. So after fourteen years as an imperial mistress, Catherine was transformed into an honest woman and Alexander's 'marriage before God' became a marriage before men. The precipitancy of this action was deeply misguided: it was Catherine who insisted on it, and it is impossible to endorse her judgement. She had nothing to gain and much to lose. St Petersburg had got used to having her about the place as the Tsar's mistress, even though it disapproved of all those children romping about inside the Winter Palace where the Tsaritsa lay dying. With a show of discretion, the Princess, still only thirty-two years old, might have won many hearts. It was the age of Mrs Keppel, who knew precisely how to conduct herself in London. As it was, she won no hearts at all. The Tsarevich was so angry that he considered carting his whole family off to settle in Denmark; Melikov, however, with that short-sighted eye for the main chance which so often goes with liberalism of the more sophisticated kind, saw an ally. Not to put too fine a point on it, he buttered Catherine up. For the moment he was very clever in retaining the favour of the Tsarevich while winning Catherine as a friend. But it could not last.

It lasted long enough for him to formalise his thinking towards the end of 1880 to the point when he could lay before the Tsar a cut-and-dried plan for a form of constitutional government which would not be a constitution. What would have happened to Melikov had his master survived is a fascinating question. He had persuaded Alexander to agree to a disguised representative assembly – a body of delegates from zemstvos, assemblies of the nobility, city councils, to work on draft legislation under the Ministry of the Interior (he, of course, was to be the Minister of the Interior). He had provided for an enlarged State Council to take in delegates from these groups to consider the draft laws and make recommendations to the Tsar (but Alexander, however, would not agree to this). He had, in a word, established at least a bridgehead for a constituent assembly, thus threatening a fixed article of dynastic faith.

By the middle of February 1881 the programme was ready and on the eighteenth of the month Melikov put the draft before the Tsar. He had not been unduly perturbed when three weeks earlier the police had uncovered yet another plot against the Tsar and arrested among others three key members of the Executive Committee of the 'People's Will'. Nobody knew quite how important they were, quite how advanced their latest plans were. Nobody knew that Perovskaya, Zhelyabov and others had been working feverishly for the completion of the most daring scheme of all.

By now Pobedonostsev and the Tsarevich were having second thoughts about Melikov. So were Katkov and many other conservatives who believed in all seriousness that he was allowing himself to be carried away by the applause of the liberals, an unhealthy breed quite cut off from the devout and simple faithful who looked to the Tsar as their father. There was a collision in the making, but it never took place. The devout and simple terrorists saw to that. Oblivious of the powerful currents and cross-currents which, released by the tensions of the dawning industrial age, were stirring the stagnant waters of Russian political life – or, if not oblivious, uncaring – Perovskaya, Zhelyabov and their friends laboured away, still intent on the supreme act of destruction, which was to annihilate the Tsar and with him the autocracy. Shooting had failed; an elaborate, ingenious and devoted attempt to blow up the Imperial train had failed; the great explosion inside the Winter Palace had failed. There had been many killings and woundings, but the membership of the Executive Committee itself had also suffered and was reduced to the merest handful now. The survivors, however, persisted with their latest plan, which was to explode a mine in a certain street, the Maly Sadovaya, along which the Tsar was accustomed to drive whenever he left or returned to the Winter Palace. It seems extraordinary that with the sort of police precautions in force after the Tsar had so narrowly escaped assassination so many times it was possible for the terrorists to rent a basement room in this street and from it carry out the tunnelling operations under cover of a very bogus-looking cheese shop which they could not stock with even seeming adequacy for lack of cash. But possible it was. The tunnelling continued. And at the same time a suicide squad of bomb-throwers – four in all – was being trained for action if the mine did not explode.

This was the position when Melikov presented his draft programme (contemptuously referred to later by the new Tsar as the Loris-Melikov Constitution) to Alexander on 18 February. The mine should in fact have been set off three days earlier, but the work on the tunnel had been delayed by the arrest at the end of January of a number of the bolder and more intelligent members of the Executive Committee. A new zero hour was fixed for 1 March. But on 27 February disaster struck the conspirators. By sheer luck the police got on the track of Zhelyabov – though not of the tunnel – and arrested him. It was some time before they realised who he was. When the news reached Melikov his relief was great. Even when Zhelyabov refused to talk or in any way inform on his comrades there seemed no reason for dismay. The Tsar would be killed, Zhelyabov insisted, no matter how many were arrested first. Nobody believed him. He was right. Melikov knew well enough from previous confessions that he had been absolutely correct in his earlier belief that the terrorists were very thin on the ground. With Zhelyabov behind bars, he was sure, the remainder were leaderless and would soon be caught.

He was so very nearly right. But he was reckoning without Sophia Perovskaya, that deeply disconcerting creature, who despised words and by her incessant urging of immediate action became the scourge and the conscience of the dreamers among the revolutionaries. Tiny, flaxen-haired, almost doll-like with pink and white cheeks and pale blue eyes, she was a revolutionary to the bone. Unlike Zhelyabov or the bomb-maker Kibalchich, who became revolutionaries by accident (Kibalchich could have been a scientist, perhaps an inventor of genius, had he not fallen foul of authority for the most trivial cause), Perovskaya cannot be imagined outside the context of her life and early death. Her family was ancient and respected. Her mother was a great beauty. Her father had been Governor-General of St Petersburg when Karakozov made his assassination attempt in 1866, and was sacked in consequence. Sophia loathed and detested the whole social and militaristic set-up into which she had been born. She hated her bully of a father. She joined the Tchaikovsky Circle and, once a revolutionary, was astounded to find so many able-bodied young men content to sit about talking, talking, planning, dreaming, doing nothing today, looking only to the future. For Sophia Perovskaya the future was now. It was she who headed the movement from reform to terrorism, and now, at the age of twenty-eight, it was fitting that she should take command on that final day. The mine was ready, and thanks to Zhelyabov's insistence and foresight the bomb-throwers had their primitive grenades and were carefully placed to cover the different routes the Tsar might follow: Ivan Grinevitsky, T. Mikhailov (no relation of Alexander Mikhailov), N. Rysakov, I. Emilyanov. The first two were twenty-four, the others eighteen and nineteen respectively. Sophia herself was to take up position outside the Michael Riding School where on Sunday mornings Alexander used to drive to applaud the horsemanship of his Guards. From there she would be able to signal to the bomb-throwers.

And so it happened. On the very day that Alexander put his signature to the Loris-Melikov reforms, within a couple of hours of what should have been an epoch-making action, Perovskaya struck. This extraordinary young woman, agonised by the arrest of her lover, knowing that the police were already on the trail of the whole group and at any moment would discover the tunnel with the bomb already wired for detonation, kept her head, deployed her forces, refused to be daunted when it was clear that the Tsar was changing his route so that all the tunnelling had been in vain, took up her position, watched with clear and steady eyes, gave the pre-arranged signal which set the action moving to destroy a Tsar. Mikhailov had already lost his nerve and moved back from his station: he should as things turned out have been the first to throw. Rysakov, fifty yards down the quayside, kept his head, but made a bad throw. The grenades were so feeble that Kibalchich had warned his comrades they must be thrown from very close, so close that the throwers would probably go up with them. Rysakov threw his from some way off. It exploded under the back axle of the Tsar's carriage, disabled it, killed a baker's boy in the crowd and wounded one of the Cossack escorts. Alexander, instead of driving on in another carriage as urged, insisted on going back on foot first to look at Rysakov, who had been seized at once, then to see the casualties. It was now that Grinevitsky shouldered his way out of the crowd, came face to face with his Emperor and, almost within touching distance, hurled his bomb.

Alexander was dead within two hours, his shattered body brought with difficulty to a sofa in the Winter Palace. Grinevitsky's own wounds were almost as bad, but he lived for over eight hours, regaining consciousness an hour or so before he died, but refusing to say a word to the police at his bedside. This much has been recorded. But in the high romantic terrorist tradition Grinevitsky's bomb killed or maimed at least a score of others, whose blood stained the trodden snow. Who these were, how many died, what happened to the survivors it is impossible to discover.

4

What happened to the conspirators – Zhelyabov already in prison, Perovskaya, Kibalchich and the three surviving bombers – is that they were all hanged. This last public execution to be staged in Russia took place before a crowd of some eighty thousand. It was the youngest of the conspirators, eighteen-year-old Rysakov, who broke down in prison, confessed, begged for mercy, exposed as many of his comrades as he could. It did not save him from the scaffold. And on the scaffold the others coldly turned away from him, exchanging last words among themselves, leaving Rysakov to die quite alone. It was the execution of the Decembrists all over again, except that one of the hanged was a woman. There was no proper drop, only stools to be kicked away, and the stools were too low for a quick kill. Worst of all, Mikhailov's noose slipped, not once, but twice. He was heavier than the executioner, who was drunk, had bargained for. He had to be lifted up and re-hanged. All took some minutes to die. Russia still had not learnt even how to hang.

CHAPTER SIXTEEN

The Peace of the Graveyard

I

WITH the accession of Alexander III Imperial Russia entered a new phase in her history. It was not simply that all effective revolutionary activity was ended for many years to come; more importantly, it was the end of serious reform from above: when, twenty-five years later, certain major reforms were at last, belatedly, undertaken, they were forced upon a desperately resisting monarch from below.

On the face of it Alexander's reign was an interlude of reaction not dissimilar in kind from earlier periods that often enough in the past had followed crises of flux and change, an interlude summed up by a distinguished British historian: 'stagnation in agriculture, progress in industry, retrogression in education, russification of the non-Russian half of the empire's population, and an overall attitude of nostalgic, obscurantist, and narrowly bureaucratic paternalism'.[1] This is true as far as it goes, but it does not go far enough. For there was a new element, which was to mark off Alexander's reign very sharply from all previous reigns. It was an element, moreover, which was to endure through the next reign, the reign of Nicholas II, the last Tsar, and beyond. This was the institutionalisation of police rule.

Of course, as we have seen, the autocracy had for long relied on the Third Section and the Gendarmerie. Shuvalov in particular had managed to exploit the Tsar's fears of revolution in the early 1870s to win for himself power and influence over a very wide front. When Loris-Melikov abolished the Third Section and put the Corps of Gendarmes under the Ministry of the Interior he acted in good faith, believing that only in this way could he get control of the political police and prevent them from continuing with the sort of repressive actions which played into the hands of the subversives. But what he did not foresee was that he would not last long as minister and that less enlightened successors would find under their hands a centralised police apparatus to use as they liked.

It took just under two months for Alexander to get rid of Loris-Melikov, rather less than six months to put the country under police rule and, in so doing, quite unwittingly deliver the autocracy itself into the hands of successive chief policemen. The direction was not at first plain to all. For a moment the survivors of the 'People's Will' seemed to have convinced themselves that with the death of the Tsar Liberator the walls of Jericho would fall. An extraordinary open letter was addressed by its Executive Committee to the new Tsar in which they loftily assured him that they would let bygones be bygones if he would do the same: forget the grief and pain we have caused Your Majesty and your family, the letter said in effect, and we will forget the grief and pain Your Majesty's family have caused so many thousands for so long. Give us freedom of speech, freedom of assembly, and everything else we modestly demand, and we will make an end of violence. But if not, then war to the knife, violence piled on violence, until you and yours are utterly destroyed in the inevitable revolution: 'Your Majesty must decide!'[2] It does not seem to have occurred to the remaining terrorists that from now on they would be hunted out of existence. But this happened. Those who were not caught and imprisoned fled abroad. There was no more organised action for years to come.

The terrorists were not the only ones to underrate the destructive power of the regime when it was single-mindedly applied. The novelist Leo Tolstoy, though he detested terrorism, was moved to write to the new Tsar imploring him to inaugurate a new era by treating the accused with clemency and sparing their lives. The letter was sent by the hand of the celebrated critic Strakhov to Pobedonostsev to bring forward to the Tsar.[3] The chief arbiter of the Christian Church in Russia was outraged. 'When I read your letter I saw that your faith had nothing in common with mine, which is that of the Church, and that my Christ was not your Christ. My Christ is a man of strength and truth who heals the weak, and yours seemed to me to be a weak man himself in need of healing.'[4]

Pobedonostsev's reply was written from a position of assured strength when the crisis was over. But he too had had his moments of anxiety when he feared that the new Tsar might too easily stray from the narrow path of total rectitude. Tolstoy was not the only one to beg for imprisonment instead of hanging. The philosopher and mystic Vladimir Solovyev, son of the great historian, a lofty and disinterested spirit who could never be suspected, as Tolstoy could all too easily be suspected, of playing a part, of exhibitionism, also wrote to the Tsar, prompting Pobedonostsev to an almost panic-stricken reaction: 'An idea that fills me with horror has just begun to circulate. . . . The Russian people are already beginning to fear that monstrous schemes may be submitted to Your Majesty to move you to pardon the criminals. . . . No, no, a thousand times no; in this moment, with the eyes of the entire Russian nation upon you, it is unthinkable that you should pardon the murderers of your father the Emperor of Russia – that you should forget the blood that has been shed, for which everyone (apart from a few weak-hearted and feeble-minded individuals) cries vengeance. . . .'[5]

Alexander did not need telling. He was more sure of himself than anyone believed at the time. And although he was to march his country steadily towards catastrophe, he was a more able ruler, in the sense of management and political finesse, than is usually believed. He was not against pragmatical reform in principle, but was determined to stop anything that smelt of liberalism dead in its tracks, and he did so with the minimum of fuss. For eleven years he achieved what so many of his predecessors had aspired in vain to achieve – peace and the tranquility of the grave – without extravagant bloodshed or spectacular cruelty. He was unimaginative and unspeculative, slow-thinking too, and was thus incapable of grasping a number of fundamental facts – on one level, for example, that nothing stands still and that a country which does not move forward must move backwards; on another level, that by giving the police the power to decide who shall be arrested, and when, and what shall be done with the body, a ruler is abdicating his own authority. But according to his dim lights he was a formidable man, and he would have pursued his course almost certainly without any help from Pobedonostsev.

The key to Alexander is that he had a strong element of cynicism. He was one of those unusual creatures, a truly honest man who does not expect others to be honest. This has confused posthumous estimates of his character. In appearance he was simplicity itself, a four-square, six feet three and broad in the frame to match, patriarchially bearded, so strong that he could perform all the strongman's tricks, such as tying pokers into knots and bending horseshoes with his bare hands, faithful and devoted in marriage to his gay and lovely Danish princess, Dagmar, the sister of the future Queen Alexandra of England, stern and loving as a father, unassuming in his interests – such as presiding over the deliberations of the Historical Society of Russia. How could such a man, not stupid but slow and amiably dull, be cynical?

The cynicism had its roots, of course, in a profound, rich arrogance, the quiet possession of which set him apart from other men, including most of his forebears. Heaven knows, the German Romanovs with their Russian pride were all arrogant enough, but in most the arrogance was in some degree forced. Alexander I had found it necessary to dazzle the world in order to believe in himself; Nicholas I had been driven to dramatise his quasi-divine regality on every suitable and unsuitable occasion; Alexander II had displayed his own inner uncertainty by swinging between imperial stubbornness and nursery sulks. But the new Tsar was truly blessed: he was so sure of himself that he felt no need to demonstrate his authority and preferred others to take the limelight and even believe that they were leading him. He was also lazy and looked to others to formulate his thoughts for him. It is hard to believe that such a man needed reassurance or example from a Pobedonostsev. But Pobedonostsev was a clever fellow who knew all the difficult words and had an answer for everything. He also had a waspish tongue and knew how to keep people in order. To the stolid Alexander his tirades, lapsing frequently into hysteria, must often have seemed absurd. But then all human beings not born into the purple were absurd. One used them. One might even become attached to them. After all, it was not their fault that they were not born Romanovs.

So Pobedonostsev need not have worried. Alexander was bound to go his way, but needed to explore the ground before he moved. People were surprised when he did not immediately throw out Loris-Melikov and countermand all his arrangements and plans. But Alexander had no wish to make a public demonstration of non-confidence in his late father's dispositions. He also needed to salvage anything he could from the ruins of those plans. It is hardly too much to say that apart from Loris-Melikov himself he was the only man in all St Petersburg who kept his head in face of the hysteria that swept the city after the assassination. And he was not the sort of man to arrive at final decisions on the impulse of the moment.

Pobedonostsev was not a good judge of character and because Alexander preferred not to dismiss Melikov out of hand bombarded him with dire warnings: 'He is not to be believed. He is a prestidigitator. He may even be playing a double game. . . . He is not a Russian patriot.'[6] Alexander continued on his path, imperturbably. The little man's day would soon come.

Indeed, it was already dawning. Unknown to anyone, Alexander now instructed him to compose a manifesto which should establish the keynote of his reign: 'The voice of God commands us to stand resolutely by the task of governing, relying on Divine Providence, with faith in the strength and truth of autocratic power, which we have been called to confirm and protect for the good of the people against all encroachments.'[7] This pronouncement went clean against the sense of the Melikov proposals, and it was printed and thrown without warning at the heads of the Conference of Ministers as they met for the third time to discuss to what extent those proposals would be implemented in the changed situation, and how. It was a clever move. To the country at large Alexander could say that his manifesto was no more than a loyal avowal of an age-old principle, an act of re-dedication which in no way precluded change within the framework of the autocracy. But to Loris-Melikov it was a direct affront, and intended as such. It was understood in this sense by conservatives all over the land. Those royal words, declared Katkov, in his newspaper, 'fell like manna from heaven! They are our salvation: they give back to the Russian people a Russian, an autocratic, Tsar.'[8]

This was on 29 April. Loris-Melikov offered his resignation on the spot. Within a few days the Grand Duke Constantine, Alexander's uncle, who had stood in the front line of reform for a generation, threw in his hand; he later removed his whole family into self-imposed exile in Paris. General Dmitri Milyutin, the veteran War Minister who had done so much to raise the army from its post-Crimean demoralisation, also departed, and with him, after only a year in office, the new Finance Minister, A. A. Abaza. Loris-Melikov, still only fifty-six, retired to live out his days in Nice (where the Princess Yurevskaya, née Catherine Dolgoruky, also went into retreat). Dmitri Milyutin decided to rusticate himself at home. Thus the three most able and enlightened men in the Imperial service were effortlessly erased from the scene, becoming for all practical purposes un-persons. Milyutin was to live on for thirty-one years, long enough to watch his beloved army shattered by an enemy he had never dreamed of, the Japanese, but spared the last ordeal by his death, at ninety-six, in 1912.

2

The man whom Pobedonostsev had been urging on the Tsar in place of Loris-Melikov was none other than that 'true Russian', the Panslav Count N. P. Ignatiev, of San Stefano fame, who now became Minister of the Interior. Here, as in the appointment of the fraudulent General Baranov to command St Petersburg and purge it of subversion, Alexander allowed his cynical streak to show. He had known very well that Baranov was an exhibitionist braggart and a liar, but he wanted someone who could put on a show of mighty resolution. He knew that Ignatiev was totally un-reliable, a compulsive liar and intriguer, and a Panslav romantic into the bargain. But he was popular with the conservative elements which needed steadying and also had a certain appeal to younger idealists believing in the Slav mission. Alexander himself had once been moved by Panslav sentiments, mainly in reaction against the powerful German influence in the administration. But it had soon dawned on him that the very idea of Panslavism was a challenge to acceptance of the divine superiority of Russia; and he was a Russian nationalist through and through: with practically nothing but German blood in his veins, he was more self-consciously Russian than any Tsar had been before him and the scourge of the Germans in high positions who had for so long had things their way.

Alexander knew how to use Ignatiev, and did so. The first task he was set was to draw up a new code of measures for combating sedition, in which one of his chief collaborators was a thirty-five-year-old career official, V. K. Plehve. It was a bad day for Russia when Plehve was picked out as a coming man. It is hard to think of a single beneficent action performed by him in the next twenty-three years, before he was killed by one of those revolutionaries his own policies had done so much to provoke into action.

This is to move ahead too fast and too far. But it is reasonable to look a little in the direction of the way we have to go. The year 1881 was a critical year indeed. The publication of the new measures for the security of the realm promulgated on 14 August of that year was a climacteric act, and the emergence of Vyacheslav Plehve on the national stage was a portent. For this hollow man was an opportunist climber devoured by ambition who lacked the self-knowledge of the proper cynic. To Loris-Melikov he had presented himself as just the sort of liberal, young functionary to supervise the state police within the Ministry of the Interior. To Ignatiev he managed to appear as a staunch authoritarian who hated liberals. He was also by blood an East Prussian who managed to soar in the service of a Tsar who loathed Germans. Clearly he was talented. As clearly he was void. When in the next reign he reached his apogee as Minister of the Interior under a weak Tsar his emptiness was exposed for all to see. He was not a man of violence and did not, as was widely supposed, personally instigate pogroms or the rounding up of demonstrating students by Cossacks, who flogged them brutally and raped the girls into the bargain. But he countenanced both these horrors and in fact encouraged them by the calculated intemperance of his condemnation of Jews and students.

For the time being he occupied a subordinate position. But he had a good deal to do with the drafting of the new regulations which he was to invoke whenever it suited him in years to come. Formally entitled 'the Statute Concerning Measures for the Protection of State Security and the Social Order', their main feature was to outlaw – there is no other word for it – political action of any kind. The regulations provided for the recognition of two distinct states of emergency known as 'Reinforced Degree of Defence' and 'Extraordinary Degree of Defence' (*Usilennaya Okhrana* and *Chrezvychainaya Okhrana*). The first could be imposed by the Minister of the Interior and Governor-General; the second needed the approval of the Tsar and Council of State. But for neither were the conditions laid down with anything approaching precision.

These 'exceptional measures', the employment of which was to become the rule, were applicable to separate localities as and when deemed necessary. Under the Reinforced Degree, governors-general and governors were empowered to override the law in a fairly wholesale manner. For example, they could imprison any individual without trial for up to three months and fine him up to 400 roubles; they could prohibit all gatherings and assemblies, private or public; they could close down factories, shops, etc., for as long as the emergency was deemed to last; they could deport any individual from his home district. On top of this they could order the instant dismissal of any paid employee on the staff of zemstvo, city or town councils.

The Extraordinary Degree, of course, was more thoroughgoing still. The affected district, region, province, would be placed in effect under military rule. For the duration of the emergency a so-called commander-in-chief was appointed, endowed with all the powers enjoyed by the governor under the Reinforced Degree, with others added. He could set up military police commands, have certain categories of offenders tried by military tribunals instead of civil courts, declare certain actions outside the law altogether, make arrests, confiscate property, imprison and fine in an entirely arbitrary manner. More spectacularly, he could formally dismiss *elected* officials from their posts, close down whole zemstvos, sack out of hand any member of the civil service below the three highest ranks, close schools, universities and technical colleges, and ban publications at will.

It is true to say, I think, that there was no time between the promulgation of the Statute of 14 August 1881 and the fall of the dynasty in March 1917 when the 'exceptional measures' were not in operation in some part of the land – often over large parts of it. It was this law which was to make a mockery of the hard-won civil rights promised after the abortive revolution of 1905 and, together with the development of the system of police informers, serve as the ready-made and indispensable base for Lenin's and Stalin's Russia, the Russia of the Cheka and the G.P.U.

3

Ignatiev had no idea of what he was doing when he sponsored these regulations, nor had Pobedonostsev, who, although he had started life as a professor of law, lacked the least understanding of what the law was about. Later on in the reign, when the graveyard calm was fairly established, he addressed a memorandum to the Tsar urging not only the abolition of the jury system, so hardly won, the irremovability of judges, the freedom of defence counsel to act and speak as they saw fit, but also the very principle of the separation of the judiciary from the executive. It was obvious that a man of this passionately obscurantist character would not put up with an Ignatiev for long. Indeed, one can only assume that he had misread the mind and character of Ignatiev, just as he had misread the mind and character of Loris-Melikov only two years earlier, perhaps because he saw they were both able men of strong and forceful nature and found it impossible to imagine that such men might not share his own ideas – or at least be induced to share them, with their self-evident righteousness in the light of the reason which he, Pobedonostsev, would be pleased to supply. At any rate, Ignatiev started to earn his disapproval even before the year was out, when in December he sponsored certain reforms designed to help the peasants by rounding off the work started by the Emancipation Act of twenty years earlier. And in May 1882 he went altogether too far. Fired again by the Slavophile dreams which had run him into trouble only a few years earlier, Ignatiev made the suicidal mistake of proposing to Alexander a restoration of that hoary old institution, the Congregation of the Lands, the *Zemsky Sobor*. This solemn assemblage of nobility and people had not been convened since the election of Michael Romanov in 1613, but in the 1830s the Slavophiles had begun to idealise it as the symbol of the sacred union of Tsar and people. Now, Ignatiev innocently thought, the time was ripe for its revival.

The proposed assembly would have been in effect a colourful pageant with a cast of two thousand, representative of all the estates, high and low, and all the institutions of central and provincial government, secular and religious. It could have achieved nothing practical and it would in no way have affected the integrity of the autocracy. But to Pobedonostsev it was anathema. The *Zemsky Sobor* was the thin end of the wedge. It would lead inevitably to demands for a constitution. 'If the will and decision pass from the Government to any sort of national assembly whatsoever, that will be the end, the ruin of government and the ruin of Russia'.[9] It would be to flirt with the notion of parliamentary government, 'the great lie of our time'.

Although the last thing anyone had wanted was for 'the will, the decision' to pass from the Government, within a matter of weeks Ignatiev was gone, his place taken, again on Pobedonostsev's recommendation, by Count D. A. Tolstoy, one-time Minister of Education and Pobedonostsev's predecessor as Procurator of the Holy Synod. There was to be no more experimenting, the nonsense was over. There had been a good deal of nonsense. Ignatiev, for example, had collaborated with, or at least tolerated, a remarkable private army run by an illustrious but slightly dotty senior courtier, Count Vorontsov-Dashkov – a sort of cross between the Lord Chamberlain and the Earl Marshal at the Court of St James. Known as the Sacred Company, this sinister organisation sought to rally the nobility in defence of the life of the Tsar against the terrorists, and in its methods it showed that the terrorists had no monopoly of conspiratorial talent. Indeed, by seeking out known revolutionaries in foreign exile and promising them certain concessions in return for a truce, at least until the Tsar was crowned, the Sacred Company entered that twilight world where all cats are grey which was to exercise such an irresistible fascination on the political police in years to come. Dashkov promised his support for the *Zemsky Sobor* and Ignatiev believed that the idea had the Tsar's blessing.

Pobedonostsev now said what Alexander wanted to hear. The new Tsar had been on the throne ten months and could see his way ahead. There must be no more fantasy – and no more hysteria. Panic had subsided. Bismarck in Berlin had stopped demanding daily news of the situation in St Petersburg, expecting the worst. Alexander and his family had virtually abandoned the Winter Palace and taken up residence at Gatchina, which (the Emperor Paul had seen to that) was easier to guard. Throughout his reign, indeed, Alexander was the Tsar who, unlike his father and his grandfather, never went among his people. When he did appear on great ceremonial occasions he presented a fine figure of an Emperor and the magnificence of his bearing during the week-long coronation ceremonies in May 1883 stirred the hearts of many who had recently felt unkindly towards the Romanovs. But for all his appearance of grave amiability he was aloof and benevolently dismissive in the grand regal manner. 'When you go home,' he said to the traditional delegation of peasant elders who came to bow low to him in homage, 'give my hearty thanks to all; follow the counsel and leadership of your marshals of the nobility; and do not believe the absurd and ridiculous rumours and stories about dividing the land, free gifts of land, and so on. These rumours are spread by your enemies. All property, including yours, must be inviolable.'[10]

He continued to hold aloof, moving, heavily guarded, between Gatchina, the Winter Palace, Tsarskoe Selo, and his beloved Crimean resort at Livadia.

The course was set.

4

It was not quite so benevolently conservative as on the surface it appeared to be. In some ways, indeed, it was rather nastily radical. When Alexander spoke of his subjects, dwelling on their sterling qualities, he was thinking of some 50 million Great Russians, who formed only half the population of the Empire. It is fair to say, as certain Slavophile writers approvingly insisted, that Alexander III was the first Tsar to recognise the special qualities of the rank-and-file Russian and to value them. Alexander I with his cosmopolitan outlook had regarded his subjects as barbarians; Nicholas I had viewed them through the eyes of a drill sergeant; Alexander II had indeed sought with the great reforms to raise them up, but chiefly for reasons of state to make good the deficiencies of the army and the economy. Alexander III, however, cared for Russians as Russians.

This was unfortunate for some 50 million non-Russian citizens of the Empire – from Finns and Lithuanians in the north to Georgians and Uzbeks in the south – who, in the past, had looked to the Tsar for protection against Russian officialdom, and had received it if only because the Tsar regarded all his peoples as equally subject to his will. Alexander's national consciousness coincided with the swift development of that popular nationalism which was such a feature of the Turkish War – and which was, of course, also rampant in other countries as the century moved to its close, in France as well as in Britain and in Germany too. It coincided also with the maturing of the vast post-Emancipation bureaucracy which was called into being by the development of industry and commerce and by the abolition of the serf-owning landlord as the effective viceroy, magistrate, administrator, of the rural population – a bureaucracy, of course, which was swollen by recruits from precisely those landowning families which had been hard-hit by the Emancipation. This bureaucracy very naturally sought to establish uniform rules and regulations, customs, attitudes throughout the vast land; so that the pressure towards russification was twofold: administrative convenience and ideology worked together. The ideology was a combination of the religious and the secular. Orthodox Christianity was the only true faith, setting its face with perfect rigidity against all other religions and sects. And of course it was the Christian sects which came in for the roughest treatment. The Moslems of Asiatic Russia, for example, although harassed and proselytised, were never anathematised: on the whole they were left in relative peace to practise their outlandish religion, regarded by their Christian overlords as gentlemen-barbarians. The Old Believers, on the other hand, the Baptists, the lesser, more specialised sects of Russia proper, above all the Catholics and the Uniats of the western lands, had the effrontery to call themselves Christians. This meant that they were heretics, to be treated as such. Subject a non-Orthodox community to the religious outrage of a Pobedonostsev, the administrative drive for uniformity of a St Petersburg bureaucrat, the genuine passion for universal law and order of a D. A. Tolstoy, and the result is a steamroller effect calculated to obliterate deviant languages, cultures, and religions. This ironing out process had been operative fairly effectively under Alexander II, especially in Poland and the Ukraine. Under Alexander III the drive was renewed, above all now against the Germanic inhabitants of the Baltic States, to whom the Russian Empire owed so much.

But the worst sufferers, for obvious reasons, were the Jews, five million of them, mostly living in the western lands comparatively recently acquired by Russia. It was under Alexander III and thanks to Alexander III that anti-semitism in Russia became institutionalised, respectable – and violent.

Here again, several currents flowed together to form a dangerous flood. Alexander himself, and passionately more so Pobedonostsev, were moved by the age-old Christian revulsion against the Jews as the murderers of Christ. 'In my heart,' he once observed, 'I am very glad when they beat the Jews, even though this practice cannot be permitted.' It was, in fact, permitted a good deal until the notorious old reactionary Dmitri Tolstoy was able to stop it for a time in the name of law and order. Most of the Jew-beating and killing – the organised pogroms – which distinguished Alexander's reign took place in the borderlands where the great bulk of Russian Jewry was congregated within the Pale of Settlement – the Ukraine, White Russia, the Polish provinces, Bessarabia in the south. Here there was genuine and endemic anti-semitism among the common people, who hated the Jews (as their descendants do to this day) as shopkeepers and money-lenders, oblivious of the fact that they had never been permitted any other occupation. Here anti-semitism trembled always on the edge of violence. But violence did not get out of hand until the last decades of the century, when a more active sort of anti-semitism became fashionable in Russia proper; there were no pogroms in St Petersburg or Moscow, but there was sympathy with the thuggery in the western provinces. (It was widely believed that the famous Sacred Company had a hand in certain pogroms.) And very soon a certain kind of official discovered in active anti-semitism a useful diversion, to be encouraged, from popular discontents, and in the Jews convenient scapegoats for a variety of ills. One of the most remarkable aspects of the anti-Jewish agitation was that for a time the pogroms, or massacres, were supported by certain revolutionaries, brimming with ideals. Their argument was that in killing

Jews the masses had embarked on the course which would end in the killing of all oppressors everywhere.

The serious growth of anti-semitic feeling had begun under Ignatiev, who had convinced himself during the run-up to the Turkish War and its aftermath at the Congress of Berlin that an international Jewish conspiracy was at work. This conspiracy had corrupted the honest Serbs, who were thus laid wide open to penetration by Jewish banks in Vienna; it had plotted behind the scenes for the humiliation of Russia at the Berlin Congress – and not so much behind the scenes . . . Look at the arch-fiend, Disraeli! Now the conspiracy was showing its hand nearer home. The Jews and the Poles had come together in a most sinister combination; and this 'Polish-Yiddish' association had already swallowed up the St Petersburg stock-exchange, the banks, the Bar as well, and important newspapers. It had deliberately engaged itself in organising terroristic acts in order to frighten the autocracy into conceding political rights and representative institutions which it could then exploit to its own advantage. It was responsible for the Tsar's assassination.

This open anti-semitism was something new. It marked the final degeneration of the Slavophile movement. It was to persist after the fall of Ignatiev, feeding on its own poison, tacitly supported by the Tsar, openly supported by Pobedonostsev, encouraged by local officials, smiled on by the police, into the next reign. Good and honest men strove to check it. Alexander II's splendid old Finance Minister, Reutern, was appalled, and said so in highly prophetic words. He was now Chairman of the Committee of Ministers. In any other country he would have been the grand old man of politics, the elder statesman, very much to be listened to. Now he spoke up for the law, but nobody heard.

'It is necessary to protect everyone from any kind of illegal encroachment. Today they hound and rob Jews. Tomorrow they will go after the so-called kulaks, who are morally the same as Jews, but of the Orthodox Christian faith. Then will come the turn of the merchants and the landlords . . . We can expect the most terrible kind of socialism in the not too distant future.'[11] Reutern got the order wrong – the merchants and the landlords were destroyed before the kulaks. Otherwise he was right enough. And what he was most right about was his insistence on the need for law.

There were now, less than half a century after the ex-serf Nikitenko's lament about the lawlessness of the rulers, very considerable numbers of loyal Russians who had come to understand the supreme importance of law. They had received little encouragement from Alexander II and were to receive none at all from the new Tsar. They were buffeted by the chauvinists on the one hand, to whom the interest of Russia was the law, on the other by the radicals intent on throwing out the baby with the bathwater. They battled on. Thus in 1883 a commission was set up under a conscientious and enlightened official, Count K. I. Pahlen, to examine the position of the Jews throughout the Empire and to make recommendations for the revision of the laws regulating their position in society. The commission to a man came up five years later with the blunt assertion that whether one liked the Jews or not, they were Russians, not foreigners, and must be treated as such. 'The existing repressive and discriminatory laws should be replaced in an orderly fashion by a gradual process of total emancipation.'[12]

Nothing happened. It is not too much to say that the official attitude towards anti-semitism and pogroms, which became more viciously irresponsible in the reign of the last Tsar, contributed as much as any other single factor towards encouraging and perpetuating that paralysing lawlessness *from above* which was to do so much to undermine the dynasty and then to set the tone for the successor regime.

It had another important by-product. Jews began to emigrate in great numbers. But among those who stayed many, driven to desperation by persecution, began to turn their minds to thoughts of revolution. When Ignatiev charged the Jews with responsibility for terrorism there was no truth in the charge. There were then a few Jews among the revolutionaries; but the whole revolutionary tradition until the 1890s was Russian to the core. It was only in the closing years of the century, when the revolutionaries began to lift their heads again, that the picture changed. In the industrial regions of the western borderlands particularly, the Jewish intellectuals and workers attracted to Marxism founded the Bund, a Jewish Social Democratic Party which was to play a large part in fomenting the strikes and demonstrations of the years to come: resolutely anti-Bolshevik, its members nevertheless played a greater part in the revolutionary education of the masses than the Bolsheviks themselves, who were later to destroy them.

Alexander's heavy-handedness was also felt beyond the borders of his own empire, and especially in the Balkans. Here his proprietorial attitude towards the Bulgarians and the bluntness of the means whereby he sought to establish his overlordship laid up trouble for the future and gave the Western world its first sight of Russia's way of imposing her will upon a weak neighbour (Russia in Poland had been another matter: the unfortunate Poles were victimised also by Prussians and Austrians). The arrangement reached at the Congress of Berlin under which an independent Bulgaria was set up in the north (Prince Alexander Battenberg was chosen as its nominal ruler), while in the south Turkey exercised suzerainty on what was called Eastern Rumelia, could not last. Bulgarian nationalism, like every other nationalism, was on the march. In 1885 a group of nationalists seized Philippopolis (now Plovdiv), the capital of Eastern Rumelia, and proclaimed the existence of a united Bulgaria under Battenberg.

Alexander, who regarded Battenberg as a creature of the British, was not going to have him parading as ruler of a greater Bulgaria hostile to St Petersburg. His anger was exacerbated by the fact that Britain and Russia had only a few months before clashed dangerously in Afghanistan. His immediate reaction was to humble the Bulgarians by ordering back to Russia all Russian officers serving with the Bulgarian army. This meant all officers over the rank of major. Serbia, contemplating the rise of Bulgaria with a jealous eye, seized the moment to attack. But the Bulgarians were not daunted. Their army, commanded by junior officers only recently under Russian tutelage, threw the Serbs back and had to be stopped in their triumphant invasion of Serbia by Austria, who for once saw eye to eye with Russia. Alexander was now very angry indeed, and he reacted in a manner unprecedented at that time, though since then enthusiastically adopted by his Soviet successors. He had Alexander Battenberg kidnapped and brought to Russia. But then the Bulgarians refused to lie down and elected Prince Ferdinand of Coburg to be their king. Now Alexander sulked and broke off diplomatic relations with the Bulgarians: there was nothing more positive that he could do without inviting a general war. This humiliating experience, however, was not enough to make St Petersburg (or, for that matter, Vienna) understand the strength and persistence of nationalist feeling among small peoples.

CHAPTER SEVENTEEN

New Wine in Very Old Bottles

I

THERE could be no Marxism without industrialisation. And it was under Alexander III that the Russian industrial revolution at last reached take-off point, to use the image of latterday economists. In the 1890s Russia's annual rate of growth, at just over eight per cent, was the highest in the world; and even after a heavy set-back at the turn of the century, it continued as the highest in Europe at an average of almost six per cent per annum until 1914.[1] This remarkable phenomenon was less widely appreciated than it should have been because of Russia's relative backwardness. That is to say, on the eve of the First World War, although her economy was forging ahead steadily and fast enough, she was still far behind the more slowly advancing West. The rate of growth was concealed from the Russians themselves by the ubiquity of the peasants: outside the relatively few and sparse factory towns it was impossible to think of this vast land as anything but a primitive peasant mass supporting a very thin top layer of cultivated or well-to-do society. As even to this day, vast industrial complexes were lost, swallowed up, in immemorial forest and steppe. Since the Revolution, of course, it has been very much in the interest of the Soviet Government to conceal the industrial achievements of Imperial Russia. It would have been more to the point if Soviet historians and economists had freely admitted the fact of growth and then gone on to query the cost. This, however, was inexpedient, for reasons which will soon be obvious.

The fundamental features of Alexander III's industrial revolution, as of Peter the Great's, were that the main drive was provided by the state, that industrialisation was carried out at the expense of agriculture and the hungry peasant, that the whole operation was inspired less by economic necessity than by dreams of national prestige. The chief architect of this industrial revolution from above, Sergei Yulevich Witte, believed with passion that he was leading his country to a glorious future beneath a reinvigorated autocracy. And indeed he performed miracles. But it may also be argued that with his crash-course of industrialisation he had a great deal to do with the creation of the conditions which made the country's stability hopelessly vulnerable to the imbecilities of Nicholas II.

Witte was not the first of the furiously industrialising Ministers of Finance. The first was I. S. Vishnegradsky, who took over from B. K. Bunge in 1886. Bunge, the last liberal of the Loris-Melikov stamp to hold office, deserved well of his country. He fathered enlightened labour laws affecting the employment of women and children; he pulled the economy together after the Turkish War; above all he abolished the detested and inequitable poll-tax, as well as the salt tax. He helped to set the country on its new course of economic dependence on French investment, which was to become increasingly important throughout the decade, as Russia and her old ally Germany, drifting farther apart, became involved in a tariff war.

Bunge came to grief when he resisted what he considered excessive demands for military expenditure to meet the absurd Bulgarian crisis of 1885-6. Vishnegradsky lacked his wisdom. He was primarily a technician, with little sense of popular feeling, let alone human needs, interested solely in strengthening the state and willing to turn the screw to this end, not seeing that he might be defeating that end by piling on indirect taxes (which hit the poor hardest), by forcing exports at the expense of domestic consumption even of essentials. He had one of those trick mathematical minds which enabled him to run his eyes over a page of logarithms and recite the figures by heart. He was ingenious in other ways too. In order to keep down the price of grain for state buyers he decreed that all taxes must be paid in the autumn, thus compelling the peasants to sell their crops quickly when there was still a glut. Vishnegradsky was to a considerable extent directly responsible for the calamitous famine of 1891; for when the harvest failed over twenty-two provinces (the worst diaster of this kind for half a century) the peasants had no reserves of grain to carry them through into the next year. And of course they had no money to buy food. So they starved and sometimes ate the corpses of their neighbours. When Vishnegradsky fell, largely as a result of this catastrophe, Witte stepped forward to take over. He had for some time been head of the Department of Railways under Vishnegradsky; and he had earned the confidence and admiration of the Tsar. He was to give his name to an epoch. He was not merely a great industrialist who had worked his way up from the bottom, he was an entirely new phenomenon, a statesman under the Tsar whose talent and determination were such that he, not the Tsar, made policy – until a Tsar invoked his supreme sanction and dismissed him.[2]

Witte was not an attractive man – boastful, coarse, self-opinionated, downright, yet tricky and evasive too, even treacherous; but he was a great and powerful figure. His mind was acute, his vision wide and far-ranging, his energy stupendous, his organising ability outstanding by any standards, by Russian standards miraculous. He was also capable of extreme pettiness. People said he was cold and calculating. In a sense this was true: he was cold and calculating as the artist is cold and calculating when realising his dream. But the dream is conceived in passion, and sustained by passion. Witte was indeed a passionate man, sometimes to the point of incoherence. It would have been better had he been cold and calculating in the conventional sense. But he was a romantic at heart. When he was trying to win Alexander's support for the greatest of all his projects, the Trans-Siberian Railway, he wrote: 'from the shores of the Pacific and the heights of the Himalayas Russia would dominate not only the affairs of Asia but those of Europe as well'. A British historian quoting those words remarks that it is impossible to tell whether Witte really thought in those terms or was flattering his master with visions of great-ness. I should say he thought in those terms for some of the time. He lacked ballast. He stood as high intellectually as he did physically above the officials and politicians of the time; this meant that he had nobody to talk to, nobody to jolt him up with the awkward question. And he was so active that he hardly gave himself time to think.

Even about his family and his family background there was the sug-gestion of the fluidity and rootlessness of a new age. His father's family came from the Baltic provinces but of Dutch, not German, stock. His father was a well-placed bureaucrat in Tiflis, who had exchanged Luther-anism for Orthodoxy in order to marry very high indeed, the daughter of a Fadeyev and a Dolgoruky princess. (To inject a slightly bizarre note, a first cousin of the great statesman was the celebrated founder of the Theosophical Society, Madame Blavatsky.) Witte himself was full of con-tradictions. Filled with a driving ambition he nevertheless risked his career by marrying a divorcee who was also a Jewess and was never happily accepted by St Petersburg society, which he pretended to despise. Practical, level-headed, sensible in many ways, he nevertheless for a short time allowed himself to be enrolled in that rather nastily lunatic organisa-tion, the Sacred Company. This element of instability in Witte surely accounted for some of his grossest errors – above all the continued and disastrous neglect of agriculture, even with the lesson of the 1891 famine under his eyes. He seems genuinely to have convinced himself that the effects of his great industrial programme would begin to work through and transform the whole of society from the peasant base upwards within a few years. So that when a succession of bad harvests culminated in yet another famine in 1897, this time accompanied by a great deal of peasant violence, he was taken by surprise.

The fact remains that for better or for worse he changed the face of Imperial Russia and brought her to the threshold of the twentieth century. Some idea of his importance may be gained from the reflection that the high plateau of his career linked two reigns and that his activity and influence were such that the natural break in any historical narrative must occur not with the death of Alexander III in 1894 but with the dismissal of Witte as Minister of Finance by Nicholas II just nine years later. More than this, Witte's influence (unacknowledged, of course) continued strongly into the new Soviet era; for Stalin was to make Witte's great mistake all over again – though on such a colossal scale as to be almost unrecognisably the same – and to employ some, though not all, of his methods. They were, in fact, the methods once devised by Peter the Great.

Witte believed with a kind of holy passion in railways. (He had worked his way up through the railway service from the lowest clerical level.) From the building of railways all good must flow in the way of material prosperity and cultural development. Railways called for industry to build them, supply them, sustain them; in turn railways provided the transport without which industry could not grow. The access of distributed wealth accruing from heavy industry created a new demand for the products of light industry. The peasantry, the landowners too, eager to buy such products, would produce more food for more cash. The machines created by industry would make possible higher productivity in agriculture. And so on. The dream was fair. What was wrong was the time-scale. This sort of development would need a generation at least to mature, even in the most favourable conditions. But besides underestimating the time element almost ludicrously, Witte failed to foresee quite a number of snags.

He should have foreseen, for example, that by putting up a high tariff wall to protect the new Russian industry from overwhelming foreign competition he was ensuring that many kinds of goods would be too dear for Russians to buy – and this applied particularly to agricultural machinery. Less easy to foresee (but surely some department in his ministry should have been on the look out for it?) was the shattering effect on Russian grain exports in the closing years of the century of the cheap grain pouring into Western Europe from the prairies of America.

2

With all his faults, he came near to salvaging the economy. The development of industry in general and of the railways in particular during the

Witte epoch was phenomenal. Railway building had been moving steadily ahead under Alexander II and in the first years of his successor; but in the 1890s it took a great leap forward. Between 1890 and the outbreak of war with Japan in 1904 the length of track was virtually doubled, from 19,000 to 37,000 miles.[3] This, of course, included the mighty Trans-Siberian Railway, Witte's supreme creation, which was intended to open up China to Russian exploitation and at the same time earn immense quantities of foreign currency as the main transport artery between Europe and the Far East. With the whole economy now deliberately geared to the growth of rail transport, the great railway boom at last made imperative the exploitation of the coal of the Donetz basin and the iron ore of Krivoy Rog in the Ukraine. Hitherto, it will be remembered, these abounding natural resources of southern Russia had been neglected in favour of imported ore and coal to be processed into steel in and around Moscow and St Petersburg. The new tariff system, so damaging in some ways, now at least gave Russian mines and furnaces their chance, and the steel town of the Donetz basin started by the Welshman Hughes and called Yuzovka after him quickly took shape as the heart of a colossal industrial complex run by entrepreneurs of many nations. At Yuzovka, the show-place of the Witte era, the young Nikita Khrushchev, a child of peasants of the poorest kind, started work as a boy of fifteen in 1909. 'I worked,' he once declared, 'at a factory owned by Germans, at pits owned by Frenchmen, and at a chemical plant owned by Belgians. There I discovered something about capitalists. They are all alike, whatever their nationality. All they wanted from me was the most work for the least money that would keep me alive.'[4]

It is interesting to think of this future ruler of Russia caught up uncomprehendingly with tens of thousands of his peasant contemporaries in the process which was to give the Empire an industrial base and, at the same time, an angry proletariat. In the last decade of the century, just before the young Khrushchev came to Yuzovka, coal output in the Donetz basin had increased from 3 million tons to 11 million tons; pig-iron from the Krivoy Rog ore from 600,000 tons to some 4 million. In the older established iron and steel regions of the Urals the increase in production was not so spectacular; but it was considerable all the same. So was the expansion in the oldest and most important of all Russia's industries, textiles. By the turn of the century there were 600,000 textile workers mostly in the Ivanovno-Voznesensk complex, for so long the main source of the Sheremetyev wealth, and Lodz in Russian Poland. Add to these more than half a million workers in the metallurgical industries and more still in the quite new oil extraction industry of Transcaucasia, to say nothing of three-quarters of a million in railway and water transport, and it would seem that here was at least the growing point of a powerful proletariat, even though still quantitatively insignificant when compared with the vast army of peasants working the land.[5]

But there were contradictions in the development of this labour force which made it easy for authority to disguise from itself the grimmer and more ominous aspects of the industrialisation drive. Right up to the turn of the century it was possible for a Pobedonostsev to believe that in Russia there was no such thing as a working class. One day Witte made some passing reference to precisely this so un-Russian concept and Pobedonostsev assailed him with his usual vehemence:

'The working class? I know of no such class in Russia. Sergei Yulevich, I do not understand what you are talking about. We have peasants. They form 90 per cent of the population. They include a relatively small number who go to work in mills and factories, but who still remain peasants. You are trying to create artificially a new class, a sort of social relationship completely alien to Russia. In this respect, Sergei Yulevich, you are a dangerous socialist.'[6]

What is particularly fascinating about this confrontation is that Pobedonostsev was in fact only echoing the terms of a secret circular issued by Witte's own ministry in 1895, which stated with admirable brevity the rationale of the refusal to recognise that Russian workers were like other workers:

In our industry there prevail patriarchal relations between the employer and the worker. This patriarchy in many cases is expressed in the concern of the factory owner for the needs of the workers and employees in his factory. . . .

In Russia, fortunately, there is no working class in the same sense and significance as in the West, *and therefore there is no labour question. . . .*[7]

This breathtaking official statement on the eve of mass strikes of tens of thousands of textile workers in 1896 and 1897 and only ten years before a major upheaval which saw the installation of workers' councils, or soviets, in St Petersburg and other cities, drew its substance from certain peculiar features of Russian factory labour and the way these features were emphasised as a consequence of that profound revulsion against the ways of Western capitalism which was shared by autocrats, bureaucrats, liberals and revolutionaries alike.

The vestigial plausibility of Pobedonostsev's view of the Russian workman derived from the special feature of the Russian factory which he went out of his way to stress: from the fact that many of the workers were seasonal, part-time, temporary, or otherwise episodic, returning to their peasant families either regularly each year for the harvest, or from time to time, retaining their status in the commune, paying their share of the taxes. By the beginning of the new century this custom was only in part superseded by full-time employment. Thus Nikita Khrushchev's father was driven by poverty to employment in the mines in winter, whereas Khrushchev himself became a real proletarian living and working at Yuzovka. Nevertheless in 1917 this tough little steel worker joined in the flight back to the land, turning up in his home village of Kalinovka, poor as it was, to take part in the parcelling out of the land 'in the name of the Revolution'.[8]

It was not merely the spirit of the commune and its compulsions, psychological and physical, which militated against the maturing of a proletariat. There was something provisional, a mood as it were of the camp, about all the industrial settlements except those most anciently established in the Urals and at St Petersburg. Russian society had never been naturally urban, and except in the few great cities there was no tradition of organic urban growth. For the most part the new proletariat were housed in factory barracks, often of extreme and desolating squalor, although there were model exceptions. It is hard to say whether the extremity of wretchedness was achieved in those working-class areas which sprang up round the perimeters of the few existing cities, or in those, frequent enough, where a factory or a mill was dumped at a convenient point in the landscape to become the nucleus of a workers' town which resembled a concentration camp without watch-towers and wire rather than a town.

It is frequently argued that the slums of Britain achieved an obscenity of inhumanity which no other society could conceivably equal. In the sense that the misery of the lowest depths in English and Scottish slums equalled the misery of the lowest depths in Russian ones, this is true. But by no means all British workers belonged to the lowest depths, while almost all Russian workers did so belong. In England there were, for a whole complex of reasons, gradations of misery. In Germany the regimentation of the workers was notorious but Bismarck's social services precluded an extreme of deprivation and degradation. In Russia there were no gradations: workers were wage-slaves in the strictest sense and their wages were insufficient to support a family. And there were no social services beyond the bounty of rare individual employers.[9]

And all the time the peasants grew hungrier. As they multiplied, so their holdings diminished, until these were not enough to keep body and soul together. And the poorer the village, the more determined were the elders to allow nobody to escape. It was a vicious circle: the more mouths there were to feed, the less there was to eat; but the fewer, the higher the taxes. All the same, more and more peasants were driven into the towns, while retaining their place in the commune and continuing to pay their taxes. The holdings of those who stayed on the land were on the average nearly twice as large as the average peasant holdings in France – ten acres as against five acres. But agricultural techniques were so primitive, and the climate so difficult, that the yield per acre had barely risen above the mediaeval level. In mediaeval Europe the typical yield was expressed in the ratio 1 : 3 – three grains harvested for each grain sown. By the sixteenth and seventeenth centuries this ratio had improved to 1 : 6 or 1 : 7. By the middle of the nineteenth century the yield in England was 1 : 10. But the Russian yield still averaged 1 : 3.[10] And almost nothing was grown but grain. It was an arable cultivation, very low on livestock – therefore low not only in meat but also in manure. Yet only half the peasants had a horse to help them with the cultivation. So long as the commune system was maintained, with its almost infinite re-dividing of limited tracts of land, this was a situation which was bound to continue. And, as we have seen, that system was favoured for its apparent stability by men as far apart as Pobedonostsev and Witte – and by most of the revolutionaries also because they saw in the commune a native institution that could be the natural foundation of a socialist state. Admittedly now there were well-to-do peasants of the class which came to be known as kulaks, men who were go-ahead, able, clever, greedy, or predatory, who managed to buy the land from bankrupt or disheartened nobles and build up their own holdings, employing their own neighbours as labourers.[11] But these were few and far between. And when the crops failed over large areas of central European Russia in the closing years of the century Witte was appalled to see that the response of the peasants was still the immemorial idiocy of burning down manor houses and destroying the landlord's barns and livestock. What was particularly discouraging for those who had devoted their energies, their lives, to improving agrarian conditions in general and the lot of the peasantry in particular by working through and for the zemstvos with no thought of self was to see drunken peasant mobs or conspiratorial moonlighters setting fire not only to the houses of absentee landlords but also to the model farms and institutes – cattle-breeding stations, stud-farms, veterinary clinics, experimental cropping centres and the rest – laboriously established and built up out of hard-won zemstvo funds to serve as signposts to a better life.

3

These peasants were not revolutionaries. They broke out in localised violent protest because the times were hard. Their fury subsided as the fires died down. Nevertheless, at the turn of the century the spectre of revolution reappeared, and there is no doubt at all that some of the agrarian riots were inspired, or stirred up, by a new generation of populist revolutionaries who took courage from the character of Nicholas II.

On the face of it, ever since the remnants of the 'People's Will' had been destroyed, imprisoned, exiled, or frightened into impotence after the regicide of 1881, the authorities had triumphed over the terrorists and at the same time proved that Loris-Melikov had been right about their numbers. Throughout the thirteen years of the reign of Alexander III there was only one serious plot to kill the Tsar. This was conceived and organised by a group of young idealists inspired by the tradition of 'People's Will', but so amateurish in their approach that their venerated heroes and heroines of 1881 would have regarded their activities with exasperated contempt. The chief point of interest about this failed attempt was that the man who made the bombs, Alexander Ilyich Ulyanov, was the elder brother of Vladimir Ilyich Ulyanov, soon to call himself Lenin. Alexander was hanged, with five of the fifteen who were arrested. The future Lenin was then seventeen, preparing for his school-leaving exams. The legend that he was immediately fired with the resolve to avenge his brother has no truth at all. Vladimir Ilyich was a notably cool and collected youngster, in spite of his reddish hair. The thought of revolution had never entered his head. He was the son of an ennobled and respected educationist, lately dead and widely mourned. He was preparing himself for a lawyer's career, and he went on doing so. While his mother travelled to St Petersburg to be with her elder son and plead for him, Vladimir Ilyich ran the household, looked after his sisters, and passed his exams with flying colours.

His headmaster at Simbirsk gymnasium was, believe it or not, the father of Alexander Kerensky who, just thirty years later, was to head the Provisional Government which Lenin was to destroy. Now Kerensky senior, who had venerated Lenin's father, gave the son the warmest possible recommendation to the university authorities. It was not until the young Lenin had become caught up almost by accident in a mild and quite harmless student demonstration at Kazan University that he found himself face to face with the system that had destroyed his brother.

Until then he had not been made to suffer for his brother's crime, but once he passed through the hands of the police for whatever trivial reason, he became the natural scapegoat. Others were allowed to resume their studies after arrest and punishment. Vladimir Ilyich Ulyanov, the brother of a would-be regicide, was not. His career was broken. His mother, whom he loved, and who had strained herself to the utmost to keep him from thoughts of revolution, still had hopes of establishing him as a modest gentleman-farmer on an estate she had managed to buy. But her son by now had started reading Marx, and re-reading Chernyshevsky; and these experiences, coupled with the blank injustice he himself had suffered and the apparent impossibility of making the career he had chosen, were decisive. His mother was desperate. Appeal after appeal she addressed to the Minister of Education, L. V. Delyanov: 'It is sheer torment to look at my son, and to see how fruitlessly these years of his life which are most suitable for a higher education pass by. . . . Almost inevitably it must push him to thoughts of suicide . . .'[12] So it may have done for a time; but soon it pushed him to thoughts of revolution. By the time his mother won through and found an official who would listen and allow her son to study at home for his degree and take it at St Petersburg, it was too late. He did well, as always. In less than a year he caught up with a three-and-a-half-years' syllabus and came out at the top of his class. The way to a professional career was open. But Vladimir Ilyich was no longer interested in a professional career. He was interested only in revolution.

4

Lenin was attracted by Marxism (which his brother had never been) in 1893 when he arrived in St Petersburg to practise law.[13] He had flirted with a small Marxist circle at Kazan, and at Samara (now Kuibyshev), lower down the Volga, where his mother had carried him off to live and work, he had found kindred spirits also interested in Marxism. Marxism was something new to the Russian revolutionary tradition, but it was beginning to take hold, if only because of its anti-romantic appeal to young men who had seen their elders on the one hand beating their heads against peasant obscurantism and on the other achieving little but their own destruction as a result of organised terrorism.

Interestingly, authority was tolerant towards the Marxist circles that began to take shape from the 1890s. This was because instead of preaching political change they, to all appearances, confined themselves to discussing problems of economic development. Even Marxist newspapers were tolerated in the middle 1890s, and although the great prophet of Russian Marxism, G. V. Plekhanov, lived in exile in Switzerland, having formed in 1883 his 'Liberation of Labour' group with P. B. Axelrod (who had been at his side when he had split the 'Land and Liberty' movement in his stand against terrorism in the late seventies) and the redoubtable but still muddled Vera Zasulich, plenty of Marxist discussion groups were popping up inside Russia. And it was one of these that Lenin joined in 1893. In the following year there appeared in a sudden flowering of energy three important and seminal works on Marxist theory, an elaborate critique by the populist Mikhailovsky in his influential *Russkoe Bogatsvo* (*Russian Wealth*) and major works by P. B. Struve and Plekhanov. The movement was launched. The police knew all about it, but because of its emphasis on economic problems, and because it did not preach immediate revolution, they left it alone. To the St Petersburg workers the Marxist agitators were welcome: their lectures about economics, sociology, and world affairs were deeply appreciated by honest working men hungry for education if only to better themselves. Not until a sudden rash of strikes against intolerable conditions broke out in the textile and cigarette factories of St Petersburg in 1895, strikes which Lenin and other Marxists sought to exacerbate with stirring leaflets, did the police hit back and pull in every Marxist known to them.

Lenin now had his first night in a prison cell and in due course was sentenced to three years' exile in remote Siberia. And it was during this term of exile that a group of nine Marxists met in Minsk in 1897 and formally founded the Russian Social Democratic Labour Party. The manifesto was composed by Peter Struve, who was not present and who was later to move to the far right of radical politics. The proceedings were blessed by Plekhanov, far away in Geneva. When the news reached Lenin in Siberia he was beside himself with joy. He was already finding himself as a polemicist. The future of the Party must depend on the establishment of a journal to be published like Herzen's *The Bell* outside Russia, and he, Lenin, was the one to found and run it. In 1900 he was out of Siberia and in Geneva with his friend Julius Martov,[14] also fresh from exile, fortified by funds from well-wishing liberals, ready to found *Iskra, The Spark* ('Out of this Spark will come a Conflagration!' exclaimed the masthead, borrowing the words of a Decembrist poet). He was now set on the course which was to lead only three years later to the bitter and fateful division of the R.S.D.L.P. into the Bolshevik and Menshevik wings.

5

Meanwhile, however, the authorities were right not to agonise too much about the Marxists in their midst. Even when revolutionary activity was at its high peak in the first decade of the new century the most immediate threat to the regime came not from the Social Democrats but from the Socialist Revolutionaries. Not by any stretch of the imagination can the bitter and noisy pamphleteering, intrigue and mutual character assassination, so soon to be the mark of the Russian Marxists, be seen as even marginally important in the history of Russia before 1917, though decisive in the shaping of the Soviet Union. Conversely, however, some appreciation of Russian history is essential for even a rudimentary understanding of Bolshevism. Lenin was very much a product of Chernyshevsky and Tkachev, who were Russian to the core.

The Socialist Revolutionaries were also, of course, Russian to the core. They were far more numerous than the Marxists, far showier too. In due course they were to be swept by Lenin from the surface of the earth; but at the turn of the century they made the running and spread terror. Some of them were killers. The Marxists did not believe in terror as an oppositional tactic: it was wasteful of energy and effort, theatrical, unhistorical. In Lenin's eyes, the shooting or bombing of individual ministers and officials achieved nothing and was no more than self-indulgence. Terror as an instrument of governmental repression, directed effectively against whole classes, was another matter: it had not yet arisen. The Socialist Revolutionaries, however, were the heirs of the Populists, especially of the 'People's Will', with its crowning achievement in the murder of Alexander II. They were far from being disciplined ideologues: their simple-minded aim was to clear away the system as quickly as possible and with as much violence as was convenient in order to establish in its place without further ado a new order of justice and equity. A number of groups had arisen in various parts of the country moved by more or less the same ideals to be pursued with more or less ruthlessness, all inspired by memories of the heroes and heroines of 1881. Some of these groups were perfectly happy to work together with any other organisation devoted to the destruction of the autocracy. They got on quite well with the primitive Marxists (if the phrase is permitted), and would no doubt have continued in this innocent comradeship had not the *Iskra* group in Geneva made it quite plain that any revolutionary who was not prepared to subscribe absolutely and in minute detail to the doctrine as proclaimed by them was not a revolutionary at all but an enemy of revolution. The Socialist Revolutionaries, who in 1901 finally coalesced into the party known by that name, laid a good deal more stress on peasant revolt than the Social Democrats, as would be expected from their Populist background. But it should not be imagined that they were exclusively an agrarian party. Far from it. Although they were so strong in the rich agricultural lands of the Volga and the Ukraine, they also recognised the power of the urban proletariat and sought to stimulate it into activity. Strikes, demonstrations, all forms of industrial protest were welcome. But almost at once the new party as such, and its leader, Viktor Chernov, were put in the shade by the very purposeful activities of one of its parts, the so-called Combat Section, a virtually autonomous and tightly-knit organisation devoted exclusively to terrorism and organised by a young Jewish scientist, G. A. Gershuni, whose first major coup, in 1902, was the assassination of Witte's nominee as Minister of the Interior, D. S. Sipyagin. It was the Socialist Revolutionaries' Combat Section which was in the years to come to be responsible for the long series of killings which astonished the world. And the most remarkable aspect of the whole bloody process was that for the greater part of the time the head of the Combat Section was the notorious Yevno Azev, who was also an agent of the secret police, the Okhrana. Azev managed to penetrate the S.R.s so deeply that he himself can hardly have known when he was acting as police agent, when as revolutionary. Time and time again he would plan the assassination of this or that official, only to warn his comrades of the police in time for them to pick up his comrades the conspirators. But sometimes he allowed the assassination which he himself had organised to be carried out, with no warning to the police, and afterwards covered up for the assassins. The high peak of his achievement was reached in the years 1904 and 1905 when he organised down to the last detail the killing of the Minister of the Interior Plehve (his own chief), and the Tsar's brother, the Grand Duke Sergei.

Nobody has yet explained the workings of Azev's mind, though many attempts have been made, some at least partially successful. But there is one point which bears on his background: he was not alone in playing a double game. Indeed, Azev himself was for a time instructed by Colonel S. V. Zubatov, chief of the Moscow Okhrana, who conceived the brilliant idea that the way to combat unrest among the workers was to guide it into relatively harmless channels, and in 1902 obtained the official backing of precisely the Grand Duke Sergei and Plehve. He set up special trades unions (in a land where trades unions were forbidden by law) controlled by police agents whose job it was to encourage the proletariat to agitate for better working conditions and more pay in order to divert their minds from revolutionary politics. Thus that strange sense of 'the romance of the police' commented upon by Herzen in connection with the celebrated police chief of the first Nicholas, General Dubbelt, seems to have grown stronger under the second Nicholas, even as corruption itself ran deeper. How else to account for the fact that Azev was directly betrayed in 1908 to the chief security officers of the Socialist Revolutionaries by none other than an ex-head of the department of police, A. A. Lopukhin? The twilight nature of the company in which we now find ourselves is illustrated once more by the fact that Lopukhin for this act of treachery was sentenced to only five years' penal servitude, which was commuted to comfortable exile in Siberia.

The S.R.s were not the only revolutionaries to be involved with the police. The Bolsheviks were also to have their own special police spy in the person of Roman Malinovsky, who got himself elected to the Duma as their chief spokesman. This time it was the official police who, exasperated by Malinovsky's noisy championship of working-class causes, decided to expose him. Malinovsky had to leave the country, but he was welcomed with open arms by Lenin in exile, who refused to believe he was guilty.

6

At the turn of the century, however, the revolutionaries were very far from occupying the foreground. Almost imperceptibly the country had been taking on a new dimension. It was opening out into a rich and complex society suspectible to influences of which the Tsar himself and most of his ministers had no conception, thinking thoughts over which the censors had no control. The country, in a word, which was still governed as though it were the Tsar's private estate, had yet developed a life of its own from which the Tsar and his administration were effectively excluded. It was a life led on many levels, but all, from the richest to the poorest, now generated their own vitality, no longer depending for the very breath of life on Caesar's pleasure. In so far as the Russians (as distinct from members of the minority races) were a united people, they were unified by love of country on the one hand and on the other by the heavy hand of the police. The Tsar himself was the living symbol whose presence elevated the mixture of profound attachment to the native soil and active fear of the consequences of unorthodoxy into a positive mystique of patriotism. But the patriotism, demonstrative as it was, was a surprisingly delicate plant. How could it be otherwise when to be a thinking Russian was to be at least in some degree in opposition to the ruling system?

Pobedonostsev and his friends, the Tsar himself, were ignorant not only about the working class; they were no less in the dark about the vague and fluctuating aspirations of all the educated and merchant classes outside the highest ranks of the civil service, the army and the Church. They were unaware of the way in which the varied elements of the educated classes – hereditary nobility, service nobility, sons of clergy, army officers of middle and junior ranks, the new professionals (engineers, scientists, technicians, teachers, doctors, lawyers, agronomists, vets, artists of all kinds, actors, journalists, musicians, to say nothing of industrial entrepreneurs and mill owners) were blending to form a sort of radical élite. It was an élite powerless to act because denied any legitimate political role, but all too ready to encourage with greater or less sympathy the subversive activities of the revolutionaries.

Numerically this élite was also relatively insignificant. The Tsar could be forgiven for thinking of his realm as a peasant mass ruled over by a loyal bureaucracy. At the turn of the century there were some 97 million peasants (which included some factory workers) plus nearly 3 million Cossacks; some 13 million small shopkeepers, tradesmen, artisans and most of the factory workers – a total of 113 million of the lower orders out of a total population of 116 million. But the 3 million of the élite formed a rich mixture.[15]

Alexander III died in 1894. Some idea of the cultural splendour of the inheritance of his successor, an inheritance of which Nicholas knew virtually nothing, may be gained from the following highly selective roll of honour:

The doyen of Russian great men was, of course, Leo Tolstoy, who was then only sixty-six, for long established as the greatest novelist in the world, and now also a cult figure and a national monument. Turgenev and Dostoevsky were dead; the newcomer Anton Chekhov was already thirty-four. His great plays were yet to come, but some of his finest short stories were already published. Maxim Gorky, twenty-six, was a raw young beginner from the slums. The symbolist poet, Alexander Blok, was a schoolboy of fourteen. Boris Pasternak, the future author of *Dr Zhivago*, was four years old; and his father, Leonid, was a highly talented painter with a marvellous circle of friends – musicians, painters, writers, actors.

There were no men of manifest genius among these painters; but in the work of a number of them we can see, as we see in Chekhov, a profound insight into the complex humanity of a Russia growing and groping forward by its own inner light, overshadowed now, but no longer protected, by the autocratic system. The one indisputable painter of genius, V. V. Kandinsky, who was born, amazing to reflect in 1866, was already out of Russia and helping to bring new life to the West. The generation of painters who had helped to establish the Russian identity – Repin, Vershchagin, and others – were in their fifties, and the generation which was to explode in the first years of the Revolution and then disperse into exile – Malevich, Tatlin, Lissitzky, Chagall – was already born.

Mussorgsky and Borodin were dead, without proper recognition, but Tchaikovsky, at fifty-four, was a national hero whose music carried the flag of Russian culture all over Europe and to America. Rimsky-Korsakov was approaching the peak of his influence as composer and teacher and preparing the way for the posthumous celebration of Mussorgsky and Borodin. Lesser composers, the Taneyevs, Glazunov and others were well established when Nicholas came to the throne, while Rachmaninov and Skryabin, twenty-one and twenty-two respectively, had already begun to compose. Igor Stravinsky was a schoolboy of twelve, his father a celebrated bass singer at the St Petersburg Opera. That opera, the conservatoires of St Petersburg and Moscow founded by the Rubinstein brothers and, of course, the Imperial Ballet, had achieved a high level of distinction for some years past. And even as Nicholas ascended the throne the elements of one of Russia's greatest gifts to the West, the sharing of it denied to her, were taking shape: Sergei Diaghilev was twenty-two and moving towards the foundation of his celebrated magazine, *The World of Art* (*Mir Iskustvo*); Bakst, to be his greatest designer, was sixteen. And the dancers who were to amaze the Western world were already in training: one of the most loved, Tamara Karsavina, was nine years old at the time of the accession and had been at the Maryinsky Theatre School already for two years. Chaliapin, born in a Kazan slum, made his operatic début in that very year, 1894, at the age of twenty-one in Meyerbeer's *Robert le Diable*.

Of the scientists, the doyen was without doubt the great chemist Mendeleyev, at sixty with his best work behind him. But A. S. Popov, for years a teacher at the Naval School of Mines at Kronstadt, now thirty-five, was to run neck and neck with Marconi in pioneering wireless telegraphy. I. P. Pavlov, ten years older, was already preparing the groundwork for his critical work on conditioned reflexes.

A rich mixture indeed, but still most sadly subject to an authority which knew next to nothing about it and understood less. Consider the case of Mendeleyev. In 1890, four years before the death of Alexander III, the then Minister of Education, the reactionary nincompoop, Delyanov, saw fit to remove this internationally renowned figure from his chair at the University of St Petersburg and for no greater offence than that Mendeleyev had dared to pass on to the minister a students' petition of which he disapproved. This great man, who was elected a Fellow of the Royal Society in London and received honorary degrees from Oxford, Cambridge, Berlin and the Sorbonne, could be effortlessly deprived of his university appointment and his livelihood by any jumped-up bureaucrat. And there was nothing that could be done to put things right. When Witte became Minister of Finance two years after the dismissal of Mendeleyev he had the sense to rescue the great scientist, take him into his own ministry as head of the department of weights and measures (a Wonderland appointment for the discoverer and formulator of the Periodic Law) and give him facilities for continuing his researches. Witte was rightly pleased with himself on this account but even he seems not to have grasped the depth of intellectual squalor of a system which permitted a Delyanov to make or break the career of a Mendeleyev. He made no attempt to change that system.[16]

It seems to me that this episode brings home with unusual clarity the sheer frivolity of the system, which was now more damaging than its brutalities. For a second example of the shadow under which all Russians lived, and particularly those individuals who brought most glory to their motherland, I shall cite the solemn excommunication of Leo Tolstoy ten years later and under a new Tsar. By the year 1900 Tolstoy was considered a thorough-going public nuisance by the secular authorities for his subversive teaching (which had included showing Russians how to organise famine relief when authority denied the existence of hunger), by the religious authorities for this blasphemous heresy. But he was so towering an international figure that nobody dared arrest him. Instead, Church and State came together in the indispensable person of Pobedonostsev and drummed him out of the community of the faithful. It was believed that honest Russians who might be deluded enough to take Tolstoy's part if he were arrested and locked up by the Okhrana would recoil from him in horror when they saw him anathematised by the Church. The Church overrated itself: the great man was now regarded widely as a martyr as well as an apostle of light.

Earlier it was remarked that Witte had the distinction of giving his name to an era and spanning two reigns. The same could be said of Pobedonostsev, whose name might stand for the seamy side of an even longer span. He stood behind Alexander III for all the thirteen years of his reign (Witte was prominent only during the last three), and he stood behind Nicholas II until well into the twentieth century.

I have referred to the shadow under which all Russia lived in the days when the richness of native talent, bursting out all over, seemed to offer much promise for the future. It would not be fair to see in the destruction of that future the hands of the Pobedonostsevs, the Delyanovs, the Plehves alone. To fill out our selective view of Russians alive at the time of the accession of the last Tsar who had either achieved or would achieve distinction, let us not forget the following: Lenin was twenty-four; Trotsky (Lev Bronstein) and Stalin (J. V. Djugashvili) were fifteen. Molotov (born V. M. Skryabin, a cousin of the composer) was four, the same age as Boris Pasternak, whose father was Skryabin's great friend.

CHAPTER EIGHTEEN

Nicholas and Alexandra

I

WE have entered a new reign, barely recording the passing of the old and without introducing the new Tsar, Nicholas II, by more than name. This is symptomatic, for the impact of Nicholas, considerable by all means, was almost wholly negative. His formidable father when he died was only forty-nine. He imagined he had many years before him, and he had done next to nothing to prepare the way for an heir he found it impossible to take seriously. But to the superficial eye the heritage he left behind him was in good running order. The industrialisation drive was reaching its peak; the grand Trans-Siberian Railway project was pushing ahead; the revolutionaries were in hiding, when they were not in prison or exiled; the Empire was at peace with an unusually peaceful Europe. It seemed reasonable to suppose that given a few more years of domestic stability and international tranquillity, and with a new Tsar to signal the start of a new era, Russia would continue to grow in prosperity, her Government moving towards less repressive policies, towards the enlistment even of all the talents into the business of government itself.

In fact the appearance of stability was an illusion. We have already seen how the industrial programme was impoverishing the peasants and depressing the conditions of the factory workers. Under the nagging, bullying pressure of Alexander's russification policy bitter resentments against central rule had built up among the non-Russian peoples, forming almost half the population of the Empire – not least in the once autonomous Finland. Active anti-semitism rebounded on St Petersburg in a number of ways – for example, the waste of much-needed undeveloped talent, especially among the tens of thousands driven to emigrate, and also the conversion to revolutionary ideas of many of those who stayed in Russia. Discouragement of the zemstvos and the curtailing of their powers, together with the repressive introduction of rural dictators in the shape of 'Land Captains', was detrimental not only to the development of the countryside as such but also to the loyalty of thousands of gifted and frustrated administrators, specialists, technicians of all kinds.

It was not only in domestic affairs that Alexander, had he had the sense to see what was going on, might have recognised that the Crown was being pushed aside increasingly. He had been, for example, irritated by newspapers which meddled in affairs of state, but he had not understood that in allowing them the freedom to comment at all he was abdicating his authority as sole guide and preceptor of his realm even while he refused to contemplate any sort of representative national assembly. The first intimation of the development of a public opinion that had to be reckoned with, the Panslav agitation under Alexander II on the eve of the Turkish War, has been followed by other consequential intrusions into what had hitherto been forbidden ground. In foreign affairs, the most important positive developments under Alexander III were the abandonment of the Three Emperors' League, the distancing of Russia from a Germany increasingly committed to Austria, and the new understanding with France. In the summer of 1891, on the occasion of a ceremonial visit of French warships to Kronstadt, the Tsar of All the Russias stood bareheaded for the playing of the revolutionary hymn, the *Marseillaise*. But this development – a series of important French loans followed by a consultative agreement and culminating in a military convention – although in the last resort forced on Alexander by the behaviour of the brash new German Emperor, William II, had been foreseen and publicly urged as early as 1886 by the unresting Katkov in his newspaper. Katkov had indeed been reprimanded for speaking out of turn, but he had not been silenced. And he had seen more of the game without realising its ultimate significance than the new Foreign Minister, Gorchakov's successor, N. K. Giers, who held out as long as he could against the unholy logic of events. It took Giers nearly four years to abandon hope of a renewed understanding with a Germany which, without Bismarck, was beginning to run wild.

Alexander's legacy, then, was by no means in such good order as on the surface it appeared. And if the powerful and downright father was no longer in control of a society which was increasingly developing a multiform life of its own, how much less in control would be the son, charming, slight, boyish (infantile his father called him to Witte),[1] not only weak of purpose but lacking all sense of purpose – except (a large exception, of course) to carry out the will of God as his obedient adjutant on earth. This involved the assertion of absolute authority in the name of the Almighty by a man who possessed no natural authority at all.

It is difficult and painful to contemplate Nicholas in the bleak light of hindsight: one is haunted always by that image of the deposed autocrat seated on a tree-stump in his drab field-service uniform, alone except for the soldiers in the background, his warders, hollow-eyed and gazing blindly into the camera and far beyond. One's memories are dragged again and again to that dreadful cellar at Ekaterinburg (Sverdlovsk) in the Urals, where Nicholas himself, the Tsaritsa, the four nice girls and their brave and cheerful little haemophilic brother were murdered by the Bolsheviks with a brutality which seemed to be a barbaric aberration, but which turned out to be prophetic. The courage to die well, however, was not enough to make Nicholas a good ruler.[2]

Nobody knew much about him when he came to the throne at twenty-six except that he was quiet, gentle, shy to excess and deeply in love with his bride-to-be, Princess Alix of Hesse-Darmstadt, the future Tsaritsa Alexandra Feodorovna. He was very small, in somewhat disconcerting contrast not only to his father but also to his three gigantic and extremely overbearing uncles. Alexander himself had thought so little of his elder son's abilities that he had done nothing to educate him as future ruler or to introduce him to the business of state. The Tsarevich himself had been, to all appearances, perfectly content to lead the existence of a junior cavalry officer. His father had sent him on a world tour to broaden his mind, which took him to Egypt, India, China and Japan. But to judge from his letters home his mind was not visibly enlarged. In India he was struck chiefly by the British presence: 'How stifling to be surrounded again by the English and to see red uniforms everywhere.'[3] He turned against Japan after an attempt on his life in Tokyo, and for ever after referred to the Japanese as monkeys. Landing at Vladivostok on his way home and proceeding to Moscow via the route prospected for the new railway, he was fêted everywhere and was filled with pride in the immensity of this vast land, without a red-coat in sight, which had been entrusted to him by God.

Back in St Petersburg he was appointed chairman of the Trans-Siberian Railway committee by a reluctant parent who considered him incapable of taking an intelligent interest in anything: it was Witte who urged this appointment, arguing that unless he was put to some sort of work Nicholas would indeed confirm his father's worst fears. In fact the only really intelligent interest recorded at this period was the Tsarevich's love affair with a future star of the Imperial Ballet, Mathilde Kschessinska, an affair pursued with more enthusiasm than was considered wise. The affair was not at first interrupted when Nicholas fell in love with his German princess, Alix of Hesse, Queen Victoria's granddaughter, to whom he clung in face of parental disapproval with all the stubbornness of his grandfather. Kschessinska wept when the engagement was finally announced but before long consoled herself first as the mistress of one of

Nicholas's cousins, then as the wife of another. She lived in great style in her own palace across the river, near the fortress of St Peter and St Paul, and it was from the balcony of this palace that Lenin, in April 1917, newly arrived at the Finland station after his long journey across Germany in the sealed train, first harangued the revolutionary mob.

2

Alexander fell ill of nephritis and died, quite unexpectedly, before the marriage of his son and heir could take place. But even before their marriage the fateful pattern of the relationship between the indecisive Nicholas and his neurotically determined bride, which was to end in calamity, began quite clearly to emerge. The Tsar lay dying in his favourite holiday palace at Livadia in the sub-tropical Crimea. The whole family hung about the echoing marble halls waiting for the end. Nicholas had sent for Alix and she arrived to discover, chagrined and furious, that her beloved Nicky, so soon to be the new Tsar, was being ignored or brushed aside. The doctors and the courtiers not unnaturally deferred to the Tsaritsa, who, stricken in her great love, surrounded by her enormous brothers-in-law, was scarcely aware of Nicholas, not at all of Alix. Alix, outraged more on Nicholas's behalf than on her own, was nearly sick with frustration. She was only twenty-two, but she was in the process of giving up her familiar existence, including her religion, in order to worship and sustain her bridegroom-to-be. To stand by and watch his authority being usurped by those abominable uncles was too much for her. She declared war on those uncles, as soon she was to declare war on the whole of official Russia, embarking on that long course of keeping Nicholas up to scratch and making him assert himself against the world. Now she wrote him little notes of encouragement and reassurance, among them the famous exhortation on a page of his own diary, written in English and largely in that baby language which was to distinguish their correspondence until it ceased in blood and fire:

Sweet child, pray to God. He will comfort you, don't feel too low. . . . Your Sunny is praying for you and the beloved patient. . . . Darling boysy, me loves you oh so very tenderly and deep. Be firm. . . . if the Dr has any wishes or needs anything, make him come *direct* to you. Don't let others be put first and you left out; you are Father's dear son and must be told all and be asked about everything. Show your own mind and don't let others forget *who you are*. Forgive me lovy.[4]

So it was to go on through a lifetime of exhortation. It never seems to have occurred to Alexandra, then or at any time, that she herself was the chief offender. Her own demands of the man she ceaselessly urged to resist all demands grew ever stronger and more extravagant, while Nicholas himself developed a protective sense of humour towards his still beloved wife (it is clear from some of her early recorded remarks – again in her husband's diary – that the marriage was built on a shared sensuality which could support any amount of spiritual fantasy) but only a spasmodic, intermittent stubbornness, or strength of will, towards the problems of government in peace and war. It is November 1916, twenty-two years later, and Nicholas and Alexandra have only four months left to them as Tsar and Tsaritsa. Nicholas has gone back to be with his generals at army H.Q. for the last time. Alexandra, with Rasputin at her side, is ruling in his absence, as his unofficial deputy. Now Nicholas, still only forty-eight, has only one role in Alexandra's eyes: to preserve his heritage so that it may be passed on intact to little Alexei.

'I am fully convinced,' she writes to her desperate, exhausted husband at a supreme crisis in the war, 'that great and beautiful times are coming for your reign and for Russia. . . . We must give a strong country to Baby, and dare not be weak for his sake. . . . Don't let things slip through your fingers and leave it to him to build all over again. Be firm. . . . How I wish I could pour my will into your veins. . . .'[5]

The remarkable thing about this sad woman is not that she came to arouse profound suspicion and hatred on a nationwide scale, so that she could be accused, quite unjustly, of acting in the German interest during the war, but that nobody in that land so inured to political murder ever tried to kill her in the interest of the dynasty, as on this occasion in November 1916 when she has been making her husband's life miserable by urging him to retain a notoriously corrupt and idiotic minister, Protopopov, because Rasputin demanded it. Instructing her husband to destroy all those who dared to object to Protopopov, she exclaimed, 'Be Peter the Great, be Ivan the Terrible, be Tsar Paul – crush them all under your feet. . . . Now don't laugh at me, you naughty one!'[6]

Nicholas did laugh all the same. It was his only defence. 'My dear,' he replied, 'tender thanks for the severe scolding. I read it with a smile because you speak to me as though I were a child. . . . Your poor little weak-willed Hubby.'[7]

It is important to establish this relationship, which need not hereafter be dwelt upon. It was a critical relationship at a turning point in history. Nicholas was weak and indecisive, but he was not absolutely an imbecile; Alexandra, if not an imbecile, was politically and socially illiterate, dominating him, and towards the end forcing upon him calamitous decisions. Great efforts have been made to find excuses for Alexandra, beginning with the generous defence offered by the last Prime Minister of Imperial Russia (apart from the vile Sturmer), Count V. N. Kokovtsev, who was broken by her, and ending with Robert Massie's study in *Nicholas and Alexandra* which, through the film, has made her one of the best-known characters in Russian history. The argument is always the same, as it must be: first the discovery that the longed-for heir, Alexei, born in 1904 after ten years of agonising, after four girls in succession, was a haemophiliac, the disease transmitted by her; then the discovery that the uncouth holy man, Gregory Rasputin (he had no surname: 'Rasputin', which means the dissolute one, was a village nickname which stuck and which he wore like a badge) had the power to relieve the child's suffering. This explains how Alexandra allowed herself to become the creature of Rasputin, even to the point of believing that he was the voice of God on earth.

It fails, however, to explain a great many things. It does not explain why the twenty-two-year-old girl from Hesse, plunged suddenly into the midst of the most overpowering court in Europe, instead of taking stock, immediately started nagging her beloved Nicky at his father's death-bed. It does not explain her instant and implacable hostility to the family into which she had entered, or her complete failure to perform her duties as Tsaritsa (duties which she freely undertook when she was old enough to know what they were) and to go virtually into hiding for the greater part of her life – trying to confine her children and Nicholas himself to a sort of everlasting cosy tea-party at Tsarskoe Selo. She was not a stranger to royal protocol and etiquette: as one of Victoria's favourite grandchildren, she had largely been brought up at Windsor Castle. It ignores the fact that long before Rasputin appeared on the scene she had patronised a series of bogus holy men, including the notorious French charlatan Philippe, whose table-turning was the rage of the sillier sections of St Petersburg society. It does not explain why she never made a worthy friend.

She was a religious *exaltée* with a strong sexual drive – a combination which is liable to colour even the most everyday transactions with a touch of the orgiastic. She had nearly drawn back from her betrothal at the last moment, recoiling from the prospect of abandoning her faith in order to be received into the Orthodox Church; but when the time came she plunged head first. It was in a mood of quasi-mystical exaltation, prophetically characteristic, that she was formally received into her new faith, standing between her future husband and the widowed Tsaritsa, in the chapel of the palace at Livadia, while Alexander's corpse lay upstairs waiting to be taken to St Petersburg. With her new religion and with all the fervour of the convert she embraced Russia. She convinced herself, not without grounds, that the court was corrupt and corrupting, and with it the whole bureaucratic system: it was on rather shakier grounds that she convinced herself that she and she alone understood the holy inwardness of the Russian peasant and that virtually the whole of educated society was engaged in a conspiracy to set barriers between Nicholas and his people. She trusted nobody and believed the worst of anyone who sought to advise or influence her husband. For many years her interest in politics was minimal and her advice, or instructions, to Nicholas was offered in general terms: it was not until the dynasty's final phase that she began to make and break ministers and generals on Rasputin's behalf. Nevertheless, the harm she did by causing Nicholas to leave St Petersburg and spend his winters at Tsarskoe Selo and his summers at Peterhof, by cocooning him in her claustrophobic apartments, visited only by inferior hangers-on, by coming between him and men and women of talent and ideas, by helping him to pretend that he was indeed the autocrat and father of his people, was past all computing. Almost the only thing that can be said in her defence is that she was treated badly by the Dowager Empress. So she was. Marie made all too little effort to help Alexandra find her feet. Furthermore, she insisted on taking precedence over the young Tsaritsa and obviously delighted in the fact that her son at first turned to her for political advice far more than he did to Alexandra. But the Dowager Empress was not a saint. She was gay, young at heart, intelligent and knowledgeable, high-spirited. She had lost a good husband in early middle life and had no intention of resigning herself to oblivion. Certainly not in favour of a large, fair, intense young woman with handsome features and soulful eyes, who was holier than anyone had any right to be, who nevertheless appeared to worship Nicholas with her body with something of the same unhealthy fervour which she brought to contemplation of the Almighty; who seemed unable to decide whether Nicholas was God's right hand and she his acolyte, or whether she was sent by God to instruct poor Nicholas; who was so shy that she could hardly utter and yet so jealous that nobody else might utter. Marie, indeed, who had never approved of this marriage, must have wondered whether Nicholas in his infatuation might not be devoured whole.

Nicholas shrank from the crown, perhaps with more genuine anguish than any of his ancestors, and said so. He seems to have been possessed by two ideas, mutually exclusive: he longed to bring happiness and prosperity to his people and to be loved by them; and he owed it to his forebears to sustain the autocratic principle. It is worth recording that there is a sea-change here: Nicholas I, Alexander II, Alexander III had in their different ways justified autocratic rule on the grounds that without it the Empire, Russia itself, would fall to pieces. But by Nicholas II the autocracy was justified not as an expedient but as a religious institution, sanctified by antiquity – and this in an age in which, for the first time, first-class politicians – Witte, already encountered, Stolypin to come – were in fact running the country subject only to the Imperial veto.

He meant well: his private sensibilities were as unexceptionable as his beautiful manners. He put himself, as he thought, in the hands of God and stood ready to do God's will as he conceived it at no matter what cost. In the end he was to face abdication, imprisonment and death in the brave and serene conviction that everything that happened to him was in accordance with the will of God which it would never occur to him to question. It was this blind faith, as much as the insensitivity which lay behind some of his remarks, which has been found most unforgivable. He had absolute trust in God and he held Russia in trust on God's behalf: he must therefore expect and extract the same obedience from his people as he himself accorded to God. Three months before the outbreak of revolution the British Ambassador, Sir George Buchanan, desperate with worry and dismay, took it upon himself to give a last warning to the Tsar: 'Your Majesty, if I may be permitted to say so, has but one safe course open to you – namely to break down the barrier that separates you from your people and to regain their confidence.'[8] Nicholas drew himself up and replied, 'Do you mean that I am to regain the confidence of my people or that they are to regain *my* confidence?' That was in January 1917 at Tsarskoe Selo. Nicholas, from all reports, had in the words of the French Ambassador already 'abdicated inwardly and is now resigned to disaster'.[9] But he was still Tsar, and so long as he was Tsar he would keep his people – and the British Ambassador – in their places.

3

The religious conviction of the sacredness of the autocracy was his own, but he looked in the early days to Pobedonostsev to give it expression. And just as this disastrous man had drafted for Alexander III a formal declaration of his autocratic purpose, so he now did the same for Nicholas II. But whereas Alexander's declaration was benign in the confidence of the new Tsar's own strength, the words put into the mouth of his son were almost shockingly ill-considered, dismissive, bad-tempered.

As always, many Russians pinned their hopes of the liberalisation of the system on the accession of a new Tsar. As so often in the past, it was the worthies of Tver who again set the pace. This time the zemstvo leaders of Tver in their loyal address to Nicholas went so far as to repeat some of the hopes expressed by their noble forebears: 'Sire, we await the opportunity and the right for public institutions to express their opinion on questions which concern them, so that the expression of the needs and thought not only of the administration but also of the Russian people may reach to the very height of the Throne.'

The reaction to this modest presumption was swift and chilling. At a reception for local government leaders on 17 January 1895, the new young Tsar spoke in greeting to his guests, many of them veterans in the service of the people, deeply experienced, some even wise: 'I am informed,' he said, 'that recently in some zemstvo assemblies voices have made themselves heard from people carried away by senseless dreams about the participation of zemstvo representatives in the affairs of internal government; let all know that I, devoting all my strength to the welfare of the people, will uphold the principle of autocracy as firmly and as unflinchingly as my late unforgettable father.'

The phrase 'senseless dreams' was never to be forgotten. It was almost universally held to characterise callousness and arrogance. In fact what it characterised was the ineptitude of Nicholas. He simply did not know how to act – nor how to think. Count Alexander Izvolsky, the future Foreign Minister, is emphatic in his memoirs that Nicholas had no stomach for a head-on collision with the zemstvos but was argued into taking the tone he did by Pobedonostsev, who insisted that he make a firm declaration of his faith in the principle of autocracy as an obeisance to his sainted father; moreover, Izvolsky goes on to say, the draft speech was prepared by Pobedonostsev, who handed it over at the last moment so that Nicholas quite clearly hardly knew what he was reading. This sounds in character.[10]

The fact remains that in acquitting Nicholas of callousness one is laying him open to a charge of ineptness of a kind which may produce worse consequences than deliberate malevolence. Only four months after the zemstvo reception the young Tsar ruined himself finally in the eyes of countless thousands by yet another display of ineptitude which had an appearance of callous insensitivity almost past understanding in the Europe of that day.

The occasion was the fearful disaster on the Khodynka Field, the vast military exercise ground just outside Moscow where, on the fourth day of the coronation festivities, on 18 May 1896, a great throng of some half a million loyal and often drunken subjects were gathered to be feasted on free beer given away in coronation mugs. Thousands had been waiting all night to cheer the newly crowned Tsar and Tsaritsa who would appear before them. And many were already drunk at their own expense. Suddenly a rumour went round that the free beer and mugs were running out. There was a stampede for the booths. The field was criss-crossed with shallow trenches dug in the course of military exercises. Into these people pitched and were then pinned down by others tripping and falling over them. Hundreds were suffocated or trampled to death – women and children above all. Nobody ever knew how many.

Nicholas when he heard the news was shattered. His impulse was to cancel all the coronation festivities and go into a retreat. Once again, and fatally, he allowed himself to be talked out of a good and natural impulse which would have established his good will. He was talked out of it this time not by Pobedonostsev but by his uncles. He must pull himself together and behave like his father's son, they said. That night Nicholas and Alexandra were to attend a ball in their honour given by the French Ambassador. It was an epoch-making occasion, a celebration of the new alliance. It was also an affair of prestige for the Government of France, which had sent pictures, silver, porcelain, all beyond price, from the national collections to adorn the occasion – and tens of thousands of roses from the south of France: the French would never forgive such a cancellation.

Nicholas agreed reluctantly. He and Alexandra appeared blazing with orders and diamonds to open the ball while the Moscow hospitals were crammed with injured and besieged by thousands looking for lost relatives. Next day the Tsar and the Tsaritsa made a round of the hospitals, and Nicholas himself paid out of his privy purse a thousand roubles to the family of every victim. But it was too late. The damage was done. The new Tsar was on the way to being written off by the people whose loyalty he most needed, not as a brute – he quite clearly was not that – but rather as despicably shallow and frivolous, good for nothing.

4

The most striking feature of the early years of the new reign was a negative one: the lack of the least sense of urgency at the start of an epoch of the sharpest possible challenge. 'But what challenge?' one can imagine Nicholas asking in his politely uninterested way, had any of his advisers suggested that the problems of a Russian autocrat on the eve of the twentieth century differed in some degree from the problems faced by his seventeenth-century forebears. Nicholas was not alone to blame. He was not invited to think in terms of challenge, either from within, arising from the discontent and disaffection of his own subjects, or from without, as the great powers in the imperial age started blundering about very wildly indeed in the unexplored territory of global strategy. Indeed, he was not invited to think at all. Witte alone among his ministers knew that great movements were in train and had to be carried through, and at speed. But they were going to be carried through by Witte, in his own way. All he needed was to have behind him the authority which could come only from the Tsar. It was to be the old, old story of revolution from above: Witte would propose, the Tsar would decree, Witte would execute; and any dilution of the autocratic power could only slow things down. Hence the paradox that the most gifted, dynamic, in a sense progressive, of Russian statesmen was no less implacably opposed than Pobedonostsev himself to any devolution of powers or any concession to the idea of elective representation.

The most vital and creative forces in Russian society at this time were still the zemstvos, whose moving spirits were a focus of genuine liberalism; they knew the people, they had valuable administrative experience of a kind far removed from the desk-bound bureaucrats of the central government. Among them were wise and able men like D. N. Shipov, chairman of the Moscow district zemstvo, with whom any statesman dreaming of a prosperous Russia at peace with herself should have been eager to ally himself. But just as the radicals were too impatient to wait for the Shipovs, as they worked quietly away to achieve representative government by easy stages, so now Witte was impatient in a different way. To the radicals the Shipovs appeared as a brake on the revolutionary transformation of society; to Witte they were a brake on his programme of industrialisation by decree. And so it was that when the new Minister of the Interior, Ivan Goremykin, the very image of cynical inertia of the most amiable kind, actually went so far in 1899 as to recommend the extension of the zemstvo system to certain parts of the Empire (above all in the western areas of the Ukraine and White Russia and on the lower Volga) where zemstvos had never been established, he came under immediate attack from Witte in his celebrated memorandum entitled *Autocracy and the Zemstvo*[11] which argued that elective local government of any kind, including the limited kind already in force, was incompatible with autocracy: either it must go, or autocracy must give way to constitutional government. It was an absurd situation in which Goremykin, blindly loyal to the Crown but possessed of no other principle whatsoever, should prove himself more open-minded than a Witte. He resigned (he was to come back later as Prime Minister) and was replaced by the shallow reactionary Sipyagin.

When Witte, some years later, desperately needed the co-operation of the zemstvos it was too late. Before that, his conversion to the need for agrarian reform had come too late. By the turn of the century he had been able to lift his eyes from the immediate problems of industrial development and budgeting and perceive that in spite of his great achievements (perhaps, indeed, because of them) in getting Russia on to the gold standard and raising loan after loan from the French, the country was in a very bad way indeed, the landowners hard-pressed, the situation of the urban workers a national disgrace and a threat to public order, the condition of the peasants a national calamity. After various committees had sat to enquire into the causes of peasant unrest and agricultural backwardness, all of them pointing to the existence of the commune as the great barrier to progress, in January 1902 a commission to end all commissions was set up, headed by Witte himself. It collected an immense volume of insights and information, but long before it came to making recommendations (and Witte by then was himself in the wilderness) it was overtaken and swamped by the very events which, had it been set up ten years earlier, and listened to, it might have forestalled.

By 1902 the tensions which had been building up since the first flush of disillusionment after the tragedy on the Khodynka Field in 1896 were such that they could no longer be resolved by any conceivable administrative action short of some surrender by the Tsar of his autocratic powers. The students who had demonstrated then had never really settled down: in all the university towns, above all perhaps in Kiev, student turbulence became a standing feature. And now the students were not alone. In the 1870s their fathers and mothers had gone to the people, to the peasants, seeking to rouse and enlighten them, in vain. Now the peasants were roused, if not enlightened, without any help from the students. And even as Witte's commission was holding its first meetings there came reports of new outbreaks of peasant violence, arson, pillage, on a greater scale than for centuries past. The workers, the peasants in the towns, were on the move too: they were discovering a new sense of solidarity, and although they were glad to listen and to learn from the educated missionaries of revolution who were ready to talk to them and instruct them for ever, their sense of power came from the discovery that the labour of their hands counted for something and that when they withheld it, it hurt. They went on strike again and again all over the land, and more and more frequently the cry for better pay, better living conditions, reduced working hours, was mingled with quite new demands – for freedom of speech, for freedom of assembly, for the overthrow of the autocracy itself. They could be intimidated now by nothing short of the Cossack's whip or the rifle bullet. Nor was it only a matter of peasants and workmen and turbulent students. In 1902 a group of zemstvo officials and radical intellectuals met in Switzerland to form the first illegal opposition party, the Union of Liberation, which was soon to lead the great movement for constitutional government.

Witte now found himself arguing for reform against men he himself had nominated to key positions, above all Sipyagin at the Ministry of the Interior. The Tsar, his master, was against him too. Nicholas had never liked Witte. The imperative need to keep him in office, at least while the finances of the country were being reorganised and stabilised on a basis of foreign loans, combined with the need to escape from his overpowering presence may very well have encouraged Nicholas in his tendency to surround himself with inferior place-men and intriguers – notably at the start of his reign the notorious Prince Meshchersky, nicknamed the Prince of Sodom, corrupt and corrupting, with his extreme right-wing newspaper *Grazhdanin (The Citizen)*, and, later on, the fortune-hunting ex-Guards officer Captain Bezobrazov. Attempts to escape from the importunities of Witte, who did in fact seek to interfere in everything and to have a finger in every pie, may also have exaggerated that unfortunate characteristic which was to earn Nicholas the reputation of being double-faced and treacherous: on the one hand he would agree on a line of policy with the official adviser of the moment – and then re-open the whole matter for discussion with that adviser's adversaries; on the other hand he was to become notorious for his inability, or refusal, to criticise one of his ministers to his face, and loyal servants time and again would return to their offices or homes after the friendliest of audiences with the Tsar only to be shocked to find awaiting them notice of their dismissal.

Of course this weakness was a deep-rooted part of the Tsar's character. I suggest only that living in the shadow of a clumsy giant like Witte in the early days of his reign may well have made it worse. Just as the curious uncertainty of purpose, a distinguishing mark of the era in Russia, which ran all the way through the public life of the country, not only reflected Nicholas's own inner uncertainties but also must have aggravated them.

In their different ways the actions of almost every official of importance were, like Witte's, shot through with contradictions and uncertainties, if not with plain equivocation. Very striking indeed among the contradictions of the period was the attitude towards industrial unrest. On the one hand, with the blessing of successive Ministers of the Interior, Sipyagin and Plehve, provincial governors using their statutory emergency powers were very free indeed with the calling up of troops to shoot down strikers – as at Batum, when fifteen oil refinery workers were killed and more than fifty wounded, and at Zlatust in the Urals where sixty-nine were killed (the responsible governor here was assassinated by Socialist Revolutionaries very shortly afterwards by way of reprisal). But even while the central authorities permitted, if they did not encourage, savage repression of this kind, they were also giving their blessing to a diametrically opposed approach, recognising the existence of legitimate grievances and experimenting with ways and means of turning the energies of the workers away from political slogans and towards economic solutions.

The hero of this operation was that Colonel Zubatov, chief of the

Moscow Okhrana, referred to earlier. With the full support of the Tsar's uncle, the Grand Duke Sergei, and with the consent of two successive Ministers of the Interior, Sipyagin and, for a time, Plehve, Zubatov organised a number of police-sponsored trades unions, exotic apparitions in a land where the trade union was illegal, if not virtually unthinkable. The workers, he argued, must inevitably agitate for more pay, shorter hours, better housing, and so on; and this was only reasonable, given their present conditions. Discontented and frustrated, they would fall to the first agitator who came along to exploit their grievances. And the agitator was all too likely to be a revolutionary who was less interested in ameliorating the worker's lot than in inflaming him to rise against his masters. The way to avoid this, surely, was to organise those same workers in an orderly, open and above-board manner, giving them a legal platform for the proclamation of their grievances and also some leverage in their perfectly reasonable struggle with too greedy employers. In this way their minds could be concentrated on the satisfaction of their immediate material needs and the revolutionaries would have nothing to work on.

This fantastic institutionalisation, under police sponsorship, of a perfectly commonplace and obvious expedient, namely to keep revolution at bay by treating your employees better (an expedient, of course, feared and abhorred by Lenin and his friends, watching from far away), was something that could have occurred only in Russia, where it was inconceivable that any action should be taken without a theoretical basis and without the approval and supervision of authority – even when such action was a challenge to authority. In fact, it was not really more far-fetched than the intrusion of provincial governors, backed by military firing squads, into perfectly ordinary industrial disputes between workers and employers.

The Zubatov experiment had spectacular results. Workers flocked to the new unions and held many enjoyable and peaceable demonstrations under the protection of the benevolent police – including one in Moscow actually inside the Kremlin walls before the memorial to Alexander II, fifty thousand strong. But the employers were soon up in arms: government support in suppressing strikes was welcome, cost what it might in loss of dignity and independence; but government support of strikers in asking for an eight-hour day and free medical attention was unheard-of. And Witte was on the side of the employers. The dream had to end. In June 1903, there was a positive explosion of illegal strikes in the south, above all among the oil workers of Baku, the most wretchedly treated of all, but also in machine shops, mines, railway depots and construction sites. Many of the Zubatov unions not only joined forces with the non-unionised workers but also provided them with leaders and organisers for what soon developed into a paralysing general strike. Zubatov had done too well.

He was sacked. But the strange ambivalent notion of police socialism lingered on, to break out a year and a half later with heavy consequences.

We are reaching the stage when foreigners for long familiar with Russian conditions and practised in discounting disturbances which in any other country would have looked threatening indeed began to fear the worst. There was an epidemic of assassinations. The first political killing of the new reign was the shooting in 1901 by a Socialist Revolutionary student of a relatively harmless Minister of Education, N. P. Bogolepov. But there was better soon to come. Witte's nominee as Minister of the Interior, D. S. Sipyagin, was killed in 1902 and two years later his successor, Plehve, went the same way – both at the hands of the S.R. Combat Section, the devoted members of which were responsible for the deaths of many lesser men as well.

Plehve, since his early days as head of Loris-Melikov's new Department of State Police, had made a reputation for himself as an administrator of extreme harshness (above all as responsible for Finnish affairs when Finland was being tortured by the brute General N. N. Bobrikov – assassinated in 1904), though not without guile and a certain superficial flexibility. Like Witte, like so many lesser lights, he bent his efforts to the impossible task of encompassing change within the rigid framework of the autocracy. Plehve put his money on what was in effect a confidence trick: if he could win the public support of leaders of liberal opinion he would be able to manipulate these and to some extent emasculate them while persuading the disaffected that he was a liberal at heart. He sought to woo the deeply respected zemstvo leader D. N. Shipov with promises of the amelioration of agrarian conditions; he went so far as to offer the Ministry of Education to the liberal historian P. N. Milyukov. But he was unconvincing as a reforming minister. Even while holding out promises to the peasants he lent his authority to the savage treatment of those of their brothers who had been involved in the peasant rioting before he was minister, without pausing to enquire, as urged by the zemstvos, into the reasons for the violence. On another level, he had to bear the blame for the atrocities of a rash of pogroms, above all the notorious Easter pogroms at Kishinev in 1900 when over four hundred were massacred over several days while the police looked on. And this was just. For although he did not instigate this or any other pogrom, as he is still sometimes charged with doing, his conviction, shared with Nicholas, that the Jews were behind all sorts of subversive activity and were anyway sub-human, was never concealed; and the anti-semitic local police and the members of reactionary secret societies felt safe, knowing that the minister would privately favour their murderous activities. Some of the societies, of course, were not so secret: Nicholas himself was to become a benevolent patron of the disreputable

Union of the Russian People, which tacitly, if not actively, encouraged the gangster-like atrocities of the notorious Black Hundreds.

Plehve was also simple-minded enough to think that he might buy a Shipov or a Milyukov, and inept enough to spoil his effects by mixing his blandishments with threats, like a caricature of a Fascist or a Communist official in the twentieth century (we are too solemn about these abject creatures who in our own time have ruled so large a part of the world: their significance should be sought not in political philosophy but in the melodrama of Eugène Sue). Pallidly embowered among actresses, ballerinas, and other less colourful aspirants to high patronage, Plehve, like his Soviet successors, was closer in style to Baron Scarpia than to Torquemada. Play along with me, he said in effect to the Shipovs and Milyukovs, and you will be surprised to find how liberal I am. But stand against me and I will sweep you off the face of the earth. And indeed, some of his last actions were to dismiss the complete membership of the Tver zemstvo (Tver getting ahead of the game once more) and to refuse to confirm the veteran Shipov himself as head of the Moscow zemstvo.

He was killed by a bomb on 15 July 1904, the second Minister of the Interior to be picked off in two years. The assassination was indeed a triumph for the Socialist Revolutionaries. The bomb was thrown by the S.R. student Sazonov, a genuine martyr, who saw himself following in the footsteps of Zhelyabov and Perovskaya. But Sazonov was only the instrument. To penetrate the very tight security round Plehve was a major undertaking, and the conspirators behind Sazonov worked long and deviously to perfect their plan. The leading lights had travelled far in spirit from the sacrificial idealism of the 'People's Will'. For the power men were taking over the revolutionary movement – among the S.R.s no less than among the S.D.s In all the cities of the Empire, and in the countryside too, there were more and more devoted young revolutionaries, men and women, children of the rich as well as of the poor, prepared to give their days and nights, their lives, for the betterment of their fellow men and women. But even as these grew in numbers, so they became increasingly the instruments of men who were more interested in destruction than in building – killers like Gershuni of the S.R.s – or others, intriguing, self-deluding demagogues like, in their very different ways, Lenin and Trotsky, who believed that they alone among all mankind knew what was good for mankind and were thereby licensed to take whatever measures seemed necessary, at whatever cost in misery and bloodshed, to win power for themselves. For the Social Democrats, Bolsheviks and Mensheviks were now increasingly active in the factories, just as the S.R.s were stirring up the peasants to violence and shooting and bombing on the streets.

It seems a fitting commentary on both the revolutionaries and the government that Plehve's killing was planned and organised by Yevno Azev, the police agent employed by Plehve himself to infiltrate the revolutionaries.

Nicholas, of course, felt and behaved like Lenin. He believed that he knew best and could do no wrong. For this he stands condemned, and justly so. But at least Nicholas inherited a long-established and widely shared delusion: he believed he was the obedient instrument and regent of God on earth. How to compare this millennial and in some sense humble fantasy with the raw lunacy of a man who, denying God, inheriting no burden of responsibility, singles himself out and unforgivably proclaims that he and he alone can succeed where all other men in the history of the world have failed?

In 1904, when Plehve was killed, the lunacy was only brewing. Nicholas had displayed his own inner uncertainty by replacing Plehve not – on his mother's urgent recommendation – with a harsh disciplinarian operating through the emergency laws but by Prince P. D. Svyatopolk-Mirsky, an enlightened, gentlemanly, bumbling moderate from one of the oldest families in the land. It was to be Mirsky's task to reconcile Crown and subjects at a time of national emergency which, it was confidently expected, would soon unify the Empire in pride of victory over the contemptible Japanese. Sadly, there was no victory; and within six months of taking office Mirsky's good intentions were trampled down by military and demonstrators as they met head on.

CHAPTER NINETEEN

Defeat in Asia

I

IN so far as the Russo-Japanese War was simply one more adventure in the riot of global imperialism which put an end to a number of familiar diplomatic assumptions after the Congress of Berlin, it tells us nothing specific about Russia. The concert of Europe was no longer even a dream: the balance of power had taken its place, and the powers themselves were looking to the oceans and the remotest corners of the globe. It was the age of Manifest Destinies and White Men's Burdens; of enraged confrontations between Anglo-Saxons, Latins and Teutons on the banks of the Nile or in Morocco. It was the age of the scramble for Africa. It was an age in which the combined wisdom of all the statesmen of all the powers, including the United States, could take it unquestionably for granted that the vast, hostile, tenacious mystery of China (by all means now an inert and crippled giant) could be kept under drugs and exploited for ever. It was an age in which all the powers could come together to crush the Chinese who had the effrontery to rebel, and then in almost the same breath sanctimoniously condemn one of their number for fighting the Boers in South Africa.

All ages have been disreputable, but there was a peculiar unpleasantness about the last decade of the nineteenth century and the first of the twentieth: popular nationalism swept Europe like a disease. Millions instead of thousands were now corrupted by the sense of power. Marxist explanations are not enough. Of course there was a drive for markets, seen very clearly indeed by some Europeans and Americans. Thus Brooks Adams, the influential and bleakly imperialistic brother of the United States Secretary of State, could write in 1899, on the eve of the Boer War: 'Eastern Asia now appears . . . to be the only district [*sic*] likely to be able to absorb any great manufactures . . . Whether we like it or not, we are forced to compete for the seat of international exchanges, or, in other words, for the seat of empire.'[1] Brooks Adams was obsessed with the urgency of America's need to forestall Russia in China. Witte in St Petersburg was thinking in very much the same terms in reverse, though less dramatically. But whereas Adams was driven by the apocalyptic conviction expressed in his *Law of Civilisation and Decay* that the United States had to engage in continuous growth or else relapse into barbarism, Witte was not troubled by philosophical nightmares: for him the Chinese trade was a means of building up Russian strength so that Russia could hold her own as a great power among the newly industrialised powers of the West. To what purpose? Simply to stop her being overwhelmed. By whom?

Side by side with fear, there was also a great deal of showing off. William II of Germany with his theatrical costumiers' uniforms, his perpetual attitudinising, his absurd telegrams, was certainly the joke-figure of prestige politics. But he was more than a joke-figure, he was also sinister; real jackboots and spurs went with those uniforms; the helmet surmounted by the glittering eagle was bullet-proof; and when after the manoeuvres of the Russian Baltic Fleet he addressed his notorious signal to poor Nicholas: 'The Admiral of the Atlantic salutes the Admiral of the Pacific!' he was already anticipating the day when his fleet, the navy of a great land-power with few maritime responsibilities, would be bringing Europe to the verge of war by trying to outbuild the Royal Navy upon which the very existence of the British Isles depended. And he was already encouraging 'the Admiral of the Pacific' into Far Eastern adventures, precisely to embroil his young cousin whom he patronised, whom he affected to love, whom he despised, in trouble with Britain, America, Japan, anyone at all away from Germany's doorstep.

And leaving aside all of what might be called rational elements in international rivalries – such as France burning for revenge and the return of Alsace-Lorraine; Austria torn between greed for more territory in the Balkans and anxiety about any change which might upset a precarious *status quo*; Germany (reasonably in an imperial age) seeking colonial outlets; Russia jealous of her own influence in the Balkans, her suspicions of Austrian designs in that quarter inflamed by the way in which the mildness of Austrian rule in southern Poland was providing a focus and a haven for Polish rebels against Russia – leaving aside all these as it were traditional elements, the spirit of the age was exacerbating a jumpy situation by its sheer vulgarity. For William II, exaggerated as his image might be, was less of an aberration than a caricature. Everything he did, from the way he grew his moustaches to the martial flamboyance of his sabre-rattling, was unreal. But it was no more unreal in its sabre-rattling way than the attitude and behaviour of Edward VII of England (whose age this really was) or Nicholas himself. At a time when the masses were achieving self-consciousness as never before, and were also downtrodden and very poor, the heir to Victoria's throne had turned London Society into a cross between an orchid house, a casino and a brothel, while expending more time and nervous energy thinking about uniforms and orders than was strictly sane; France, not long recovered from the Boulanger affair, was torn by the Dreyfus case; Nicholas, modestly living out his narrow, remote existence surrounded by the mahogany furniture and mauve hangings which were Alexandra's contribution to the glories of Peterhof and Tsarskoe Selo, nevertheless spent money like water on keeping up a suffocatingly brilliant court, far more elaborate and spend-thrift than his father's. So that it might be said not unfairly that as far as the Little Father of all Russia was concerned the net result of Witte's industrialisation and the new opening to the Far East was a collection of Fabergé's Easter eggs, those perfect symbols and crowning glories of the Winter Palace in decline.

A collection of Easter eggs, a shameful military defeat, countless dead, maimed, widowed, orphaned, and something very like a revolution thrown in. For the war with Japan was real.

2

Urging him to be bold, William assured Nicholas that Russia had a holy mission in Asia – in the Defence of the Cross and the old Christian Euro-pean culture against the inroads of Mongols and Buddhists. 'I would let nobody try to interfere with you and attack you from behind in Europe during the time you were fulfilling the great mission which Heaven has shaped for you.'[2] The Kaiser was thinking of China, his celebrated 'Yellow Peril'; but Japan would do just as well: anything to keep Russia tied down and depleted on the far side of the world. That, of course, was not in fact the reason why Russia went to war with Japan; but William's urgings undoubtedly helped to ease Nicholas into a position from which it was difficult to draw back.

War when it came was a mistake as far as Russia was concerned. In the months preceding the Japanese attack on Port Arthur in January 1904, Nicholas had been dithering more than was usual even for him. But although he was being urged to war by one faction, prominent among them Plehve, by a majority of his advisers he was being heavily restrained, above all by Witte himself and, most significantly, by General Kuropatkin, his Minister of Defence. Yet it was Witte with his great Trans-Siberian enterprise who had made the war possible and carried Russian commerce and Russian arms over the threshold of China herself and into challenging proximity with Japanese interests in Korea.

At the turn of the century all the powers, of course, were on the make at the expense of China. But Russia was in a different position from the others because China was her neighbour, and in seeking to expand into Manchuria she was simply continuing the process which had brought her all the way from Muscovy to the Pacific and, in more recent times, deeply into sovereign Chinese territory. She was also in direct confrontation with Japan, then in a fury of modernisation and explosive growth, and needing more space and control of the waters round her islands with a desperation far exceeding Russia's need to penetrate still farther east and south. Korea, in the process of being wrested from Chinese sovereignty by Japan, was very much a point of contention. It was separated from Japan by narrow waters, from Russia only by part of Manchuria. Japan therefore needed a foothold on the mainland, and after defeating China in 1894 demanded the cession of the Liaotung Peninsula with Port Arthur, Manchuria's superb natural harbour. Witte, who saw the main purpose of his great railway project being defeated if Japan once established herself in Manchuria, managed to persuade Nicholas to resist; and Germany and France were persuaded to join with Russia to stop Japan, who gave way to *force majeure* and contented herself with taking Formosa, the Pescadores, and a heavy indemnity.

Russia could now present herself as the protector of China, and the relationship was soon formalised as an alliance against Japan. Its first fruits were the agreement for the construction of what came to be known as the Chinese Eastern Railway across northern Manchuria, a short cut for the Trans-Siberian Railway across Manchuria to Vladivostok. Witte built this railway, and also paid China's indemnity to Japan, largely with French loan capital. She retained control of a strip of territory to be patrolled with her own military guards on each side of the railway.

Witte had thus established a military presence in Manchuria. Three years later the operation was crowned by Russia's seizure of the very prize, Port Arthur and the Liaotung Peninsula, she had forced Japan to relinquish after her successful war. This was made possible when a German foray into Shantung, ostensibly to avenge the murder of two missionaries, gave the green light for other powers to take what they could (Britain's share of the loot was Weiheiwai). It was an action which Japan would not forgive.

Witte, through the Ministry of Finance, was now controlling what amounted to a private empire in Manchuria. He was content with this. But other Russians were not; so that even while Witte and Count Lamsdorf, his nondescript colleague at the Foreign Ministry, were protesting that Russia had no further designs in the Far East, something like an organised war party was crystallising round the Tsar. Its members coveted

Korea, not simply because of its strategic importance *vis-à-vis* Vladivostok, but also because it was going to make them rich. The leading light of this cabal was the disreputable ex-Guards officer Bezobrazov, who had organised a colossal timber concession on the Yalu river into which he had persuaded far too many high-born individuals who should have known better to put their money. Worse, he managed to talk Nicholas himself into patronising the scheme, investing in it personally, and instructing Witte, who was furious, contemptuous, apprehensive and resentful, into providing treasury funds in support of an enterprise that was to be backed by Russian troops and was bound to lead to direct conflict with the Japanese.[3] Another prominent member of the Far Eastern war lobby was a vain and incompetent sailor, Admiral Alexeyev, who was reputed to be the Tsar's uncle, an illegitimate son of Alexander II. The lobby also had the backing of Plehve, an imperialist by nature, who was ready for any opportunity to thwart Witte or intrigue against him, and who also imagined, as he himself was to explain to Kuropatkin shortly before his own assassination, that what was wanted to avoid revolution at home was 'a little, victorious war'.[4]

War was brought a very long stride nearer when, consulting nobody, telling nobody except Plehve (leaving his other ministers, including the Foreign Minister, to read the news in the newspapers), Nicholas appointed Admiral Alexeyev to be Viceroy of the Far East, responsible to the Tsar alone, and owing no allegiance to the Foreign Ministry. With Alexeyev sitting in Port Arthur more than five thousand miles from St Petersburg communicating only with the Tsar and his own coterie in the capital, and with Nicholas refusing to take his ministers into his confidence, the Far East had become a stamping ground for adventurers of every kind. The dismissal of Witte in 1903 meant the removal of the last restraints, and Nicholas showed his contempt for the decencies by insisting that this very great man should accept the purely honorific post of Chairman of the Council of Ministers.

All this occurred when the situation with Japan was more acute than ever before. Three years earlier, during the Boxer Rebellion, Russia, as her contribution to the international effort to put the rising down, had occupied virtually the whole of Manchuria. Once there she was in no hurry to get out, and it was soon clear that Witte and Lamsdorf, who wished to behave correctly *vis-à-vis* other interested powers, were being undermined and overruled by Nicholas himself. Britain and America were alarmed, as well as Japan, and by the end of 1901 those Japanese who had striven to make a deal with the Russians came to see that there was little hope of Russia's abandoning interest in Korea. In January 1902 Japan at last gave up trying and, not without apprehension, concluded her celebrated defensive alliance with Britain. Here at last was action to sober up the Russian adventurers and make Nicholas think again. It had no effect at all. Nicholas, while certainly not desiring war, went on behaving as though Japan was an insignificant offshore island whose claims and pretensions could be ignored. The occasion of the collision, when it came, was provided by Manchuria. Even after making a definitive promise for a phased withdrawal the Russians dragged their feet, demanding ever greater concessions from the Chinese. Japan, who had a war party of her own, decided that the sooner she asserted herself and struck the better. On 9 February 1904, without any declaration of war, she struck, sending ten fast destroyers under cover of darkness deep into Port Arthur harbour to wreak havoc on a Russian fleet lying peacefully at anchor and silhouetted against the lights of the fortress town beyond. It was a rehearsal for Pearl Harbor.

3

It was not as successful as Pearl Harbor. Three Russian ships were damaged, only one of them seriously, but the moral shock was severe. The Russians had an extremely powerful fleet based on Port Arthur, including seven battleships. It had never occurred to anyone in St Petersburg that these might be seriously challenged. But when next day, recovering from the first shock, the fleet put to sea to encounter Admiral Togo's ships drawn up in battle array, after a brief half-hour's exchange of fire (in which the Russian guns in fact did a good deal of damage) the Russian admiral was only too pleased to break off the action and return to harbour. On that same day the Japanese attacked a Russian squadron off Chemulpo in western Korea, sinking two cruisers.

The Japanese, commanding the sea for the time being, were now in a position to start the war in earnest. There were to be two lines of attack: a push through Korea and across the Yalu river into Manchuria towards Mukden, and a direct landing on the Liaotung Peninsula to cut off Port Arthur and invest it.

Even after the shock of the original naval reverses it never seems to have occurred to Nicholas or those around him (with the solitary exception of General Kuropatkin himself) that Russia was in peril. They knew, of course, that the army had deficiencies, especially that transport facilities left much to be desired. But they had a splendid navy; they had what was perhaps the best artillery in the world; and they had the quasi-mystical sense of untold masses behind them. And who were these Japanese monkeys, as Nicholas habitually called them? How could these toothy, jabbering, yellowish, undersized little islanders, only just emerged from centuries of mediaeval seclusion, hope to make an impression on mighty Russia once she had decided to stir her vast and torpid frame to vengeful action? Nobody knew or cared that since the imperial restoration in 1860 the Japanese had set themselves as the most urgent task basic to all others precisely the undertaking which had been and still was so desperately needed in Russia – the introduction of universal primary and secondary education of the highest attainable quality. So that those 'children of coachmen, servants, cooks, washerwomen, small shopkeepers and persons of similar type' contemptuously and deliberately denied educational opportunities in Russia as recently as 1887 by the egregious Delyanov[5] were in Japan given the chance, urged indeed, to develop their potential. Authority in Russia was so unsure of itself that it dared not encourage literacy among the children of the poor. Authority in Japan dared quite recklessly, and now had its reward in the shape of a great body of skilled and intelligent labour and an army and navy to match. Russia had no excuse for her ignorance of this, or of the giant strides made by Japan in building up the machinery of modern warfare and developing the techniques to employ it. Russia, however, did have some excuse for not understanding that the modern Japanese were somehow managing to combine Western technology with their own unique brand of patriotism, sacrificial to the point of suicide. The Russian conscript would endure the most fearful punishment in defence of his homeland; the Japanese were no less extreme in their offensive courage. The Russians were to rely, as they had always relied when it came to the pinch (and were to rely again – how soon! – in 1914), on there being such a lot of them. The Japanese knew all about this and were determined to shatter the Russian forces in Manchuria before the slow but almost limitless build-up of reinforcements could begin to tell. They went at their task in a positive frenzy of single-minded violence which threw the Russian command into confusion.

Confusion was increased by an almost ludicrous division of command. The Russian commander-in-chief in control of both army and navy was Admiral Alexeyev, sitting to begin with in Port Arthur. The army commander was General Kuropatkin, who had resigned his appointment as Minister of War to take the field. Many of the initial tribulations of the Russians were due to Alexeyev, who could communicate directly with the Tsar and his own particular circle round the Tsar. Poor Kuropatkin, who had to do the fighting, was constantly overruled and as constantly issued with contradictory orders. He was not a brilliant general, but he was a good soldier and he understood the traditional Russian way of making war and sought to apply it in Manchuria. Patience was what he asked for, but patience he was never allowed to practise. He did not much mind giving up territory for the time being, provided he could keep his forces intact and let the enemy beat himself against a defensive wall until he was exhausted – or until the Russian army was so strong that it could take the offensive with the certainty of victory. Kuropatkin had more reason than anyone else to know about the deficiencies of armaments and transport. Some time before the Japanese attack he had urged on the Tsar his conviction that Russia would be in no condition to fight until the late spring of 1905: certain matters of re-equipment had to be completed, but, above all, there was still a worrying gap to be closed in the Trans-Siberian Railway. Given the command of the sea, the Japanese with their short sea passage would have had an immense advantage over the Russians with their 5,000-mile haul along a single-track railway, even had that track been complete. But it was not yet complete: all rail traffic came to a halt on the shores of Lake Baikal, and men and material had to be off-loaded and transferred to boats in summer and to a light railway crossing the ice in winter – then loaded into trains again on the other side. And closing the gap of a hundred or so miles was going to be a slow job: the country round Baikal is mountainous, and something like twenty more tunnels had to be drilled and blasted before the line could be completed.

The Russian army as such was, of course, far bigger than the Japanese. Alexeyev had an army of two and a half millions at his back, Togo much less than half that number. But when war broke out the Japanese had 180,000 men in Korea with the immediate promise of a further 30,000 across the narrow sea, while the Russians had only 100,000 fighting troops in Manchuria, plus another 30,000 railway troops, used to police the Chinese Eastern Railway and scattered far and wide.[6] It was obviously correct for Kuropatkin to concentrate his forces on holding the Yalu river line, ready to retreat slowly and in good order if necessary on Mukden, pending the arrival of reinforcements (he was desperately short of field artillery as well as men). It was obviously correct for the Japanese to follow up their naval assault with a whirlwind attempt to force the Yalu river and make a landing behind Port Arthur while the Russians were still weak. It was obviously inevitable that the disastrous viceroy, egged on by his disreputable friends in St Petersburg, should insist and insist again on a swift and immediate Russian offensive and that this should not only fail but leave Kuropatkin vulnerable. It was less obviously inevitable that the Japanese should have been allowed by Alexeyev to make an unopposed landing behind his back. This, however, is what happened. And in no time at all they had cut off the end of the peninsula, isolating Port Arthur.

It was also less obviously inevitable that to add to the misfortunes due to their own incompetence the Russians should have been punished by sheer bad luck, almost without cease, from start to finish. The most severe blow of this kind was the loss on 31 March of Admiral Makarov and his splendid flagship the *Peter and Paul*. Makarov was incomparably the most gifted commander on the Russian side, and also the boldest. He had taken hold of a demoralised Pacific fleet and turned it into a fighting force, giving Admiral Togo serious cause for worry about his own communications. But putting back into Port Arthur after a routine foray, his ship hit a mine and blew up. Thereafter during a most critical period the Pacific fleet feared to move from the shelter of Port Arthur's guns. It made one major sortie in August, when the Japanese were drawing the net round Port Arthur itself. But the imposing force of six battleships and five cruisers was scattered. The new admiral was killed, his flagship disabled, and with it four more of the battleships, which just managed to limp back glumly into harbour. The sixth battleship and a number of cruisers finished up interned in neutral ports. After this the Pacific fleet was never to show itself again, locked up in harbour until battered to destruction by Japanese guns firing down on it from the hills.

Kuropatkin fought two great battles in the hope of relieving Japanese pressure on Port Arthur. The first was at Liao-Yang, to the south of Mukden, opening on 26 August and continuing for over a week, with 150,000 Japanese facing the same number of Russians on a sixty-mile front; the second and still more terrible clash occurred when Kuropatkin at last started his major offensive on the Sha Ho river to the south of Mukden. Here a total of 350,000 men and 1,500 guns were deployed against each other on a forty-mile front. In both battles there was no outright victory, but the Russians were pushed back a little, suffered very heavy casualties, and were farther than ever from coming to the help of the Port Arthur garrison, which from the middle of August came under repeated and almost desperate attack from General Nogi's forces.

Hope flared a little when Alexeyev was recalled after the Sha Ho river battle and Kuropatkin was at last given supreme command. But it was too late now for clearer orders to make much difference. Alexeyev's final legacy was to leave a certain General Stoessel in command of the fortress city and its well-equipped garrison of nearly fifty thousand. It is conceivable that there were worse officers than Stoessel in the Russian army of the day, but, if so, they have not been heard of. The whole burden of the defence was assumed by a courageous and gifted subordinate General Kondratenko, who was killed in the early days of the fourth and final major assault which opened at the end of November. When Kondratenko died Port Arthur was doomed, and Stoessel in fact surrendered at the end of December; without Kondratenko to organise and inspire the defence against the last overwhelming hand-to-hand assaults, Stoessel simply crumpled up. His junior officers and men, whose performance was in the same class as that of the heroes of Sevastopol, were eager to continue the fight, and the fortress still had plenty of food and ammunition; but the commander's will gave out. Perhaps it was inevitable. General Nogi was evidently prepared to sacrifice his men in tens of thousands to secure Port Arthur and finally destroy the Pacific fleet as a fighting force, and his men were prepared to die without question. But already the slow, relentless accumulation of Russian men and material in Manchuria was beginning to tell. The Trans-Siberian Railway was now handling fourteen trains a day, instead of only four, which was all it could manage at the start of the war. And Japan with her strictly limited resources was beginning to feel the strain; so that it is possible to believe that a Kondratenko could have held on until the corner was turned.

The fact that the Japanese were to hold their own, indeed to advance, in the battles that followed the fall of Port Arthur proves nothing. The Russians were now fighting without the immediate spur of relieving the fortress and saving the fleet; so that when after the costly failure of an unnecessary and premature offensive in January the two armies stood face to face in mid-February at the outset of the battle for Mukden, the confrontation was seen by Kuropatkin not as the final test, which it turned out to be, but, rather, as an important stage in a grand strategy of attrition which must inevitably end in Russian victory. Poor Kuropatkin was so far from St Petersburg and Moscow that it was easy for him to forget that wars of attrition depend very much on public morale. Nor could he foresee that the Imperial navy, in the shape of the Baltic fleet, at that moment resting in Madagascar before continuing its long voyage towards the Yellow Sea through half the oceans of the world, was heading inexorably towards a disaster unmatched in naval history.

Mukden was, in terms of the numbers involved, the biggest battle until then recorded, bigger even than Leipzig, 'the Battle of the Nations', in 1813. Over six hundred thousand men, more than were ever engaged in any nineteenth-century battle, fought desperately for over two weeks instead of for a day. Neither Kuropatkin nor Oyama on the Japanese side had any clear idea of how to handle such numbers, divided by the Russians into three armies, by the Japanese into five. But on the whole the Japanese commanders were the more flexible, and none of them got their troops into such a mess as General Kaulbars in command of the Russian Second Army. Oyama, what is more, did keep a clear enough picture of what was going on to embark on a bold and extremely threatening encircling movement, which forced the Russians to retreat, though in remarkably good order and under full discipline, behind Mukden. The battle ended with both armies intact except for very heavy casualties (90,000 Russian, 70,000 Japanese) and with the Japanese in Mukden; but also with both armies in no condition to resume the offensive for some time to come, and with the Japanese wondering very apprehensively indeed how they could weather another holocaust of this kind when the Russians had regrouped and reinforced themselves, as they undoubtedly would. Kuropatkin was recalled and replaced by a senior and more gifted general, Linevich, who had commanded the First Army at Mukden.

The final test never came. The Japanese never had to discover how their dwindling resources could withstand the relentlessly growing pressure of superior numbers. Relief came to them from the sea and, ironically, from the very quarter which they had most feared.

Perhaps the greatest spur to the successful storming of Port Arthur had been Togo's constant dread that what was left of the Pacific fleet would be reinforced by the Russian Baltic fleet. And indeed, when Port Arthur fell, the Baltic fleet was already on its way though not so close as Togo feared. It had sailed from Kronstadt under Admiral Rozhdestvensky at the beginning of October. The Tsar in person had said farewell to the fleet with colourful and moving ceremony as it set out on a virtual circumnavigation of the globe. For the voyage ahead was long indeed: one end of the Baltic to the other; out into the North Sea and down through the Straits of Dover; thence round the coast of Africa to Madagascar; thence across the Indian Ocean and out into the Pacific and the South China Sea. Then the remaining ships of the Pacific fleet would issue forth from Port Arthur, join forces with the Baltic fleet, and be ready to challenge the Japanese on level terms.

It did not happen like that at all. At the very outset Admiral Rozhdestvensky suffered a humiliation which all but turned farce into tragedy; and this set the tone for a voyage which, in the end, was to turn tragedy into farce. The first thing was the celebrated incident off the Dogger Bank in the North Sea, when the Admiral, all nerves and fearing a torpedo attack from the diabolical Japanese, found his fleet in the darkness of the October night surrounded by an unknown number of unidentifiable small craft – and gave the order to fire first and ask questions afterwards: unfortunately what he was firing at was a harmless concourse of English fishing-boats. Luckily there were very few casualties (two men killed and one boat sunk), and although the uproar was tremendous and for a moment it looked like war between Britain and Russia, tempers calmed down and nerves were soothed. The Admiral ploughed on, and on, and on. At last, in December, he put into Madagascar to refuel, and almost at once came the news of the fall of Port Arthur and the total destruction of the Pacific fleet. Was there any further purpose in the Baltic fleet's continuing its voyage? The Admiral thought not, so did many cool heads in St Petersburg. But the war party had the bit between its teeth. It not only wanted Rozhdestvensky to continue but also urged Nicholas to defy all Europe to do its worst by sending the Black Sea fleet out through the Dardanelles to join him, thus breaking the international Straits Convention. Nicholas, however, for once steadied by his more professional advisers, drew back from the prospect of embroiling his country with all the powers simultaneously. Instead, it was decided (this time in the teeth of sober advice) to tell Rozhdestvensky to sail on and to send after him an auxiliary fleet consisting of every fighting ship, obsolete or not, so long as it could keep afloat, that could be scraped up from the Kronstadt dockyards. It was in the China Sea on 22 May that the two fleets made their junction.

There was no Port Arthur to receive them now, of course: the combined fleet could not rest until it reached Vladivostok. To attain this safe haven Admiral Rozhdestvensky chose to sail through the narrow Tsushima Strait, between Japan and Korea, rather than make a wide sweep to the east of the Japanese islands. His was a formidable array ploughing steadily northwards, even though many of his ships were old and slow: eight battleships; twelve cruisers; nine destroyers. All went well for five days and nights, but then, on the afternoon of 27 May, they were intercepted by Togo with a fleet almost identical in numbers, not quite so heavy in armament, but on the whole very much faster. Within an hour Russia's sea power had been blasted off the face of the waters.

So accurate and deadly was the Japanese gunnery that with almost the first salvo a dozen Russian ships went up in flames or were sunk. When darkness fell the fast Japanese destroyers finished off the survivors with torpedoes. When it was all over four of the eight Russian battleships were sunk and four captured; seven cruisers were sunk; five destroyers were sunk and one captured. One cruiser and one destroyer got through to Vladivostok, their crews the sole survivors to set foot once more on the native soil they had left so many months before. The last remnants of the fleet found their way to internment in foreign ports. All that remained of the Imperial Russian navy was the Black Sea fleet locked up behind the Straits. And within a month the pride of that fleet, the very new battle-cruiser *Potemkin*, was to be the cockpit of a mutiny which, in years to come, through the genius of a film-maker, was to be transformed into the very symbol of revolution triumphant and the tragedy of civil strife; so that all that remains of the navy of Nicholas II in the minds of most people today are the camera images of the red flag being run up over a battle-cruiser in Odessa harbour, a terrified mob being fired at on Richelieu's great stone staircase leading down to the quayside – and a solitary perambulator bobbing its way to destruction down those same steps.

There were several lessons to be learnt from the Russo-Japanese War. The first, of course, was that Japan was materially a more formidable power than even her admirers and champions had realised and morally possessed by the spirit of total and unquestioning self-sacrifice, the nature of which had to be learnt all over again by the allies in the Second World War, a discovery which was the cause of a good deal of sober reflection in London, still more in Washington. The second was that mass armies supported by modern fire-power were, in the hands of any commander who was not a genius, well on the way to bringing the battlefield to a halt: nobody absorbed this lesson, not even the Russians who paid for it. Ten years later two not ungifted Russian generals, Samsonov and Rennenkampf, who had both commanded divisions at the shambles of Mukden, embarked on the offensive in East Prussia in command of immense bodies of troops, treating corps like battalions for all the world as though Mukden had never been. The third was the discovery that it was possible for a fleet admiral to lose not only a battle but a war in the course of an afternoon. The Russians were too preoccupied to think much about this – or, indeed, anything else; but the revelation hit the British and the German naval strategists very hard indeed: after Tsushima no senior naval commander was going with a song in his heart to expose his ships to a free and gallant engagement which might abruptly end with the loss of the entire fleet after an hour or so (and when the Germans and the British did at last engage at Jutland the lesson was rubbed home). The Russians profited little from any of these lessons because their thoughts were elsewhere.

CHAPTER TWENTY

'Impossible to Live Thus Any Longer'

I

WHAT they were thinking about was revolution.

It is a vivid commentary on the size and the resources of Russia that the huge and costly war in Manchuria might well have been taking place on another planet as far as St Petersburg and Moscow were concerned, to say nothing of Kiev and Odessa. Throughout the first year of the war the agitation against the autocracy continued along the lines already projected before the Japanese attack. Plehve's 'little war', victorious or not, had next to no effect on the growing demand for radical change which he had hoped to drown in a torrent of patriotic euphoria. Certainly when the Union of Liberation met illegally in the first days of the war, the moderate majority, as opposed to the radicals who prayed for Russia's defeat, agreed to hold back from harassing the Government for the duration of the war. This resolution was soon blunted by Plehve's high-handed treatment of even the most widely respected of the moderates. When he was assassinated in the mid-summer of 1904 and succeeded by Svyatopolk-Mirsky there was new hope. Mirsky quickly made it clear that he wished to work with the zemstvos, removed the restrictions placed upon them by Plehve, and allowed even the comparative radical I. I. Petrunkevich back into the official fold. Shipov for his part saw the chance of influencing the Tsar through Mirsky. Both men understood each other well; what neither understood was that both were almost equally out of touch with current reality.

It was not simply that the revolutionaries were gaining influence in the factories, among the intelligentsia and elsewhere: this was understood and could be combated, it was thought, by enlightened co-operation between zemstvos and central government. The new and runaway development was the increasing readiness, even eagerness, of reform-minded liberals to unite with revolutionary parties in total hostility to the regime. It was a development most clearly expressed in the emergence in the immediate aftermath of Plehve's murder of the deeply respected but uneasy, alienating, damaging figure of P. N. Milyukov.

Milyukov, born in 1859, was a professor of history, the son of an accomplished architect, raised in the liberal tradition, taught by the great Klyuchevsky, endowed with a first-class brain and profoundly imbued with what he understood to be the Western democratic ideal. Unfortunately he proved to be as rigid, as absolutist, as hectoring, in his demands as Lenin himself. After suffering exile, more than one spell in prison, and much petty-minded harassment on trumped-up charges (mainly he was accused of being a bad influence on his students), he was allowed back into circulation after ten years, now wholly convinced that the salvation of Russia lay in the creation of an elective parliament, or constituent assembly. Since Nicholas would never conceivably agree to this, then Nicholas must go. Thus it was that while the best-respected zemstvo leaders and the moderates of the Union of Liberation pinned their hopes on a gradual but steady development of persuasion of popular participation in government, Milyukov, for whom liberalism meant not slow organic growth but the springing into existence of a parliament like Minerva fully armed, decided that the first task was to sweep away everything that stood in the path of such a consummation. This meant destroying the regime. And if the destruction of the autocracy was the first task, then it followed that the proper, if temporary, allies for all good liberals were the extreme radicals and revolutionaries. It was at a special conference of a majority of radical and revolutionary groups held in Paris in September 1904 that Milyukov formally subscribed to a resolution calling for the overthrow of the autocracy and the installation of 'a free democratic system on the basis of universal suffrage'. But even earlier than that, unconsciously echoing the words used by Witte from the opposite corner of the ring, he had declared: 'Between autocracy and constitutionalism there is no halfway house'.[1] Thus it was that this very upright but overbearing man, this very contradiction of liberalism, the doctrinaire liberal, found himself in odd company thereafter. He was embarked on a course as champion of the liberal cause which it was his fate to undermine to its final destruction by more practically-minded men who knew all about halfway houses: what Lenin was to ensure was that there should be no halfway house between one autocracy and another.

It was not only in Paris that conferences were being held. Inside Russia itself the second half of the year, and particularly the final months, were marked by an extraordinary and increasingly open demonstration of the way in which the ideal of constitutional government of some kind had taken hold of 'society', including many sober-minded individuals who would not have dreamt of having any truck with radicals or revolutionaries. The process whereby in so short a time it came to be taken almost for granted that critics of the system could speak their minds with impunity is almost beyond analysis. It began for all practical purposes when the well-meaning but uncomprehending Svyatopolk-Mirsky showed that what he meant by concessions to liberalism was minimal change within the rigid framework of the autocracy. It was accelerated by the bad news from Manchuria as Kuropatkin's first offensive failed and Port Arthur was directly threatened. It was stimulated by the felt but unexpressed need on the part of the moderates to counter the radical extremists by putting forward some sort of a positive programme instead of on the one hand simply exhorting the Government to action and on the other offering counsels of moderation to the impatient. By an overwhelming majority vote the Union of Liberation, though far from subscribing to Milyukov's doctrine of collaboration with the extreme Left, decided to call on all zemstvos and all professional bodies to organise special conferences and 'banquets' (formal public meetings being prohibited) at which resolutions calling for constitutional government would be passed. Early in October Shipov himself presided over a special conference of nation-wide zemstvo leaders in Moscow. It was illegal, and it had to change its meeting-place each day to keep a jump ahead of the police. But Mirsky knew about it and tolerated it. How indeed to stop it without invoking the full force of the emergency laws against a broad assembly of some of the most respected citizens in the land? Perhaps the mood would be all the better for the letting off of steam.

But the zemstvo leaders did not merely talk, they acted. On 9 November they delivered to Mirsky himself a document that came to be known as the Eleven Theses – an eleven-point resolution which demanded all the freedoms (of person, conscience, speech and assembly), the reorganisation of the zemstvos and the urban Dumas on strictly democratic lines, the repeal of the notorious 'state of emergency' laws (under which at least half the country was at that moment governed), and the setting up of a representative legislative assembly.[2]

Poor Mirsky, being unable to conceive that any responsible citizen could conceivably harbour such revolutionary desires, let alone express them, was taken completely aback. At the same time he had to suffer the anger of Nicholas, who was required to wrench his mind from contemplation of his military reverses on the other side of the world to face what must have seemed to him a grave and disloyal affront to the Crown on a scale which reduced the earlier offences of the liberal stalwarts of Tver to the point of insignificance. Angry as he was, however, he also for a moment lost his nerve. Reports from the police were pouring in telling him in effect that 'society' had gone off its collective head. All over the land the response to the Liberationists' appeal for conferences and banquets had been overwhelming, timid and tentative at first, then almost recklessly bold. All over the country meetings of sober citizens were putting on record demands far exceeding the modest conditions of the Eleven Theses. After consulting with brothers, cousins, uncles, courtiers and senators Nicholas showed himself willing to bend a little to the storm. And then retracted. For when in mid-December he issued his decree outlining 'measures for the improvement of the regulation of the State' it turned out to be more or less meaningless: vague promises of vague reforms to be considered in due course.[3] Such anodyne words were no longer enough; but the Tsar compounded his offence by coupling his inadequate assurances with a warning couched in minatory terms to the zemstvos to mind their own business and keep quiet about all matters outside their immediate jurisdiction.[4] Alexander II had been able to talk like that. Alexander III had found it unnecessary to do so. But times had changed, and the liberals were not going to be told that the very constitution of society had nothing to do with them. What they did not know was that Nicholas had sruck from the original draft of the decree as agreed by the State Council a clause granting a really important concession: the Council itself was to be reorganised to include members directly elected by the zemstvos. Nobody except Pobedonostsev, who egged him on, knew that Nicholas had gone behind the back of all his advisers to delete from the decree the one point that mattered – and, at the same time, to issue his crass warning. Svyatopolk-Mirsky was so appalled when he read the published decree that he tried in vain to resign.[5] Nicholas had finally proved himself to all who knew the inside story unfit to rule.

Within a matter of days he was to prove it to the country at large. His deception of his own Imperial Council was proclaimed to them on 12 December. On 21 December (O.S.) Port Arthur fell, piling national humiliation on national anger. On 9 January the Tsar demonstrated that he could not even receive a petition from the workers of St Petersburg without shooting them down in the streets.

Of course Nicholas did not do the shooting himself, or even order it; but he allowed it to happen. He is supposed to have been a man who detested violence, and no doubt he would have found it hard to wring the neck of a chicken. The fact remains that his diary, his letters, his marginalia, are sprinkled with exclamations of zestful approval of acts of violence on the part of his subordinates great and small. His scribbled words, violent in themselves, encouraged violence and never rebuked it, whether violence against the Jews, or violence against strikers and other demonstrators. His shrinking from personal violence, one may believe, meant no more than his shrinking from telling the truth to his ministers and advisers. It is desirable to be clear about this. Nicholas was not fit to rule, and by

1905 he had finally demonstrated that his conduct after Khodynka Field was a fair sample of what was to come. That he was a dear and loving father of his family is not in question. And very soon now he was to be faced with the tragic and desperately painful burden laid upon his shoulders by the discovery that the infant Tsarevich was a haemophiliac. For after ten years of married life, after bearing four daughters in succession, Alexandra Feodorovna, amid scenes of almost hysterical emotion, had given birth to a son and heir in July 1904. But although the stresses of the Tsar's private life contributed much to what appeared to be the collapse of his authority and the delivery of Russia into the hands of the Tsaritsa's favourites, venal or vile, towards the close of his reign, that authority in fact never existed. He had nothing to stand on but his inherited majesty.

2

His inherited majesty received a knock from which it never fully recovered on what came to be known as 'Bloody Sunday' on 9 January 1905. After that there was a new cry to add to 'Down with the Autocracy!'

'Down with the Tsar-Murderer!'

By that time, without anyone yet realising it, there was a revolution in being.

The explosion when it came owed nothing directly to the liberals or even to the radical and revolutionary intelligentsia, although all these between them had in past months been creating an atmosphere in which politically motivated individuals, or groups, among strikers or demonstrators could shift the emphasis of slogans from economic to ideological demands. And this is what seems to have happened on 9 January when the petition which most of the demonstrators conceived to be a plea to the Little Father for an improvement of their material conditions and the punishment of their oppressors turned out to be a set of revolutionary demands.[6]

The hero of the occasion was yet another of those strange, ambivalent figures moving obscurely between two or more opposed worlds whose activity does so much to obscure and confuse the turning points of Russian history. Father George Gapon was a priest and one time prison chaplain, an associate of Zubatov too, who after the dismantling of Zubatov's empire, for some reason which has never been made plain, was allowed by Plehve himself to build up an organisation called the Assembly of Russian Factory and Mill Workers, financed by police funds, and dedicated to improving living and working conditions. Gapon fancied himself as a worker-priest and also, more justly, as an orator. Small, but possessed of a magnetic personality and a good voice, he was intoxicated by the discovery that he could lead, and although he had started as a police agent, building up an organisation of workers which no Jew or socialist was allowed to penetrate, insisting on the holiness of the Tsar, who alone could bring to heel corrupt and greedy officials and factory bosses, soon he had started to identify himself with those same workers and, in effect, to lead them in revolt.

What happened on 'Bloody Sunday' arose from a strike at the great Putilov works in St Petersburg which was concerned not with politics, but with the management's alleged victimisation of certain members of Gapon's organisation. The strike spread. Gapon conceived the idea, or had it put into his head, of a personal appeal to the Tsar. He organised a monster demonstration which was to bear, in all humility and reverence, a petition to lay at the feet of Nicholas Alexandrovich in the Winter Palace. Revolutionary in its demands, the petition was almost abject in its phrasing. Most of the demonstrators lacked even an inkling of an idea of the inflammatory nature of their plea: they thought they were prostrating themselves before the Tsar and begging him for his protection. It was 1825 all over again, with mutinous soldiers convinced by the rebel leaders that they were calling for the true Tsar, Constantine, when what they were really calling for was a constitution. Gapon, of course, knew what he was doing, but it has never been decided whether he was master or tool. Since he was very shortly, in exile, to show himself megalomanic to the point of insanity it does not seem to matter very much. The idea that he had become so uplifted by the discovery of his power over large audiences that he believed himself to be the chosen one who would, on behalf of the Almighty, open the eyes of the Tsar to his true path is not in itself farfetched. On the other hand, the duplicity and peasant cunning he displayed when being lionised in Geneva by the émigré revolutionaries suggests that at heart the man was more charlatan than man of God.[7]

Be that as it may, Gapon certainly convinced himself that he would be allowed to march to the Winter Palace and present his petition unmolested.[8]

He knew his march was illegal, but officialdom and the police had had every opportunity to warn against it and had not done so. On 8 January Gapon himself informed the Government of the nature, time and route of the proposed march. And nothing happened. Neither he nor anybody else knew that a most peculiar sort of paralysis had fallen upon the Government and the municipal authorities. Even when Mirsky at last decided to order the arrest of Gapon and a score or so of his lieutenants, the order was not obeyed by the Prefect of Police, General I. A. Fullon, another rather indecisive gentleman not unlike Mirsky himself in character. Even the Tsar's senior uncle, the Grand Duke Vladimir, military commandant of St Petersburg and normally savage in his views about demonstrators and subversives, refrained from urging Mirsky to take action to stop the performance while there was still time or from warning Nicholas of what was in store. Was he hoping that the march would indeed take place so that his troops might teach the workers a lesson? Nicholas himself slipped out of St Petersburg to be with his family at Tsarskoe Selo, where he now spent almost all his time: nobody, apparently, had seen fit to tell him of the magnitude of the challenge: there was trouble, he was told, with a subversive priest who was agitating among the strikers. He would be dealt with. It was not until the last minute that counter-measures were worked out, and these seemed calculated to encourage the largest possible disturbance to be put down with the greatest possible amount of bloodshed.

There were to be five columns of marchers, all converging on the great square in front of the Winter Palace. The authorities knew their routes because Gapon had told them. No attempt was made to break up the columns and divert them early in their march. The troops were so disposed that they would come into collision with the marchers only when each column was nearing the Palace Square; so that if there was trepidation in the hearts of many of the demonstrators as they set forth, very soon their fears were quietened, and all were swept by the euphoria of peaceful togetherness as they shambled along behind chanting priests, holding aloft banners, holy ikons, portraits of the Tsar: 200,000 of them in those five columns, singing hymns and unarmed, the main column led by Gapon himself in his priestly vestments. As they marched the city police actually cleared the way for them and held up traffic, while onlookers made the sign of the cross and bowed as the ikons went by. It was not until the separate columns were within sight of their goal, some of them already converging, that they found their way barred by cordons of troops and police. They were ordered to stop, but by now were so sure of themselves, so lifted above themselves indeed, that they paid no attention – until the leading files were forced back and broken up by a squadron of cavalry. But they reformed and came on, even when the order to fire was given – not over the heads of the crowd but into it. It took repeated volleys to break the momentum of the column and disperse it in terror. Gapon was among the first to flee.

This is the picture of 'Bloody Sunday' which has become legendary – masses of unarmed, hymn-singing petitioners being shot down as they approached the Winter Palace. But it was not so much this initial massacre that filled Russian hearts with a bitterness against the Tsar that was quite new, but rather what happened next. What happened next was that the Commander of the Guards, Prince Vasilchikov, who was responsible for the disposition of the troops, had held back a considerable reserve from his 20,000 men to keep watch over the Palace Square and adjoining buildings in case the demonstrators succeeded in breaking through the main barricades. And this reserve was still posted long after the processions had been shattered and dispersed: nobody had told them that the danger was past. Later in the afternoon, however, little groups of workers on their way home after the disaster, mingled with indignant students and inquisitive passers-by, began to penetrate into the square from the Alexander Gardens to see what was happening. Vasilchikov, fearing a dangerous build-up of a hostile mob, ordered the crowd to disperse. Some turned away, but others came back to jeer at the soldiery. So after warning shots there was yet more shooting and killing, shooting and killing that before long spilled out into the Nevsky Prospect itself.

In this way a peaceful demonstration was transformed into the first act of a revolution. For Nicholas now began to lose his magic for that mass of simple-minded workers who were not caught up in the revolutionary movement but simply looked to the Tsar for succour. A monarch cannot allow his personal guards to shoot down in droves in front of his own house an unarmed assembly of working-men, to say nothing of harmless onlookers, and continue to be revered as the source of all wisdom and kindness. A great deal has been written about who was most to blame for 'Bloody Sunday'. It seems clear enough. Svyatopolk-Mirsky for his incompetence and lack of understanding; General Fullon for his failure of nerve which prevented him from acting in time; the Grand Duke and Prince Vasilchikov for the savagery of their reaction, whether impelled by panic or calculation – all these were to blame. But the man who was most to blame was the man who had least immediately to do with the affair, who had an alibi, who was the least fitted to understand the true inwardness of the rising tide of dissent, but who insisted all the same that he was the sole repository of all authority:

'To the Emperor of Russia belongs the supreme autocratic and unlimited power. Not only fear, but also conscience commanded by God Himself, is the basis of obedience to this power.'

Article One of the Fundamental Laws was still very much in force. Either the Tsar was responsible for everything that happened in Russia, including his absence from the Winter Palace and the massacre in front of it, or else he was a hollow shell. 'A sad day', he was to write in his diary that night. 'Serious disorders took place in St Petersburg when the workers tried to get to the Winter Palace. In several parts of the city troops were compelled to fire: there were many killed and wounded. Lord, how sad and painful.'[9]

That was one way of putting it.

3

To be fair to Nicholas, although he had no clear conception of the enormity of the events of 9 January, he at last began to see that problems had arisen which could not be solved by simple police action. At the same time he rejected the urgings of some that he should publicly dissociate himself from the actions of his troops. Svyatopolk-Mirsky was immediately replaced by Count Bulygin, a colourless, orthodox bureaucrat whose thinking had reached much the same level as his master's – namely that straight repression would no longer do, but what to put in its place? What indeed? Nicholas was to display the poverty of his imagination almost immediately. He accepted the suggestion of his new Governor-General of St Petersburg, General D. F. Trepov, a heavy-handed but honest police-chief, that it would be a good thing for him to meet a deputation of factory workers to assure them that in spite of appearances to the contrary he felt for them; but when the deputation appeared before him amid the eighteenth-century splendours of Tsarskoe Selo he found himself chiding them like children, quite unable to change the old, old record: they had been led astray by wicked men, but he, Nicholas, knew that they were good and loyal at heart and would strive to make up for the harm they had done. This meeting, and the Tsar's words, made no impression at all, but Nicholas himself was so moved by his own unprecedented act of condescension that he easily believed Trepov (who himself believed what he said) that it had been an epoch-making occasion.

A little more serious was the commission of enquiry set up under a member of the Council of State. It was not a very effective commission, but the fact that it was set up at all indicated that in Nicholas's eyes there was something that called for an enquiry.

Activities of this kind could be only peripheral to a Russia that positively seethed with indignation and frustration. Strikes broke out with perfect spontaneity wherever men worked in factories, mines, dockyards. The burning anger at the events of 9 January was like the breaking of a great wave of resentment, augmented by domestic misery and disgust at the conduct of the Japanese War. From Warsaw to Samara, from Helsingfors to Tiflis, almost a half-million workers had downed tools before the month was out. They were joined by the students in their thousands, so that for all practical purposes the universities ceased to function. And surprisingly often their professors and teachers stood by the students. Sixteen members of the very official Academy of Sciences issued a formal declaration calling for a change of government. Three hundred and twenty-six professors and university lecturers joined them in a written demand calling for the power to make laws and check the workings of the bureaucracy to be given into the hands of 'freely elected representatives of the people'. More than a thousand distinguished scholars all over the country endorsed this 'Statement of the 342'. When the Directorate of the Russian Musical Society came down with a heavy hand on the Conservatoire students in St Petersburg, the man who found himself labelled not merely as a revolutionary but as an inciter of student revolt was the sixty-one-year-old Rimsky-Korsakov, now the revered doyen of Russian composers. All he had done was to write a letter to the Press criticising the Directorate for its failure to understand his students' motives. It is a commentary on the hysteria of the time that the Directorate was goaded into dismissing him. The uproar of protest was deafening. All the same, the police managed to stop a concert of Rimsky-Korsakov's work put on by his students, and blocked off the stage by lowering the safety curtain. Further performances were banned. The composer Taneyev resigned from the All Russian Musical Society in protest, and he was soon followed by Glazunov and Liadov.[10]

Nor was it by any means a matter for workers, students and intellectuals. One of the most remarkable episodes was the unheard-of decision of the Merchants' Club to close its doors to all Guards officers because of the part they had played in the massacre.

But even while Nicholas was showing that he understood the need for conciliatory action he still did not perceive the need for speed. His mood was in fact more reasonable, his mind more open than at any time in his career. When, for example, his Minister of Agriculture, Alexander Yermolev, a man of apparently nondescript character and inconsiderable talents, took his life in his hands and delivered to his sovereign at his weekly audience a solemn and circumstantial warning of the kind of trouble that was brewing, the reasons for it, and the sort of concessions that would have to be made, Nicholas accepted this unprecedented lecture with calm good-humour. But he seemed to feel that his broad-mindedness and generosity in so doing were in themselves action enough for the time being. He allowed things to drift until the shock of the murder of his uncle, the Grand Duke Sergei, who was also the Tsaritsa's brother-in-law.

The assassination (by no means the first attempt to kill this very much hated man, until recently Governor-General of Moscow) was carried out by a student called Kalyaev, but, like the killing of Plehve it had been organised by Boris Savinkov and the police agent Yevno Azev. For obvious reasons Nicholas was hit especially hard. Only the day before the murder (4 February) he had been in session with his Council of Ministers trying to work out a formula which would announce the promise of an elected advisory assembly. After his uncle's death he hurried on with the drafting of a series of documents intended to take the country by storm: a

Manifesto to his people; a Decree, or Ukase, addressed to the Senate; a Rescript, or personal instruction, to the Minister of the Interior, Bulygin. The general sense of this broadside was the momentous (for Nicholas, revolutionary) decision to permit the establishment of a consultative assembly, consisting of 'elected representatives of the people to take part in the preliminary discussion of legislation'. This was the formal message to Bulygin, who would be responsible for setting up the machinery. The message to the Senate affirmed the right of all citizens to be heard by the Crown and invited suggestions for 'the improvement of the public welfare'. Unfortunately the impact of these proposals, which marked the first retreat from the 'immutable' principles of the Tsar's forebears, was muffled by an apparently contradictory emphasis in the Rescript on precisely that immutability and, above all, by a positive tirade denouncing all those who offended against the Fundamental Laws as treasonable and summoning 'all right-thinking persons of all classes and conditions' to uphold the throne. It was afterwards discovered that Nicholas, urged on, of course, by Pobedonostsev (but it was almost this old man's last effective action) had inserted these passages into the draft at the last moment, without informing his ministers. So what was society to believe? That the Tsar was seriously prepared to consult with his subjects? Or that his will was to remain absolute and unquestioned?

In fact, even had the Tsar's intentions been unambiguously stated, it would have been too late. Already the moderates who a few months before would have regarded the promise of a consultative assembly as a major step towards the millennium were beginning to join in the radical clamour for nothing less than a constitution and a constituent assembly to be elected by 'universal, direct, equal and secret franchise'. The Tsar's gesture, half-hearted as it was, could not have been more unfortunately timed. All these documents were published on 18 February, just a week before the sad and humiliating end to the battle of Mukden with its 90,000 casualties. Ever since the fall of Port Arthur public indignation had been growing at the corruption and profiteering in the supply services, the bad leadership in the field (though Kuropatkin himself was a popular hero), and the usual catalogue of military insufficiencies. With the retreat behind Mukden indignation came to the boil. In March and April almost all the zemstvo members, some reluctantly still, fell in behind the formal demand for a constitution and were now joined by the professional unions which Milyukov had been successfully wooing. With the catastrophe of Tsushima in the following month the train was lit for a major explosion. And even while the moderates were still striving to keep lines open to the Tsar and prevent a final and irreparable collision between the liberals and the system, the workers were taking charge.

The agonisings of liberals and radicals now seemed almost irrelevant beside the sudden, convulsive movement of the mob. They had tried so hard. And a measure of their almost obsessive single-mindedness is the fact that even after Tsushima domestic politics still came first. While Milyukov on the left suceeded in combining all the professional unions into one imposing Union of Unions, a completely unheard-of and illegal grouping, on the right the moderate zemstvoists were giving the monarchy a last chance. On 6 June they sent a fourteen-man delegation to Tsarskoe Selo to pledge the loyalty of the zemstvos and urge the imperative neces- sity for the establishment of a legislative assembly. It was in fact the first time that Nicholas had ever met these intelligent, responsible, deeply troubled and patriotic men. But he was unable to recognise them for what they were, received them politely but without lively interest, and sent them away empty. It was the last chance he was to have of winning the more sober elements of 'society' to his side. He was unable to recognise either the occasion or the men for what they were.

Meanwhile, immediately after Tsushima, Nicholas had appointed General Trepov to be Assistant Minister of the Interior with personal control over the police. This made him virtual dictator in the Tsar's name, with more power than his nominal chief, Bulygin – whose resignation Nicholas, however, refused to accept. It was Trepov who, as Governor- General of St Petersburg, had dreamed up the idea of the workers' depu- tation to Tsarskoe Selo for a reconciliation with the Tsar after 'Bloody Sunday'. He was a curious mixture of a repressive disciplinarian, an ingenious fool and an intriguer. He liked to think of himself as a man who knew how to talk to the troops. The troops in this case were striking and demonstrating workers, who did not take at all kindly to the General's attempts to cajole and frighten them into remembering their better selves (but it was at least to Trepov's credit that he recognised that factory workers were in fact human beings). There were riots all over the place; and where there were riots there were shootings. In Lodz alone some three hundred were killed and a thousand wounded on the streets in three successive days of turbulence (and this was only the climax of weeks of sporadic violence). Soon, however, all lesser incidents were put in the shade by the major upheaval in the great Black Sea port of Odessa. After nearly three months of fairly decorous strikes the first blood was shed when an individual demonstrator fired at a squad of Cossacks, who at once retaliated with their characteristically savage and exhibitionist violence. Then the storm broke, and for two days and nights there was civil war, with members of the Black Hundreds joining forces with the police and the military, and secret revolutionaries of all the parties emerging from hiding to organise, lead, or egg on the strikers. On 15 June after many deaths and much destruction by fire the city was put under martial law.

And it was on 15 June that the pride of the Black Sea fleet, the very new battle-cruiser *Potemkin*, put into Odessa harbour flying the red flag. The mutiny had been an independent operation. Though obviously influenced by the climate of the times, including Tsushima, the ratings of the *Potemkin* had in fact risen against their officers in protest against an issue of bad meat, though obviously there was a great deal more than this behind the revolt, which involved the shooting, throwing overboard or locking up in the cells of every single officer on board. When the *Potemkin* arrived in port (the mutiny took place when the ship had been detached from the fleet for a separate exercise) the ring-leaders, who all said they were Social Democrats, were soon in consultation with secret party members ashore. But plans for concerted action came to nothing. That night the street fighting in the city reached a new pitch and there were scenes of major carnage, with some two thousand dead, as the military and the police fought hard to drive the revolutionaries out of the parts of the city they had mastered. But the sailors in the *Potemkin* could not land and looked on helplessly.

It was not until next day that a detail was allowed ashore to bury one of their comrades who had died in the mutiny. They were fired on by the police, and their comrades on board retaliated by opening up with the ship's big guns on the city. Without their officers the gunners did not know how to lay the guns correctly and the shells went so wide of their targets that they soon gave up. The third day for the mutineers was also ignominious. The rest of the fleet was due to enter harbour, and the plan was to give the signal to their comrades in the other ships to rise against their officers too. But only one ship responded, and she was run aground. The others were withdrawn by their admiral who had no desire to be blasted out of the water by the *Potemkin*'s superior guns (he did not know that her shooting was so bad), and the *Potemkin* was left alone. Not knowing what else to do, the mutineers put to sea and sailed their ship to Constanza in Roumania, where they scuttled her by opening the sea-cocks and fled inland.

This was the substance of the great *Potemkin* legend. The real fighting was done by the people of Odessa without any help from the fleet, and it was at Odessa that a number of dedicated revolutionaries who had been praying for an armed uprising had their baptism of fire. But not of course their leaders, who were all far away in western Europe arguing about ways and means, Bolsheviks and Mensheviks locked in venomous conflict. Nominally the conflict was about the extent to which they should co-operate with S.R.s, radicals and liberals. And, indeed, there were genuine differences in this matter, the Mensheviks being in effect collaborationists with the bourgeois reformers, the Bolsheviks seeking to use them only to devour them at once. But behind these high-sounding theoretical arguments lay a question that was deeper, more elemental, more real: who was to run the Social Democratic Party? And the real split was between those who accepted Lenin as the unquestioned leader, and those who questioned his infallibility and his right to lay down the law. The number of Lenin's followers, of Bolsheviks, that is to say, was far from constant. It went up and down. There were to be moments before the final amazing triumph in October 1917 when Lenin was so isolated that of all the considerable revolutionaries he was the solitary Bolshevik. This did not deter him.

And now, in the summer of 1905, he was not to be diverted from his doctrinal power struggle within the party – not even by the thought that while he could find nothing better to do than pursue a slanderous vendetta against his old mentor and friend, Plekhanov, and pronounce anathema on Martov, the closest of his contemporaries, now leader of the Mensheviks, the workers whose cause he claimed as the sole justification for his being were fighting and dying on the quayside of Odessa and elsewhere. Many of the most distinguished international socialists, especially in Germany, were shocked by the spectacle of the man who proclaimed himself the true leader of all Russian Marxists wasting so much of his own (and other people's) energy on endless introverted quarrelling, while Russia herself seemed to be poised on the very brink of a titanic upheaval.[11] They would have been still more shocked had they been able to see the incessant flood of nagging, admonitory letters on pettifogging organisational points directed in Lenin's name by his devoted, humourless wife, secretary and chief of staff, Nadezhda Krupskaya, to the Bolshevik committees working underground in Russia.[12] They would have been shocked yet again had they known the true strength of the active Bolsheviks in Russia in 1905 when Lenin in Geneva was claiming to be the natural leader of the whole revolutionary movement. At a conspiratorial dinner given by members of the revolutionary organisation of Guards officers, referred to earlier, the question was finally put: in the event of an armed uprising how many fighting revolutionaries could the party leaders promise? Immediately the S.R.s promised 10,000; the S.D.s (Bolsheviks and Mensheviks together) could only muster a few hundred.[13]

In a word, the revolutionary turbulence of 1905 owed next to nothing to the professional revolutionaries, and when some of these came forward later to exploit the situation, they were new men thrown up to meet the hour. After the suppression of the Odessa riots and the failure of the Black Sea mutiny (but the commanding admiral was so apprehensive that he put his fleet into dock and sent five thousand of his ratings and petty-officers on indefinite leave in order to replace them with more reliable crews) there was no more major violence until the autumn. Assassinations were frequent. But army and police had for the time being established their ascendancy over the masses. The ferment of dissent was kept working by the liberals and radicals of 'society'.

On 6 July, driven to desperation by the polite snubbing they had received from Nicholas in May, the zemstvo leaders, defying Trepov's explicit ban, mounted in Moscow a united conference of all zemstvos and urban Dumas. When, after three days, the police finally intervened and closed the proceedings down, the extremists among them, those that is to say who demanded nothing less than a constitutional monarchy with a sovereign constituent assembly, held together under the leadership of Milyukov and formed themselves into the first political (as distinct from revolutionary) party in Imperial Russia: the Constitutional Democrats, or Cadets, as they came to be called. And the first act of the Cadets, who were to play so prominent and damaging a part in the fight for freedom in the years to come, was to formalise the position already adopted by Milyukov himself: they declared themselves ready to join in action with what they called 'the broad masses'. The liberals had sought to work for reform in collaboration with the Tsar; the Tsar had rebuffed them. Themselves, they were powerless. Was it not therefore immoral to refuse to join forces with those who had the power and would use it in the attempt to achieve the end desired by all right-thinking liberals? It is easy to condemn the short-sightedness of these turn-of-the-century Russian liberals. But at least they were pioneers in error. They were exploring wholly new ground, with no help from anyone. Nobody then had heard of the young lady of Riga. And if today, after a lifetime of mourning the fate of comrades who went for rides on tigers, latterday radicals, liberals, 'progressives' to use their own quite meaningless label, can still take up the cry *pas d'ennemis à gauche*, how much more tempting must this view have been to the Milyukovs in their all but virginal innocence?

There were some liberals, nevertheless, who contemplated this development with misgiving. The most subtly intelligent of them all, a young lawyer, V. A. Maklakov, diagnosed the situation perfectly. Looking back in his memoirs (which were not published until 1954), he could recall the day when it seemed blasphemy to question the people's will. Which means that by the middle of 1905 for any intellectual to question the proposition that all problems could be solved by the importation into Russia of the British parliamentary system was to breach an absolute taboo – as in our own immediate time for any individual even to wonder aloud about the possibility of fundamental genetic differences between different races.

Maklakov saw very clearly that the liberals had no power of their own, that they might achieve great things 'in alliance with . . . the established regime' when it was (as it was in the autumn of 1905) ready to make concessions. But if the regime repulsed the advances of the liberals, then they would have to join forces with 'the only real power, that of Acheron'. If this happened, then revolution one day would inevitably ensue, and liberalism would be the loser in either victory or defeat.[14]

This, of course, is what happened. Except that in the autumn of 1905 it was the liberals, in the form of the Cadet party, who repulsed the advances of an established regime ready to make concessions because, said Milyukov, the concessions were not enough. And by that time even the cool, detached, truly liberal (in the Western sense) Maklakov had ridden down his own scruples and, against his better judgement, joined Milyukov.

4

While all this was going on Nicholas had been seriously addressing himself to the problems involved in honouring the Bulygin Rescript – in setting up a consultative assembly, that is. He was very far from being able to bring his whole mind to bear on this matter because during that chaotic and terrifying month of June when most of his subjects seemed to be preparing for civil strife he had been compelled to think a great deal about the winding up of the war with Japan. This affair had been brought to a climax five days after Tsushima on the initiative of that eccentric potentate William II of Germany, who, at heart very much less warlike than he usually sounded, was now seriously worried about the chances of revolution in Russia and feared for the personal safety of the Tsar. America, like Britain, was alarmed at the sudden emergence of Japan as a major Pacific power and thought it time to put a check on her advance. France was distressed by the beating her ally, Russia, was receiving. So when the American President, Theodore Roosevelt, took his cue from the German Emperor and offered to mediate, sighs of relief went up all round the world – not least from Japan herself. Having administered a thrashing to one of the great powers of the Western world, and in so doing turned upside down all past assumptions about the proper relationship between East and West and Yellow and White, she was only too pleased to conclude a magnanimous peace before she was totally ruined and exhausted.

Not that the fighting ceased immediately. Kuropatkin was convinced that Russia was bound to win if she continued to send her own hordes against Japan with her limited manpower. No doubt he was right; but

Nicholas knew that neither the people nor the peasant army would stand for much more sacrifice. He wanted peace; but he was determined not to concede an inch of Russian territory or pay a kopek in indemnity. Clearly he needed a man of exceptional parts to conduct the peace negotiations, and he was forced reluctantly and bitterly to recognise that the only man who measured up to the task was that same Witte whom he had sacked two years before largely for his opposition to the Far Eastern policy which had ended in war. So Witte it was who went off with plenipotentiary powers to represent Russia at Portsmouth, New Hampshire.

The American invitation was received on 8 June, but the conference did not open until 10 August. Then Witte performed prodigies at great speed. His master's conditions were obviously impossible to sustain, even though Japan was eager to end the war, even though America did all she could to minimise Russia's humiliation. Japanese military and economic overlordship in Korea was formally recognised. Japan received the southern half of Sakhalin island, a territory used by Russia only as a convict settlement. Russia ceded the lease of Port Arthur and the Liaotung Peninsula, a stretch of the South Manchurian Railway, and all Russian industrial properties and concessions in the peninsula. The treaty was signed on 5 September. Witte was rewarded by being made a count. Theodore Roosevelt in due course became the first head of state to receive the Nobel Peace Prize for his part in the affair. After a leisurely journey home Count Witte arrived in St Petersburg on 15 September to find the country on the edge of a new upheaval, with himself very shortly to be cast as saviour.

Two things had happened in his absence. On 6 August a special conference (Grand Dukes, ministers, some others), convened among the fountains and cascades, the rococo fantasies of Peterhof and presided over by the Tsar, had announced the conditions and procedures for the election and duties of the new consultative assembly, or State Duma. For the first time elected representatives of the Russian people would be permitted to examine new laws and comment on them to the Tsar through the Council of State. To the conservatives this spelt red revolution. To the liberals and radicals it was an insult; but they were divided all the same as to whether to boycott the elections, whether to co-operate with the Duma in the hope of better things, or whether to seek to destroy it. The electoral roll was so rigged that the urban workers and the professional classes (including the Third Element, the professionals of the zemstvos) were scarcely represented. The assembly was to be heavily weighted in favour of property owners in town and country and the peasants. The peasants were supposed to be unassailably loyal to the throne. And this alone showed how very much out of touch the Government was with current reality. For all through the spring and early summer peasant unrest and peasant violence had been growing. Starting with the usual burnings and pillagings it was beginning to take on a political flavour as the Socialist Revolutionaries made their influence felt. And in May things had moved so fast that a Peasants' Union was established. All these activities had been overshadowed by the rioting in the cities, and minimised by local officials who, successful enough in putting down their own local revolts, were individually and collectively unaware of what was going on in other areas.

The next thing that showed the Government's ignorance was the quite extraordinary decision announced on 27 August to restore to the universities that autonomy which had been taken from them in 1884. Since that date a constant outcry had been kept up for a return to the *status quo*, and now in that difficult summer of 1905 Nicholas and his advisers seem to have believed that in gratitude for this concession the students would stop striking and go back to their lecture rooms. They went back to their lecture rooms, certainly (although the S.R.s and the S.D.s both shortsightedly urged them to continue striking), but to create a level and intensity of agitation possible to sustain only in sacred enclaves where the police could not penetrate. While the students found their own sanctuary in their assembly halls and lecture rooms, they were also able to throw open their doors to agitators, to orators of all kinds, to illegal revolutionaries, who in that privileged and inviolable forum could say what they liked. And in the wake of the speakers new audiences came crowding in to hear them. As Nicholas himself saw it: 'God knows what has happened in the universities. Every kind of riff-raff walked in from the streets, riot was loudly proclaimed – nobody seemed to care.'[15] No work was done. The debate was continuous and endless. And more and more the voice of the moderates was drowned by the extremists. And very soon the most extreme demands of the most extreme constitutionalists were outbid by the open calls for an armed uprising.

It was this sudden and unforeseen opportunity for nation-wide agitation which led directly into the new series of strikes which spread throughout the Empire all through September. These began harmlessly enough with a printers' strike in Moscow. But by the end of the first week in October St Petersburg itself was paralysed and the Government effectively neutralised. There was no transport, gas, water, electricity; all shops were closed; there were no newspapers; all factories were at a standstill. It was the start of a general strike on a stupendous scale, a total shut-down of all activity. Even the *corps de ballet* at the Maryinsky Theatre gaily and excitedly joined in. And it happened with no trade union organisation, with no central direction – a simultaneous and spontaneous downing of tools over all the vast area of the Empire. And when tools were downed and shops were closed and trains ceased to run, the workers took to the streets and marched and counter-marched with banners and militant slogans.

How militant, too! At first those groups of workers who had a coherent idea of what they wanted presented perfectly reasonable demands for better pay, shorter hours, reforms of this and that. But within a matter of days the street demonstrations had transformed a strike into a revolution. The railway workers now were demanding the immediate proclamation of a democratic republic, the transfer of the arms of the police and the military to the workers. And so far gone was the mood of irresponsible euphoria that even the professional unions came out in support of this fantasy. Milyukov liberals, in a word, were now demanding that the workers should be armed against the state. In some cities the mob was already in charge, manning barricades in the streets. The police went into hiding.

On 9 October Nicholas, fatalistically calm as always, but foreseeing the end and surrounded by panic-stricken advisers, was forced once more to call upon the man he so much disliked, the newly created Count Witte. And four days after Witte took over he was faced with a wholly new development, the establishment in the heart of St Petersburg of a workers' council, or soviet, originally an elected body of forty delegates each said to represent 500 workers, set up to co-ordinate and lead the masses – in a word, to govern the city in the absence of all normal communications, chains of command, and so on. The workers' soviet was not invented in St Petersburg. The original concept, which had such a bitter future in store, had first arisen six months earlier, when the textile workers at Ivanovno-Voznesensk staged a strike that was almost a little revolution in itself and called its *ad hoc* strike committee a soviet. Soon the idea was taken up elsewhere. But it was natural for the St Petersburg soviet to be seen as the progenitor of all soviets and the headquarters of revolution. It was, when all was said, organising an alternative government in the very seat of government. And very soon it was to win especial fame as the arena in which the young Trotsky, then calling himself a Menshevik, first appeared as the supreme demagogue of revolution – much to the disgruntlement of Lenin who had at last decided it was time for him to get back into Russia and assert himself, and was stuck in Stockholm fuming as he waited for a forged passport that did not come.

Dire as the situation was in St Petersburg, and swiftly as Moscow and other cities seemed to be advancing towards a similar paralysis, the worst threat of all lay elsewhere. From all over the country came reports of the peasants rising to burn and murder as never before since the days of Pugachev. It was no longer a question of what one might call selective incitement by S.R. agitators on the ground, but a widely based upheaval, a long pent-up explosion of discontent and desperation, which threatened to sweep the country and destroy all authority. And the most boding question of all was how would the army respond when peasant troops were ordered to shoot their brothers?

This was the fear which made Nicholas bow to Witte when the latter proposed an admission of defeat and a retreat from the principle of autocracy which the Tsar had sworn to uphold.

It was a bizarre situation. In the heart of St Petersburg the workers' soviet behaved like a noisy and unruly parliament, but a parliament acting with emergency powers. The Tsar and his family were marooned at Peterhof (they had not in fact dared set foot outside Peterhof or Tsarskoe Selo all the summer), which could now only be reached from St Petersburg by a short steamer trip. The hurried, repetitive consultations of the next few days were punctuated by the shuttling to and fro of ministers and senior officials, some of whom thought even Peterhof unsafe and urged the Imperial family to take refuge with the Dowager Empress's family in Copenhagen.

Witte, even before Nicholas asked him formally to take charge of the Government, had made up his mind what had to be done. It was too late, he believed, to stage a head-on collision between authority, resting on bayonets, and the people. Himself authoritarian by nature, he believed with passion that the proper, the only certain way to hold Russia together, vast, shambling, heterogeneous, backward as she was, was through autocratic rule. But the autocracy had been betrayed by a feeble autocrat who listened to irresponsible and sometimes sinister advisers. It would cost too much bloodshed to restore it, even if in fact the army could be relied upon. And to restore it for what? To be betrayed again by the same Tsar repeating his past mistakes . . . Therefore there was only one thing to do. This despiser of constitutionalism must press a constitution upon his master.

And this he did. He went about it cleverly, coldly, deviously. He offered Nicholas alternatives. I will be your Prime Minister, he said in effect, provided I am granted prime-ministerial powers under a constitutional monarchy. But there was still an argument for some sort of military dictatorship the validity of which he, Witte, was prepared to concede; he, however, could personally have no part in such a government. Nicholas was still fighting for his sacred inheritance, but he was now alone. He turned to the flaccid Goremykin; but Goremykin could only produce a feeble copy of Witte's scheme. He turned in desperation to his cousin the Grand Duke Nicholas, urging him to take over the Government as a military strong man. The Grand Duke refused: the story is that he took out his revolver and threatened to shoot himself on the spot if he was pressed any further. Nicholas gave way, put his destiny into the hands of Witte, and a few days later, on 17 October, issued the Imperial Manifesto whereby he formally turned himself into a constitutional monarch.[16] He did not believe it for a moment.

CHAPTER TWENTY-ONE

Stolypin and the Thirteenth Hour

I

WITTE saw farther and more clearly than any of the Tsar's advisers, but even he did not see clearly enough. The October Manifesto conceded more than anyone had demanded even a few months earlier, apart from revolutionaries and extreme radicals. It conceded liberty of conscience, freedom of speech, freedom to hold meetings, freedom of association. It guaranteed freedom from arbitrary arrest and imprisonment without trial. It promised a wide extension of the franchise in the elections to the new State Duma to include 'those classes who are now completely deprived of electoral rights'. It proclaimed 'the immutable principle that no law may come into force without the approval of the State Duma' and declared that the people's elected representatives would henceforward 'participate in supervising the legality of the actions of any appointed authorities'. Characteristically, Nicholas insisted against Witte's advice on introducing these revolutionary changes as a personal act of autocratic power.

What Witte did not see was that the liberals were now in a mood to reject any form of government short of a sovereign constituent assembly, or that the workers and revolutionaries were not going to abate their demands and surrender their intoxicating sense of mastery in return for the promise of a paper parliament by a monarch they distrusted absolutely. On the very day of the Manifesto the St Petersburg soviet had elected a responsible executive committee, which included representatives of the S.R.s and the S.D.s. On that day, too, the soviet managed to bring out the first issue of its own organ, *Izvestia (News)*, in which Trotsky declared his undying hostility to all representatives of the regime: 'The proletariat knows what it wants and what it does not want. It wants neither the police thug Trepov nor the liberal financial shark Witte, neither the wolf's snout nor the fox's tail. It spurns the police whip wrapped in the parchment of a constitution.'

The proletariat appeared to be widely in agreement with this ebullient young man's diagnosis of its wishes, and the peasants were feeling much the same. As if this was not enough, the subject nationalities, some of whom had been in a state of open revolt against St Petersburg throughout the summer, were quite ignored in the October Manifesto. Nobody would have expected Nicholas to exercise his imagination in this direction, but the failure of Witte to take account of the troubles in the Baltic States, in the Ukraine, in the Caucasus and Transcaucasia, in Turkestan and elsewhere, and to persuade the Tsar to make concessions indicated another blind spot in this remarkable man of the kind he had exhibited ten years earlier when in his single-track drive for industrialisation he ignored the condition of the countryside. He seems to have half-forgotten the minority nations. But Ukrainians, Georgians, Turcomans, Armenians, Latvians, Lithuanians and Esthonians, all of whom had been demanding with varying degrees of violence varying degrees of political or cultural autonomy (in Latvia a full-scale civil war was raging with the indigenous urban workers and the peasants united against the largely alien landowners, Baltic Germans) were quite excluded from the purview of the Manifesto, which recognised only Russians. Not even Finland received a special mention, although in fact the hated Finnish conscription law had been repealed earlier in the year, and in a special November Manifesto the Finns were to be granted not a constituent assembly, as they demanded, but an institution called the Constituent Senate, with authority to reorganise the Diet. Before that happened the extraordinary situation arose in which a Russian Governor-General of this weak but heroic country was forced to bolt from his residence in Helsingfors and seek sanctuary in a Russian warship in the harbour.

It took Witte nearly two months to break the revolution (longer to clear up the aftermath), and during this time he was wrestling with defeat on the front that mattered most. He was very much isolated. Nicholas had indeed signed the Manifesto, but almost at once he was overcome with a sense of guilt and shame, expressed in agonised letters to his mother, and his dislike of Witte hardened. As Witte formed his Government, and its members could see for themselves that the Prime Minister, far from being favoured by the Tsar, was hated by him, many of them found it expedient to go out of their way to please Nicholas and his favourites at the expense of their political chief. The most extreme example of unprincipled nastiness was the behaviour of P. D. Durnovo, who became Minister of the Interior and took over control of the police from General Trepov. It was Durnovo who was most active in encompassing the downfall six months later of Witte, to whom he owed his job: to his very great surprise he fell with the man against whom he had plotted. On the face of it it was an extraordinary aberration on the part of Witte to appoint this wretched time-server to rule over the domestic affairs of a country which had torn itself to pieces and was now officially being wooed by its monarch at the instance of a Prime Minister who had staked everything on reconciliation. Witte himself called it his biggest mistake. It was more than that; it was catastrophic. It is impossible to read Witte's own evasive and rambling explanation of his reasons for urging the appointment of Durnovo (resisted by almost everyone round him, including even Nicholas himself) without a growing feeling that there must have been some truth in the tenacious rumour that Durnovo had some sort of hold on him.[1]

But Witte was to pay a great deal for this error when Durnovo turned against him. It was the country that paid most, however; for the really lasting harm done by Durnovo's appointment was not the frustration of Witte himself nor the immediate consequences of the many savage and bloody repressive actions carried out by troops and police on Durnovo's instructions, but the refusal of the liberals to enter any government in which Durnovo held a portfolio. This refusal, and the consequent delivery of the new administration into the hands of the old discredited bureaucracy, marked one of those sharp stages in the long descent into the abyss; and for once it was not Nicholas who was responsible, but his first minister, the first Prime Minister (in everything but name) of a Russia in the process of transforming itself into at least a semi-constitutional monarchy. It is possible, even probable, that the great mass of the liberals would have shrunk from participation in any government of Witte's. Milyukov himself was in a very high and mighty mood and insisted that before doing so he must have a specific assurance that the provisions of the October Manifesto were to be understood as conceding a constitution. Since the use of that word was still forbidden by Nicholas, and everybody knew it, this was plain silly: the urgent task of the liberals, if only they could have seen it, was to seize with both hands the opportunity to share in government for so long dreamed of by their forerunners; and, by sharing, change it. But the appointment of Durnovo made it virtually impossible for even the most cautious and moderate liberals to dissociate themselves from Milyukov and accept the burden of shared responsibility for the running of the country.

So it was that at the very moment of hope for a more liberal future the liberals were excluded, partly by their own actions, partly by the actions of the man who most needed their support. And the ear of Nicholas was open to the poison dripped into it not only by Durnovo and Trepov, not only by conservatives of profound and loyal conviction, but also by the leaders and spokesmen of a riff-raff of melodramatic absolutists, black reactionaries and corrupt adventurers whose one aim in life was to bash the Jews, bash the socialists, bash the liberals, bash Witte. It was from these that the Jew-murdering Black Hundreds were drawn, and the more intellectual among them (those who could read) formed a political party of sorts, the Union of the Russian People, which one would be tempted to label as a precursor of fascism, if that term had not become so corrupted as to mean nothing: it did mean something once, and so did the Union of the Russian People, then led by a demagogue-on-the-make of quite unusual destructiveness, V. M. Purishkevich.

The really rather wretched Government which Witte finally managed to scrape together had to run the country on its own for six months before the first Duma could be elected and assembled. For six weeks, Durnovo notwithstanding, the St Petersburg soviet managed to keep in being, functioning almost as a parallel government, which the workers obeyed. But its charms were fading. It took an extremely dedicated revolutionary to go on striking and demonstrating and living dangerously at a high pitch of emotional intensity forever and a day. The first warning came when the soviet called for a new general strike on 1 November. This time the response was half-hearted and muddled, and the whole affair petered out in less than a week. By the end of November Durnovo felt strong enough to order the arrest of the chairman of the soviet, and on 3 December troops made a swoop on its building, broke into it, and made nearly two hundred arrests, including all the important leaders – including especially Leon Trotsky.

2

In St Petersburg there was little heart left for resistance: the arrest of the soviet was the end. In Moscow, however, which had all along presented a tougher proposition to the authorities, where for lack of any natural leaders the forces of order had long been demoralised and where even rich business magnates, most notably the multi-millionaire Savva Morozov, had been financing the revolutionaries (sometimes in the rather curious hope that with the smashing of the autocracy restrictions on commerce and private enterprise would also be swept away), there was a flare-up of extreme violence. The Moscow uprising achieved nothing at all, could never hope to achieve anything but a good deal of bloodshed (more than a thousand died); but it became a legend for the Bolsheviks. From 8 to 20 December there was heavy street fighting with artillery against rifles and home-made bombs, whole districts were gutted by fire. But it was essentially destructive, negative fighting, a demonstration rather than a rational campaign. It has been argued that the revolt stood a very good chance because practically the whole of Moscow, alienated by years of misrule by repressive governors-general, military governors and chiefs of police (e.g. the Grand Duke Sergei, General Trepov, P. D. Durnovo himself), was against the regime; further that in the whole of Moscow there was no strong man to take charge; further that a great proportion, perhaps the greater part, of the garrison troops were disaffected and might very well join the revolutionaries. In fact none of these considerations carried much weight. It was one thing for the nobility, 'society', the bourgeoisie, to condemn the regime and sympathise with the radicals, quite another for them to view with satisfaction the spectacle of barricades manned by gaunt and hungry figures emerging from the slums and backstreets, all too copiously armed. There were plenty of strong men among senior army officers, and it was the easiest thing in the world for Witte to persuade the Tsar to despatch a General Dubasov to Moscow to break the revolt; and while it is true that Dubasov found himself at first quite unable to deploy against the revolutionaries the powerful forces he commanded for fear that many of the troops would go over to the other side, once it was clear in St Petersburg that decisive action was really necessary and that troops must be spared from guarding the precious person of the Tsar, the Semyonovsky Guards were very quickly put at Dubasov's disposal. They soon cleared up the mess, behaving with exemplary ruthlessness and shooting everyone they came across who was in possession of weapons of any kind.

It was on the occasion of the Moscow rising that Lenin for the first time unequivocally revealed that element in his very complex make-up which was to find its fullest expression in the unloosing of wholesale terror in 1918: an obsession which bordered on hysteria with the necessity of what he called 'hardness', an urge towards demonstrative and unnecessary violence which was at odds with Marxist teaching and much more akin to the demonology of Nechayev. Even at the time comrades found it odd that the leader of a party which condemned the use of terror as practised by the Socialist Revolutionaries should in 1905 be urging recourse to an armed uprising as a short cut to revolution. The Bolsheviks were more active in the Moscow rising than at any time during 1905, trying to make up for lost time. But they did not lead it. Lenin, however, encouraged and applauded it, and later celebrated it as the 'general rehearsal for the revolution' (Plekhanov, his one-time mentor, castigated it as 'criminal folly').

Soon Lenin was to shock the comrades again by his expressed approval of the rash of 'expropriations' – bank-raids and other bandit-like operations – with which local Social Democrat committees sought to build up their fighting funds. One of the most notorious of these raids, in 1907, was master-minded by the young Georgian Bolshevik J. V. Djugashvili, then known as Koba, soon to be reborn as Stalin. Lenin, firmly opposed in his patronage of violence by all the Mensheviks and many of the Bolsheviks, developed a warm spot for Stalin as a man uninhibited by scruples of any kind.

It is not necessary, I hope, to assure the reader that I am aware of the power, incisiveness and range, the subtlety indeed, of Lenin's intellect or the unsurpassed strength of his will: in the sense of being elemental in force and larger than life he was indeed a great man. But like so many great men, as opposed to great spirits, he destroyed more than he built. Further, his purely intellectual processes, powerful as they were, were always at the service of his instincts; and these were the killer instincts of a power-seeker. He was also a very jealous man. At the time of the 1905 revolution he was thirty-five and almost absurdly jealous of Trotsky, who was nine years younger and yet had swayed immense crowds and won fame in the St Petersburg soviet.

But what Trotsky had done chiefly was to talk (there was nothing visible in him then to suggest the future organiser and commander of the Red Army). And Lenin, until then for his whole political lifetime surrounded by endlessly talking revolutionaries, now that the time for action had come was determined to prove to himself and to others that he, the great theoretician, was also a man of action (in fact he was not a profound theoretician: he was a highly articulate opportunist of genius who had a highly developed talent for rationalising his opportunism). People who talk a great deal about the necessity for hardness are liable to be more dangerous than the naturally hard. Be that as it may, the Moscow uprising was a costly failure. At least half of the two thousand or so actually engaged were killed, and many more were executed afterwards. And whole areas of the city were left in ruins. (In certain districts of Moscow the scars were still visible until well after the Second World War.)

3

This was the end of the revolution as a mass movement. But it was by no means the end of sporadic violence all over the country, and the severity of the repressive measures, the 'pacification' as Witte called it, exceeded anything experienced in modern times. As a rule the local outbreaks of resistance were quickly subdued by troops; then came the executions, with or without a drumhead court-martial. In the Baltic provinces alone over two thousand rebels were shot or hanged by Major-General A. A. Orlov. Another spectacular operation was mounted against troops returning from the Japanese War who mutinied and not only joined the strikers who had brought the Trans-Siberian Railway to a standstill but also spread disaffection far and wide all along the line. Generals A. N. Meller-Zakolemsky and P. K. Rennenkampf (then only a divisional commander, but later, as commander of the Army of the Niemen, to play an important, perhaps a decisive, role in Russia's first great defeat of the 1914 war) were despatched with strong loyal forces along the line, the one starting from Manchuria, the other from western Russia, putting down insurrection all the way until they met in Chita. This was a notoriously harsh action, popularly attributed to Durnovo. But in fact Witte himself in his memoirs blandly claims full responsibility, and the plan had his personal mark.[2] Certainly Nicholas too held Witte responsible. Even he was mildly shocked at the harshness of the pacification measures which he attributed entirely to Witte, petulantly exclaiming to his mother that Witte's attitude passed all comprehension. 'I never knew such a chameleon!' One day he was urging his Imperial master against all his convictions to yield to popular clamour, the next he was shooting down all opposition like a maniac.[3]

Witte in fact was deteriorating fast, mentally and physically, though he was to live on for another ten years. He had, when all is said, been terribly wrong in his prognostications. He had convinced Nicholas that all dissension would cease with the promulgation of the October Manifesto. Faced with the turbulence that followed he must have felt vulnerable to anyone who cared to charge him with persuading the Tsar to dilute his authority by making false promises. He had been left in the lurch, as he saw it, by the liberals, who should properly be hailing him as their champion and hero. It is hardly to be wondered at if he hit out, and hit hard and a little blindly, at any focus of opposition.

He was to make one more mistake. The new electoral system, proclaimed in December, was heavily weighted in favour of the peasants: in spite of the outbreaks of violence all over the country, St Petersburg's faith in the absolute loyalty and devotion of the peasant masses remained unshaken. All concerned seemed to have convinced themselves that agrarian disturbances were due to a handful of born trouble-makers worked on by evilly disposed revolutionaries. But it was not like that at all. And when, in April, it became apparent that the peasant representatives (forming a sort of electoral college) were casting their votes not for the conservatives but for the radicals, above all for the Cadets, the game, as it were, was up.

Witte was isolated. He was disliked by his master, abhorred by the reactionaries who regarded him as a traitor and, like the Tsaritsa, accused him of plotting to set himself up as a dictator. He was distrusted by the moderates. In the eyes of revolutionaries he was a monster of repression and a tool of international capitalism. He had quite discredited himself in the eyes of the Cadets, not only by his choice of Durnovo, but also because he had connived at the Tsar's very noticeable betrayal of the spirit, if not the letter, of the October Manifesto. It was not so much that Nicholas broke his word as that he qualified it out of existence. It was a process which marched happily with the resurgence of Imperial confidence after the smashing of the Moscow rising and the success of the many punitive expeditions throughout the Empire.

In fact it was Witte himself who insisted on the exclusion of the Duma from the whole area of military and foreign affairs. In March it was announced that the Duma would have no powers at all over the military and naval estimates, the vast expenditure of the Imperial Court, or the activities of the Ministry of Foreign Affairs. The Chairman of the Council of Ministers, or Prime Minister, could himself be removed at will by the Tsar and another appointed in his place. So could all the other ministers. According to the new Fundamental Laws published on 23 April all ministers were accountable only to the Tsar, not at all to the Duma, which, moreover, could take no action to amend the Fundamental Laws. The Duma was permitted to express its disapproval of individual ministers, or indeed, of the whole Government, but the Government need pay no attention. Individual members of the Duma could put questions to the Prime Minister and other ministers, but there was no obligation on these to reply. The President of the Duma, or Speaker, had right of personal access to the Tsar to acquaint him with the Duma's hopes and fears, but the Tsar need do no more than listen, or appear to do so. Finally, Nicholas dug his feet in very firmly when faced with any attempt to amend clause one of the old Fundamental Laws which was the legal basis of his autocratic power: 'To the Emperor of All the Russias belongs the supreme autocratic and unlimited power...' This categorical statement could not be retained without making total nonsense of the October Manifesto. Nicholas, who until then had clearly been determined never to abate his formal powers by one jot, whatever people cared to think about Dumas and representative assemblies, was adamant. In the end he consented only to the deletion of the words 'and unlimited', which, in any case, might seem to be tautologous.

Nicholas would have got rid of Witte quite early in the new year if he could have done, but this was a luxury he could not afford. There was an immense French loan in the offing, which was to pay for the Japanese War. Witte had to be retained as the one great confidence-inspiring figure until that was safely negotiated. Then he could go. And so he did, on the very day the new Fundamental Laws were published and four days before the opening of the first State Duma – this huge, strange, ambiguous rock of a man, who had called down on himself the fear, jealousy, resentment of the Tsar, the hysterical hatred of the Tsaritsa, the envy of mean-spirited intriguers like Durnovo and Trepov, the distrust of the moderates, the contempt of the radicals, the loathing of the revolutionaries. His faults and failures have been recorded here. But in the context of turn-of-the-century Russia his achievements had been very great. He was not a Bonaparte or a Bismarck, a man of the kind that, at least for a period of years, seems capable of doing anything, overlooking nothing, providing for every contingency, perceiving with the speed of light the likely consequences and side-effects of any action. He was essentially a man of great parts with unbalanced talents and blind spots to set against great vision – a man, in a word, who would be at his best when kept up to scratch by friction with two or three colleagues of scarcely inferior gifts. Witte did not fail Russia. Russia failed Witte: from among all her millions she was unable to produce another man, let alone more than one, fit to work with him.

So the first Duma was inaugurated on 27 April, not in its designated home, the brilliant Tauride Palace built by Catherine the Great for her favourite, Potemkin, but in the Winter Palace itself, in the shining white St George's Hall, resplendent with its Corinthian pillars and superb chandeliers. Here all down one side of the vast room, 150 feet long, the elected representatives of the people stood in drab suits, peasant blouses, or exotic national costumes, facing an assembly of courtiers, nobility, bureaucrats, soldiers and sailors, all brilliant in dress uniforms while the Tsar, heavily robed, tiny under the great bulbous crown, with the far more imposing Tsaritsa at his side, offered a formal address of welcome, almost embarrassing in its coldness. That was all. There was not a breath of spontaneous feeling in his words. No contact was made. None was intended. Nicholas said what he had to say and vanished, and with him the Tsaritsa who throughout the proceedings had preserved an air of sulky aloofness (it is fair to say that this was her usual demeanour in the presence of all but her own chosen friends).[4] There was no communication. And so it remained.

The Duma soon showed that it had no desire to enter into a dialogue with the Government and the Tsar. Under the domination of the Cadets it showed itself from the beginning not so much a debating chamber as an unyielding, aggressively uncompromising enemy of the administration. And the administration was delighted; it governed while the Duma talked. With Witte's dismissal (technically, his resignation) Nicholas had shown where his true tastes lay. He had immediately seized upon that idle old cynic Goremykin, approaching seventy now, who did not intend to pay the least attention to the Duma and could not understand why anyone thought he should do so. Sir Arthur Nicolson, very recently installed as the new British Ambassador to St Petersburg, was horrified by what he found when he paid his first call on Goremykin only a week or two after his elevation. There he was, the First Minister of the Tsar of All the Russias, without any pretence, 'reclining on a sofa surrounded by French novels'. This hero of the hour, Nicolson recorded in his diary, was 'an elderly man with a sleepy face and Piccadilly whiskers. He treated the Duma with the greatest disdain: "Let them babble," he said. "The Government alone knows the country." He was very indignant with the tone of *The Times* and the *Daily Telegraph* in regard to the Jews, whom he characterised as the vilest of people, anarchists, extortioners and usurers. I went away with a sad heart: the Russian bureaucracy is incorrigible.'⁵

This interview, it should be mentioned, occurred at a time when Russia was just beginning to wake up after the trauma of the Japanese War and try to decide what to do to secure and improve her position in the outside world. It was a moment when the French Ambassador was going about predicting total collapse and the consequent ruin of millions of French investors. Nicholas, wrapped away at Peterhof, might not have existed. The Duma ranted. The Prime Minister read French novels. He had in fact attended the Duma, which had endorsed the complete programme of the Cadet Party's demands as its own (amnesty of all political prisoners, compulsory break-up of the great private estates, the repeal of the Emergency Laws, ministers to be responsible to the Duma, and so on). There was no obligation on either Nicholas or his First Minister to reply, but Goremykin decided to answer in person and once and for all. He tottered into the chamber, exaggerating his age and the feebleness of his voice, bowed down, it seemed, by the longest and bushiest Piccadilly whiskers in the world, rheumy-eyed, husky-voiced, implacable. Every single one of the Duma's proposals, he regretted to say, inadmissible. He was courteous enough to give reasons. His voice expired, drowned in the general uproar, and he went away. The Duma continued to function demonstratively and uselessly in a vacuum. It compounded silliness with silliness by demanding the instant resignation of the Government. That was on 18 May, after it had been in session for just three weeks. Within a couple of months the first Duma itself was dissolved.

4

In fact the country had already shown that it had outgrown the Goremykins. The deadlock between Duma and Government notwithstanding, there were political stirrings of quite a new kind, a reaching out on the part of the bureaucracy, even (to all appearances) in a half-hearted way on the part of Nicholas himself, towards the concept of compromise with the new forces they feared and did not understand. It is impossible to be dogmatic about certain very peculiar overtures made in the mid-summer of 1906 because nobody knows how seriously they were intended. General Trepov of all people, still very close to the Tsar, made a direct approach to Milyukov (who, although he dominated Cadet policies as a result of some procedural muddle, had not been elected to the Duma) and suggested that he should form a Cadet Ministry to replace Goremykin's administration. Milyukov, of course, responded by laying down impossible conditions. At the same time, however, the new Foreign Minister, Alexander Izvolsky, a career diplomat (the replacement for Lamsdorf), and the new Minister for Internal Affairs, Peter Stolypin, who was to dominate Russia for the next five years, were urging the hero of the moderates, D. N. Shipov, now an elected zemstvo representative on the State Council, to form a coalition ministry. Shipov was obviously attracted by the idea, but he doubted very much whether the Cadets would be prepared to work with any coalition, and he was right. He was also magnanimous. When he knew the worst, namely that Milyukov would allow the Cadets to take no part in government unless they had things all their own way, Shipov urged Nicholas in private audience to give them a trial. Anything was better than deadlock and the constant demoralising, unsettling uproar in the Duma. Shipov when he came away was convinced that he had persuaded the Tsar to send for Professor S. A. Muromtsev, once the liberal head of the Law Society, now Speaker of the Duma, in order to ask him to form a Cadet administration. Nobody knows whether Nicholas really intended to do this, but was dissuaded by others after Shipov had taken his leave, or whether his apparent sympathy for Shipov's proposals had all along been meaningless. Either way, one more chance (how many there had been!) of developing some sort of symbiotic relationship between the monarch and his subjects, between the bureaucracy and 'society', was lost.[6]

Towards the end of June the Duma laid itself wide open to total defeat. Infuriated, as well it might have been, by the formal and absolute refusal of the Government to countenance on any terms at all the compulsory break-up of private estates, the Cadets exceeded their powers and appealed to the people over the heads of the administration, issuing a proclamation declaring that the land question could not be settled except with the Duma's participation. This was seen for what in fact it was, deliberate infringement of the Imperial prerogative. Nicholas was enraged: the Duma must be dissolved, and quickly. Before dawn on Sunday, 9 July, the Tauride Palace was surrounded by troops and the ukase announcing the dissolution posted up on the doors. Milyukov had expected some action of this kind and had prepared for what is now-adays called a sit-in. This came to nothing because the members were all at home on Sunday. They found themselves not sitting in but locked out. What to do? Nearly two hundred of them, mostly Cadets, hurried across the frontier into Finland (the tactic so soon to be immortalised by Lenin), assembled in the Belvedere Hotel at Vyborg, and declared themselves to be in full session. Their first act was to issue what became known as the Vyborg Manifesto, a document drafted by Milyukov calling upon all Russians to refuse to pay taxes or provide recruits for the army until the Duma had been recalled. The only upshot of this quite useless gesture was to associate the liberal Cadets still more closely with the revolution-aries and their methods and to provide the authorities with a perfectly good excuse for arresting all those they could lay hands on.

5

Eight months were to pass before the convening of the second Duma, and those eight months, from July 1906 to March 1907, stamped the Empire with the image of a new man and produced reforms which promised to revitalise it. The man was Peter Stolypin, the second strong man to take upon himself the task of saving the Romanov dynasty from itself; he was also the last.

That task was appalling in its magnitude. Order had to be restored in a land where all the signs indicated the build-up of a new revolutionary situation; then the whole framework of Russian rural life – the life of nine-tenths of the population, that is – had to be turned upside down and refashioned, so that agrarian Russia might begin to catch up with urban Russia and the two sides balanced and harmonised. This was to be done not by a dictator but by a Prime Minister with no powers built into his office, a Chairman of the Council of Ministers, who was pledged to work with the Duma when it was in session while at the same time retaining the confidence of a master who detested the very idea of the Duma and could dismiss him at will.

At forty-three Stolypin, who came from an old landowning family, had already made a name for himself as Governor of Saratov province on the lower Volga. He was a superb organiser, and he was tireless; he was also swift, decisive and harsh in the repressive measures he had brought to bear to defeat the rioting, the arson, the killing, which was such a feature of his region. But he understood the peasants, even as he chastised them. He was a burning patriot, and this meant that he had no choice but to believe in the peasants, who *were* the country. He was dedicated to the task of releasing what he believed to be their full potential by getting rid of the restrictions and restrictive practices, the closed shops and the traditional rituals – above all that sacred cow the village commune, or Mir – which held back agricultural development, isolated the peasant from contemporary reality, and preserved him, drunk or sober, with his traditional village culture like a rather squalid, shaggy, very muddy exhibit in a museum of primitive cults and customs. It was not for this that he had been brought to St Petersburg to replace Durnovo as Minister of the Interior after Witte's fall, but because of his reputation for toughness. With the dissolution of the first Duma, Goremykin threw in his hand and Stolypin took over as First Minister – at first enjoying, as so many lesser men had done before him, the enthusiastic admiration of his Imperial master. This did not last very long.

His first task was to check disorder. In that high summer of 1906 the situation was threatening enough to justify almost any expedient. The new British Ambassador, Sir Arthur Nicolson, a man not easily alarmed, found it necessary to write to Sir Edward Grey on 3 July warning him that if the peasants responded with violence to the revolutionary agitators, and the urban workers rose simultaneously, there would ensue 'a catastrophe such as history has rarely witnessed'.[7] Such a consummation seemed far from improbable in 1906. There was a very great fear of a general peasant rising once the harvest was in. There were frequent mutinies in the armed services, among garrison troops in the provinces, among the Guards at St Petersburg, in the fleet at Kronstadt. Lenin, now in hiding but still in Russia, was urging the chances of a more successful armed rising than the abortive Moscow one. The new 'Maximalist' wing of the Socialist Revolutionaries had launched a campaign of indiscriminate terror more wholesale than anything known before.

Stolypin met violence with violence. Between the late summer of 1906 and the spring of 1907 there were more than a thousand executions officially recorded, ordered by the special summary courts-martial set up all over the land with instructions to try each prisoner within twenty-four hours of arrest and carry out the sentence of the court immediately: it was a common thing for an assassin to be tried and hanged before his victim had been buried.[8]

On the other hand, in the two years 1906 and 1907 there were nearly four thousand murderous acts of terrorism with victims all down the line from provincial governors to ordinary policemen: by the Maximalists everyone in uniform was regarded as fair game and, by virtue of the uniform, excluded from human kind.[9]

The calm which Stolypin brought to his deliberate policy of exterminating the terrorists and the notorious 'expropriators', or bank robbers, and other active revolutionaries, was uncanny. Although he was a man of passionate feeling, nothing was allowed to affect the seemingly clinical detachment with which he applied himself to a distasteful task. 'There is no vengeance in politics; there are only consequences,'[10] he once said in quite another context; but that saying could be applied to his own attitude towards all enemies of the system. His calm and his subsequent behaviour were unaffected even by the terrible injuries to his own children when the Maximalists tried to kill him on 21 August.

Two men disguised as police officers drove up to his private house in St Petersburg, walked up to it as though they had every right to do so, and lobbed an unusually powerful bomb through a ground-floor window. The whole front of the house was demolished by the explosion, which blew the terrorists to bits, killed twenty-five others and wounded another thirty-two, six mortally. The children were playing on a balcony which came down as the house collapsed, killing their two nurses, burying them in rubble – badly injuring the small boy and crushing the legs of the fifteen-year-old daughter. Stolypin himself was in his study at the back of the house and, although thrown to the ground, was unhurt. He emerged to search in the rubble for his children, who were feared dead. Even after this he retained his outward detachment and did nothing to suggest in the relentless pursuit and execution of terrorists that he was moved by any personal feeling.

To quote one of Sir Harold Nicolson's admirable portraits from the life:

A tall stiff man with a dead white face and a dead white beard. He entered a room stiffly, carrying a top hat and kid gloves, looking straight in front of him, bowing like an automaton over the hand of his hostess, passing rigidly from guest to guest. He spoke in a cold and even voice, as cold as the clasp of his white hand.... He gave no impression of ferocity. He left an impression only of cold gentleness, of icy compassion, of saddened self-control.[11]

There was indeed no ferocity in this man who came to bear upon his shoulders, without glory, the whole weight of the accumulated sins of an inadequate dynasty, a selfish nobility, a venal bureaucracy, a sycophantic and frivolous court, an alienated 'society', a hungry peasantry and a brutalised working class.

Sir Arthur Nicolson, who came to know him well and understood something of the magnitude of his task, put it on official record that Stolypin was a great man. 'He was, in my opinion, the most notable figure in Europe.' He did not claim for him high intellectual qualities, 'but he possessed, what was far more important, an ardent love for his country, and a most earnest desire to steer her safely through the troubles and difficulties by which she was surrounded.'[12] To this should be added honesty. Certainly he lacked Witte's brains, but in character he was very much superior to that tarnished genius who indeed was so deeply to resent his successor's achievement that he intrigued venomously against him and was in large part responsible for the disfavour into which he fell before he died.

Stolypin may very well have been 'the most notable figure in Europe' of his day. But with all his aloof grandeur and the passionate loyalty he inspired in those who saw him as his country's hope (these were above all the soberer and more conservative of the idealistic zemstvoists) he had great flaws. I do not refer now to his repressive measures, but rather to the inconsequent facility with which he broke the new and fragile, laboriously constructed statutes which represented Russia's first stumbling steps towards the rule of law, and also to his blind and intolerant nationalism. The objection is not that he so readily broke certain laws (naturally with the enthusiastic approval of the man who had signed them into existence, the Tsar); the temptation was very great, perhaps indeed irresistible. The objection is that he broke the law without appearing to understand what he was doing – taking Russia straight back to the days of Nicholas I and Nikitenko's lament over governmental lawlessness.

Of course he ran the country better when the Duma was not in session. His greatest reforms, those for which he will be remembered and celebrated one day in Russia by Russians – the reforms which, but for the impact of a shattering war, might have saved Russia from that 'catastrophe such as history has never witnessed' foreseen, a little prematurely, by Sir Arthur Nicolson – were concerned with the liberation of the peasant from his bonds and the transformation of the agrarian economy. These reforms, the most important of them, were promulgated in a series of five enactments very early in the Stolypin era, between 12 August and 9 November 1906. They completed and crowned the process begun by Witte in November of the previous year with the waiving of peasant indebtedness to the state. They released the peasant from his commune together with his own land which was to be consolidated from a series of scattered strips into a compact holding. They brought into the Peasant Bank for the subsequent purchase by individual peasants all the lands belonging to members of the Imperial Family and so far rented. They brought into the same vast pool all the immense crown-lands in Siberia; they removed all legal restrictions on the peasants as a class and curtailed the powers of the land-captains over individuals. In a word, their aim was to transform poverty-stricken and wretchedly-run collectives in which there was scope neither for initiative, for the development of individual responsibility nor for modern agricultural practice – to transform this age-old monument to institutionalised inefficiency into a yeoman peasant system with individuals free to buy or to sell, to sow what they liked, to reap when they liked, to merge, co-operate, employ their neighbours. The whole scheme as Stolypin himself once put it, was 'a gamble not on the drunken and the feeble but on the sober and the strong'.[13]

Of course it was hard on the wretched and the weak. The strong, the able, the energetic, the greedy, forged swiftly ahead, buying up the land of the feeble, the feckless, the gentle, who were either reduced to near starvation, bankrupted, or driven to the factories or to work for their powerful neighbours. These, of course, grew into the celebrated kulak class, which effected a remarkable improvement in agricultural productivity, until it was destroyed by Stalin only twenty years later in order that the old collectives should be restored, but this time controlled not by village elders but by Communist Party officials who, as often as not, did not know a plough from a handsaw. Then the level of production achieved by the kulaks was halved in one year, and it was not until the 1960s that it once more, with the aid of modern machinery, reached the volume of output achieved by the Stolypin system – but now with a vastly increased population to feed.

These enactments, and many more besides, were carried through by Stolypin under article eighty-seven of the new Fundamental Laws, which provided for legislation by decree when the Duma was not in session, on condition that all such decrees be submitted to the Duma within two months of its reconvening. The interesting thing was that although he was happiest and at his best governing without the Duma, and although a convinced monarchist, Stolypin had no intention of ignoring the Duma as Goremykin had ignored it and as Nicholas would have liked to ignore it. Indeed, he did his best to impress on Nicholas the need to show respect for his own creation, and he worked long and assiduously with the co-operation of the newly-founded League of 17 October, a conservative offshoot of the Cadets led by A. I. Guchkov supported by Shipov. In vain. It was the easiest thing in the world, and probably true, for a Guchkov to convince himself that Stolypin simply wanted him for his name, as once the insufferable Plehve had tried to win Shipov and Milyukov for their names. The Octobrists refused to participate in the administration unless they were allotted seven portfolios. It was too much. Thus it was that Stolypin almost in spite of himself became the second Duma's scourge.

It opened in March 1907. Stolypin had hoped that he had so managed things that the opposition parties would be heavily reduced. But he was disappointed. The Tauride Palace was no longer dominated by the Cadets, largely because so many of their deputies were still in prison after the Vyborg Manifesto, but Milyukov who (quite unfairly) had not been arrested with them, had his seat this time and appeared as the leader of his party. It was a far more mixed and confused assembly than the first. There were some ninety supporters of the Government, including the violent right-wing; but this time Lenin had told the S.D.s to use the Duma as a sounding board and, led by the Georgian Menshevik N. S. Chkeidzke, they had sixty-five seats, twelve of them held by Bolsheviks. The S.R.s had thirty-four seats, including twenty-two of the violent left. There was virtually no constructive discussion. The extreme right and the extreme left were united in shouting down everybody else, and even though some of the Cadets were more in a mood to co-operate with the Government than in the previous Duma, it was easy for intransigents to turn them against Stolypin, not only for his rule by summary courts-martial but also because of his absolute ignoring, in the land statutes promulgated in the absence of the Duma, of all demands for the expropriation of the landowners, either with compensation as the Cadets desired, or without, as the S.R.s demanded.

That second Duma came to an abrupt end when it was dissolved in July 1907, after a stormy and useless life of three and a half months. The heaven-sent pretext for Nicholas to order a dissolution was a treasonable incitement by an S.D. deputy to the army to mutiny. One would have said that by now Stolypin as well as Nicholas would have been considering putting the Duma indefinitely into cold storage. But not a bit of it. No sooner was the second Duma dissolved than Stolypin, operating once more under article eighty-seven, introduced a new electoral law. This had quite obviously been in preparation for some time past: it directly contravened the Fundamental Laws, and so transformed the franchise that Russians (still only half the population of the Empire) were greatly favoured over non-Russians, and landowners had the most commanding position of all.

Here the two great flaws in Stolypin's character – his lack of respect for law and his Russian nationalism – came together. At first not unfruitfully. The third Duma, conservative as it was, actually worked. The Cadets and parties to the left of them were furious and loud in condemnation of what, correctly, they called a *coup d'état*. The regime from then on was referred to by them contemptuously as the Third of June Monarchy. But the Duma lasted its five-year term and did useful work. It was, of course, a highly conservative assembly, with the 150 Octobrists the dominant body, for all practical purposes acting as a liaison force between the administration on the one hand and the 140 assorted right-wing and the scarcely more than a hundred left-wing deputies in permanent and noisy opposition. The Cadets were reduced to fifty-four, the S.D.s to fourteen. The S.R.s had decided to boycott this Duma; but there were thirteen members of a new workers' party, the Trudovniks. The new President of the Chamber, or Speaker, was N. A. Khomyakov, son of the great and gifted Slavophile; the Octobrist leader Guchkov was a man of remarkable gifts and considerable eccentricity, the son of a business tycoon. Devoured by ambition, skilled in intrigue, he was nevertheless the prey of impetuous ideals, and his combative nature made him fight for them. It drove him, for example, in his late thirties, all the way to South Africa to fight for the Boers against the British. Before he passed out of history in flight from Lenin's Bolsheviks he was to be one of the two Duma leaders to travel from St Petersburg to Pskov to receive the abdication of the Tsar in February 1917; and he was to be Minister of War in the first Provisional Government before Kerensky took over from him.

It was obvious that any close relationship between Stolypin and such a man as Guchkov would be uneasy in the extreme, and so it was. As early as 1908 Guchkov, backed by most of his party, violently assailed the Tsar (which meant Stolypin too) for ignoring the Duma when it came to granting new credits for the much-needed reorganisation of the armed forces. He went so far as to demand the resignation of the Grand Dukes from their military commands. Nothing happened to him; but Nicholas was so impotently furious that he dismissed his own Minister of War for his failure to deal with Guchkov – and Stolypin was the target here too. For, predictably, the Tsar was tiring of his great minister, as sooner or later he tired of everything except his family, his crown and the toys of M. Fabergé. The extreme right – the Union of the Russian People and the Society of Michael the Archangel – with their thuggery, their pogroms, their Black Hundred gangsters, their bullying, corruption and blackmail, above all their vile and perpetual anti-Jewish activity, were flourishing as never before, largely because of Stolypin's own careful and devious manoeuvring to exalt the right wing at the expense of the left in the Duma. The left he had virtually destroyed for the time being, but to the right, who regarded him as a traitor and little short of a revolutionary, he was now falling victim. And the right had increasingly the ear of the Tsar.

There was another complication, and a very sinister one. It was the growing influence on Tsar and Tsaritsa of the notorious 'man of God', Gregory Rasputin. When Rasputin had first been picked up, as it were, by the two silly Montenegrin princesses (married to Russian Grand Dukes), ever on the look-out for new sensations, and introduced to Nicholas and Alexandra, he had appeared to them as no more than an unusually impressive example of a phenomenon characteristic of Russia and greatly loved by Russians, the wandering holy man. Such men were to be found hanging about on the fringes of almost every noble household. Virtue accrued through caring for them, and, for those Russians with a quasi-religious sense of the nobility of the peasant, communion with these characters was held to signify communion with the very soul of Russia. Rasputin, the insolently dissolute son of a peasant from a village near Tobolsk, was outstanding in his brazenness and boldness, and in the mesmeric quality of his gaze. He appealed strongly to the debatable idea that the bigger the sinner the nearer he is to God.

It was not until four years later, in 1908, that Rasputin was insinuated into the Tsar's family circle by a foolish young maid of honour called Anna Vyrubova, who was the nearest thing the Tsaritsa then had to a confidante. He knew how to talk to Nicholas to make him feel that here at last he was in contact with the real Russia; he knew how to exploit the Tsaritsa's religious mania; above all, and as time went on, he was able to help the young Tsarevich Alexei in his haemophilic agonies when doctors could do nothing at all.[14]

This development did not reach its climax until 1912, when the eight-year-old Tsarevich, at death's door, was 'cured' by the famous telegram from Rasputin, assuring the Tsaritsa that all would be well. After that his ascendancy over Alexandra, and therefore over Nicholas, was complete. But long before then, gossip about his influence was running so freely and scandalously that great damage was being done to the reputation of the Crown. Stolypin alone found the courage to warn Nicholas of the dangers of the association. He did more. He presented a circumstantial report on the man's disreputable activities and at the same time personally ordered Rasputin's banishment from the capital. The Tsaritsa was beside herself with fury, but she could not move Nicholas, who refused to rescind Stolypin's order – a fact which tells us that from 1911 onwards Nicholas knew precisely the sort of man 'Our Friend' really was. But the most soundly based of ministers could not now for long survive Alexandra's displeasure.

And at this time Stolypin was not soundly based. He had long been hated by the extreme right and by the extreme left. Now he had run into trouble with many of his moderate conservative supporters as a result, curiously enough, of his uninhibited Russian chauvinism. Already he had shown himself as bad as Alexander III in his determination to continue the russification of the minority lands, earning the justified hatred of the Finns for quite arbitrarily withdrawing concessions made in 1905. Now he was determined to set up zemstvos in the western provinces, where they had not hitherto existed, by procedures which were nothing less than humiliating to all non-Russians. Although the great landowners in those provinces were mostly Poles, this was seen as a deliberate assault on the nobility, and Russian landowners rallied to the support of their Polish peers. Stolypin suddenly found that his bill was rejected not only by the Duma but by the aristocratic State Council whose support he had always taken for granted.

This looked like being the end. He tried to resign. Nicholas refused to accept his resignation. But it was a cat and mouse game. Stolypin was ill. The strains of the past five years had been all but intolerable even for this giant of a man. Now he was not merely trying to sustain the whole great edifice of the Russian Empire on his own broad shoulders, he was under attack from every side. It could only be a matter of time before he went. Russia was not yet ready for a Stolypin. It would be ready only when it could produce at least a handful of politicians who were strong and steady and detached enough to work with a leader of his calibre, support him, and wrestle with him in the hammering out of policies. A single man left to dominate or to fight quite alone is liable to go mad.

Stolypin did not go mad. He was murdered. The occasion was a memorial gala for Alexander III at the Kiev Opera House. Nicholas was in the Imperial box; Stolypin in the stalls. The security precautions were of the most stringent kind imaginable. They did not, however, prevent yet another of those twilight figures who blur at every turn the sharp edges of Russian history, from entering the theatre and shooting Stolypin dead. The assassin was a Jew called Bogrov, a Socialist Revolutionary turned police agent. He had invented news of an imaginary assassination project and had been allowed into the theatre to report the latest developments to the chief of police in person, who had then dismissed him and told him to leave the theatre. Instead he remained. In the interval he walked up to Stolypin and shot him at point-black range, in full view of the Imperial box. Stolypin, who was standing with his back to the stage, turned towards Nicholas, his Imperial master, made the sign of the cross, and fell, mortally wounded.

Nicholas tried to visit him in hospital but was not allowed to his bedside. No member of the administration attended the services of prayer held on his behalf. Bogrov was executed before any effective enquiry could be made. So nobody knows to this day whether he was acting on behalf of the police conspiring with the extreme right, or on behalf of the S.R.s to rehabilitate himself as a revolutionary. But Stolypin himself had prophesied that he would be killed by his own police. In any case, there could have been no Bogrov if Stolypin himself had not personally encouraged the continued and intensified use of police informers, infiltrators, double agents.

CHAPTER TWENTY-TWO

The End

1

STOLYPIN had never hoped for immediate results. He knew that his great agrarian reforms would take a generation to mature and fructify. Give us twenty years of peace at home and abroad, he declared, and Russia will be wholly transformed. Witte before him had also needed peace for the realisation of his own particular vision – and had been given the war with Japan. Stolypin had guaranteed peace at home, at least for a decade ahead, by virtually exterminating the active terrorists and driving all those revolutionary leaders who were not in prison to flee the country – including Lenin once again. His own assassination when it came in 1911 did not contradict this picture. The charnel-house attempt on his life in 1906 had been part of the great wave of terrorism which was now spent. Bogrov's crime had been out of series, as it were: it sparked off no new movement.

For peace abroad, however, Russia depended not on Stolypin but on the Tsar himself, and for some time on the rather engaging but unsteady person of Alexander Izvolsky. A career diplomat with wide experience in the foreign service, Izvolsky had been appointed Minister of Foreign Affairs in the Goremykin administration in succession to Count Lamsdorf. He did in fact keep the peace during his tenure of office, which expired suddenly and sadly in 1910. But he sowed dragon's teeth, and his successor, the unfortunate, timid, relatively inexperienced S. D. Sazonov, was unable to cope with the subsequent crop. For Sazonov was a connection by marriage of Stolypin's, and after the murder of his great patron was so dominated by the desire to please that he was all too ready to allow his better judgement to be overruled. In July 1914 he allowed this to happen once too often. Knowing that his surrender to the demands of the General Staff for full mobilisation would mean war, and hating the idea of war, nevertheless he surrendered.

Russia did not start that war which was her undoing, but she was active in creating the situation which made it possible and then in helping to convert possibility into certainty. And in the beginning was Izvolsky, dapper, immensely vain, very much on his dignity, undoubtedly well-meaning and with a shrewd eye for the realities of behaviour when he himself was not affected, but too clever by half, indeed, mistaking cleverness for subtlety and deceit for finesse, and always desperately afraid of being taken in. These shortcomings were to cost his country very dear.

He began quietly enough. His first job was to re-establish civilised relations with Japan, which involved mutual agreement on future spheres of influence in China. And this was accomplished quite sensibly. His second job was to mend fences with England. This took rather longer.

The general pressure of events had been forcing England and Russia towards some sort of an understanding for some years past. The face of the general pressure of events was the face of the Emperor William of Germany who was asserting his presence and threatening the equilibrium of Europe by stamping on everybody's toes. France, as we have seen, had achieved an alliance with Russia under Alexander III, which meant that she could never again find herself isolated as she had been in the war of 1870. It was the most natural thing in the world for a Britain waking up somewhat belatedly to her own vulnerability if she continued to pursue her policy of splendid isolation first to seek an understanding with France, then to extend that understanding to France's ally, Russia.

The process would have got under way sooner but for Russia's bitter resentment against England for her support of Japan. Without the alliance of 1902, it was thought (no doubt correctly) Japan would not have dared attack. The German Emperor had worked hard and enthusiastically to exploit this ill-feeling. But in 1905 he badly overreached himself in the farcical episode of the Treaty of Björkö which left the Russian Foreign Ministry with a nasty taste in its mouth and at the same time demonstrated to an inner circle at that ministry the hopeless insufficiency of Nicholas which had been proved to a larger public in the matter of 'Bloody Sunday'.

According to Izvolsky, Nicholas was invariably in a state of nerves well in advance of any meeting with his eccentric German cousin, whose persuasive rhetoric, barrack-room humour, theatrical posturing and overbearing familiarity he found at the same time repellent and hard to resist.[1] But William was not all clown: he knew how to flatter effectively, and he had moments of brilliant perceptiveness. It was he, for example, who threw off in one of his marginal comments what was perhaps the most devastating of all reflections on the character of Nicholas: 'The Tsar is not treacherous, but he is weak. Weakness is not treachery, but it fulfils all its functions.'[2]

The Björkö fiasco arose from William's persistent determination to engage Russia in an alliance directed at England at the expense of going behind the back of France, Russia's formal ally, who was already in close accord with England. Unable to achieve his objective at long range, William decided to use his summer cruise in the Baltic to swoop on Nicholas, then cruising off the Finnish coast in an attempt to recuperate his forces after the shock of Tsushima, alone with his family and far from Foreign Ministry advisers. For three days Nicholas put up a spirited resistance to this unwanted, unheralded guest, but in the end signed a treaty already prepared by William in which the two signatories promised to go to the help of each other if attacked by any other European power. What finally told with Nicholas was his resentment against Britain, his gratitude to Germany for assisting in various semi-clandestine ways in the war against Japan, his feeling of forlorn isolation (for the French alliance had not helped in the matter of Japan), and William's assurance, written into the treaty, that France in due course should be invited to subscribe. But he very soon had second thoughts and realised that he had been duped and railroaded, even before he confessed, belatedly, to Lamsdorf, who was duly horrified. The French alliance, with all that it stood for in the way of financial support, was what counted most, and, in the teeth of bitter reproaches from William, the Björkö Treaty was denounced by Russia before it even took effect.[3]

Since that summer of 1905 Germany had done her level best to conciliate Russia. Sir Arthur Nicolson was to comment on the very marked difference between her habitual bullying and hectoring attitude towards most countries, including France and Britain, and her cosseting and soft-soaping of Russia. And it was against this background that the long series of conversations between Nicolson and Izvolsky were brought to a successful conclusion with the Anglo-Russian Convention of 1907. Because these conversations were conducted so quietly and because the Convention was technically no more than a threefold agreement about spheres of influence in Persia, Afghanistan and Tibet, Germany was not seriously alarmed, although in fact it marked a critical staging post on the way to the Triple Entente. What worried the German Chancellor, von Bülow, much more was the meeting of Edward VII and the Tsar on board the royal yacht *Victoria and Albert*, in the roadstead at Reval in June of the following year, and the subsequent banquets on board the imperial yacht *Standart* and the Dowager Empress's yacht *Pole Star*.

And indeed the occasion was so dazzlingly brilliant, so blatantly public, so different from the hole-in-corner meeting in *Pole Star* between Tsar and German Emperor three years earlier, that Berlin had some excuse for alarm. On the British side were present the King and Queen and Princess Victoria; the head of the Foreign Office, Sir Charles Hardinge, the

Inspector-General of the British Army, General Sir John French, the eccentric First Sea Lord, Admiral Sir John Fisher, the British Ambassador of course, and a glittering assortment of high-born equerries, ladies-in-waiting, etc. This remarkable party had already put in at Kiel and been received by Prince and Princess Henry of Prussia, which somehow made it worse when they then sailed straight on to Reval to be fêted by the Tsar and Tsaritsa, the Dowager Tsaritsa, the little Tsarevich and his four sisters, to say nothing of Messrs Stolypin and Izvolsky. The Queen of the Hellenes went along for the ride.[4] Next to nothing of any importance was said. This was quite deliberate. When it came to buttering up foreign potentates Edward VII was in a different league from the Germans, who could never resist the temptation to interrupt their flattery with a minatory harangue on whatever topic happened to be uppermost in their minds. But the Germans themselves knew very well that Nicholas was immensely reassured by Edward's devilish tact, his unerring skill in having himself briefed on whatever topics, however trivial, were dear to the heart of the potentate he wished to please; they knew that he was heartened and encouraged by his elderly uncle's expressed approval. They were quite right to believe that this meeting marked a new stage in Anglo-Russian relations at the ultimate expense of Germany, quite wrong to assume that such an array of top brass would never be called together without a specific agreement in view. And so it was that only a few days after the Reval gathering William burst out uncontrollably at, of all things, a cavalry review, with the accusation that 'they wish to encircle and provoke us', and the rhetorical declaration that he knew how to break the ring.[5]

Certainly the British were not thinking at all in terms of encirclement, only of insurance against possible German aggression; certainly the last thing Izvolsky wanted was to alienate further a country traditionally and for obvious reasons a natural ally. But there can be little doubt that Germany's rather apprehensive indignation over the Reval meeting was to have a bearing on her very stiff behaviour towards Russia when, within a matter of months, poor Izvolsky found himself so humiliatingly embroiled in his desperate row with Austria-Hungary over the annexation of Bosnia-Hercegovina, which also, by throwing a match into the Balkan powder barrel, was the first definite step towards the 1914 war.

2

Izvolsky brought it on himself. His action in seeking out his opposite number in Vienna, Baron Lexa von Aehrenthal (who had been a highly respected Austrian Ambassador to St Petersburg), in order to gain support for his plan to reopen the question of the Straits was gratuitous and, in the circumstances, asking for trouble. It was the action of an underemployed minister determined to carve out a place for himself in history – of a minister, moreover, who had spent so much of his life in foreign embassies that he was completely out of touch with domestic public opinion. He imagined, erroneously, that to solve the question of the Straits would bring him instant applause and lasting fame. The Eastern Question had been the classical diplomatic problem of his formative years, and it never occurred to him that times had changed. The Panslav movement had passed him by: in so far as it meant anything to him it was simply a convenient cover for active Russian interest in the Balkans as the key to the Straits. He had been quite untouched by the growth of Panslav feeling as an aspect of Russian nationalism. So he walked into a hornet's nest.

The question of the Straits was not at that time important on the level of *Realpolitik*, as distinct from sentimental aspiration. The Russian navy would take years to recover after Port Arthur and Tsushima. The Black Sea fleet, which was all that was left of it, was, after the revolutionary upheaval of 1905, more a concept than a reality. Stolypin's demand for twenty years of peace was not excessive, and it should have been Izvolsky's primary task to provide him with them. This meant, among other things, letting sleeping dogs lie on Russia's own doorstep and keeping well away from the noisy confrontations of rival imperialisms farther from home. Russia's own doorstep, of course, was the Balkans, and the dogs there were indeed at last quiescent. That is to say, nothing was happening or was likely to happen to offer a threat to Russian security. This had been the case for many years past, or Nicholas would never have dared embark on his forward policy in the Far East which led to war with Japan. The last crisis in the Balkans had been the Bulgarian crisis during his father's reign, which had looked ugly for a time until it was successfully damped down – its only lasting consequence being the alienation of a greater Bulgaria from a St Petersburg very conscious of the fact that Bulgaria owed her independent existence to Russia and Russia alone, and very surprised and affronted when the Bulgarians turned out to be stubborn nationalists ungrateful enough as to demonstrate that by independence they meant, precisely, independence – and were prepared to fight for it.

In the third year of Nicholas's reign the traditional hostility of Russia and Austria had become for once so muted that the two powers had been able to make an agreement – to preserve the *status quo* in the Balkans, to consult harmoniously together, not to take Balkan territory themselves (although Austria reserved the right to annex Bosnia-Hercegovina and the Sanjak of Novibazar in case of need), to prevent others doing so, and to combine in opposition to the domination of the Balkan peninsula by any other Balkan nation.

This understanding survived the Macedonian upheaval in 1903 when Greeks, Serbs and Bulgarians fell to slaughtering one another with great ferocity. It survived the replacement of the pro-Austrian Obrenović dynasty in Serbia by the pro-Russian Karageorgevič dynasty, as a result of the peculiarly atrocious murders of King Alexander and Queen Draga. It survived the really dangerous tension between Austria and a newly assertive Serb nationalism which led to economic warfare of a most damaging kind. It even survived Aehrenthal's first irresponsible *coup de théâtre*, when he shocked opinion all over the world and had the Panslav Press screaming for a holy war on behalf of Slavdom by announcing as a *fait accompli* his deal with Turkey to run a railway of great strategic and economic importance across the Sanjak of Novibazar, thus linking Austria-Hungary and the rest of Europe with Salonika.

This was in January 1908, and Izvolsky – who had the greatest difficulty in calming popular Panslav and nationalist opinion, which he despised – should have been warned not only of the mood of his own people but also of the trickiness of Aehrenthal, who to all outward appearances was the untrickiest man in the world (mournfully resigned rather), but was driven by a high romantic conviction that a master of classic diplomacy must prove himself by pulling off spectacular deals, even though the desired result could as well be obtained by sober and routine procedures.

Izvolsky, who in his way was afflicted by the same disease, was not warned.

Both he and Aehrenthal were tempted into action in the summer of 1908 by what seemed to them the possible consequences of Enver Pasha's Young Turk revolution. If indeed the old Ottoman regime was swept away and the new one carried out the reforms for so long resisted by successive Sultans, then the dying Ottoman Empire would be transformed; the problem of Turkey in Europe would be solved; turmoil in the Balkans would subside; there would be no case for Vienna's continued occupation of Bosnia-Hercegovina, let alone the annexation of those provinces; while, at the same time, Russia's chances of solving the problem of Constantinople and the Straits in her favour might well be reduced.

The sensible policy for both powers was wait and see. But it was not a sensible age. The Foreign Ministers of two powers which for very different reasons were in no position to participate in the fashionable games and exercises of the moment – scrambling for Africa for example – found in the Balkans their own opportunity to make a little inessential hay. Very amicably, if a little coyly after his recent violent tirades against Austria, Izvolsky suggested that it might be a good idea if he and Aehrenthal were to meet to discuss 'in a friendly spirit of reciprocity' the two things that interested them most. If he gave his support to Austria's annexation project, he believed he might obtain from Aehrenthal backing for his campaign to get the Straits opened to Russian warships. That both men half understood that they were playing with fire was shown by the fact that neither was ready to issue a formal invitation: the meeting when it took place in mid-September was informal and unofficial and was contrived when Izvolsky was taking the cure at Carlsbad and was offered the opportunity of meeting Aehrenthal at the neighbouring country seat at Buchlau of Count Berchtold, then Austrian Ambassador to St Petersburg, who also happened to be at Carlsbad.

Precisely what the two men said to each other nobody will ever know: no record was kept. All that was known was that three weeks later, on 6 October, the Emperor Franz Joseph, apropos of nothing, proclaimed his annexation of Bosnia-Hercegovina and his simultaneous evacuation of the Sanjak. Berlin, London, Paris, St Petersburg reeled. Here was a direct breach of the provisions of the Treaty of Berlin, which forbade unilateral action in the Balkans. Serbia, which had a claim to the provinces, made martial noises of the most menacing kind. Russian public opinion, driven to a frenzy by the powerful Panslav Press, demanded instant action in support of suffering and insulted fellow-Slavs and Christians (the two provinces contained, as well as Orthodox Serbs, a high proportion of Moslem Serbs and Catholic Croats). France and Britain were alarmed and angry at this upset to the *status quo*. Germany, indignant that her ally Austria should take independent action without her permission, was also concerned lest this irregular development should upset her own careful planning for the famous Baghdad Railway.

Aehrenthal, already a sick man and badly shaken by the consequences of what was an essentially frivolous action, dug his toes in and presented himself as a responsible statesman, deeply aggrieved. Austria, he declared in effect, had done nothing that was not in the book. Since the Treaty of Berlin she had occupied the two provinces by consent of the powers, governing them in a beneficial and orderly manner; it was always understood that in certain circumstances she might one day annex them. The only other interested party was Russia, and His Excellency, M. Alexander Izvolsky, had freely indicated at Buchlau that Russia had no objection.

Izvolsky, desperate, said he had done nothing of the kind. He had indeed discussed the matter with His Excellency the Herr Baron von Aehrenthal. But what he had said was that Russia would have no objection in principle to the occupation in return for Austrian support for the opening of the Straits to Russian warships, which Aehrenthal had promised. There had, however, been no question of immediate action.

Aehrenthal said, yes, the matter of the Straits had certainly been discussed, and Austria would by all means support any demand for their opening. But what M. Izvolsky appeared to understand by the opening of the Straits was a one-sided arrangement: namely that Russian ships should be free to move out of the Black Sea, while foreign ships would not be free to move into it. This he, Aehrenthal, had not realised. The Straits open to all ships of all the powers was what he had in mind.

It is very doubtful whether this was true. Aehrenthal had seen a chance to achieve the annexation quickly by outsmarting Izvolsky, and he took it, undoing all his own good work of the past two years towards achieving neighbourly relations with Serbia. Izvolsky on his side was not taken by surprise by the news of the annexation, no matter what he said. On his leisurely way back from Carlsbad to St Petersburg he had met the German Foreign Minister, von Schon, and confided the imminence of the annexation to him, mentioning 8 October as the probable date of its announcement. He was forced to call Aehrenthal a liar to save his own face. It simply had not occurred to him that Russian public opinion at that time, the epoch of Stolypin's conservative third Duma with the very strong right-wing nationalist extremists making a great deal of the running, was far less interested in the Straits than determined that Russia should throw her weight about in the Balkans as the protector of all the Slavs.

Both Izvolsky and public opinion had their feet well off the ground in their different ways: Russia was in no position to throw her weight about or make any demands at all to protect Christians and Slavs, to support a forward Serbian policy, or to force the opening of the Straits. She had no choice but to back down in the most humiliating and public circumstances.

Aehrenthal was adamant. To the proposal by Britain and France for the convening of a European conference he agreed, providing it was understood that the annexation would be formally confirmed without question: now he looked for support from the very faction in Vienna he had striven against in the past, the war party led by the Chief-of-Staff von Hötzendorf who for long had been demanding a preventative war against Serbia. Germany, in spite of her irritation with Austria, decided that the alliance must come first and refused to intervene when Izvolsky journeyed to Berlin to plead. Britain worked hardest to prevent a war which nobody except the Austrian war party and the uninstructed Russian nationalists wanted. She did her best to help Izvolsky and also to restrain St Petersburg from committing itself too far in support of Serbia. So Serbia in the end was left on her own, powerless to challenge Austria without Russian backing. The crisis had lasted from the autumn of 1908 to the spring of 1909. Its happy ending was of the kind that could not be repeated.

3

It is hard to realise that this drama of great-power diplomacy was initiated by a Russian Foreign Minister only two years after Tsushima and the Treaty of Portsmouth and barely eighteen months after the suppression of the St Petersburg soviet and the Moscow rising. After the more or less forcible dissolution of the First and Second Dumas and Stolypin's illegal *coup* in changing the electoral law, the Third Duma, which was to run its full course until 1912, had only recently settled down to pursue its relatively fruitful and sober existence. This highly conservative assembly, beset by violent and disreputable extremes on left and right, was to approach more closely for better or worse the Western idea of good government than Russia had ever come before – or has since come. It was the Duma of which that great Russophile Sir Bernard Pares was to write in sadness:

> May an Englishman, bred in the tradition of Gladstone, to whom the Duma was almost a home with many friends of all parties, recall that vanished past? At the bottom was a feeling of reassurance, and founded on it one saw a growing courage and initiative and a growing mutual understanding and goodwill. The Duma had the freshness of a school, with something of surprise at the simplicity with which the differences that had seemed formidable could be removed. One could feel the pleasure with which the Members were finding their way into common work for the good of the whole country.... Some seventy persons at least, forming the nucleus of the more important commissions, were learning in detail to understand the problems and difficulties of administration and therefore to understand both each other and the Government. One could see political competence growing day by day. And to a constant observer it was becoming more and more an open secret that the distinctions of party meant little, and that in the social warmth of their public work for Russia all these men were becoming friends...[6]

'Some seventy persons at least...' In a country of 120 million in the year 1908 some seventy persons at least were beginning, with wonder in their hearts, to discover the joys and techniques of national self-government, still of a very limited kind – limited because there the autocrat still was able to dismiss them when he liked; and far closer to the autocrat than to the Duma was still the formal administration, the Council of Ministers under Stolypin.

That the Foreign Minister of such a country, its finances ruined, its navy sunk, its army in desperate need of reorganisation, should embark gratuitously on what can only be called a forward policy in the Balkans with all its so well-known risks, that the response to Izvolsky's failure should have been not dismissal for taking unnecessary risks but censure for failing to succeed and a furious uproar of violent jingoism or hurrah patriotism on the part of an important section of the educated public, who had recently shown themselves incapable of fighting tiny and parvenu Japan or of keeping any sort of order in their own land – all this indicated, by all means, a striking resilience on the part of great Russia. But it is permissible to wonder whether such resilience is a mark of the highest type of life and also whether such behaviour does not argue in the population at large the sort of failure to understand the facts of life which was so manifest in the autocrat himself.

Stolypin's enlightened reforms, which would in time transform Russian agriculture, were just beginning to bite. By 1915 there had emerged from the miasma of primitive peasant collectivism the astonishing number of 7,300,000 households of individual peasant, or yeoman, farmers, proud of their own standing, their own land, their own skills – and with a vested interest in the unfamiliar concept of public order.[7] But this was very much a beginning. It was a beginning that had been favoured by the remarkable luck of an uninterrupted succession of good harvests. And it was backed by a new leap forward in industrial development, which depended also on the rule of law, on good harvests (with plenty of grain for export), and on a period of calm to attract foreign investment.[8] The revolutionaries (exiled when they were not in prison), hopelessly divided, frittered away their lives, it seemed, in sterile controversy: they despaired. If conditions in Russia continued to improve as they were improving in Stolypin's last years, and even after his murder, there was no hope for revolution.

4

This idyll was interrupted in April 1912 by the notorious massacre on the Lena goldfield. The Lena is an immense and even today almost inconceivably remote river flowing to the Arctic Ocean through the forest and the tundra of north-eastern Siberia. The workers in the goldfield, virtual prisoners of their employers, struck in desperation because nobody would pay attention to their fairly modest demands for better food and living conditions in that harsh climate. In the time-honoured manner troops were called in. Confronted by a crowd of some five thousand sullen workers they opened fire in the time-honoured manner, not once but many times. When the shooting stopped some two hundred lay dead on the ground and another two hundred at least were wounded.

This sort of thing had happened often enough before, but Russia was changing, and when the news came through there was an immediate upset in the Duma. The fairly recently installed Minister of the Interior, A. A. Makharov, was one of many who had not properly registered the significance of change. Instead of showing concern and regret and the will to enquire into the reasons for such excess of overkill, he took the line that the military had been perfectly justified in their conduct: what could soldiers do but shoot when confronted with a demonstrating mob? He then summed the matter up with the classic remark, which would also serve as an epitaph for the regime: 'So it always has been, and so it always will be.'

Much to Makharov's surprise the Duma was not impressed with this elegant formulation. It was furious. The Government, forced on to the defensive, was compelled to set up a commission of enquiry under an ex-Minister of Justice. The commission produced a report which was a thorough-going indictment of the management of the goldfield. One of the members of that commission was a brilliant young lawyer, Alexander Kerensky, who made his mark as a rhetorician of impressive power during the course of the subsequent debate.

The Lena goldfield was a British concession. So Britain could claim a modest share in the creation of the climate of bitterness, hatred and despair which, after a brief interlude of patriotic euphoria at the beginning of the First World War, was to breed the hurricane of revolution. For the Lena massacre, in relative terms no more than yet another bloody act of repression among many, was critical in its timing. It came at a moment when soberly conservative Russia had decided with the liberals that enough was enough when it came to troops shooting down unarmed fellow-countrymen. The workers all over Russia were also affected. Instead of being intimidated they were aroused. So that the Lena massacre turned out to be the prelude to a new movement of strikes which swept the country on the eve of the great war so soon to come. And it was this new wave of proletarian militancy, more politically inspired than ever before, which gave their first chance to a new generation of revolutionaries.

These were not bourgeois intellectuals but shop-floor conspirators and demagogues, men who worked with their hands, had a rough edge to their tongues, and found intellectual sustenance in a sort of kindergarten

Marxism. They tended to despise the exiled heroes in Zürich and Geneva endlessly talking and quarrelling over endless cups of coffee. It was from among these that in years to come Stalin was to find the men he needed in his bid for power: men like the nineteen-year-old Lazar Kaganovich, employed in a shoe factory in Kiev, or the slightly older Nicholas Shvernik, who had started work at fourteen in a metallurgical plant in St Petersburg; and many others. They were as different in attitude and background from the cultivated Marxists and Socialist Revolutionaries grouped round Lenin, Martov, Chkeidzke, Chernov, as it is possible to imagine – as different indeed as they were from that anonymous and growing host of devoted, angry, gentle, confused, humanitarian idealists, many of them women, who wore out their lives and risked their freedom to succour the poor and downtrodden in the name of a revolutionary movement they did not understand and from which they would have shrunk in horror had they been given an inkling of its future.

5

It was also in 1912, the year after Stolypin's murder, that Gregory Rasputin became a major public issue. The first newspaper mention of his name had occurred two years earlier. In 1911, as already noted, Stolypin found it necessary to warn Nicholas that the Rasputin connection was bringing the Imperial family into disrepute and that the man should be banished from the capital. An ominous row had arisen when the Chief Procurator of the Holy Synod, a decent functionary called Lukyanov, made a move with Stolypin's backing to put down a savagely reactionary and scurrilous monk called Iliodor who had established such an ascendancy in Stolypin's own province of Saratov that he had succeeded in virtually terrorising the authorities from the Governor downwards into subservience. The moment Lukyanov took action to remove this wretch it was discovered that Iliodor had very high protection indeed: the Tsaritsa herself, instructed by Rasputin. Stolypin had his work cut out to argue Nicholas into postponing the dismissal of Lukyanov on his wife's insistence and his replacement by a Rasputin protégé, V. K. Sabler, a man of a nastiness remarkable at that time, but soon to be surpassed by a multitude of Rasputin's nominees. With Stolypin out of the way Lukyanov went and Sabler was brought in. For the first time a large public began to realise that this bogus holy man with his disgusting manners and lurid reputation was a figure to be reckoned with.

There is no known evidence of Rasputin's influencing of government appointments before the Sabler scandal. But very soon after this came the miraculous 'cure' of the Tsarevich and Alexandra's total surrender to the miracle-worker. It was pure chance that at this moment the wretched Iliodor quarrelled with Rasputin and put out copies of the Tsaritsa's letters to Rasputin which made plain her almost worshipping dependence on him. Alexandra only made things worse when she flew into a rage and demanded that all public reference to Rasputin be forbidden. She, like Makharov, had forgotten about the Duma: the Octobrist majority might be conservative and loyal to the throne, and were; but they were also highly critical of the court's excesses. The Speaker of the Duma, now M. V. Rodzyanko ('the fattest man in the Empire', Nicholas had jocularly remarked of him in easier times) was moved in private audience to offer a solemn warning to the Tsar. The Octobrist leader, Guchkov, delivered himself of a powerful public denunciation of Rasputin in the Duma. Most disturbing of all from the Tsar's point of view, for reasons of his own the unscrupulous right-wing extremist, leader once of the Union of Russian People, now of the Society of Michael the Archangel, patron of the Black Hundreds, scurrilous anti-semite and absolutist of the deepest dye, Vladimir Purishkevich, joined in the attack. And it was this same Purishkevich who nearly five years later was to act as the political member, as it were, of the little group of conspirators who murdered Rasputin in the basement of the Yussupov Palace, feeding him first with poisoned cakes and drink and then, when he did not die, shooting him in the back again and again and finally beating him to death. That was in the last week of December 1916: it may be seen as the first act of the revolution, carried out not by revolutionaries but by fanatical monarchists seeking to purge the court of Nicholas and Alexandra.[9]

In 1912 nothing whatever came of the warnings and denunciations. The Tsar was still the Tsar, an autocrat still under the new Fundamental Laws, and if he chose to pay no attention to the concerted demands and pleadings of his advisers there was nothing the Duma or anybody else could do about it. Nobody knows what Nicholas in his heart of hearts thought of Rasputin. Alexandra was now wholly under his spell, convinced, perhaps rightly, that he could help poor Alexei in his terrible affliction as nobody else could (Rasputin certainly had hypnotic powers. He seems to have had some sort of second sight too. He was never investigated by a committee of scientists as might happen to a similar apparition now, in or out of gaol). She believed that he was divinely inspired in all he said and did. Nicholas cannot conceivably have shared this conviction: he knew all about Rasputin's private life – if private is the word for the exercises of an exhibitionist sensualist. But for whatever reason – to please Alexandra, for the sake of a quiet life, for the sake of his small son – he deliberately sacrificed his trust, his country and his people to his own domestic convenience, turning his face against the urgings of the only men who could sustain him.

It was very bad luck for the new Prime Minister, Count V. N. Kokovtsev, Stolypin's Minister of Finance, that he stepped into so much serious trouble at the start of his term. He was a good man, able, upright, courageous, but neither a spell-binder nor a bulldozer. In a land which apparently had so much difficulty in producing the happy mean – anything, indeed, between the genius and the imbecile, the dreamer and the bully, the fanatic and the apathetic – he was precisely the sort of man most needed. He would have made a splendid, steady, not very imaginative but by no means inconsiderable prime minister in a land with an established constitution and settled ways. His courage he had shown immediately after Stolypin's murder, which was openly seized upon by the Kiev authorities as a perfect opportunity to organise a massacre of the local Jews (the assassin Bogrov, the policeman revolutionary, was a Jew). They were affronted and uncomprehending when Kokovtsev on his own initiative bluntly forbade any such action and ordered up three regiments of Cossacks to police the city (the Jews were already packing their belongings in a panic to be gone). On whose authority? he was asked. 'On the authority of the head of the Government!' he replied, and ordered the despatch of telegrams on the same authority to all governors of the region instructing them to use force if necessary to check pogroms before they started anywhere. It was a brave act for a man who had not yet been appointed Prime Minister.[10]

Russia was beginning to breed such men. But instead of being the first of a line of decent, honest, competent prime ministers Kokovtsev was to be the last. In no time at all he found himself up against Rasputin. On his induction Kokovtsev had been received with quite unusual warmth by the Tsaritsa, who in her deep Christian manner radiated quiet pleasure in Stolypin's demise. 'I am sure that Stolypin died to make room for you, and that this is all for the good of Russia,'[11] this extraordinary woman confided to his successor, who did not know where to look. But Alexandra soon changed her mind, instructed by Rasputin. And to the enmity of the first lady in the land was added the venom of the extreme right, baulked of their pogroms and other thuggish enjoyments.

Nicholas was quite unable to withstand such pressures. It is to be doubted whether he tried very hard. But he could not afford to let Kokovtsev go immediately: there were affairs of state which even Alexandra and Rasputin did not fully understand. The state needed money, and, as had been the case with Witte before him, Kokovtsev could not be sent packing until he had completed the negotiations for a new French loan. So once again the Autocrat of All the Russias had to hold his hand while he waited on the pleasure of hundreds of thousands, millions indeed, of French peasants who, with their careful savings, were all that stood between the glories of Imperial Russia and total bankruptcy.

Kokovtsev was dismissed on the last day of January 1914, not at all the colourless person he has often been made out to be, but insufficiently strong to make his personality prevail, even for a few over-strenuous years, as Witte and Stolypin had been able to do before him. The formal pretext for his departure was his objection to the Tsar's sudden determination to abolish the tax on vodka. This was the major source of revenue in a land where drunkenness was a national disgrace. Nicholas was no doubt correct in deciding that it was a bad thing for the state to depend for its finances on the encouragement of alcoholism. But where, asked Kokovtsev, was the money otherwise to come from? Russia could not rely on foreign loans for everything.

There was to be no more decency in official Russia. With Kokovtsev's departure Nicholas gave the game away and displayed, once and for all unmistakably, the almost awe-inspiring shallowness, the incorrigible silliness of his mind. He showed what he thought of the Duma, of his people, by recalling of all improbable relics of the past poor old Goremykin. Even so, the manner of the appointment surpassed in unconscious insolence the simple fact of it. Characteristically, Nicholas found himself unable to tell Kokovtsev to his face that he must go. He wrote him a letter instead. And the letter contained these words: 'the swift tempo of our domestic life and the striking development of the economic forces of our country both demand the undertaking of most definite and serious measures, a task which should be best entrusted to a man fresh for the work.'[12]

Kokovtsev was then sixty-one and the best financial brain in Russia; Goremykin was seventy-five, and he would have been the last to suggest that he had a brain at all. It does not matter whether Nicholas was temporarily insane when he wrote that letter, or had fallen asleep in the middle of composing it, or had taken it down from dictation by Alexandra or Rasputin or anybody else. The only point to be made is that it is profitless and absurd to take any further account of his actions for the remaining three years of his reign. He was at sea and out of control. Even Goremykin had more sense and a clearer view of what was going on.

'I am like an old fur coat,' he remarked. 'For many months I have been packed away in camphor. I am being taken out now merely for the occasion; when it is passed I shall be packed away again till I am wanted next time.'[13] He lasted until 1916 and there was to be no next time. He was a loyal old boy, idleness, cynicism, French novels, Piccadilly-weepers and all. And he had a sense of humour. It was Rasputin, of course, through Alexandra, who got him out for the last time. They got him out not to replace him with a wartime premier of energy and vision but because Rasputin decided that the premiership was the very place for the most boorish and corrupt of all his protégés, B. V. Sturmer.

Goremykin had an unexpected end. In 1918 he was set upon by a mob in a St Petersburg street. Although the revolution was successfully concluded, the Bolsheviks with their October *coup* having destroyed the Provisional Government and established themselves in power some months earlier, the mob was still bloodthirsty, and had no great respect for grey hairs. Poor Goremykin, at seventy-eight, was lynched on the spot.

Kokovtsev was luckier. Some very dreadful things happened to members of his family, but he himself, after being imprisoned by the Bolsheviks, managed to escape, to live in Paris until well after the Second World War. In prison, heavily interrogated by the first of the notorious Chekists, Uritsky, he refused absolutely to denounce his late Imperial master, insisting that Nicholas, who had so wretchedly betrayed him, had himself been betrayed by others and was not to be blamed for any of the crimes of the regime.

To strike a lighter and more cheerful note, Uritsky himself was murdered, in the best tradition of Russian police chiefs, later in that same year; and the assassin of this detested Bolshevik was, again in the best traditions of the revolutionary movement, a Socialist Revolutionary. So it will be seen that the S.R.s went down fighting bravely: tyrants of whatever colour were all one to them. But the sands were running out. When in that same year Fanny Kaplan shot at Lenin and wounded but failed to kill him (she shortened his life, however, by some years), it was almost the last act of protest by the Socialist Revolutionaries. Before very long the Bolsheviks had liquidated the lot.

6

Our story may seem to have run ahead of itself again. But in fact it is the subject that is disintegrating, vanishing into thin air, leaving nothing but the terrible memory of that blood-stained cellar in Ekaterinburg and the haunting image of the last Tsar, deposed, and staring past the camera into nothingness as he sits under guard on his tree stump. For the action of Nicholas in dismissing Kokovtsev and installing Goremykin for all practical purposes brings the story of the Romanov dynasty to a close. The only thing remaining for the last autocrat to do was to die: he was to have a holocaust for a funeral pyre.

From the beginning of 1914 he ceased to play any effective part in the government of the country. That is why the events immediately leading up to the war are of little relevance to the history of the dynasty, which was already over. Russia, desperately backward, had in the past twenty years made a supreme effort to catch up with the world and had fallen back. By many it has been held that Imperial Russia would have survived but for the shattering impact of the 1914 war. It seems to me that the events as narrated in these pages declare otherwise.[14]

It is the harder to say this because under Witte and Stolypin the country had indeed made a great effort to pull itself together. But how could two great ministers in so short a time hope to restore the damage done by successive autocrats who flatly prohibited active participation in government and by generations of nobles who submitted tamely to this ban? Russia was indeed changing, but not fast enough. As we have seen, she was only just beginning to develop a rational and productive agricultural system, and her business men and entrepreneurs, with the rarest exceptions, still looked to the state for protection and direction as they had done for centuries past. It was not vital for Russia to catch up with the West as a modern industrial power if only she would have been content to drop out of the international competition for a generation or two and cultivate her own immense and largely virgin garden. But she was not prepared to drop out. Indeed the whole dynamic behind Witte had been the determination to compete. Yet how could a society of obedient functionaries form a suitable stock on which to graft artificially the technological profusion of the West, the organic product of native skills and enterprises expressing itself with chaotic but infinitely productive spontaneity?

The sad thing was that Russia was dying even as she was being discovered by the West. For it was in those last pre-war years that Europe was suddenly electrified by the sheer vitality and intensity of the creative spirit that came out of the East. It was a point built up with a sort of pressure-cooker effect on the eve of catastrophe, stimulating the outside world, and beckoning it, with the vision of life-enhancing wonders, quite new and unheard-of before, springing up from the depths of that remote and forbidding and mysterious hinterland. It was in 1909 that Russian ballet burst on Paris, in 1911 on London. Much of the music was old, but some belonged to a new age. The young Stravinsky was the first Russian artist of any kind to find himself under attack in the West for his originality. The great Russian novelists, of course, had made their indelible mark, but for all their very special and eccentric qualities they could be referred to a familiar tradition. The impact of this music and dance was more immediate, and challenging in quite a different way. Russia was indeed beginning to repay the West for all that it had taken from it in the past. Everything seemed possible in a land that had produced a *Boris Godunov* fifty years before and could now send a Chaliapin to recreate it.

It was a false impression. Diaghilev with his *World of Art*, his dancers, designers, composers, was a revolutionary, not a celebrant. The dancers themselves were not the wave of the future but the ornaments of a dying age. Those marvellous abstract painters and sculptors, the Tatlins and the Sternbergs, were the heralds of a new age, which would be denied by Russia, not the standard-bearers of a culture that could rejuvenate her. It was Chekhov in his great pieces for the theatre who reflected the dying of the old society. Ominously, but not yet known abroad, one of the most agonisedly sensitive poets in any language, Alexander Blok, was turning from delight to despair and from despair to prophetic violence.

The war when it came, came quietly. The assassination of the Austrian Archduke Franz Ferdinand at Sarajevo in the middle of July caused very little stir. Perhaps some *Schadenfreude*: Sarajevo was the capital of Bosnia, and it served Austria right for behaving so treacherously over Bosnia six years earlier. The Russian foreign office was still being run by Stolypin's unfortunate relative, Sazonov, unhappy, indecisive, still trying to please, weighed down by responsibility. Russia had weathered the Balkan wars of 1912 and 1913 without getting into trouble. After 1908 she had tried to put together a Balkan bloc to stand against Austrian pretensions and encroachments; but Serbia and Bulgaria so heartily disliked each other that the only thing to hold them together was a mutual hatred of Turkey. Sazonov had no wish at all to back the Balkan Slavs against Turkey, but his Minister in Belgrade, Hartwig, was an ardent Panslav and did his best to encourage the belligerence of the Serbs.

Distrust and dislike of Austria, however, did not imply an equal hostility towards Austria's ally, Germany. And up to the very brink of war there were strong voices in Russia insisting that Britain was and must be the real enemy, that Anglo-German rivalry was the cause of all the real conflict in the world, that only Jews could benefit from Russia's alliance with France and understanding with England. Aehrenthal, for his part, until his death in 1912, profoundly believed that no Anglo-Russian agreement could possibly last and that sooner or later Russia would inevitably start wooing Austria once more. It was an expensive illusion.[15]

Inside Russia, one of the chief proponents of the view that Germany's staunch support of Austria sprang not from conviction but because she resented what she saw as Russia's flirtation with Britain was P. D. Durnovo, Witte's one-time Minister of the Interior.[16] It was an arguable view, but it happened to be wrong. Certainly there was every reason for Russia to keep out of conflict with Germany, and every possibility of her doing so if she played her cards correctly. But first she had to settle with

Austria and make it clear that for an indefinite period she would stop worrying about the Balkans in general and the Serbs in particular. In a word, that she would turn in upon herself and develop her own resources.

How much Russia in the person of her representatives in Belgrade had to do directly with the assassination at Sarajevo is unknown. Hartwig's anti-Austrian activities are well documented in general terms, and so are those of Captain Artamanov, the Russian military attaché, who gave money and encouragement to the Black Hand, the secret society which supplied the weapons to the assassin Gavrilo Princip and his associates. The details do not matter. When Austria, with the death-wish on her, rejected as insufficient Serbia's all but abject submission to the terms of her ultimatum she knew very well that Russia was too deeply committed to allow the Serbs to be wiped off the map. Public opinion in Russia was such that it would have taken a monarch or a prime minister of exceptional power to have climbed down a second time, as had been done in 1908. When Germany backed Austria, after much hesitation, with her celebrated 'blank cheque', she knew very well that Russia would mobilise. Of course she also knew that Russia was not ready for war, but in the circumstances this could make no difference. And France would go to Russia's help, that was understood: there was a superb German plan for dealing quickly with France. England, however, it was believed, would not go to the help of France or Russia.

Sazonov made one last attempt to stave off war (he was not alone; the Emperor William and Bethmann-Hollweg had had second thoughts) – in vain: when the Russian defence chiefs demanded immediate mobilisation he got Nicholas to urge that mobilisation should be limited to the southern armies, proof that Austria, not Germany was the foe. But Sazonov had not the courage or the conviction to stand up to the soldiers when they confronted him with the sobering technicalities of the mobilisation plan, and Nicholas was now fatalism itself, sadly laying the whole burden of decision on the shoulders of the Almighty.[17]

The armies marched. The Tsar invoked the support of his people, for whom he had done so little; and they rallied, first to their country, then to their monarch, even the radicals and most of the revolutionaries calling off the struggle for the duration. Nicholas then betrayed them by sending them to fight under inferior generals and with a feeble supply system against what had long been known to be the finest army in the world – though perhaps this cannot be held particularly against him, since every other belligerent government did the same. Against Austria the Russians performed prodigies in battles, deploying millions, advancing deep into enemy territory. But Germany came to Austria's rescue and broke the Russians in a series of battles almost unimaginable in their intensity and magnitude.

Even so, and even though all the material achievements of Witte and Stolypin were not enough to sustain the Russian armies, the troops endured. They went on enduring as St Petersburg (Petrograd now) became a mad-house. Rasputin was more in control than ever. After the disastrous summer of 1915 Nicholas, urged on by Alexandra, assumed personal command of his armies in the field and went forward, leaving the Tsaritsa in effect to rule in his name. She ruled in Rasputin's name. The job of no minister, no official was secure for a day. Corrupt fools succeeded corrupt oafs in the highest positions in the land, and fools were removed to make room for imbeciles.

Even so, the end was unexpected when it came. Imperial Russia simply rotted away from the centre outwards until the shell fell in.

Vast armies of peasant conscripts, ill-supplied, ill-cared for, ill-commanded, were still sticking it out all through the winter of 1916–17, and most of them kept at it for much longer. But in St Petersburg the people were demoralised, cold, weary, hungry. They started demonstrating as they queued for bread. There were near riots all over the city. Troops detailed to suppress the disturbances refused and joined the demonstrators (the Guards regiments were at the front, as well as the best regiments of the line: these were inferior back-area soldiers). This happened in March 1917. In a few days the troubles spread. The Duma was paralysed: something, it knew, should be done; Nicholas ought to go; a new Government should be formed; but it was very difficult to know just how. Nicholas by now had heard what was going on and decided to come back from his headquarters at Mogilev to St Petersburg. To his surprise his train was stopped in the station at Pskov, and he was politely told he could go no further. His mood was a mixture of fatalism and extreme hauteur. We remember his words to the British Ambassador, quoted earlier – that it was not for him to reconcile himself with his people: they must ask to be forgiven. He still felt like this and made no gesture to acknowledge that grievances might be real. But neither did he struggle. When nine days after the start of the great revolution representatives of the Duma (that colourful figure Guchkov was one of them) arrived in their top-hats and frock-coats to demand his abdication he conceded it willingly because clearly God wished it. But he really did not know why.

NOTES ON SOURCES

Chapter 1

A Moment of History

1 The literature in Russian on the Decembrist conspiracy and its aftermath would fill many shelves. The most circumstantial and complete account in English is in Anatole G. Mazour, *The First Russian Revolution, 1825* (Berkeley, 1937).

2 Alexander Herzen, *My Past and Thoughts*, translated by Constance Garnett (London, 1924) vol. I, pp. 11–12. For all references to *My Past and Thoughts* I have used this six-volume (1924–7) edition, which is still the most widely circulated. Mrs Garnett's admirable translation has been in some measure revised and in some particulars added to by Humphrey Higgins for the latest four-volume edition, which also has an introduction by Sir Isaiah Berlin (New York, London, 1968). Mr Higgins was able to work from the definitive Russian collected edition of Herzen's works (A. I. Gerzen, *Sobranie Sochinenii*, in 30 volumes, Moscow, 1956). For the only discrepancies between the old and the new in the passages referred to hereafter see notes 3, 4 and 5 to chapter 13 below.

3 The only authority for these remarks is Nicholas I himself, cited in N. K. Shilder, *Imperator Nikolai I, ego Zhizn i Tsarstvovanie* (St Petersburg, 1903) vol. I, p. 200.

4 An illuminating and compendious study of the four main revolts is Paul Avrich, *Russian Rebels 1600–1800* (London, 1973).

Chapter 2

The Doomed Conspiracy

1 N. K. Shilder, *Imperator Pavel I, Aleksandr I, ego Zhizn i Tsarstvovanie* (St Petersburg, 1897) vol. I, p. 172.

2 Grand Duke Nikolai Mikhailovich, *Le Comte Paul Stroganov* (St Petersburg, 1905) vol. II, pp. 61–2.

3   For a savage portrait of Speransky from a very Russian point of view see Tolstoy's *War and Peace*, bk II, chaps 2 and 10.

4   The Speransky Statute is in *Proekty i Zapiski* by M. M. Speransky, edited by S. N. Valk (Moscow, 1961) pp. 143–221. The best account of Speransky's life and work in English is Marc Raeff's *Mikhail Speransky, Statesman of Imperial Russia* (The Hague, 1957).

5   A. N. Pypin, *Obshchestvennoe Dvizhenie v Rossii pri Aleksandre I* (St Petersburg, 1900) p. 172.

6   A. S. Pushkin, *Dnevnik*: entry for 9 April 1821, vol. x. p. 6 of the 1882 St Petersburg *Sobranie Sochinenii*, ed. P. A. Efremov.

7   For a good account of the military colonies in English see Richard Pipes, 'The Russian Military Colonies 1810–1831' in *The Journal of Modern History*, vol. XXII (Chicago, 1950).

8   There is a full account of the Semyonovsky incident in Mazour, op. cit. pp. 59–61.

9   The argument of *Russian Justice* is summarised in ibid., pp. 100–16.

10 Much of the correspondence between Nicholas and Constantine is in N. K. Shilder, *Imperator Nikolai I*, op. cit., vol. I, pp. 177–212.

11 Mazour, op. cit., p. 202.

Chapter 3

The Autocratic Inheritance

1   Joseph Conrad, 'Autocracy and War' in *Notes on Life and Letters* (London, 1921, republished New York, 1972) pp. 130–1.

2   Sigismund zu Herberstein, *Notes Upon Russia*, translated by R. H. Major in *Hakluyt Society Works*, 1st ser., vols. x and XII (London, 1851–1852).

3   Vasili Klyuchevsky, *The Rise of the Romanovs*, translated by Lilian Archibald (London, 1960) p. 87. See Bibliography.

4   Carlyle's letter to Herzen was published for the first time in E. H. Carr, *The Romantic Exiles* (London, 1933) pp. 371–2.

5   Quoted in Constantine de Grunwald, *Tsar Nicholas I*, translated by Brigit Patmore (London, 1954) p. 74.

6   Shilder, op. cit., vol. I, p. 111.

7   *Letters of Queen Victoria 1837–1861*, edited by Christopher Jenson and Viscount Esher (London, 1908). Victoria's impressions of the Tsar are in letters of 4 June and 11 June 1844, vol. II, pp. 12–16.

8   Herzen, op. cit., vol. I, p. 63.

9   Marquis de Custine, *Le Russie en 1839*. See Bibliography. I have used the abridged translation by Phyllis Penn Kohler (Chicago, 1951, London, 1953) pp. 72–3.

10 Mazour, op. cit., p. 206.

11 The correspondence between Nicholas I and Franz Joseph I is in the Hause- Hof- und Staatsarchiv, Vienna. Much of it is quoted in Josef Redlich's *The Emperor Franz Joseph* (London, 1929).

12 A. V. Nikitenko, *Zapiski i Dnevnik 1804–1877*, (diary entry for 27 March 1859 (St Petersburg, 1906) vol. 1, p. 553.

13 Henri Troyat, *Pushkin*, translated by Nancy Amphoux (London, 1975) p. 310.

14 Adolf Schwarzenberg, *Prince Felix zu Schwarzenberg* (New York, 1946) p. 4.

15 Grunwald, op. cit., p. 64.

16 Ibid. and Mazour, op. cit., p. 206.

17 Kakhovsky to General Levashev, 24 February 1826. Quoted in Mazour, op. cit. p. 274.

18 A. Bestuzhev to the Tsar, undated. Ibid., p. 278.

19 N. V. Riasanovsky, *Nicholas I and Official Nationality in Russia 1825–1855* (Berkeley, 1961) p. 202.

20 Grunwald, op. cit., pp. 69–70.

21 N. V. Riasanovsky, op. cit., p. 5.

22 The embezzlement of 1,200,000 silver roubles belonging to the Fund for Invalids of the Napoleonic War by the much-decorated privy councillor and courtier, Politkovsky. See Nikitenko, op. cit., diary entry for 31 January 1853, vol. 1, p. 415.

Chapter 4

The State of the Empire

1 Herzen, op. cit., vol. 1, p. 299.

2 Ibid., vol. 11, p. 164.

3 Sydney L. Monas, *The Third Section: Police and Society in Russia under Nicholas I* (Cambridge, Mass., 1961) p. 107.

4 This celebrated phrase is usually given in English as 'Autocracy, orthodoxy, nationality'. But 'nationality' is not a true rendering of *narodnost*, which has no English equivalent. Professor Hugh Seton-Watson (see note 5 below) prefers 'the national principle', which is better but still not quite right. Sir Isaiah Berlin in his Romanes lecture on Turgenev *Fathers and Children* (Oxford, 1972) note 1 on pp. 3–4 suggests 'the national way of life', and I have followed him.

5 Report dated 4 December 1832, discussed in Hugh Seton-Watson, *The Russian Empire 1801–1917* (Oxford, 1967) pp. 219–20, and M. T. Florinsky, *Russia: A History and an Interpretation* (New York, 1953) vol. 11, pp. 797–800.

6 Storch's chief work was *Cours d'Économie Politique* (St Petersburg, 1815).

7 The building of this railway is well described in William L. Blackwell's *The Beginnings of Russian Industrialisation 1800–1860* (Princeton, 1968) which is an invaluable study of every aspect of its subject and highly readable into the bargain. It contains an elaborate bibliography.

8 Blackwell, op. cit., p. 296.

9 Ibid., p. 298.

10 Mary Chamot, 'A House Round a Russian Theatre' in *Country Life* (London, 21 November 1968) p. 1137.

11 Mary Chamot, 'A Russian Count's Palladianism' in ibid. (12 September 1968) p. 635. These two valuable articles, well-illustrated, give the best visual impression known to me of the style of the great Russian nobility and their architectural taste.

12 Blackwell, op. cit., pp. 202–3.

13 Ibid., p. 311.

14 Ibid., pp. 160–2.

15 N. A. Rimsky-Korsakov, *My Musical Life*, translated by Judah H. Jaffe (London, 1924) pp. 20–1.

16 Nikitenko, op. cit., diary entry for 11 March 1841, vol. I, p. 310.

Chapter 5

The Growth of the Mind

1 Custine, op. cit., p. 105.

2 Quoted by Raeff, op. cit., pp. 121–2.

3 Florinsky, op. cit., vol. II, p. 755.

4 *The Oxford Book of Russian Verse*, chosen by the Hon. Maurice Baring (Oxford, 1924) pp. xxviii–xxix.

5 Troyat, *Pushkin*, op. cit., p. 321.

6 Konstantin Paustovsky, *Story of a Life*, six volumes in English translation have been published in London (1964–74) under various titles.

7 P. A. Chaadayev, *Sochineniya i pisma*, ed. M. Gershenzon (Moscow, 1912) vol. I, p. 84.

8 Ibid., p. 81.

9 Ibid., p. 171.

10 Ibid., p. 188.

11 V. G. Korolenko's autobiography, *The History of my Contemporary*, extremely moving as a character study and full of invaluable sidelights on his period, has recently been well translated into English by Neil Parsons, (London, New York, 1972).

12 Incomparably the best study in English of Belinsky in particular and the writers of the period in general is contained in four essays by Sir Isaiah Berlin. See Bibliography.

Chapter 6

The Imperial Mission

1　J. S. Curtiss, *The Russian Army under Nicholas I 1825-1855* (Durham, N.C., 1965) p. 57.
2　Ibid., p. 65.
3　Nicholas to the Grand Duke Constantine, 3 December 1831, Theodor Schiemann, *Geschichte Russlands unter Kaiser Nikolaus I* (Berlin, 1904-1905) vol. III, p. 69.
4　Shilder, op. cit., vol. II, pp. 582-4.
5　*Russian Journal of Lady Londonderry 1836-37*, ed. W. A. L. Seaman and J. R. Sewell (London, 1973) p. 130.
6　Schiemann, op. cit., vol. IV, pp. 1-25.
7　Count Karl de Fiquelmont to Metternich, 6 November 1830, Grunwald, op. cit., p. 130.
8　Nikitenko, op. cit., vol. I, p. 461, diary entry 30 August 1855.
9　Florinsky, op. cit., vol. II, p. 846.

Chapter 7

The Slow Drift to Disaster

1　*The Times*, London, 16 March 1835, quoted in the Editors' introduction to *Russian Journal of Lady Londonderry*, op. cit., p. 7.
2　G. H. Bolsover, 'Nicholas I and the Partition of Turkey', in *The Slavonic and East European Review*, No. 68 (London, 1948) p. 11.
3　Ibid., p. 127.
4　Ibid., p. 128.
5　Ibid.
6　Ibid., p. 133.
7　Ibid., p. 134.
8　Riasanovsky, op. cit., p. 139.
9　Herzen, op. cit., vol. II, pp. 185-6.
10　Nikitenko, op. cit., vol. I, p. 461.
11　E. Ashley, *Life and Correspondence of Henry John Temple, Viscount Palmerston* (London, 1876), vol. I, p. 104-5.
12　Grunwald, op. cit., p. 243.
13　*Letters of Queen Victoria 1837-1861*, op. cit., vol. II, pp. 165-6.
14　Schiemann, op. cit., pp. 1-25.
15　Bolsover, op. cit., p. 139.

Chapter 8

The Crimean Fiasco

1 See note 11 to chapter 3.
2 Ibid.
3 Ibid.
4 Monas, op. cit., pp. 153–5.
5 Troyat, *Tolstoy*, translated by Nancy Amphoux (New York, 1967), pp. 113–14.
6 Ibid., p. 116.
7 Ibid., p. 121.
8 Curtiss, op. cit., p. 132.
9 Ibid., pp. 135–6.
10 Personal observation. For the first eighteen months of the Second World War Soviet military transport was almost exclusively horse-drawn and indistinguishable from the transport of the Crimean era.
11 Curtiss, op cit., pp. 124–5.
12 Evgeny Tarle, *Krymskaya Voina* (Moscow, 1950), vol. II, pp. 268–9.
13 The most useful Russian sources on the Crimean War, apart from general histories and Tolstoy's *Sevastopol Sketches* are Tarle, op. cit., in two volumes and A. M. Zaionchkovsky, *Vostochnaya Voina* (St Petersburg, 1908–13) three volumes. Curtiss, op. cit., has broken new ground for English readers with his scholarly exploitation of a host of Russian sources.

Chapter 9

The New Tsar

1 V. A. Zhukovsky, *Polnoe Sobranie Sochinenii*, edited by A. G. Archangelskov (St Petersburg, 1902). Letter to Alexander Turgenev, vol. I, pp. 463–8.
2 S. S. Tatishchev, *Imperator Aleksandr II, ego Zhizn i Tsarstvovanie* (St Petersburg, 1903) vol. I, pp. 17–18.
3 Zhukovsky, op. cit. (St Petersburg, 1906), vol. III, p. 169.
4 M. E. Almedingen, *The Emperor Alexander II* (London, 1962) p. 35.
5 Tatishchev, op. cit., vol. I, p. 82 and Almedingen, op. cit., p. 54.
6 For Herzen's own account of this episode see Herzen, op. cit., vol. I, pp. 344–52.
7 This report is printed in full in an appendix to A. P. Zablotsky-Desyatovsky's life of Count Kiselev; *Graf Kiselev i ego Vremya* (St Petersburg, 1882) vol. IV, pp. 270–344.

Chapter 10

Revolution from Above

1. Quoted in Troyat, *Tolstoy*, op. cit., p. 140.
2. Ibid., p. 141.
3. A. A. Kornilov, *Modern Russian History from the Age of Catherine the Great to the end of the Nineteenth Century* (New York, 1943) vol. II, p. 39.
4. *Kolokol* (*The Bell*) (London, 15 February 1858).

Chapter 11

Limits of Tolerance and Vision

1. The text of this letter is in Kornilov, op. cit., p. 116.
2. They spent five months in the fortress before being tried and found guilty. But their sentences were quashed by order of the Governor of St Petersburg, P. Suvorov.
3. Tatishchev, op. cit., vol. I, pp. 525-6.
4. Korolenko, op. cit., pp. 179-83.
5. B. H. Sumner, *A Survey of Russian History* (London, 1944) p. 83.
6. Quoted by Seton-Watson, op. cit., p. 366.
7. Alexander Solzhenitsyn, *A Letter to the Soviet Leaders* (London, 1974).
8. Troyat, *Tolstoy*, op. cit., pp. 220-1.
9. The most illuminating account of Herzen's life is still E. H. Carr's *The Romantic Exiles* (London, 1937).
10. A unique and hair-raising insight into the life of seminarists training for priesthood (a milieu from which so many revolutionaries came) may be obtained from N. G. Pomyalovsky's *Seminary Sketches*, translated and introduced by Alfred R. Kuhn (Ithaca and London, 1973).
11. For a sympathetic account of Count D. A. Tolstoy's life and thought see *The Classroom and the Chancellery* by Allen Sinel (Cambridge, Mass., and London, 1975).

Chapter 12

Peace Abroad; Prosperity at Home

1. Korolenko, op. cit., pp. 28-39.
2. Jocelyn Baines, *Joseph Conrad* (London, 1959) pp. 14-15 and Joseph Conrad, *A Personal Record* (London, 1919) pp. 58 and 127-34.

3 W. F. Monypenny and G. E. Buckle, *Life and Letters of Lord Beacons-field* (London, 1910–20) vol. IV, p. 337.

4 An interesting first-hand impression of this almost unknown episode is given by the composer, Rimsky-Korsakov, who in his seafaring days sailed in one of the ships. Rimsky-Korsakov, op. cit., p. 44.

5 Quoted by Almedingen, op. cit., p. 175.

6 Tatishchev, op. cit., p. 289.

7 Circular note of 21 November 1864. In Tatishchev, op. cit., p. 115. Much of it is in Almedingen, op. cit., pp. 173–4.

8 12 May 1859. Quoted in Heinrich Friedjung, *The Struggle for Supremacy in Germany*, translated by A. J. P. Taylor and W. L. McElwee (London, 1953) p. 33.

9 Bismarck, in the Prussian Landtag (30 September 1862); in *Bismarck's Reden* (Stuttgart, 1892) vol. II, pp. 126–7.

10 Monypenny and Buckle, op. cit., vol. IV, p. 337.

Chapter 13

Aspects of Self-Love

1 N. G. Chernyshevsky, *Polnoye Sobranie Sochinenii*, ed. M. N. Chernyshevsky (Moscow, 1906) vol. VI, p. 491.

2 Ibid., vol. III, p. 186.

3 Herzen, op. cit., vol. VI, p. 226. See also note 2 to chapter 1 above. There are certain small differences between the Garnett and the Garnett-Higgins translations of the *Letter to J. Michelet* ('The Russian People and Socialism') from which this and the quotations referred to in notes 4 and 5 below are taken. This is because the Letter was written in French and then translated into Russian (the translation being authorised by Herzen). Mrs Garnett translated from the Russian, no copy of the French then being available. Mr Higgins has translated from the French, as printed in vol. VII of *Sobranie Sochinenii* referred to in note 2 to chapter 1 above. Those interested will find the French original there, pp. 271–306, followed by the Russian, pp. 307–39.

4 Ibid., p. 236.

5 Ibid., p. 241.

6 Rimsky-Korsakov, op. cit., p. 29.

7 Ibid., p. 29–30.

8 V. V. Stasov, *Selected Essays on Music*, translated by Florence Jones (London, 1968) pp. 78–9.

9 Ibid., p. 103.

10 Ibid., p. 71.

11 Ibid., p. 70.

12 M. Pogodin, *Rechi* (Moscow, 1872) p. 272.

Chapter 14

'How Great is Russia!'

1 Monypenny and Buckle, op. cit., vol. VI, p. 24.
2 Quoted by Sidney Harcave, *Years of the Golden Cockerel* (New York, 1968, London, 1970) p. 221.
3 Quoted by Seton-Watson, op. cit., p. 449, from R. A. Fadeyev, *Mnenie o vostochnom voprose* (St Petersburg, 1870). N. Y. Danielevsky's *Russia in Europe* was published in 1869.
4 V. S. Solovyev, *Sobranie Sochinenii*, edited by S. M. Solovyev and E. L. Radlov (St Petersburg) vol. V, p. 228. This passage, which is quoted by Seton-Watson, op. cit., p. 486, occurs in the chapter '*Slavyanofilstvo i ego vyrozhdenie*' in Part 2 of '*Natsionali Vopros v Rossii*' which seems to me one of the most important contributions to the history of Russian thought and feeling. See also Hans Kohn, ed. *The Mind of Modern Russia* (New Brunswick, N.J., 1955) pp. 27 and 212-23.
5 Harcave, op. cit., p. 221.
6 Russian and Austrian texts of this agreement are in B. H. Sumner, *Russia and the Balkans, 1870-1880* (London, 1937) pp. 584-7 and 601, which is the most elaborate account of the whole affair. A good and lucid summary against the background of the whole historical process is to be found in M. S. Anderson, *The Eastern Question, 1774-1923* (London, 1966).
7 *The Saburov Memoirs*, edited by J. Y. Simpson (London, 1929) pp. 52-3.
8 Lord Salisbury to Lord Loftus, 16 October 1878, quoted by Lady Gwendolen Cecil in *Life of Robert, Marquess of Salisbury* (London, 1921) vol. II, p. 344.
9 *The Saburov Memoirs*, op. cit., p. 45.
10 To Lady Salisbury, 4 October 1879. Quoted by Lady Gwendolen Cecil, op. cit., p. 89.
11 *The Letters of Disraeli to Lady Bradford and Lady Chesterfield*, edited by the Marquess of Zetland (London, 1929) p. 179.
12 Harcave, op. cit., p. 225.
13 Monypenny and Buckle, op. cit., vol. VI, p. 325.
14 Dmitri Milyutin to William I. In Anderson, op. cit., p. 215.

Chapter 15

The Impact of Terror

1 D. A. Milyutin, *Dnevnik* (Moscow, 1950), vol. III, p. 41.
2 Quoted in Tibor Szamuely, *The Russian Tradition* (London, 1974), p. 341.

3 P. A. Zaionchkovsky, *Krisis Samoderzhavia na Rubezhe 1870–1880* (Moscow, 1964), p. 148.

4 Herbert Weinstock, *Tchaikovsky* (London, 1946, New York, 1959), p. 188.

5 *Dnevnik A. S. Suvorina*, ed. M. Krichevsky (Moscow, 1923), pp. 15–16. The whole passage is quoted in translation by Isaiah Berlin, op. cit., pp. 61–3. There is a French translation of the journal: *Journal intime de Alexis Souvorine*, translated by M. Lichnevsky (Paris, 1927).

6 Weinstock, op. cit., p. 208.

7 There is a very good account of Nechayev in Robert Payne's *The Fortress* (New York, 1957), which is a fairly comprehensive and detailed study of the careers of all those revolutionaries who served time in the fortress of St Peter and St Paul. For the conspiratorial aspects of Nechayev, as of the Russian revolutionaries in general, see particularly Tibor Szamuely's brilliant but sometimes perverse *The Russian Tradition*, op. cit.

8 For the most elaborate account of the extraordinary relationship between Bakunin, Nechayev and Natalie Herzen, with much new material, see *Daughter of a Revolutionary*, edited by Michael Confino (London, 1974).

9 The most complete account in English of the life and work of Lavrov is Philip Pomper's *Peter Lavrov and the Russian Revolutionary Movement* (Chicago and London, 1972).

10 He was later to achieve notoriety under the name Stepniak.

11 For the development of Axelrod's thought, see Abram Ascher's valuable study, *Pavel Axelrod and the Development of Menshevism* (Cambridge, Mass., 1971).

12 A brilliant illumination of the Populists in general and Zhelyabov in particular is in D. J. Footman, *Red Prelude* (London, 1944).

Chapter 16

The Peace of the Graveyard

1 Seton-Watson, op. cit., p. 466.

2 The full text of this letter is in P. A. Zaionchkovsky, op. cit., p. 302.

3 For the letter itself and a good account of this episode see Troyat, *Tolstoy*, op. cit., pp. 403–5.

4 Ibid., p. 406

5 Ibid.

6 Harcave, op. cit., p. 248.

7 Seton-Watson, op. cit., p. 463.

8 Harcave, op. cit., p. 251.

9 Seton-Watson, op. cit., p. 465.

10 Harcave, op. cit., p. 255.

11 Ibid., p. 255.

12 S. M. Dubnow, *History of the Jews in Russia and Poland* (Philadelphia, 1916), p. 368.

Chapter 17

New Wine in Very Old Bottles

1   John P. McKay, *Pioneers for Profit: Foreign Entrepreneurship and Russian Industrialisation 1885–1913* (Chicago and London, 1970), pp. 4–5.

2   The best study of Witte as an industrialist is *Sergei Witte and the Industrialisation of Russia*, by Theodore H. von Laue (New York, 1963). Witte's own memoirs, fascinating but unreliable, have been translated by Avrahm Yarmolinsky as *The Memoirs of Count Witte* (New York and London, 1921). For Witte as statesman see *Count Witte and the Tsarist Government in the 1905 Revolution*, by Howard D. Mehlinger and John M. Thompson (Indiana University Press, Bloomington and London, 1972).

3   Seton-Watson, op cit., pp. 581–2 and Theodore H. von Laue, 'Problems of Industrialisation' in *Russia under the last Tsar*, edited by T. S. Stavrou (Minneapolis, 1969), p. 128.

4   N. S. Khrushchev speaking to a group of foreign visitors quoted by Harold M. Martin in *The Sunday Times Magazine* (London, 13 December 1964).

5   Figures are taken from P. A. Khromov, *Ekonomicheskoe razvitie Rossii v. XIX–XX vekakh* (Moscow, 1950), p. 462.

6   Cited Harcave, op. cit., p. 278.

7   Lionel Kochan, *Russia in Revolution 1898–1918* (London, 1966), p. 27.

8   *Polityka* (Warsaw, No. 28, 11 July 1959), quoted by Lazar Pistrak in *The Grand Tactician Khrushchev's Rise to Power* (London, 1961), p. 10.

9   For a vivid description of urban working conditions under Nicholas II see Kochan, op. cit., part 1, chapter 2.

10   Richard Pipes, *Russia under the Old Regime* (London, 1974).

11   The best account in English of conditions in the villages is in *Rural Russia under the Old Regime* by G. T. Robinson (London, 1932).

12   Adam B. Ulam, *Lenin and the Bolsheviks* (London, 1966), p. 97.

13   For Lenin's waverings on the way to Marxism see Richard Pipes, 'The Origins of Bolshevism' in *Revolutionary Russia*, ed. Richard Pipes (Cambridge, Mass. and London, 1968).

14   For the place of Martov in the revolutionary movement, see *Martov*, by Israel Getzler (Cambridge, 1967).

15   Figures taken from the census of 1897. Cited in Seton-Watson, op. cit., pp. 534–5.

16   *Memoirs of Count Witte*, op. cit., p. 51.

Chapter 18

Nicholas and Alexandra

1 Preface to *Dnevnik Imperator Nikolaya II*, ed. anon., extracts (Berlin, 1923), p. 7.
2 I am aware that the precise circumstances of the annihilation of the Imperial family are still, nearly sixty years later, in dispute. What is not in dispute, I believe, is that a crime of remarkable vileness, involving the murder of children in cold blood, was committed by Bolsheviks and acknowledged by Trotsky in his *Diary in Exile* (Cambridge, Mass., 1955).
3 *Journal intime de Nicolas II* (extracts), translated by A. Pierre (Paris, 1925), p. 36.
4 Ibid., p. 101. Also *Dnevnik Imperator Nikolaya II*, op. cit., p. 83
5 *Letters of the Tsaritsa to the Tsar 1914-1916*. Introduction by Sir Bernard Pares (London, 1923) pp. 453-5.
6 Ibid.
7 *Letters of the Tsar to the Tsaritsa*, ed. C. E. Vulliamy (London, 1929) p. 307.
8 Sir George Buchanan, *My Mission to Russia* (London, 1923) vol. II, pp. 243-9.
9 Maurice Paléologue, *An Ambassador's Memoirs*, translated by F. A. Holt (New York, 1925) vol. III, pp. 151-2.
10 *The Memoirs of Alexander Izwolsky*, edited and translated by Charles Louis Seeger (London, 1920) pp. 253-5.
11 *Samoderzshavie i Zemstvo*, with an introduction by P. B. Struve (Stuttgart, 1903).

Chapter 19

Defeat in Asia

1 Quoted by W. A. Williams, in *American Russian Relations 1781-1947* (New York, 1952) pp. 23-4.
2 Sir Bernard Pares, *The Fall of the Russian Monarchy* (New York, 1961) p. 167. *Der Briefwechsel Wilhelm IItens mit dem russischen Tsaren* (Berlin, 1920) pp. 328-35.
3 *Memoirs of Count Witte*, op. cit., pp. 116-20.
4 Ibid., p. 250.
5 Circular of 18 June 1887 to provincial officials of Ministry of Education. Quoted by Florinsky, op. cit., vol. II, pp. 1113-14.
6 Ibid., p. 1271.

Chapter 20

'Impossible to Live Thus Any Longer'

1   Milyukov's memoirs were published in Russian in New York in 1955: P. N. Milyukov, *Vospominaniya 1859-1917*, edited by M. Karpovich and B. I. Elkin, two volumes.

2   The text of the Eleven Theses is in Sydney Harcave's *First Blood: The Russian Revolution of 1905* (London, 1965) pp. 279-81.

3   For the text of this ukase see ibid. pp. 282-5.

4   V. I. Gurko, *Features and Figures of the Past* (Stanford, 1939), p. 317.

5   Richard Charques, *The Twilight of Imperial Russia* (London, 1958), p. 110.

6   For the text of this petition see Harcave, *First Blood*, pp. 285-9.

7   His career was brief. Friends hid him and helped him to slip out of the country. In Switzerland Lenin made much of him for a short time. He flirted with both the S.D.s and the S.R.s and finally settled for the latter. Returning clandestinely to Russia he made a secret approach to the Minister of the Interior expressing his desire to act as a police agent. But before long he was rumbled by his revolutionary companions, and Peter Rutenberg, a dedicated S.R. who had marched with him to the Winter Palace, organised his escape and then his return to Russia, now, to make amends, convened a secret tribunal of workers, who condemned Gapon to death and carried out the sentence by hanging him on the spot in a wood near St Petersburg. That was in March 1906. For Rutenberg's account see Kochan, op. cit., pp. 73-4. For what it looked like to one of those devoted revolutionaries of the rank and file, whose ideals were soon to be trampled down by Lenin, Trotsky and others, see the most moving and illuminating *Memoirs of a Revolutionary* by Eve Broido, translated and edited by Vera Broido (London, 1967) pp. 66-67.

8   Harcave, *First Blood*, contains a good account of 'Bloody Sunday' set in its full context, pp. 69-97.

9   Nicholas II, *Dnevnik*, op. cit., 194.

10   Rimsky-Korsakov, op. cit., pp. 346-7.

11   Ulam, op. cit., pp. 225-6.

12   The best indication of Krupskaya's preoccupations and limitations is in *Bride of the Revolution* by Robert H. McNeal (London, 1933), which has a useful note on sources.

13   Ulam, op. cit., p. 218.

14   Quoted by Harcave, *First Blood*, p. 163.

15   *The Letters of Tsar Nicholas and Empress Marie*, edited by E. J. Bing, (London, 1937) pp. 185-6.

16   The text of the Manifesto itself as well as Witte's account of the whole

affair is in Witte, op. cit., pp. 231–49. Nicholas's own account of his thoughts and feelings is in a long letter to the Dowager Empress contained in Bing, op. cit., pp. 184–5.

Chapter 21

Stolypin and the Thirteenth Hour

1 Witte, op. cit., pp. 320–4.
2 Ibid., p. 291.
3 Bing, op. cit., p. 201.
4 See, for example, S. D. Sazonov, *The Fateful Years 1909–16* (London, 1928) p. 44.
5 Harold Nicolson, *Sir Arthur Nicolson, Bart, First Lord Carnock* (London, 1930) pp. 210–11.
6 For Shipov's own account of this episode see his own memoirs: *Vospominaniya i Dumy o Perezhitom* (Moscow, 1918), pp. 50–7.
7 Nicolson, op. cit., pp. 222–3.
8 Robinson, op. cit., p. 198.
9 Kochan, op. cit., p. 114.
10 Observation addressed to the Poles in the second Duma, quoted by Charques, op. cit., p. 160.
11 Nicolson, op. cit., p. 226. See also pp. 227–8 for the author's own memory of the scene immediately after the bombing of Stolypin's house.
12 Ibid., p. 225.
13 To the Duma on 5 September 1908.
14 The most complete and perceptive account of this relationship is in Robert K. Massie's *Nicholas and Alexandra* (New York, 1967, London, 1968) to which the Rasputin story is central.

Chapter 22

The End

1 Izwolsky, op. cit., p. 52.
2 Nicolson, op. cit., p. 214.
3 For a full and circumstantial account of the Björkö affair from the Russian point of view, see Izwolsky, op. cit., pp. 40–83.
4 Nicolson, op. cit., pp. 269–70.
5 Ibid., p. 275.
6 Pares, op. cit., p. 117.
7 Robinson, op. cit., pp. 214–16.

8 Useful figures showing industrial growth are in Florinsky, op. cit., vol. II, pp. 1224-32.

9 The assassination of Rasputin is treated by Prince Felix Yussupov himself in *Rasputin* (New York, 1927); in Paléologue, op. cit.; in A. Vryubova's *Memoirs of the Russian Court* (New York, 1923) etc., etc.

10 V. N. Kokovtsev, *Out of My Past* (Stanford, 1935) pp. 273-4.

11 Ibid., p. 283.

12 Ibid., p. 418.

13 Ibid., p. 439.

14 For the most informed and lucid argument in this sense see the writings of Theodore H. von Laue.

15 Edward Crankshaw, *The Fall of the House of Habsburg* (London, 1963) p. 32.

16 Seton-Watson, op. cit., pp. 695-6.

17 For the wild interchange of telegrams between Nicholas and William II, seeking to avert disaster, see Buchanan, op. cit., vol. I, pp. 200-4.

BIBLIOGRAPHY

General

The basic general history of Russia for English students for many years has been Sir Bernard Pares's *History of Russia*, revised edition (London, 1955). Outstanding among more recent histories is M. T. Florinsky's *Russia: A History and an Interpretation* (New York, 1953) two volumes. For a compressed but lucid introduction, Richard Charques's *A Short History of Russia* (London, 1959) cannot be beaten. Probing and very revealing indeed is B. H. Sumner's *Survey of Russian History* (London, 1944). In Russian one of the world's masterpieces of historical writing is Vasili Klyuchevsky's *Kurs Russkoy Istorii* (St Petersburg, 1904-21) five volumes. Volumes 3 and 4 are now available in a good new English translation by Lilian Archibald as *The Rise of the Romanovs* and *Peter the Great* (London, 1960 and 1958 respectively).

For the student of the period covered by this book, Hugh Seton-Watson's compendious *The Russian Empire 1801-1917* (Oxford, 1967) is indispensable. The same author's earlier volume dealing with post-Crimean Russia, *The Decline of Imperial Russia* (London, 1957) is also useful. Sydney Harcave's *Years of the Golden Cockerel, the Last Romanov Tsars* (London, 1970) covers the period 1814-1917 in a more vivid and impressionistic manner. In Russian one official and two unofficial collections of documents, letters, memoirs, etc., are major sources of information. These are the 148 volumes of the Imperial Russian Historical Society, *Sbornik Imperatorskogo Russkogo Istoricheskogo Obshchestva* (St Petersburg, 1867-1916) and two periodicals published by private enterprise, *Russkaya Starina* and *Russkii Archiv* (St Petersburg, 1870-1917 and 1863-1916 respectively). In *Russkaya Starina*, for example, the memoirs of A. V. Nikitenko, N. A. Milyutin, P. A. Valuyev, and many others were published for the first time. To these periodicals may be added the post-revolutionary successor, *Krasny Arkhiv* (Moscow, 1921-1941) which although strongest on foreign affairs is especially rich in documents relating to the Third Section and its various chiefs. Valuable for economic development is P. A. Khromov's *Ekonomichskoe Razvitie Rosii v xix i xx Vekakh* (Moscow, 1950). The Marquis de Custine's celebrated travel-book was first published in Paris in 1843, *La Russie en 1839*. For the English reader Phyllis Penn Kohler's abridged translation of the 'definitive' French edition of 1846 appeared in London in 1951 as *Journey for Our Time, the Journals of the Marquis de Custine*.

The best life of Alexander I in English is Alan Palmer's (London, 1974). The standard Russian biography is N. K. Shilder's *Imperator Aleksandr I ego Zhizn i Tsarstvovanie* (St Petersburg, 1897), four volumes. Marc Raeff's *Michael Speransky* (The Hague, 1961) is good for the whole reign as well as for Speransky himself. A. N. Pypin's *Obshchestvennoe Dvizhenie v Rossii pri Aleksandre I* is good for social conditions. Outstanding among the political memoirs of the period are *Mémoires du Prince Adam Czartoryski*, ed. Charles Mazade (Paris, 1887) two volumes. The literature on the Decembrists is immense. The fullest account of the whole affair in English is Anatole G. Mazour's *The First Russian Revolution, 1825* (Berkeley, 1937) which contains an elaborate bibliography of Russian sources. In *The Rebel on the Bridge*, Glyn Barratt's life of the Esthonian Decembrist Baron Andrei Rozen (London, 1975), much interesting material is made for the first time available in English. The most comprehensive collection of material in Russian is *Dokumenty po Istorii Vosstaniya Dekabristov*, ed. M. N. Pokrovsky and M. V. Nichkina (Leningrad, 1925–58) eleven volumes.

Constantine de Grunwald's *Tsar Nicholas I* translated from the French (London, 1954) is a great deal more serious than its rather tiresomely dramatic style suggests. It is the only life in English, but there are a number of works, scholarly and at the same time highly readable, on different aspects of the reign which illuminate the character of Nicholas himself. N. V. Riasanovsky's *Nicholas I and Official Nationality in Russia, 1825–1855* (Berkeley, 1961) is brilliant and deeply perceptive; Sydney L. Monas's *The Third Section; Police and Society in Russia under Nicholas I* (Cambridge, Mass., 1961), J. S. Curtiss's *The Russian Army under Nicholas I* (Durham, N.C., 1965) and William L. Blackwell's *The Beginnings of Russian Industrialisation, 1800–1860* (Princeton, 1968) are invaluable studies, between them exploring a great part of the fabric of the Russian State and the men who served its institutions. All command Russian sources until recently largely untouched by Western scholars. In Russian, N. K. Shilder's quasi-official biography *Imperator Nikolai I ego Zhizn i Tsarstvovanie* (St Petersburg, 1903) breaks off, after two volumes, in 1830. It contains superb illustrations. The most complete life of Nicholas is in German: Theodor Schiemann's *Geschichte Russlands unter Kaiser Nikolaus I* (Berlin, 1904–9) four volumes.

Among memoirs available in English Alexander Herzen's *My Past and Thoughts*, translated by Constance Garnett (London, 1924–7) six volumes, has a great deal to say about the state of Russia in the early years of the reign. A. V. Nikitenko's *Zapisky i Dnevnik, 1804–77* (St Petersburg, 1904) two volumes, is a mine of information about every aspect of literary, academic and bureaucratic life over a long period. It is entertaining into the bargain. An abridged English version by Helen and Saltz Jacobson has been brought out under the title, *The Diary of a Russian Censor* (Amherst, Mass., 1975). Also very useful are the memoirs of Baron Korf in *Russkaya Starina*, volumes 99–102, and the journal of P. A. Valuyev, *Dnevnik P. A. Valuyeva* (Moscow, 1961) two volumes. All these, of course, extend into the next reign, as does A. P. Zablotsky-Desyatovsky's life of the liberal Count Kiselev, with its important appendix on the condition of the serfs, *Graf P. D. Kiselev i ego Vremya* (St Petersburg, 1882) four volumes.

It would be out of place here to list the collected or selected works, often in many editions, of the thinkers and writers of the age: the student of Russian philosophy and literature will know where to look. But for the English reader there is a two-volume edition of V. G. Belinsky's *Selected Philosophical Works* (Moscow, 1948). Sir Isaiah Berlin's four Northcliffe Lectures, published under the general title 'The Marvellous Decade' in *Encounter* (London, June and November 1953; December 1955 and May 1956) form incomparably the best studies of Belinsky in particular and the writers of the period in general. With these should be read the same author's Romanes Lecture on Turgenev, *Fathers and Children* (Oxford, 1972). On a more workaday level Richard Hare's *Pioneers of Russian Social Thought* and *Portraits of Russian Personalities* (London, 1961 and 1959 respectively) offer useful introductions to the thinkers and critics of the century.

On international affairs, the Eastern Question commands a whole library which can be safely left to students of this important but rather drearily repetitive subject. M. S. Anderson's *The Eastern Question 1774-1923* (London, 1966) offers a very clear and lucid account. His volume contains an elaborate bibliography. Relevant for our immediate period are P. E. Mosely's *Russian Diplomacy and the Opening of the Eastern Question* (Cambridge, Mass., 1934) and G. H. Bolsover's article, 'Nicholas I and the Partition of Turkey' in *Slavonic and East European Review* No. 68 (London, 1948).

The Crimean War is another of those massively documented affairs. A. W. Kinglake's *The Invasion of the Crimea*, first published 1863-87, still immensely readable, eight volumes, remains the classic account from the Allied side. E. V. Tarle's *Krymskaya Voina* (Moscow, 1950) two volumes, is the best account of the actual war in Russian. A. M. Zaionchkovsky's *Vostochnaya Voina* (St Petersburg, 1908-13) is the most complete on the diplomatic side. With the Crimean War we find ourselves well into the period covered by A. J. P. Taylor in *The Struggle for Mastery in Europe, 1848-1918* (Oxford, 1954), essential reading for the general European picture and not seriously invalidated by the author's interesting conviction that Russia has never wanted anything other than to be left alone. Prince A. G. Shcherbatov's *General Feldmarshal Knyaz Paskevich* (St Petersburg, 1888-1904) seven volumes, is full of documentary interest, and so it should be at that length.

E. H. Carr's *Bakunin* (London, 1937) and *The Romantic Exiles* (London, 1933) remain the best and most entertaining studies of the early revolutionaries. Michael Confino's *Daughter of a Revolutionary* (London, 1974) exposes the inside story, through diaries and letters, of the extraordinary relationship between Bakunin, Nechayev and Natalie Herzen. The critic P. V. Annenkov's *Literaturnye Vospominaniya* (Moscow, 1960) offers an especially vivid impression of the intellectual life of the time. An idea of Pogodin's rhetoric can be gained from a single volume, M. Pogodin *Rechi* (Moscow, 1872). M. P. Barsukov's surely record-breaking biography, in no less than twenty-two volumes, *Zhizn i Trudy M. P. Pogodina* (St Petersburg, 1888–1910) is in effect a repository of recorded thoughts and actions from the last years of Alexander I to the twentieth year of the reign of Alexander II.

Alexander II

The standard biography of Alexander II is S. S. Tatishchev's *Imperator Aleksandr II* (St Petersburg, 1903) two volumes. For English readers E. M. Almedingen's *The Emperor Alexander II* (London, 1962) is a fair and perceptive study, conscientious and very readable.

A. A. Kornilov's *Obshchestvennoe Dvizhenie pri Aleksandre II* (Moscow, 1909) is good for the peasant situation at the time of the Emancipation. V. Zhitova's *The Turgenev Family*, translated by A. S. Mills (London, 1947) throws a shocking light on the powers of a tyrannical serf-owner, the novelist's widowed mother. Turgenev's own *Sportsman's Sketches* (many editions) offers the best insight into the peasant mind before the Emancipation. *The Peasant in Nineteenth-Century Russia*, ed. Wayne S. Vucinich (Stanford, Cal., 1968) is an outstanding contribution to recent studies in English, bringing together essays on many aspects of peasant life by nine distinguished scholars.

The most useful memoirs of this period are Dmitri Milyutin's journal, *Dnevnik D. A. Milyutina* (Moscow, 1947–50) four volumes, and B. N. Chicherin's *Vospominaniya* (Moscow, 1929) four volumes. Chicherin was a conservative-minded liberal, who was also a man of affairs, a friend of Herzen and Turgenev among many others, a dedicated foe of the Education Minister, Count D. A. Tolstoy. He throws a good deal of light on the zemstvos. A very recent study of Dmitri Tolstoy himself is Allen Sinel's *The Classroom and the Chancellery* (Cambridge, Mass. and London, 1975). This does not seek to whitewash, but it does set Tolstoy's ideas in their proper context and helps the reader to understand how the more responsible elements of the Tsarist bureaucracy made sense to themselves. Baron B. E. Nolde's *Yuri Samarin i ego Vremya* (Paris, 1926) is an interesting study of one of the most intelligent and thoughtful men of his generation who, nevertheless, succumbed to the mystique of Great Russia. The best account of Russia's Balkan entanglement is perhaps B. H. Sumner's *Russia and the Balkans, 1870–1880* (London, 1937). W. N. Medlicott's *The Congress of Berlin and After* (London, 1963) and M. B. Petrovich's *The Emergence of Russian Panslavism* (New York, 1956) are spoken for by their titles.

It is now that the vast literature of revolution starts up in earnest. I can do no more than pick out a limited number of works; I shall, for example, leave it to the interested reader to discover for himself the formal writings of professional revolutionaries from Chernyshevsky to Lenin. About the non-revolutionary reformers there is next to nothing in English and precious little of any distinction in Russian. The splendid N. A. Milyutin was one of the great figures of the nineteenth century: nothing about him has been published other than a brief but illuminating biography in French: Leroy-Beaulieu's *Un homme d'état russe* (Paris, 1884). A. A. Kornilov's *Krestyanskaya Reforma* (St Petersburg, 1905) and I. V. Gessen's *Sudebnaya Reforma* (St Petersburg, 1905) are useful on the Emancipation and the reform of the judiciary. For the 'new men' E. Lampert's *Studies in Rebellion* (New York, 1957) is useful. For the Populists Franco Venturi's *Roots of Revolution*, an abridged translation of *Il Populismo Russo* (Turin, 1952) is first-class. So in its way, and concentrating on Zhelyabov, is D. J. Footman's *Red Prelude* (London, 1944). For an example of modern Soviet historiography at its all-too-rare best, P. A. Zaionchkovsky's *Krizis Samoderzhaviya na Rubezhe 1870–1880 godov* (Moscow, 1964) is outstanding. Two useful memoirs of revolutionaries of that epoch are *Memoirs of a Revolutionary* by Prince Peter Kropotkin (London, 1899) and *Mémoires d'une révolutionnaire* by the redoubtable Vera Figner (Paris, 1930).

Alexander III and Nicholas II

I run the two reigns together because there is no clear-cut dividing line. Father and son were both deeply influenced by Pobedonostsev, while the economy during the latter part of Alexander's reign and the first part of that of Nicholas was dominated by Count Witte, whose memoirs, though by no means wholly reliable (he wears his hates on his sleeve), are central for the period 1888–1906. The latest Russian edition is *S. Yu. Witte, Vospominaniya* (Moscow, 1960) three volumes. A. Yarmolinsky's English translation, *The Memoirs of Count Witte* (New York and London, 1921) is in one volume. Pobedonostsev's correspondence is important for an understanding of both Tsars. A great deal of it is published in *K. P. Pobedonostsev i ego Korrespondenty* (Moscow, 1923), two volumes, and *Pisma Pobedonostseva k Aleksandru III* (Moscow, 1925–6) two volumes. In English a collection of his writings is published in translation as *Reflections of a Russian Statesman* (London, 1898).

There is no major biography of either of the last two Tsars, although the characters of Nicholas and his consort are open for intimate public inspection in published letters, diaries and innumerable accounts, more or less sensational. Within its own terms of reference Robert K. Massie's *Nicholas and Alexandra* (London, 1968) is sensible, honest and, of course, compellingly readable: its immense popular success in no way detracts from its essential seriousness. But the nearest thing to a sober and balanced 'life and times' of Nicholas II is Richard Charques's modest but extremely penetrating *The Twilight of Imperial Russia* (London, 1958). Parts of Nicholas's journal have been published in Russian as *Dnevnik Imperatora Nikolaya II* (Berlin, 1923); other parts in the overlapping French version, *Journal intime* (Paris, 1925). The most important letters are *Letters of the Tsar to the Tsaritsa*, ed. C. E. Vulliamy (London, 1929); *Letters of the Tsaritsa to the Tsar*

1914–1916, Introduction by Sir Bernard Pares (London, 1923); *Letters of Tsar Nicholas and Empress Marie*, ed. E. J. Bing (London, 1937). *At the Court of the Late Tsar* by A. A. Mossolov (London, 1935) and *Memories of the Russian Court* by A. Vyrubova, (New York, 1923) accomplish what they set out to do, to cite only two among many.

On Witte's industrialisation Theodore H. von Laue's *Sergei Witte and the Industrialisation of Russia* (New York, 1963) is essential. The author reverts to the same theme in his contribution, 'Problems of Industrialisation' to *Russia under the Last Tsar*, ed. T. G. Stavrou (Minneapolis, 1969), a collection of studies of aspects of the last decades of the monarchy by American scholars who wrestle with the problem, was the Revolution inevitable, or would it have been staved off but for the 1914 war? In this connection a paper by George Kennan, 'The Breakdown of the Tsarist Autocracy', contained in yet another symposium, *Revolutionary Russia*, edited by Richard Pipes (Cambridge, Mass. and London, 1968) is very much to the point. This whole symposium – papers presented by a galaxy of international scholars, followed by discussions, on the fiftieth anniversary of the Russian Revolution – is of great importance for the understanding of the Soviet Union. Most of the papers deal with post-revolutionary phenomena, including Lenin's *coup d'état*, and are thus outside the scope of the present volume. But Richard Pipes himself in his own paper, 'The Origins of Bolshevism', offers new material concerning Lenin's own conversion to Marxism in the last decade of the nineteenth century.

For a general understanding of the condition of Russia during the last fifty years of the monarchy as it appeared in foreign eyes Sir Donald Mackenzie-Wallace's *Russia* is in a class by itself, describing many institutions and elements of society from the inside, from zemstvos to the higher bureaucracy, from the peasantry to the nobility. First published in 1877, revised, enlarged and brought up to date in 1912, it was reprinted in New York in 1961 in paperback with an introduction by Cyril E. Black. This edition is now available in London. Anatole Leroy-Beaulieu's *L'Empire des Tsars et les Russes* (Paris, 1881–9) three volumes, is also very good in this sense. G. T. Robinson's *Rural Russia under the Old Regime* (London, 1929) is the best study in English of the Russian peasant and his existence from early days to the Revolution. All these three books illuminate life as it is still lived by countless millions in the Soviet Union today. This also applies very much to a recent account, description, explanation of the historical, social and ideological matrix of the Russian reality, *Russia under the Old Regime*, by Richard Pipes (London, 1974) notable for its boldness, penetration and learning.

For the Far East, B. H. Sumner's *Tsarism and Imperialism in the Middle and Far East* (London, 1940). General Kuropatkin's diary is scattered through several volumes of *Krasny Arkhiv* as 'Dnevnik Kuropatkina' — volumes 2, 5, 7 and 8 between 1922 and 1925; volume 48 in 1935. Kuropatkin's own account of the war, *The Russian Army and the Japanese War* (London, 1909) two volumes, is largely an essay in self-justification, but not notably more so than the memoirs of most military commanders and politicians. It is full of interest. So is Sir Ian Hamilton's *A Staff-Officer's Scrap-Book during the Russo-Japanese War* (London, 1907) two volumes. Hamilton was even then a very senior officer (after seeing much active service he was appointed Quarter-Master General in 1902) attached to the Japanese army as the representative of the Government of India. He wrote with unusual knowledge and authority.

Back to the revolution: the 1905 revolution is well treated in Sydney Harcave's *First Blood: the Revolution of 1905* (London, 1964) and, in a wider setting, by Lionel Kochan in *Russia in Revolution 1890–1918* (London, 1966). The development of Marxism is particularly well handled in J. H. L. Keep's *The Rise of Social Democracy in Russia* (London, 1963), which contains an excellent bibliography. S. H. Baron's *Plekhanov, the Father of Russian Marxism* (Stanford, 1963), and Israel Getzler's *Martov* (Cambridge and Adelaide, 1936) are good on individuals as parts of movements. From the Menshevik standpoint, Theodor Dan's *The Origins of Bolshevism* (London, 1964) is of very great interest; from the non-Marxist standpoint L. B. Schapiro's *The Communist Party of the Soviet Union* (London, 1960) is a model of clarity. Leopold Haimson's *The Russian Marxists and the Origins of Bolshevism* (Cambridge, Mass., 1955) and George Fischer's *Russian Liberalism, from Gentry to Intelligentsia* (Cambridge, Mass., 1958) are both worth reading. For Lenin I shall mention Adam B. Ulam's brilliant *Lenin and the Bolsheviks* (London, 1966) and leave it at that, except for an interesting volume, not well enough known, of first-hand impressions: *Encounters with Lenin* by Nikolai Valentinov (London, 1968) and a volume of essays, *Lenin, the man, the theorist, the leader*, ed. L. Schapiro and P. Reddaway (London, 1967). Those who think Lenin was a splendid man will know just where to read all about him. Essential for the collapse of the monarchy and the coming of revolution is George Katkov's *Russia 1917, The February Revolution* (London, 1967).

The proceedings of the Duma are recorded from the beginning to the end of its short existence in *Gosudarstvennaya Duma, Stenograficheskie Otchoty* (St Petersburg, 1906–16). But there is not a great deal in English other than Sir Bernard Pares, especially *The Fall of the Russian Monarchy* (London, 1939). The memoirs of Stolypin's successor, V. N. Kokovtsev's *Out of my Past* (Stanford, 1935) are of very great interest, so are those of V. I. Gurko, *Features and Figures of the Past: Government and Opinion in the Reign of Nicholas II* (Stanford, 1939). In Russian, D. N. Shipov's *Vospiminaniya i Dumy o Perezhitom* (Moscow, 1918) is revealing for the dawning and swift eclipse of official liberalism in Russia. For the last phase, two works by the British and French Ambassadors to St Petersburg are sadly important: Sir George Buchanan's *My Mission to Russia* (London, 1923) and Maurice Paléologue's *La Russie des Tsars pendant la guerre* (Paris, 1921–3) three volumes. Two volumes of memoirs by Russian Foreign Ministers important for an understanding of the run-up to the 1914 war are *The Memoirs of Alexander Izwolsky*, edited and translated by Charles Louis Seager (London, 1920) and *The Fateful Years, 1909–16* by S. D. Sazonov (London, 1928).

CHRONOLOGICAL TABLE
Intended as a Guide to the Period

	Affairs outside Russia	At Home	The Arts and Sciences
	NICHOLAS I: 1825–55		
1825		Decembrist Revolt	
1826		Execution of conspirators; organisation of political police (Third Section of Imperial Chancery)	
1826–8	War with Persia. Treaty of Turkmanchai		
1828–9	War with Turkey. Treaty of Adrianople		
1830–1	Suppression of Polish revolt		
1832–3	First Mohammed Ali crisis. Treaty of Unkiar Skelessi		Birth of the composer Borodin
1833	Münchengrätz agreement		
1834		Alexander Herzen banished to Vyatka. New radical intelligentsia from now on at grips with censorship and police	Birth of the scientist Mendeleyev
1836		P. A. Chaadayev declared insane by Nicholas for critique of Russian backwardness	First performance of Gogol's *Government Inspector* and Glinka's *A Life for the Tsar*
1837			Pushkin killed in a duel at 38
1839			Birth of the composer Mussorgsky
1839–40	Second Mohammed Ali Crisis		
1840	Bakunin leaves Russia for Germany		Birth of the composer Tchaikovsky
1841			Lermontov killed in a duel at 27
1844			Birth of the composer Rimsky-Korsakov
1846			Dostoevsky publishes *Poor Folk*

1847		Turgenev publishes *A Sportsman's Sketches* Death of V. G. Belinsky
1848	Revolution in France, Austria, Italy and Germany. Chartist Petition in England. Publication of *Communist Manifesto*	
1849	Nicholas intervenes to help Austria put down Hungarian revolt	Dostoevsky and others sentenced to death and reprieved Birth of I. P. Pavlov
1851		Opening of St Petersburg–Moscow railway
1852	Louis Napoleon proclaimed Emperor of France	Leo Tolstoy publishes *Childhood* Death of Gogol
1854–6	Crimean War	
1855		Death of Nicholas I
ALEXANDER II: 1855–81		
1856	Treaty of Paris ends Crimean War	
1857	Indian Mutiny. Herzen founds *The Bell* in London	
1858–60	Russian penetration in S.E. Asia: acquisition of Amur and Maritime Provinces from China	
1859	Shamil surrenders: conquest of Caucasus complete except for Circassia (1864)	Foundation of Vladivostok
1860		Emancipation of the serfs. Formation of first revolutionary groups
1861		Start of railway boom
1862	Bismarck becomes Chancellor of Prussia	Birth of Anton Chekhov Turgenev publishes *Fathers and Sons*
1863	Poland again rebels	Tolstoy begins *War and Peace*

	Affairs outside Russia	At Home	The Arts and Sciences
1863-4		Reforms of law, education and local government (zemstvos) N. G. Chernyshevsky banished to Siberia	
1864	Conquest of Central Asia		
1864-8	Prussia defeats Austria at Königgrätz		
1866	Sale of Alaska to America	First attempt on Alexander's life	Birth of the painter Kandinsky
1867			
1868			Birth of Maxim Gorky War and Peace finished.
1869			Tchaikovsky's first opera The Voivoda performed. The Russian musical flowering (Balakirev, Rimsky-Korsakov, Borodin, Mussorgsky, etc.) a feature of the years to come
1870		Birth of V. I. Lenin	
1870-1	Prussia defeats France Bismarck unites Germany under William		
1871	London Convention on the Straits		
1873	Three Emperors' League		Birth of the musician Rachmaninov
1873-4		'Going to the People'	
1877-8	Victorious war with Turkey Treaty of San Stefano	Mass trials of radicals and revolutionaries	
1878	Bismarck presides over the Congress of Berlin		
1878-81		Development of terrorist activity. Dynamiting of Winter Palace; wrecking of imperial trains	
1879		Birth of J. V. Stalin	Birth of Alexander Blok
1880			
1881		Alexander II assassinated	

ALEXANDER III: 1881–94

Year			
1881		Reaction. Institution of Emergency Powers. Ascendancy of Pobedonostsev	
1882	Anglo-Russian crisis over Afghanistan		Birth of the composer Stravinsky
1885	Bulgarian crisis		
1885–7	'Reinsurance Treaty' between Russia and Germany		
1887		Execution of Lenin's brother for participating in attempt on Alexander III	Birth of the painter Chagall
1890		Famine Start of Trans-Siberian Railway	Birth of Boris Pasternak
1891			
1891–3	Maturing of Franco-Russian alliance		
1892–1903		Witte revolutionises industry, commerce and transport	
1894		Death of Alexander III Birth of N. S. Khrushchev	Birth of V. Mayakovsky and Isaac Babel

NICHOLAS II: 1894–1917

Year			
1896	Expansion into Manchuria: Chinese Eastern Railway		
1897		Foundation of Marxist R.S.D.L.P. (Social Democratic Labour Party)	
1898			Foundation of Moscow Arts Theatre
1899			Diaghilev founds *Mir Iskustvo* (*The World of Art*)
1900	Boxer Rebellion in China		
1899–1902	Boer War		
1902		Foundation of Socialist Revolutionary Party. Assassination of D. S. Sipyagin (Minister of Interior)	
1903		Lenin splits Social Democratic Party into Bolshevik and Menshevik wings. Kishinev pogrom	

	Affairs outside Russia	At Home	The Arts and Sciences
1904	The struggle for Port Arthur	Assassination of V. I. Plehve (Minister of Interior)	
1905	Fall of Port Arthur (January) Battle of Mukden (February–March) Destruction of Russian Fleet at Tsushima (May)	Bloody Sunday (9 January) Assassination of Grand Duke Sergei. Abortive revolution (general strike; establishment of Soviets of Workers' Deputies; violent repression. Concession of representative assembly, or State Duma, 17 October)	
1906	Treaty of Portsmouth (August)	Birth of Leonid Brezhnev	Birth of composer Shostakovich
1906–11		The Stolypin era. Successive Dumas convened and prorogued. Revolutionary agricultural reforms. Industrial progress. Rasputin gains ascendancy over Tsaritsa and Tsar	
1907	Anglo-Russian Entente		
1908	Annexation of Bosnia-Hercegovina by Austria		
1910			Death of Tolstoy
1911	Agadir crisis	Assassination of Stolypin	
1912		Massacre on Lena goldfields. Strikes. First issue of *Pravda*, V. M. Molotov heads editorial board	
1914–17	War with Germany and Austria		
1916		Rasputin murdered (December)	
1917		Nicholas abdicates (February)	

Index